The Year 2000 Software Crisis:

Challenge of the Century

Selected Titles from the
YOURDON PRESS COMPUTING SERIES
Ed Yourdon, *Advisor*

The Year 2000 Software Crisis:

Challenge of the Century

William M. Ulrich
and
Ian S. Hayes

To join a Prentice Hall PTR Internet mailing list, point to
http://www.prenhall.com/register

YOURDON PRESS
Prentice Hall Building
Upper Saddle River, New Jersey 07458
http://www.prenhall.com

Library of Congress Cataloging-in-Publication Data

Ulrich, William. M.
    The year 2000 software crisis : challenge of the century / William M. Ulrich
and Ian S. Hayes.
        p. cm. — (Yourdon Press computing series)
    Includes bibliographical references and index.
    ISBN 0-13-655664-7
    1. Software maintenance. 2. Year 2000 date conversion (Computer systems)
I. Hayes, Ian S. II. Title. III> Series.
    QA76.76.S64U38   1997
    005.1'6--dc21   96-38030
                                                     CIP

Editorial/production supervision: *Joanne Anzalone*
Manufacturing manager: *Alexis R. Heydt*
Acquisitions editor: *Paul Becker*
Editorial assistant: *Maureen Diana*
Marketing Manager: *Dan Rush*
Cover design: *Design Source*
Cover design director: *Jerry Votta*

© 1997 William Ulrich and Ian Hayes
Published by Prentice Hall PTR
A Simon & Schuster Company
Upper Saddle River, New Jersey 07458

The publisher offers discounts on this book when ordered in bulk quantities.
For more information, contact:
        Corporate Sales Department
        Prentice Hall PTR
        1 Lake Street
        Upper Saddle River, NJ 07458

        Phone: 800-382-3419, Fax: 201-236-7141
        E-mail: corpsales@prenhall.com

Printed in the United States of America
10 9 8 7 6 5 4

ISBN 0-13-655664-7

Prentice-Hall International (UK) Limited, *London*
Prentice-Hall of Australia Pty. Limited, *Sydney*
Prentice-Hall Canada Inc., *Toronto*
Prentice-Hall Hispanoamericana, S.A., *Mexico*
Prentice-Hall of India Private Limited, *New Delhi*
Prentice-Hall of Japan, Inc., *Tokyo*
Simon & Schuster Asia Pte. Ltd., *Singapore*
Editora Prentice-Hall do Brasil, Ltda., *Rio de Janeiro*

JAN 20 '98

Dedication

To Kathy and Catlin

—William Ulrich

To Anne and Jessica

—Ian Hayes

Contents

Chapter 8
Management Issues, 187

Chapter 12
Year 2000 Enterprise Assessment, 273

Chapter 14
Validation Strategies,   367

Chapter 15
Year 2000 Tool and Technology Selection,   399

Chapter 16
Small Information Technology Organizations,   437

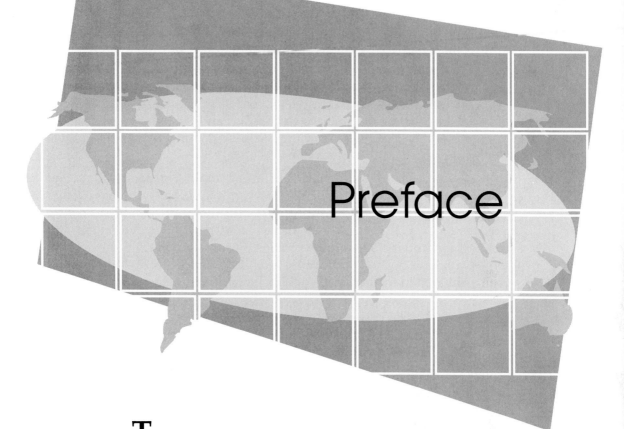

Preface

This book is about the pending Year 2000 software crisis. It is a surprisingly mundane problem with far-reaching consequences. When the first business programs were written in the 1950s, who would have believed that the decision to store years as two digits, say, 57, rather than four digits, 1957, would have tremendous ramifications forty years later? These programmers would have been astonished to find that many of their programs and the data associated with those programs are still in use. Unfortunately, the Year 2000 issue is not limited to 40-year-old programs. Originally devised to save expensive hardware resources, this shortcut found its way into the standard programming methods employed throughout the computer industry. Even the newest PC software may still reference years in a two-digit format.

In one way or another, Year 2000 issues touch the life of almost every person who directly or indirectly relies on computers. Many computer professionals will spend a large percentage of their time over the next five to six years reprogramming software to correctly process century-related data, or handling the consequences of incorrect date processing. Businesses will face a multitude of expected and unexpected problems. Reports will be sorted incorrectly, date-based calculations will be wrong, and data comparisons that include date values will produce unwanted results. Some of these consequences will be minor annoyances. Other consequences will cause serious financial losses as inventory systems order unnecessary replacements, financial transactions are incorrectly posted, and customers are dropped from master files. And given our litigious society, many of these issues will end up in court.

The pervasiveness of computers and computer-generated data and services in modern society means that even individuals who have never used a computer can and will be affected. They will suffer the consequences of Year 2000-related breakdowns within both government and business institutions. Even if the problem is corrected in time, they will in some way pay a portion of the bill. The worldwide cost of the problem has been estimated in the hundreds of billions of dollars.

After a slow start, the Year 2000 crisis is finally gaining public attention. In our travels and work with clients, we have been surprised to find people from all walks of life who have heard about the problem. While a few leading edge companies and government agencies recognized the problem early, much of the Information Technology (IT) industry has been in a state of denial. The first individuals who raised Year 2000 issues publicly were derided as millennium moaners and were viewed simply as consultants seeking a new way to make money. Many IT organizations simply felt that their applications would be replaced before century dates became a problem. In 1995, reality began to hit. In that year, there was one major industry conference on the topic. In 1996, there were over fifty. The topic has become front page news in the business press as well as in the computer media. Suddenly, a major market appeared for consulting vendors and software firms.

IT organizations have progressed from inaction to panic as they begin to comprehend the magnitude of the problem. Their panic has been fed by the media and the public relations efforts from the growing multitude of software vendors and consultants in the marketplace. Conflicting stories abound. Rumors of magic bullets and other shortcuts are interspersed with horror stories of impending failures and outrageous costs. Lost in this maelstrom is a coherent method for solving the problem. Providing that method to a wide variety of organizations is the goal of this book.

We began work on the Year 2000 issue at the insistence of our client base. Our consulting efforts focused on helping clients assess their degree of exposure, related costs, understanding their options and constraints, and developing strategies to achieve Year 2000 compliance. Exposure to many IT organizations taught us that there are no magic solutions; there isn't even a single best strategy. There are, however, basic building blocks and guiding principles that apply to all Year 2000 initiatives. We found that by following these principles, an IT organization can assemble the right set of strategies, tools, internal resources, and consulting services to meet the unique needs of their organization. This knowledge is the foundation of this book.

Our intent is to expose our readers to the full range of possible issues and the multitude of solutions for those issues. Armed with this information, readers can separate market hype from reality as they develop the optimum Year 2000 solution for their organization.

Audience for this Book

This book is written for IT managers, business managers, software vendors, consultants, and other individuals that require an in-depth understanding of Year 2000 issues. It is written in four major sections: Year 2000 Overview, Issues and Strategies, Assembling a Solution, and Strategic Implications. These sections are designed to communicate multiple levels of understanding. Sectional chapter overviews are provided for readers requiring high-level knowledge, while more detailed information is provided for the project managers charged with implementing a Year 2000 project. This book is not intended to replace the need for a proper methodology. The breadth of the topic prevents the authors from duplicating the implementation knowledge available within a detailed Year 2000 methodology.

Nontechnical readers or senior executives requiring a high-level understanding of Year 2000 issues may wish to read the first section in its entirety and the overviews for each remaining section. Those charged with implementing a century-date compliant effort will want to read all sections in detail and use this book as an ongoing reference guide on the Year 2000 topic.

Summary of Contents

The Year 2000 overview section provides a high-level explanation of the Year 2000 issue and its effect on IT organizations. It provides readers with a realistic idea of what is wrong, the extent of the problem, what it will take to solve it, how to justify a solution effort and the importance of beginning immediately. It describes the specific ramifications of the Year 2000 problem and how these issues can affect a typical organization. These include ramifications outside of IT as well as internal issues. These ramifications can be positive as well as negative, offering hope for gaining value from the migration effort. Finally, the overview section discusses impacts on specific industries and why some organizations and industries are at more risk than others.

The Issues and Strategies section describes the building blocks of a Year 2000 strategy. It demonstrates that Year 2000 projects encompass a wide range of issues that extend beyond simply changing code. These issues include:

- **Asset management issues.** Application software no longer exists solely on large, central computers. Nor is it the only software impacted by the Year 2000. Different issues arise, based on system type, age, technology, platform, and support levels.

- **Migration issues.** Selecting the optimal migration approach for each application requires an understanding of the most common strategies and application characteristics that lead to optional approach selection. If multiple strategies are available, this section describes the benefits and risks of each choice.

- **Environmental issues and support technologies.** The quality of the software and testing environment that supports the operation, maintenance, and migration of production systems is critical to the success of a Year 2000 migration. This section describes the type of environment needed to support a Year 2000 project and approaches for achieving this type of environment.

- **External organizations.** Year 2000 compliance projects are not completely under the control of the IT organization. Companies share data and interfaces with many external organizations. Even when a century date conversion is the responsibility of an external entity, the timing and approach may have a profound impact on organizational functions. This section describes strategies for assessing and mitigating the risks associated with external organizational interfaces.

- **Management issues.** The size and scope of a Year 2000 project is significantly larger than any single project previously faced by IT organizations. Studies have shown that most IT organizations are notoriously poor at meeting deadlines and budget commitments.

Unless corrected, this weakness will be fatal in Year 2000 projects where there is no latitude in project scope or delivery dates. This section explores project management issues that must be overcome to ensure the success of major Year 2000 initiatives.

Part 3, Assembling a Solution, describes the tasks needed to implement a Year 2000 project. It emphasizes the importance of planning and methods for creating a cost-effective, implementable solution. The chapters in this section are arranged by the phases of a typical Year 2000 project and are followed by guidance for selecting tools and consulting assistance. A chapter is included to cover the special requirements of small IT organizations. This section includes:

- **Strategies.** High-level strategies for a formal process to guide Year 2000 planning, project implementation and tool utilization are covered in depth in this section.

- **Year 2000 budgeting.** The size of the Year 2000 issue makes accurate, one-shot budgeting impossible. The reader is taken through a strategy of building a rolling budget that provides accurate and obtainable goals through the use of multiple industry budget models.

- **Project mobilization.** Project Mobilization is the process of setting up a Year 2000 project. This section offers the reader guidance on the activities to be performed, the work products to be produced, office setup, and guidelines for estimating the effort required to implement the phase.

- **Enterprise assessment.** The enterprise assessment phase of a Year 2000 project gathers the detailed information needed to select strategies, formalize a more concrete budget, and scope and conduct the implementation phase.

- **Implementation and deployment.** This section describes the execution of the implementation phase of a Year 2000 project. This phase conducts the actual conversion of data and system and the production implementation of the software systems. The tasks and deliverables of this phase are described at a project management level along with analysis guidelines for conversion specialists. Techniques are described broadly but without excessive technical details. This section also includes a discussion on application package and system software upgrade projects.

- **Validation.** Testing and validation will use as much as 50 percent of the typical Year 2000 migration budget. This section discusses the tools, infrastructures, and techniques needed to guarantee that the migrated applications will truly function in the year 2000. Two major approaches are covered.

- **Tool and technology selection.** Year 2000 projects are too large and complex to be conducted without tools. This section describes the tool characteristics needed to support a Year 2000 project and the criteria for selecting and acquiring the right tools.

- **Small IT organizations.** Small IT organizations may not have the budget or the resources available to establish a comprehensive Year 2000 delivery capability. This section is aimed at those organizations and should allow them to look toward various alternatives that will keep their systems running. This section also addresses the PC user.

- **Services selection.** Most IT organizations will rely heavily on outside services to implement their Year 2000 strategies. This section guides IT management through the many variations of conversion assistance available for Year 2000 projects. It describes the pros and cons of each service option, as well as describing how to write a valid RFP to obtain these services.

The fourth section of the book describes the strategic implications of the Year 2000 initiative. Many organizations view Year 2000 projects as pure overhead—no business value is gained. Fortunately, this view is incorrect because IT organizations can take advantage of a Year 2000 project to position themselves for the future. This section describes how to apply the knowledge, tools, and techniques from a Year 2000 project to the long-term advantage of the IT organization. It also explores how the lessons from the Year 2000 project can be a catalyst for strategic change. The high cost of obtaining century compliance in legacy applications should inspire IT management to move beyond their traditional caretaker role to initiate strategic change.

Following the last section of the book is an appendix containing sources of assistance. This supplement provides a noninclusive list of tool vendors, consulting firms, and conversion companies. The appendixes also include sample forms and a meta-model for project tracking deliverables. A glossary defines terms used in the book.

Acknowledgments

This book could not have been written without the help of many dedicated individuals and companies. First, we would like to thank our wives, Anne Hayes and Kathy Ulrich, for their masterful job of editing the first drafts of each chapter and for putting up with many nights and weekends of their husbands working on their PCs.

The ideas within this book were not developed in a vacuum. Rather, they evolved over many years from many collective discussions, experiments, and use on consulting projects. It is impossible to acknowledge everyone by name, but we want to express our gratitude to our clients, Year 2000 conference attendees, software vendors, and consulting firms that have contributed to these ideas. Hopefully, we are able to repay some of this favor through this book.

Many software vendors and consulting firms contributed literature on their products and services as background materials for this book. These vendors are listed in Appendix A. These materials were very helpful for understanding the range of tools and services on the market. We greatly appreciated this assistance. We apologize in advance to any vendors who were inadvertently omitted.

We also wish to thank Paul Becker from Prentice Hall for believing in this project and supporting our writing efforts. We especially appreciated his astonishment at our ability to deliver the book manuscript on time. In addition, we want to thank Joanne Anzalone, our Prentice Hall production editor, for her efforts in turning our mingled prose into proper English.

Finally, we would like to thank the readers of this book. We sincerely hope that it helps you and your organization successfully survive the Year 2000 crisis. We wish you the best of luck on your projects.

Ian S. Hayes
Clarity Consulting
Marblehead, MA

William M. Ulrich
Tactical Strategy Group, Inc.
Soquel, CA
August, 1996

Year 2000: Crisis or Opportunity?

There is a crisis in the information technology (IT) industry. It is called the Year 2000 problem. As computer systems begin to encounter dates that occur after December 31, 1999, they will begin to misinterpret time-dependent events. This includes pension eligibility, birth dates, stock option dates, license renewal dates, credit card expiration dates, and a list of other scenarios that is virtually endless. Part 1 of this book introduces this topic.

It normally takes the IT industry a couple of years to gather steam when it comes to hyping a new topic. Computer-Aided Software Engineering (CASE) and, more recently, client/server markets were the product of an overly zealous computer press that needed something to talk about. In the last 12 to 18 months, however, the Year 2000 problem has created more attention, "expert" opinions, startup ventures, industry hype, financial analyst interest, and mainstream press coverage than most IT topics generate in a lifetime. In 1995, for example, there was one Year 2000 conference. In 1996, there were dozens. This sudden attention to the problem is due to the fact that the Year 2000 issue is real and that it must be addressed within a very short span of time. For an industry that rarely meets project deadlines (less than 9 percent of the time according to Standish Group International), this is a rather ominous thought.

Part 1 of this book deals with an introduction to the Year 2000 problems and solutions. We provide a brief history of the evolution of the problem, discuss the implications to IT and to the world in general, dispel six common myths, and outline a "call to action." Topics include legal risks, a breakdown in auditing capability, financial implications, and the stress that the Year 2000 problem will place on corporate and government infrastructures. Many of the terms are IT related, and we make every attempt to explain terms that are commonly used by IT professionals and people chartered with addressing the Year 2000 problem.

If you are responsible for IT functions, hold a position of potential liability, or depend on information technology for your pension, paycheck, investment portfolio, or health care, you will want to review Part 1 of this book.

Separating Hype from Reality

It is very easy for organizations and individuals to become consumed by the Year 2000 issue as the industry struggles through this difficult challenge. Chapter 1 clears the air on a multitude of Year 2000-related concepts as we define what the problem actually is, how it evolved, and the real-world implications. We also discuss and dispel many of the myths that have grown up within the industry. Comparing and contrasting the role of outsiders further helps to put into perspective what many vendors and service providers are claiming.

We also examine the explosive requirement for budgetary funding and personnel resources required between now and the end of the century, and define basic terminology, including many of the concepts integral to a Year 2000 solution, to provide a common framework for discussions in future chapters. Finally, this chapter closes on a hopeful note: although this is a very real problem, some silver clouds are hidden within the gray skies ahead.

1.1   What Is the Year 2000 Issue?

The information technology (IT) industry is facing the largest crisis in its brief, 50-year history. Systems are beginning to malfunction as they encounter events that project past the end of 1999. These malfunctions occur because most computer systems store only a two-digit, versus a four-digit, year value. As we draw closer to the end of the century, virtually all systems are expected to have some problems. Analysts estimate that correcting the Year 2000 problem will collectively cost the industry between $400 to $600 billion. The question is, how did this occur and what can be done about it?

The Year 2000 problem, for all of the activity that it has generated, can be stated in simple terms. Computer *data* is stored in databases and files. Data must be defined within the computer programs that process that data. Date-related data fields are normally defined in computer databases and programs as year/month/day or as some variation of this format. When the majority of today's computer systems were first created, the original designers defined the year field by a two-digit, rather than a four-digit, format. This means that 1996 looks like a "96" to the majority of computer programs in existence. When the computer compares one date to another date that occurs after December 31, 1999, a "00" (as opposed to "2000") in the year field will distort the computer's concept of time. Figure 1.1 highlights this point, using an example from an insurance company program.

IF CURR-YYMMDD < EXPIRATION-YYMMDD
      PERFORM PROCESS-LIFE-INS-CLAIM
ELSE
      PERFORM REJECT-LIFE-INS-CLAIM.

This example checks to see if an insurance policy has expired by comparing today's date (961201) to the policy expiration date. If renewal date occurs after 1999 (010101, for example), a valid claim is rejected.

Figure 1.1   Why Computers Think Tomorrow Is Yesterday

How this situation evolved is not a big surprise when examined in an historical light. Abbreviated dates appear as 12/12/96 on forms and checks that are unrelated to computers. Shorthand representation was already a habit for our society when computers were developed in the 1950s. If computers were built just prior to the turn of the century, short-hand representation would not have been a problem because designers would have accommodated the difference in century values. But early computer designers were hampered by memory limitations on the machines where the original software programs were intended to operate. The limitations of early computers are staggering by today's standards. A computer that took up an entire room had less memory than even the most archaic personal computer in use today.

Limiting representation of the year to two digits was common sense to systems designers 30 years ago. After all, society already used two-digit year abbreviations, and the end of the century was a lifetime away. But a strange thing happened. Many of the original programs and corresponding data were brought along from one generation of machine to another. Even when replacement systems were developed, they used the old data formats. As late as the 1980s, most software analysts still viewed the impending millennium as a distant concern. The first known article on the Year 2000 was published in ComputerWorld in 1984. The author was an analyst at an auto manufacturer and lost his job for pushing management past the point of irritation on the subject.

By the 1980s, systems were no longer being replaced at the same pace as in the 1960s and 1970s. At the time, a revolution in computing technology promised a utopian world where users would specify require-ments and computers would write the software for us. This phenomenon has yet to occur and most organizations are still running these older sys-tems along with a newly added generation of client/server software. Cli-ent/server systems are most noted for their ability to distribute computing workloads across networks in order to simplify user access to information. Distributed environments add another level of complexity to an already complex problem.

Worldwide estimates state that the information industry has cre-ated 150 billion lines of code to date. Since these systems primarily use existing data, the two-digit year format continues to live on long after early memory limitations were eliminated. Even standards committees failed do anything about the problem until a couple of years ago. Worst of all, industry executives have, until very recently, turned a deaf ear to the problem.

Two things have caused the IT industry to take notice of the Year 2000 problem. Over the last couple of years, systems have been encounter-ing date-related errors on an increasingly regular basis. For example, expiration dates set in the next century force time-dependent criteria to be misinterpreted, which in turn results in the rejection of otherwise valid transactions. Other, more publicized, date-related problems have helped highlight the seriousness of the Year 2000 issue. A state lottery computer could not process ticket acquisitions on 2/29/96 because leap day logic was not programmed into the system. This failure cost the state, and ultimately the company that built the system, more than $60,000 in lost revenues. Compared to shutting down an airline reservation system, the federal government, or a hospital because of Year 2000 problems, the loss of revenue due to miscalculating a leap day is almost insignificant. Even though the year 2000 is a leap year, see Figure 1.2 for a complete set of leap year rules, many programmers may not have considered this when building a system.

2000 is a Leap Year according to the Gregorian Calendar—many systems are unaware of this!

• *It is Leap Year if the year is divisible by 4*

• *Unless the year ends in "00"—then it is not a Leap Year*

• *Unless the year is divisible by 400—then it is a Leap Year*

• *Unless the year is 3600—then it is not a Leap Year*

Figure 1.2   2000 is a Leap Year

The second thing that has occurred is that people discovered that fixing the date problem involves more work and coordination than can be reasonably managed under a single maintenance project. Every system has thousands of dates contained in files and databases, programs, screens, and reports. Dates are normally passed to and from many other systems that are not under the control of a single maintenance team. When a given maintenance team decides to address the date limitation, the pervasive nature of the challenge results in a ripple effect on all systems directly or indirectly tied to that system. When system software or hardware upgrades are required, the problem is magnified.

Unless management has been on a year-long retreat on a desert island, they are aware of the Year 2000 problem. The stage that many find themselves in is one of denial. Denial comes from rationalizing away the ultimate impact of the Year 2000 problem on one's own organization. People that must pay for the problem have convinced themselves that it is not a big deal or that they can deal with it in a couple of years. But it is a big deal because the problem has the potential to reach well beyond the IT world to affect all of us.

1.2 Implications and Risks Beyond the IT World

The nature of the problem and the solution makes the Year 2000 problem the challenge of the century to both the IT industry and the worldwide infrastructure that the industry services. It is important for managers, investors, the legal profession, auditors, government leaders, stock analysts, and others to understand the breadth and criticality of the Year 2000 challenge because it reaches beyond the IT community. Cost increases, investment risks, failure of key government services, and the collapse of communication systems are just a few things that can cause a slight inconvenience to, at worst, total chaos in our lives.

The most glaring aspect of this problem, at least within a given organization, is the cost to correct it. This is generally stated to be $1 to $2 per line of source code within an enterprise. A small organization may have 5 to 12 million lines of code, while a medium-sized organization may have 12 to 25 million lines of code. Anything larger than this number of lines of code is considered to be a large IT shop. Many government agencies and Fortune 500 companies have 50 to 100 million lines of code or more. This means that a conservative estimate places the cost to fix the problem at $30 to $60 million for many shops. This is not an insignificant amount of money and typically requires board- or CEO-level approval.

The aggregate cost of the solution on a worldwide basis is said to be between $400 to $600 billion, according to the Gartner Group research organization. The question for stockholders, mutual fund managers, and ordinary citizens is "Where is this money going to come from?" For commercial companies, the money will come from an increase in the cost of goods and services. For governments, the money will come from increased tax revenues. Many companies may suffer financially. The worldwide economy may be impacted as well. Furthermore, the longer an organization waits, the more it will cost, because consulting rates will increase due to personnel shortages that will occur as we near the end of the century. One certainty is that budgets for IT, and on an overall basis, must be increased and reworked substantially.

A second, and more critical, aspect of the problem is the risk of not having systems Year 2000 compliant at all. Compliance is defined as the ability to accurately process dates and related events that span multiple centuries. Organizations that are not fully, or even partially, compliant by 2000 will encounter major disruptions in their business cycles. These disruptions could have the direct effect of lowering stock or bond ratings for the noncompliant organization. Mutual fund managers are already tracking companies that are working on Year 2000 compliance and those that are not in order to determine the resulting impact on investment portfolios. Dealing with the problem in an expeditious manner is, therefore, more important than most CEOs or CFOs may imagine.

One commonly mentioned statistic is that 25 percent to 50 percent of all computerized organizations will not be compliant by 2000. If this is true, and we concur with these statistics, the implications on the global economy could be catastrophic. It would only take a couple of major airlines, international banks, key government agencies, and health care providers to trigger major chaos. These risks, coupled with the vulnerability of highly automated stock and bond trading systems to date problems, could be enough to trigger a major ripple effect throughout international markets. That is why the urgency of the situation cannot be overstated.

Figure 1.3 depicts key impact curves associated with the year 2000. As implementation resources become increasingly scarce and costs to solve the problem go up, the value of certain stocks and bonds could conceivably go down. This means that those organizations that wait too long will see an even greater impact on the bottom line than those that pursue a solution near term. Many companies are waiting to see what happens to other companies to determine the impact on their systems. This is a high-risk proposition for any organization dependent on information technology. Executives that pursue this approach are risking total collapse of their information infrastructure and failure of the organization as a whole.

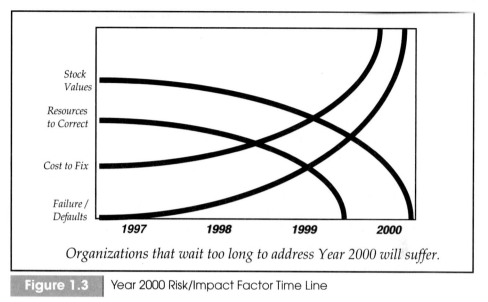

Organizations that wait too long to address Year 2000 will suffer.

Figure 1.3 | Year 2000 Risk/Impact Factor Time Line

There are an increasing number of industry examples where date handling problems have crept into production software systems. These examples foretell the potential impact on other organizations that have yet to encounter Year 2000 problems. The most common situations involve claims, forecasting, subscription, or similar systems that project forward in time. Insurance and credit card providers have experienced glitches in their software systems that had to be patched to get the systems to work properly. One type of patch used by software maintenance personnel to solve date handing problems is to leave errant dates untouched and add procedural logic to work around the problem. In other cases, a small number of selected dates are corrected to keep the system functioning. In almost all cases, problems were corrected by using an isolated approach that left these systems vulnerable to future Year 2000 problems.

Another option that companies exercise is to delay the impact of the problem by changing business procedures to work around computer system limitations. For example, a state department of motor vehicles (DMV) agency recently changed drivers license expiration dates to 12/31/99 to keep renewal systems from failing. This is clearly a stopgap measure. In another case, subscription renewal time frames for a magazine were shortened to avoid renewal dates that occurred in the next century. These "solutions" are clearly designed to delay inevitable problems that must be corrected in computer systems themselves.

1.3 Six Common Myths of Century Compliance

Given the potential consequences of date failures and the overwhelming predictions of the effort level required to achieve Year 2000 compliance, why haven't more IT organizations attacked the problem? There are many underlying reasons, including IT reluctance to invest in legacy applications at the expense of building flashy new systems. Six common myths, used by IT organizations to justify why century date compliance is not a priority in their shop, are discussed below.

1. It's a simple technical problem; just expand the date field by two digits.

This myth is true only for freestanding applications that contain few dates. Most business applications rely heavily on dates and share date data with numerous internal and external systems. Expanding date fields creates significant timing and testing issues throughout the conversion process because of these data interdependencies. Other approaches avoid date field expansion but require major modifications to legacy systems rife with poor naming conventions and nonexistent documentation. Numerous additional considerations such as system software compliance, database conversion, and unstable test environments create a technology migration and coordination problem far beyond a simple field expansion.

2. We have plenty of time.

Although it is rapidly closing in, January 2000 is still several years away. This gives an illusion of security that is fake for the following reasons:

- Systems that process dates in the future will confront 2000-related dates well before 1/1/2000. For example, a five-year leasing system had to deal with the year 2000 in 1995.

- One year of processing for testing and contingency will be needed. Prudent companies plan to complete conversion by the end of 1998.

- The sheer magnitude of the effort requires long lead times.

The lead time issue is significant. A medium-sized IT organization with 5,000 programs must convert more than 8 programs per business day starting in January 1996 to complete conversion before 1999. If each program requires only one person-day on average for analysis, coding, testing, and debugging (an overly conservative estimate), this task requires 25 person-years of effort for code conversion alone. Significant additional time is required for file conversion, interface routines, system testing, and numerous other activities.

As the deadline approaches, the volume of work stays the same, but the number of people needed to complete the effort within the required time frame increases. Qualified people will become increasingly difficult to obtain as procrastinating companies compete for scarce resources.

3. *Our systems will be replaced before 2000.*

This solution may not be mythical if the new applications are all designed and implemented to be century-compliant and delivered on schedule. Given the long lead times for building new applications, any significant project that has not started by the publication date of this book is unlikely to replace its predecessor in time. If replacement applications miss the 01/01/2000 deadline by even a few weeks, the original application must be converted to handle century-date values. Without careful contingency planning, there may not be enough time or resources to convert older applications. According to Gartner Group research and in our opinion, fewer than 5 percent to 10 percent of the systems that existed in 1995 will be replaced by 2000.

4. *We are already compliant; all of our applications are new.*

There are numerous examples of brand-new client/server applications that are not century compliant. Even if an application is 90 percent compliant, it will fail to process century dates correctly. Many new applications that claim compliance contain code copied from older noncompliant applications. Unless a new application was specifically designed and tested for century-date compliance during development, it must be validated to ensure its ability to handle all century-date scenarios. Validation testing alone is a highly time-consuming task.

5. *We will be saved by an automated solution.*

The quality and level of automation for Year 2000 software tools is increasing daily. Off-site conversion factories combine tools and consultants to offer additional options for turnkey conversions. While the degree of automation will increase over the next few years, tool coverage will be restricted to the most common languages and environments.

Waiting for the perfect solution may not leave enough time to pursue other options should such a solution fail to arrive. Furthermore, automation covers only the most rote portions of a century conversion—the code translation. Project management issues, coordination of interfaces, software package upgrades, data conversion, testing, and numerous other time-consuming activities will not be automated by a tool or turnkey conversion service.

6. *We are going to outsource the entire conversion project.*

Outsourcing all or part of a Year 2000 conversion is a valid strategy for companies with resource constraints. This does not relieve IT management from responsibility or ultimate accountability for the project. Numerous in-house management and coordination issues remain. Contracts for software packages and relationships with outside organizations providing and receiving data cannot be turned over to outsourcing vendors. Other tasks, including testing, configuration control, and production turnover, are difficult to perform without the involvement of in-house staff.

Unlike development projects, which can be self-contained, the Year 2000 migration affects production code that is typically modified every day. Reconciling maintenance changes performed by internal staff with century compliance upgrades performed by the outsourcing or consulting service is cumbersome and risky for highly volatile applications.

As the six common myths illustrate, there are no "silver bullet" solutions to make the Year 2000 problem vanish. This is a bitter pill to swallow for a project where no time extensions are available and the business cost of failure is high.

1.4 Outside Help Is Available—But Beware of False Prophets

Many people are talking about the Year 2000 problem, but it is not always clear as to who has or has not done real work on projects. Very soon, if not already, conference and seminar pundits that commonly use witty sound bites to warn people of the problem will become old hat. People are tired of hearing the same thing over and over again—they want solutions. These pundits, some of whom should be thanked for building early industry awareness, are quickly falling by the wayside as solution providers gain sophistication. The market now has enough momentum that these individuals must either get on board with solutions or step out of the way and let the vendors that can help, do their job.

The Year 2000 market is a service provider's market, because in-house IT staff must continue to focus on maintenance requests, user support, and other key initiatives. Who wants to train in-house staff for a one-time project that they will not have to repeat again? The answer is, very few IT executives. As a result, a host of companies are entering the Year 2000 market to help solve the problem. Personnel shortages within IT organizations and across the industry have made this a very lucrative market for consulting and outsourcing vendors. Given all of the advertising and promotional hype, however, it is difficult to know where to turn for help.

One reason for the confusion in finding and selecting skilled outside help is that the market is growing so quickly—it is already dwarfing the client/server package and data warehouse markets. As firms manage more and more Year 2000 projects, they hone their approach and become increasingly overwhelmed with additional work, thus opening the door to novice Year 2000 service providers. The skill levels of novice Year 2000 consultants are continuously suspect because a learning curve must be mastered. In some cases, novice service providers are barely one step ahead of their clients.

For example, early entrants in the service market incorrectly focused and diverted Year 2000 projects by performing overly-detailed, impact analysis across massive amounts of code. This effort provided clients with too much detail (irrelevant to enterprise planning projects), left them with no deployment plan, and delayed efforts to launch critical, enterprisewide initiatives. This misfortune was compounded by the fact that early clients continue to be reluctant to admit that mistakes were made by these firms on these projects. If you were responsible for a $50 to $100 million project with the company's financial survival at stake, would you admit that you made a major misstep during project initiation? These service providers are still out there working with novice clients and delaying their ability to launch projects.

Supply and demand continue to play a key role in the Year 2000 market and will affect the ability of both IT organizations and outside service providers to staff Year 2000 initiatives. While this may sound a little like the challenge facing the application package implementation market at the time of this writing, the Year 2000 personnel drain is just in the early stages. The resource shortage will become critically apparent within 2 to 3 years of the century mark. Where will the people needed to do this work come from and how will they all get trained? The answer at this point is not entirely clear.

Another challenge to staffing Year 2000 initiatives is that the IT industry is notorious for requiring long lead times for learning new technologies. In the Year 2000 area, the technology tends to be mainframe-based COBOL, PL/I, Assembler, IMS, and CICS systems. Recent college graduates probably did not learn COBOL in school, as many professors believe the only way to succeed in the IT market is to learn C++. Nor are young professionals lining up to acquire this mainframe training which they consider a potential career dead end. This phenomenon, coupled with the early retirement of skilled mainframe programmers, leaves a severe shortage of language and platform skills to support the Year 2000 market. Offshore outsourcing holds some answers to the general shortage of in-house staff and consulting resources.

Massive outsourcing will be required as traditional consulting firms and in-house staffs are drained of resources. Outsourcing companies are gearing up for this effort by teaming with in-house staff and on-site consulting firms. Outsourcing vendors provide services in two main ways. Some firms provide offshore or off-site resources, using various tools and techniques, to access in-house systems via satellite links and fiber-optic cables. Other service firms employ an approach whereby the client ships the system to be upgraded to an off-site, Year 2000 conversion "factory." The service firm then upgrades the system, using proprietary tools and techniques, and returns the compliant system to the client when finished. Both options require close coordination. Even with these firms providing Year 2000 conversion support, resources will grow scarce in the latter part of the century.

Software tool vendors can help with automating some of the more mechanical tasks of Year 2000 migration. Automation tools facilitate the systems inventory work, the impact analysis, the conversion work itself, and some of the validation. Automation, although it will not solve the problem itself, can help with the more mundane and repetitive analysis and conversion tasks. As this occurs, resources should be freed up to focus on project management, interface coordination, status tracking, and third-party vendor coordination. These people are already in short supply and the situation will get much worse before it gets better.

At some point, near the end of this century and in the first year of the next, it will seem like everybody will be in the Year 2000 market. This market, contrary to popular belief, will spill over well into 2001. Fixing backward-looking systems, retiring noncompliant software, and sorting through convoluted solutions will keep many IT professionals occupied for some time after the market is supposedly going to dry up.

Vendor support for this market will be examined in more detail later in this book. While choosing among these vendors may be confusing to organizations just beginning their Year 2000 research, these companies can and will help address the major resource shortage that the industry will experience.

1.5 Terminology

Certain terms that are used on an industry-wide basis should be clarified before we go further into the Year 2000 problem. Although these terms are defined in the glossary, the definitions are repeated here to facilitate further discussion.

Several types of systems must be considered during Year 2000 analysis. *Application* software describes a system that is maintained by in-house personnel. *Package* software describes a system that performs application functions, such as accounts receivable or payroll, and that was obtained from and is maintained by a third party. If a package is no longer on third-party maintenance, it is considered in-house, application software. *System* software includes all operating system, compiler, database, and telecommunication software. System software also includes tape, library, or other types of systems management utilities. Finally, *real time systems* refer to command and control systems or process control systems that address problems related to noninformation processing. These are commonly used in the Department of Defense, in manufacturing organizations, or facilities management.

The solution to the Year 2000 problem is commonly termed the *century date change*. A century-date change project would, therefore, involve all of the activities required to make an organization Year 2000 compliant. *Compliant* is the term used to describe the state of a given system that properly processes date values that span multiple centuries. Year 2000 compliance tends to be uniquely defined within a given enterprise, based on their needs. Specific standards are discussed later in this book. An entire organization may be considered Year 2000 compliant upon completion of a Year 2000 migration project.

Another term used frequently is *enterprise*. An enterprise is the all-encompassing set of systems that support the organization facing the Year 2000 challenge. This may be a government institution, a multidivisional corporation, or an individual company. Enterprisewide planning is a critical success factor for a Year 2000 migration initiative.

An *event horizon* is the amount of time remaining to an application area to begin a Year 2000 migration that will prevent that system from failing due to misinterpretation of time-dependent events. Assessing event horizons is a critical planning step that occurs early in a century-date change project.

Expansion or *date field expansion* is a term used to describe the increase in the physical or logical size of a data element and the corresponding physical data that is referenced by that element. Figure 1.4 shows an example of expanding a date field format as well as expanding the corresponding data in a database or file. Date field expansion is a common approach to addressing this problem, since it turns a two-digit year field into a four-digit year field containing a century indicator. Other date formats—and there are hundreds used around the world—involve some variation on the 2-character-to-4-character theme.

Change:

        YYMMDD   to   CCYYMMDD

And Change:

        961231   to   19961231

Date field expansion requires expansion of physical data and the definition of that data.

Figure 1.4 | Date Expansion Requirements

A *procedural workaround* is the alternative to the date field expansion approach. This approach works around the date problem by performing some type of procedural modification to the system so that the system properly processes dates that cross century boundaries. This approach does not expand the date field but makes appropriate logic changes to keep the system working properly.

The terms *methodology, process* and *blueprint* are all used interchangeably. A *methodology* is a detailed approach, containing generic and tool-related, step-by-step guidelines for building, upgrading, improving, or replacing application systems. In this case, the term *methodology* refers to a detailed approach for planning and implementing the Year 2000 solution. We will discuss a consistent approach for addressing this problem throughout this book and refer to industry methodologies, processes, and blueprints as needed.

A software product that supports one or more tasks within a Year 2000 project is called a *software tool* or *tool*. Tools are generally off-the-shelf, commercially available software products that assist with the analysis, upgrade, improvement, or rearchitecting of legacy applications.

Year 2000 migration efforts involve upgrading multiple systems, over time, in groups that make the most sense from a timing and economic standpoint. These groupings are called *upgrade units*. An upgrade unit is a system, or a group of related systems, treated as a single unit of work for a given scenario. The process of defining upgrade units across an enterprise is called *segmentation*.

The term used for Year 2000 testing and certification is called *validation*. The process involves running selected input data through an original program and then running that same data through a program that has been upgraded during a century-date change project to ensure that the modified program has retained functional equivalency. The output data of the validation tests should be identical, barring expected differences such as field size variations. The second main phase of validation within a century-date change project is to certify an upgrade unit to be Year 2000 compliant. Validation is covered in depth in later chapters of this book.

1.6 Real Problem, Real Solutions, Real Opportunities

The Year 2000 problem is real and will affect virtually every company and government agency in some way. It will also affect many individuals before the problem is fully resolved. Before a final solution is achieved, many IT organizations will see a significant drain on their budgets and their staff. They will also encounter disruptions in business-critical operations if action is not taken soon. Despite these pressures, management teams should not panic.

Help is available to review, plan, and implement a solution to the Year 2000 problem. If organizations systematically establish a clear strategy to inventory and correct in-house applications, packages, and system software, there is still time to blunt the impact of the year 2000 on information infrastructures. Time, however, is of the essence.

Chapter 2

Ramifications of the Year 2000 on Organizational Infrastructures

    This chapter describes the ramifications of the Year 2000 problem and how it might affect different types of organizations and the people involved. This discussion includes ramifications to the business as a whole, as well as to various information technology functions. The Year 2000 can have both positive and negative effects on the overall operations of a business. Negative effects are directly related to inaction, delays, or incomplete approaches in dealing with the problem. Positive impacts are linked to deploying an effective and efficient response to the challenge. This chapter encourages readers to pursue Year 2000 projects with a clear sense of urgency and introduces the concept that the migration effort itself can provide organizations with long-term value.

2.1 Breakdown of Information Management Capability

    In order to assess the overall risks of a Year 2000-related problem, it is important to recap the immense grip that information technology holds on the world today. Futuristic authors write that companies are evolving into a highly intertwined mix of technology and people—where one becomes inseparable from the other. This prediction, to a great extent, is already true. Organizations that have, for example, undertaken efforts to reengineer their business processes have learned that business processes are inextricably linked to information systems technology. The failure of this technology will, therefore, have an irreparable impact on critical business functions.

The external impact of the year 2000 is another major concern. It is easy to speculate about the loss of automated teller machine capability in a corporate planning session. It is a very different feeling to be standing at a broken cash machine with your family on a Sunday afternoon and telling them that the day at the theme park is canceled because you have no money. The risk of credit card failures, communication problems, or other more personalized impacts are significant. The loss of corporate goodwill in such cases cannot be predicted but must certainly be considered. Only when problems occur en masse can the full ramifications be felt.

A loss of goodwill means that customers will switch to other banks, insurance firms, and telecommunication providers. Service providers are at greater risk in this area than manufacturing companies that sell more tangible products. While no organization is risk free from the Year 2000 problem, the competitive edge that service companies once maintained because of strong information processing capabilities will become a double-edged sword if those same systems fail. Once customers are lost, they are difficult to regain. The loss of customers, coupled with the rapidly spreading news that policies are not adequately tracked, credit cards are no longer valid, or that some other service is below par, means that a corresponding drop in stock values will follow.

It is likely that some companies will not survive the year 2000 intact. This is truer for companies with certain high-risk factors. Companies, for example, that entered into a merger and doubled the size of their software portfolio may have inadvertently doubled the scope of their Year 2000 upgrade project. Shedding duplicate systems should be an urgent priority for these organizations. Companies that have reduced or eliminated senior staff positions may not have the systems knowledge required to complete an upgrade project on time. In companies where management feels that IT spending is, at best, a necessary evil, delays could extend project startup beyond critical event horizons.

Additionally, companies with limited control over central IT functions will face political constraints to mobilizing and sustaining an enterprisewide, Year 2000 upgrade. Other organizational issues that impact Year 2000 efforts include losing the chief information officer (CIO), not having a senior-level candidate to lead the project, matrix reporting structures that hinder decision-making ability, and continuous reorganizations. Many IT organizations reorganize at least once every two years. This also happens to be the average tenure for a CIO. All of these issues must be addressed or sidestepped to rapidly get to the real heart of the problem.

In addition to management issues, every organization has technical issues that complicate a Year 2000 project. The complexity of most IT environments makes a compliance upgrade a difficult job in the best of cases. Companies that have let software or hardware releases lag behind the general market face even greater Year 2000 challenges than companies that are technologically current. The scope of this problem across most companies, even those already addressing the issue, has yet to be fully realized because of the interwoven nature of systems. Every system is connected to some number of other systems. This, by the way, is one of the main reasons that legacy applications continue to outlive predictions of their demise.

This interconnectivity revolves around data that is passed and shared among systems. Many systems creating or updating a given database or file are unaware of other systems that actually use that data at another time. Figure 2.1 depicts a typical cross-section of data store usage in the relatively closed architecture of a human resources application. Propagation of erroneous data across major databases has already resulted in lost customer data and lost revenues. In response, many IT groups have stated that they will fix critical mainframe systems as a safeguard against Year 2000 problems. But if errant data is passed to a mainframe system from a client/server system, that data will quickly corrupt major databases and files. This type of corruption is a problem that is difficult or impossible to correct once it has occurred.

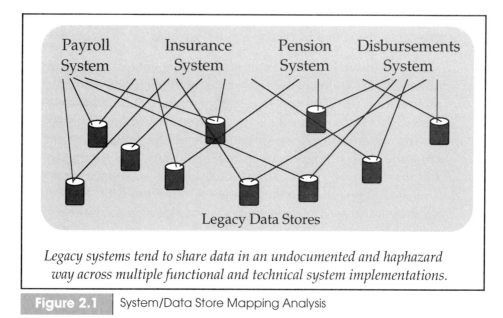

Payroll System   Insurance System   Pension System   Disbursements System

Legacy Data Stores

Legacy systems tend to share data in an undocumented and haphazard way across multiple functional and technical system implementations.

Figure 2.1   System/Data Store Mapping Analysis

Data-sharing issues are not limited to internal risk factors. Most companies regularly share data with outside entities. Even if a company was 100 percent Year 2000 compliant—a goal that is difficult to achieve—errant data can enter an IT environment through external interfaces. A company might sell, for example, a database of names and addresses representing a certain age group to an insurance company. The individuals identified, however, may be outside of the required age range, based on miscalculations performed by systems at the originating company. The receiving company may have no way to verify how many of these records are valid or invalid. The dates upon which this errant information is based may not even be contained in the data received.

Another concern faced by organizations is that IT personnel, the individuals with the most knowledge about the Year 2000 dilemma and related solutions, are focusing only on mainstream information systems. IT coordinators have stated that they cannot guarantee support for user-developed systems, distributed applications, process control systems, embedded systems, microchip devices, automated teller machines, and nonstandard hardware and software. In fact, IT people are so consumed with internal issues that they may not have spoken with the individuals responsible for these non-IT systems. This means that the people who know the most about the Year 2000 problem have not had the time, or the inclination, to transfer their knowledge to the non-IT professionals that can focus on these issues.

Even within the IT function, organizations are being caught off-guard by system failures. Some application groups believe they are not at risk because they fixed a 30- or 15-year mortgage problem several years ago. In other cases, entire industries are claiming not to have a problem. Viewing the problem from an industry-specific focus is one way to bring a sense of urgency to corporations and government agencies that need additional education about the risks of delaying work on the Year 2000 challenge.

2.2 Industry-Specific Risks and Levels of Readiness

Year 2000 risks vary according to processing requirements, whether a company is privately or publicly held, whether the organization is a government agency, distribution of information functions, and the criticality of computers to the bottom line. Opportunities vary as well. For example, large banks or insurance companies should view Year 2000 compliance as a competitive advantage. Government agencies, on the other hand, may just be concerned with survival. The manufacturing industry may see the expense to upgrade systems as a difficult budget item to sell to management. The travel industry, on the other hand, must keep reservations systems working properly to keep customers from going to another airline.

One thing that is emerging from all of the Year 2000 discussions is that certain industries seem to be communicating widely-varying responses to the year 2000. The pharmaceutical industry, for some curious reason, is claiming that they do not have a problem. The insurance industry, on the other hand, has displayed a very open approach with respect to starting work early and having a long way to go to achieve compliance. Wall Street firms are displaying a cautious attitude when speaking publicly about the Year 2000 topic. This caution will likely be emulated across other industries as the problem is more widely communicated by the media to senior executives.

Numerous industries share certain Year 2000 issues. One example can be found in pension, payroll, and human resource systems that project events beyond 1999. Another cross-industry example involves accounting systems that maintain financial aging schedules. Many industries also share common event horizons and a general level of readiness. Figure 2.2 depicts event horizons for certain industries to become Year 2000 compliant. General levels of preparedness, by industry, are also shown in Figure 2.2. Lead times and readiness levels will shift frequently as 2000 nears. Specific discussions will help clarify some of the unique issues that selected industries will encounter as they pursue Year 2000 solutions.

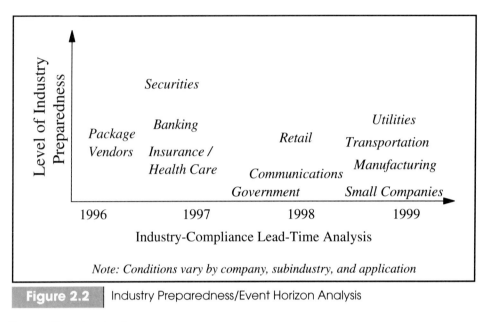

Figure 2.2 Industry Preparedness/Event Horizon Analysis

2.2.1 Securities Industry

The Wall Street securities firms are on the front lines of the Year 2000 battle. Speaking at a congressional subcommittee hearing held on April 16, 1996, Mr. Nick Magri, senior vice president of Post Trade Processing at Securities Information Automation Corporation (SIAC), shared common concerns over what the trading industry is facing. Post-trade processing involves the posting of trades that must be reconciled after each trading day and involves numerous transactions that project into the future as well as into the past. "Calculations involving trade processing must be calculated to the exact penny at the end of each processing cycle," according to Magri.

Just a few of the date-dependent issues required of securities systems include the ability to accurately clear and settle accounts in a timely manner, provide ongoing access to accounts, and calculate interest and dividend payments. Processing complexities are increased by the fact that multiple companies such as SIAC, which handles trades for the New York and American Stock Exchanges, the Deposit Trust Corp., and the Options Clearing House share common data. One major concern continues to be the complexity involved in testing these highly integrated environments.

In the securities industry, the complexities associated with a typical Year 2000 upgrade project are further complicated by the regulatory environment governing the industry. The Securities and Exchange Commission is the driving force behind recent regulatory changes, including a push to share data formats in an 8-character date format. Competition is another major factor that forces IT organizations within the securities industry to constantly be at the forefront of technology.

These issues are echoed across the securities industry where information is time sensitive, shared across the industry on a high-speed, high-volume basis, and where regulators never rest. The issues were significant enough to prompt the securities industry to establish a vehicle for dealing with the issue through the Securities Industry Association's (SIA) Data Management Division (DMD). Michael Tiernan, of CS First Boston, indicated that "the SIA DMD has created practices and procedures for dealing with the Year 2000 problem within the securities industry."

The IT industry may want to view the securities industry as a bellwether industry with respect to establishing funding, setting priorities, mobilizing teams, establishing industry standards, and delivering bottom-line results. If this industry cannot deliver upgraded systems, the financial world, as well as the rest of us, will certainly be made aware of it soon enough.

2.2.2 Insurance and Health Care

Insurance companies are faced with a staggering volume of data and applications compared to that found in other industries. Many large insurance companies have 50 to 100 million lines of code in their portfolio. One company calculated that upgrading 80,000 source programs over the next 2.5 years would require that 128 programs per work day be converted, tested, and placed back into production. With this statistic looming over the industry, insurance companies must determine which systems will not be upgraded, based on business units to be sold off, business units to be de-emphasized, systems deemed expendable, and systems that can be eliminated in favor of other options.

Rapid identification and elimination of duplicate systems is key to streamlining the list of systems that will and will not be made Year 2000 compliant. Duplicate or overlapping systems are common in many insurance companies. For example, the software that processes personal and commercial lines of coverage may have originated from identical core applications and still share many common routines. This problem is compounded where recent mergers or acquisitions are involved. An abundance of duplicate systems, common in the acquisition-driven health care market, demands special consideration. In many cases, consolidation strategies may not be as elegant as management would like because of an extremely short compliance window.

Another factor common to the insurance market is that the lead times for converting policy-based applications is relatively long. These systems typically have much longer time projection windows than systems in other markets because of policy expiration dates and other forward-looking logic that projects three years or more into the future. Comparison logic that determines if a current date is greater than a policy expiration date could cause a series of claim rejections that should have been accepted and processed by the system. The rejection of valid claims would not sit well with the holders of these policies.

These same systems also have an extensive backward-looking window based on birth date tracking. For example, insurance providers showing a birth date of 01/01/00 would not know if the person was just born or if the person was one hundred years old. Actuarial systems, which are highly oriented toward age-related risk factors, are particularly vulnerable if they misinterpret birth dates. Age miscalculations in these systems may result in higher premiums for young people and lower premiums for older individuals. Older individuals would probably not bring this to the attention of the insurance provider until millions of dollars were lost in policy revenues. On the other hand, overcharging younger policy holders on premium rates would likely result in class action suits against these companies.

Insurance companies clearly face a monumental task in dealing with massive, highly date-sensitive systems during a time when regulatory changes are at a peak. While the securities industry is on the front lines of the year 2000, the insurance industry is clearly the one to watch to see how quickly very large IT organizations can establish implementation teams and produce results. If any industry must be creative in mobilizing work teams, streamlining portfolios, shedding nonessential applications, and building contingency plans, the insurance industry is that industry.

2.2.3 Banking

Many of the major banks have a portfolio of large mainframe systems along with numerous state-of-the-art client/server systems. Mergers and acquisitions are as prevalent in banking environments as in the insurance and health care industries creating the same problems with duplicate and overlapping systems. These banking systems have the same, long lead times to correct and can certainly benefit from elimination of duplicate or overlapping systems. Distributed systems are quite prevalent in banks as well. This mix of systems means that a broader range of solutions is required across banking architectures.

Past efforts have been made to change mortgage processing functions to accommodate 30-year and 15-year mortgages. These solutions, in many cases, support only certain types of mortgages and do not constitute a comprehensive Year 2000 correction. Many of these fixes may, in fact, complicate a Year 2000 upgrade because they used a procedural workaround that will take time to decipher and correct. Similar corrections for 3- and 3.5-year credit card renewals are being implemented right now. Some of these adjustments may be embedded in date routines, which tend to be quite specialized in banking systems. Each of these routines must be examined, corrected, or replaced with routines that can support the Year 2000 rollover.

Other challenges in banking system environments involve determining if multiyear loans are maintained intact, verifying that interest credits are properly tracked, and ensuring that customers have ongoing access to accounts. Another difficult and often costly challenge is in the ATM environment. While most people would agree that the systems supporting the cash machines should be reviewed and scheduled for an upgrade, the ATM machines themselves may be in trouble. Some of the chips and the microcode in certain ATM machines may not recognize a 4-character year field and therefore not function at all. The added cost for the hardware upgrade, along with the complex testing process that this would entail, may require banks to spend more time and money than they had originally considered.

One final consideration for the banking industry is the massive amount of data that is transferred via electronic data interchange (EDI) and other means around the world each day. The sharing of synchronized information is critical to the ongoing viability of world financial markets. According to participants at the April 16, 1996, congressional hearing, a standard recommended by the SIA DMD, regardless of the internal approach employed, is that all externally transferred date formats be in an 8-character format. The interconnectivity of these environments is nonetheless going to be a major challenge. All of these factors set the stage for one of the most complex information environments to be made Year 2000 compliant.

2.2.4 Government

As mentioned earlier, the United States Government held a congressional subcommittee hearing on the Year 2000 problem. The concerns expressed by those testifying included a perceived lack of urgency on the part of Congress to take rapid action to address the Year 2000 across various agencies. Those familiar with the typical government procurement processes know that project startup generally takes longer and ultimately costs more than similar efforts in the commercial marketplace. Procurement rules make the process of initiating and sustaining a long-term project particularly difficult.

In federal and state agencies, for example, internal resources are normally unavailable to perform the work required in a Year 2000 project. This means that many agencies will turn to traditional procurement methods to obtain help from contracting firms. Existing procurement rules at the federal, state, and local level, however, will force agencies to squeeze most of the required upgrade work into a very narrow window of time. This is particularly true for those agencies that have large information infrastructures (more than 30 to 40 million lines of code) and that have not yet begun implementation. Fortunately, discussions are underway at a number of government levels to temporarily sidestep certain procurement rules to expedite Year 2000 project startup.

As far as the event horizons within various government systems is concerned, the situation varies according to type of agency and system. For example, the United States Internal Revenue Service performs significant analysis on past due accounts and on historic data, while focusing little processing effort on events that occur in the future. This means that as long as the bulk of the systems are converted by 2000, any date-related processing problems should be minimized.

The Social Security Administration (SSA) is an example of an agency that is extremely date sensitive. Much of the agency's 30 to 40 million lines of code revolves around the eligibility of recipients—which is based on age. Fortunately for U.S. senior citizens, the SSA has been working on fixing the Year 2000 problem since 1989. According to individuals at the agency, "The SSA is at the forefront of the Year 2000 effort, has already upgraded all major databases, and plans to be completed with the project by December 31, 1998." SSA has taken a leadership role within the federal government by organizing internal conferences and an interagency committee that allow various agencies to share information about the year 2000.

The United States Department of Defense (DOD) is responsible for one of the largest collections of systems in the world. Numerous hardware platforms and languages have been employed over the years to meet all of the information, real-time, and defense-related tasks required across the various branches of the U.S. armed services. Individuals familiar with various defense environments believe that weapons systems contain limited date sensitivity. The issue of weapons maintenance requirements, however, has led some analysts to suggest that these systems require close inspection prior to 2000. Defense officials have indicated that any information that they uncover will be forwarded to all allies, particularly those that have purchased U.S.-based weaponry.

As far as information systems are concerned, the DOD is consolidating operations across various command structures. This consolidation should prompt the DOD to quickly integrate and eliminate redundant systems in order to greatly reduce the overall upgrade costs associated with making systems Year 2000 compliant. This conjecture assumes that the different branches of the armed forces can determine which systems should stay and which systems should be phased out. As with most commercial environments, the DOD and other government agencies have many difficult and politically charged decisions ahead as they move toward Year 2000 compliance.

2.2.5 Transportation

The transportation industry is driven by schedules, and these schedules normally involve dates. Airline reservation systems, railroad routing systems, and truck scheduling systems all focus on time- and date-related events which tend to have fairly short windows. This may lead to short-term workaround strategies in many of these systems. One major airline is using this approach as its main strategy and is expanding date fields to a full 8-character format only on an exception basis. Other airlines are planning to migrate to a full 8-character date representation.

Lou Marcoccia, former director of the Year 2000 effort at the New York City Transit Authority, has taken an early and proactive approach to the Year 2000 problem. "We cleaned up our infrastructure first so that the inventory of systems we were working with was well defined and of high integrity. This allowed us to streamline Year 2000 planning and implementation because we did not have to deal with legacy problems such as unused, dead, or redundant application components. This infrastructure cleanup process took a couple of years to complete but has established a foundation for our Year 2000 project."

The transportation industry, for the most part, is concerned with accommodating a limited Year 2000 compliance window. In other words, the Year 2000 problem is only a problem for reservation and scheduling systems that track activity spanning the century mark. Once these activities begin to occur in the next (the same) century, problems will subside. The challenge is surviving that cross-century window of time, which may span up to one year or more.

Other applications may have longer windows of risk. This means that each system must be reviewed to ensure that problems are handled proactively. Shipping, railroad, trucking, and other transportation industries must all face the fact that schedules are time and date dependent. Unless the Year 2000 issue is resolved, the early part of the next century is going to be a difficult time for the transportation community and all travelers.

2.2.6 Telecommunications

The telecommunications industry, which includes local telephone and long-distance service providers, is another example of a highly competitive and rapidly changing technological environment. But for all of the leading edge dynamics and technological innovations at these companies, numerous legacy systems still exist. For example, almost all Regional Bell Operating Companies (RBOC) are still using the same, customer-revenue information systems that they have been using for the last two decades. Numerous attempts to replace these systems have been largely unsuccessful. Other legacy systems, as well as many newer client/server systems, abound.

One might contend that acquisition activity in the communications market, Pacific Bell, Southwest Bell, and Bell Atlantic/NYNEX being notable cases, would result in the elimination of redundant systems and streamline efforts to become Year 2000 compliant. But according to Patricia Seymour, Principal at Technology Innovations in Danville, CA, who worked at Pacific Bell for over 20 years, "the duplicate systems that result from the merger of two RBOCs are, at least initially, difficult to integrate."

"The Public Utilities Commission (PUC), which is institutionalized at the state level, governs the regulated portion of an RBOC. PUC determines service rates, service options, credits, charges, discounts, and other profit- and billing-related issues. All new products and services must be approved by PUC at the state level. Each state commission, therefore, establishes a different set of rules for each state that it governs. Systems were customized over time to accommodate this structure. It would be difficult to integrate these systems or to create an overriding system to handle all of these variances before the Year 2000 window closes," according to Seymour.

Ms. Seymour, who also worked as a strategic advisor to various long-distance providers, believes that there are Year 2000 complications ahead for long distance carriers as well. "Long-distance carriers maintain extremely distributed IT environments. This results in a more complex inventory process in the early planning stages. Another consideration is that time-to-market for a new product drives the long-distance carrier's prioritization process. If there is no direct customer benefit linked to an IT expenditure, it may not get the attention, funding, and sponsorship required to succeed. In other words, executive attention will not be focused on the Year 2000 problem," according to Seymour.

The good news according to most analysts is that hardware switching equipment will not be adversely impacted by the century rollover. The bad news is that the bulk of the software systems, particularly those that are time dependent, will be impacted, albeit for a short period of time. One piece of advice is to stay off the phone at midnight on December 31, 1999, because you may end up with a 100-year phone bill. If the call crosses multiple time zones, you may just want to avoid making that phone call for a 24-hour period of time.

2.2.7 Utilities

Utilities, including power companies providing electricity, gas, water, and other services, have large systems that tend to date back 20 to 30 years. Rate structures and billing cycles are largely based on historic usage. This means that, for many utility systems, event horizons and corresponding project lead times are limited to a year or so. This is a shorter period of time than is found in other industries. These systems, however, must be fixed in time to support any forward-looking logic that they may encounter. This means that the standard default target date used by the industry, December 31, 1998, is a valid target date for many utilities. Finally, regulatory environments and past downsizing of key IT staff, common in utility companies, are clearly potential roadblocks to progress.

2.2.8 Pharmaceutical Industry

The pharmaceutical industry is very much at risk in terms of legal issues relating to Year 2000 problems. Medicine labels must reflect accurate expiration dates so that people do not get ill from old medicine. This means that a label indicating "02/09/01" must be expanded to "02/09/2001" (depending on the country in which the label is produced) to accurately reflect the actual expiration date. The internal systems dealing with pharmaceuticals should also be expanded to 8-character dates to provide the most accurate level of processing when human lives are at stake.

Interestingly enough, the pharmaceutical industry is being very quiet about the entire situation. Numerous vendors that have approached companies in this industry have been told that their systems are Year 2000 compliant. This is very difficult to believe because all of the IT organizations that have opened up their systems to scrutiny are not compliant. The only exceptions are those few organizations that have proactively gone through the conversion process already.

Risks in this industry involve human lives and it will not come as a big surprise if company lawyers have told these firms to keep quiet on the topic of the year 2000. If these companies are not compliant (a likely situation) and they are trying to cover up this fact, they are definitely doing themselves more harm in the long term. It is one thing to make a best effort to address an issue and fail. It is a very different situation when a company tries to smooth things over when there is a real problem. The courts will not look favorably on this situation if it comes down to litigation in the early part of the next century.

2.2.9 Manufacturing

There is good news and bad news for manufacturing companies. The good news is that software portfolios for these companies are generally smaller than they are in other information-dependent industries and are also less date dependent. This means that lead times to correct systems are shorter, that the project requires fewer resources, and that project costs are lower than they would be at an insurance company or a bank. The other good news is that many of these companies are using or migrating to off-the-shelf application packages that can be maintained and upgraded by package vendors.

The bad news is that many of these companies do not have large IT budgets and may own systems that could easily be overlooked during the scope of this effort. Process control systems, for example, may have been physically developed on microchips that do not support the century rollover. Costs and lead times to correct these "nonstandard" systems may be extraordinary. The manufacturers of a given chip may no longer make that technology or may not even be in business. These process control systems may even be completely overlooked in the initial Year 2000 assessment process because they do not show up in an inventory of IT systems. New hardware may be needed and may have to be commissioned on a customized basis. This introduces a clear spike into the Year 2000 budget model.

Similarly, many companies build and sell machines that contain computer chips embedded in the equipment itself. If these chips fail around the turn of the century, the manufacturer will be liable for that failure. For example, will cars using computerized dashboards start on the morning of January 1, 2000? Are trains, trucks, or even airplanes that contain these chips going to continue operating without a problem? No one

can answer these questions until each and every piece of equipment produced by a company is examined. The legal responsibility lies with the
manufacturer of these items. Verifying compliance in advance could determine the ultimate survival of these companies.

Another important characteristic of IT environments of many manufacturing companies is that they make heavy use of third-party software.
If software packages are deemed noncompliant, and have been modified
or are not up to the latest release level, the costs and lead times to upgrade
these systems may be more than the cost to correct similar in-house applications. Manufacturing companies that believe they have limited exposure
to the Year 2000 problem should aggressively determine the state of their
packages as soon as possible.

2.2.10 Package Vendors

Third-party software vendors fall into two general categories: system
software vendors and application software vendors. Virtually all computerized companies contract with software vendors that sell system software,
utilities, and related tools. These vendors are defining compliance time
frames for each of their products on a case-by-case basis. IBM, for example,
has published a 200-page, Year 2000 white paper identifying compliance
schedules for various IBM products. It is critical that companies closely synchronize all system software upgrades with in-house efforts.

Most companies do not have much latitude with respect to switching hardware platforms, operating systems, and system support utilities
in the next 2 to 3 years. This means that vendors whose products are currently installed in a given IT environment will benefit to whatever degree
they can become Year 2000 compliant. In many cases, organizations that
may have neglected system software upgrades in the past will be forced
into these upgrades in order to keep systems working. As funding for
these upgrades is released to ensure that systems continue to function
beyond 2000, system software vendors will profit.

Application software vendors are in a very different position than
are system software vendors. Application packages, such as accounting or
human resource software, can be exchanged more readily than an operating system or embedded utility. Moreover, application software is more
likely to have been modified than system software because the source
code is typically available to in-house support teams. As the in-house version of a package becomes more and more out of date, that version
becomes more difficult to synchronize with a vendor's latest release. Thus,
the in-house version has more value than the vendor's version. At this

point, maintenance payments are usually stopped. This factor, coupled with the availability of competing packages, will reduce overall revenue streams to a given vendor, depending of course, on contractual agreements between the parties.

Many application package vendors survive on slim profit margins. The cost of being Year 2000 compliant may be too much to bear for investors and for the corporate balance sheet. The only revenue source most of these companies have is their software sales. If their software asset is not Year 2000 compliant, it has limited market value. Many of these vendors are, not surprisingly, remaining quiet about their Year 2000 support, most likely because they do not want sales to decline because of not being compliant. The Year 2000 problem makes a shakeout in the application software market almost inevitable.

On the other hand, if certain package software is Year 2000 compliant, that package may be a valid upgrade option if implementation lead times are within Year 2000 event horizons for that company. Some package vendors have attempted to make the Year 2000 issue a plus from a proactive marketing perspective. This is clearly a wise move if the competition is remaining silent on the topic.

2.2.11 Small Companies

Small companies are at risk for the Year 2000 problem, too. These companies range from dentist offices, automotive repair shops, and local retail chains, to small IT shops at manufacturing and other companies. Companies using PC-based technologies have a difficult enough time getting small-time package vendors to keep PC DOS systems technologically current, let alone having these companies rework a system to support the year 2000. Many of these small package vendors will likely rewrite these systems from scratch—given that they are made aware of the Year 2000 problem in the first place.

Other small companies, particularly in the manufacturing arena, may be running systems on IBM DOS VSE machines, have a limited staff of two to five people, and be constrained by relatively small technology budgets. These organizations may find that a Year 2000 upgrade is going to cost them 10 to 15 times their annual IT budget. These situations, which are discussed further in Chapter 16, *Small Information Technology Organizations*, tend to warrant very different solutions than larger organizations. For example, it may be more cost effective to scrap old hardware and software systems, downsize to a client/server or an IBM® AS/400® system, and acquire new applications that are Year 2000 compliant.

2.3 Legal Ramifications of Noncompliance

While each industry and every organization has unique Year 2000 challenges, one thing they all have in common are the legal risks associated with problematic systems. Legal exposure involves potential litigation that may be filed by shareholders, customers, business partners, or other entities because a system failure or errant data somehow caused them financial harm. Other potential incidents, involving weapons systems, airplane software, and health care systems, could be life-threatening. Because of these many factors, legal considerations are an integral component of the Year 2000 solution.

Examples of risk factors to corporations include system failures that result in:

- A manufacturing company that cannot process new product orders

- Field representatives that cannot accept insurance claims

- Customer service representatives that cannot handle service requests

- Businesses that lose customers because of misinformation to users and end customers

The result of these failures could motivate customers or other affected parties to file lawsuits against the company. If the situation results in large revenue losses, stockholders may decide to file a class action suit against the board of directors and corporate officers. Corporate board members are vulnerable in these situations—particularly if they were found to have been idle in the face of media warnings about the year 2000. If a company fails completely, vendors and other creditors will likely file suit as well. State, local, and federal governments are also at risk, with their constituents. Hopefully, few situations will escalate to this point.

Other situations may involve a noncompliant system passing errant data outside of the organization through EDI or other interfaces. This data may initially appear correct, but may have been created based on a miscalculation in date processing logic. For example, a file may be loaded with ineligible retirees and passed to companies offering retiree services. Imagine all of the people in the list being children under the age of five. Once errant data is loaded into the receiving company's database, it is very difficult to remove it. The situation could cause the company receiving the bad data to file a lawsuit against the originating company if real damage results. In these cases, corporations will be battling with other corporations, or even government agencies, over the contamination of strategic data.

Examples of other potential risks are even more frightening. For example, weapon systems, onboard computers on airplanes, and air traffic control systems, while at minimal risk, must be carefully examined to ensure that date problems are identified and corrected. Hospital admitting systems could fail and stall patient services. Food inspection tracking software may inaccurately determine that there are problems with certain foods, based on errant expiration dates. Senior citizens or pensioners not receiving checks could become homeless. Communication facilities, so critical to society, could fail and cause a wealth of problems. Other unforeseen issues may pose additional unknown risks.

Corporate and government legal teams must have an executive mandate to begin working with IT professionals on the process of reviewing all of the risks to their organization. Proactive legal options include a wide range of activities. The most immediate directive is to have legal teams monitor the aggressive pursuit of Year 2000 compliance on mission-critical systems. A second task requires analysis of all external interfaces to determine how corrupt data could be sent to or received from an outside entity. A third requirement involves communicating progress on the Year 2000 solution to corporate officers, stockholders, and board members to avoid surprises.

One immediate area that legal teams should focus on is contract management. Any new contracts, written for third-party software or hardware, must contain language stating a requirement to be Year 2000 compliant. Year 2000 compliance requires that software and hardware properly handle time-dependent events that cross the century mark. Existing contracts, including outsourcing agreements, must be reviewed on a case-by-case basis to determine potential exposure. Conversations with each vendor will dictate how each of these agreements is handled. Most hardware and software contracts contain language indicating that a product must function properly or "as specified." This is a good starting point for the legal team in bringing pressure on these vendors to specify a compliance time frame.

Outsourcing contracts create a special problem for both the vendor and the company that has contracted for the service. It is unclear at this point where the liability lies, because most of these contracts were written without reference to the year 2000. As far as outsourcing goes, it is probably not in anyone's interest to get into a drawn-out legal battle. Companies should concentrate on negotiating a solution with their outsourcing vendor. The bottom line on legal issues is that legal counsel must be directly involved in the discussion of the Year 2000 problem as well as the solution. External legal firms are gearing up for litigation against organizations that are unprepared to deal with the year 2000.

2.4 Global View of the Year 2000 Challenge

It is important to discuss how organizations in different parts of the world are dealing with the year 2000 issue. With so much data being interchanged across international boundaries, multinational corporations must coordinate compliance efforts with overseas divisions, customers, and partners. One thing that is generally agreed upon is that the United States is well ahead of the rest of the world in the area of Year 2000 awareness and in progress made thus far. Canada is rapidly coming to terms with the Year 2000 problem. This is particularly true for Canadian banks, many of which have projects well underway. The Canadian federal government is also pursuing work on this effort.

Europe is just now coming up to speed on the problem—particularly in the United Kingdom. With nongovernment systems being generally smaller in European countries, the lead time difference is not really that significant. One complication in Europe is that many countries are pursuing monetary conversion to a common currency called the Euro. The year 2000 will definitely complicate these efforts and drain resources slated for other projects. Coordination across Europe is even more important because of the multinational nature of many European-based companies. Federal governments in many regions are beginning to pursue Year 2000 assessment and compliance projects.

Asia is another rapidly growing Year 2000 market. In Japan, software systems calculate dates based on the emperor's birthday. Because Japan processes a wealth of international data, however, one must assume that many systems contain western date representations. Other Asian markets are just beginning to understand the impact of the year 2000. This is also true of South American and South African markets. One thing is clear in many of these countries: companies are slowly becoming aware that they need to begin addressing the problem expeditiously. These efforts will hopefully be coordinated as needed across international boundaries.

2.5 Business Case for Correcting Year 2000

The business case for the Year 2000 should be examined in light of the potential winners and losers in this market. Table 2.1 lists some of the potential benefactors of the Year 2000 market. The main winners are companies that are in information-critical markets and that are Year 2000 compliant within required event horizons. These companies, including banks, securities firms, and insurance companies, will be able to win over customers that leave companies that are not Year 2000 compliant. One can easily imagine that frustrated ATM customers and policyholders will switch to a different bank or insurance company if service is severely restricted at their current company.

The "Losers" column, shown in Table 2.1, presents a more motivating business case. As discussed in section 2.3, *Legal Ramifications of Non-compliance*, stockholders and government constituents may file suits against anyone that they consider responsible for their losses or their problems. This includes boards of directors, government entities, and corporate officers. The business case for performing a Year 2000 upgrade on critical information systems can be very simply stated: if the Year 2000 problem is not accommodated in some way, key company functions will likely fail and render the organization impotent.

Table 2.1 | Year 2000 Winners and Losers

Year 2000 Winners	Year 2000 Losers
• *Companies that are compliant in time* • *Year 2000 vendors and service providers* • *Hardware/storage manufacturers* • *Offshore outsourcing companies* • *Lawyers and legal firms* • *Investors in compliant companies* • *Investors in Year 2000 vendors* • *Customers of compliant companies* • *Constituents of government agencies that are compliant*	• *Companies not compliant in time* • *Stockholders of noncompliant companies* • *Boards of directors of companies that are not compliant* • *Insurers of noncompliant companies* • *Unprepared software vendors* • *Constituents of noncompliant government agencies* • *Vendors not in Year 2000 market*

Companies will want to take the business case to heart as they review Year 2000 strategies across individual business units. One company sold an entire leasing division reportedly to avoid Year 2000 upgrade costs. The business unit was supposedly providing marginal profits, and it was more judicious to sell the entire division than to spend the money to upgrade its outdated Assembler systems. This divestiture option will make continued sense as the year 2000 looms. The company acquiring the aforementioned business unit may be able to scrap the systems from the newly acquired leasing division and consolidate the leasing business into its existing business unit.

The leasing division sale exemplifies something that every business case must have—contingency plans. Another example of a contingency plan, suggested by an analyst, involved the Internal Revenue Service (IRS) and proposed that in the event that the IRS does not meet c ompliance dates, the government may want to institute a flat tax. These contingency plan examples demonstrate why senior executives must be involved in the Year 2000 decision-making process. While IT planning is a topic many executives do not want to discuss, the CEO, CFO, and other senior management team members must turn their attention to these matters. Without high-level oversight, IT organizations may make ill-advised decisions on how to spend Year 2000 budgets, wasting precious time and budget dollars on non-strategic systems.

Another, more positive, business case for the year 2000 focuses on the IT area. Some people have suggested that the year 2000 is a blessing in disguise. For example, a Year 2000 project offers a rare opportunity because it is one of the few projects capable of sustaining the commitment levels needed to produce a comprehensive accounting of all software assets. This information is invaluable to configuration control and systems planning teams. Obsolete technology, inactive source code, and missing components contribute to project delays and cost overruns. Once identified, appropriate areas can cleanse the portfolio and ultimately streamline the overall information delivery capability.

The Year 2000 assessment similarly examines various support functions across application areas. The Year 2000 project requires that these functions be stabilized prior to upgrading a given set of systems. This means that codification of standards, test environments, change control, and quality assurance procedures must be incorporated into the deployment plan. Once infrastructure items are corrected as part of the Year 2000 plan, they become a permanent fixture of the systems management process.

In addition to the infrastructure-related benefits from a Year 2000 project, there are strategic benefits as well. Many executives like to believe that aging architectures will eventually be migrated to a more strategic target, but the same systems continue to run in production year after year. If management truly wants to rectify this situation, they must have an in-depth understanding of legacy environments and a strategy to transition beyond those environments. The Year 2000 project, when positioned properly, provides the foundation to meet these objectives. Chapters 18 and 19 discuss these benefits in more depth.

While the bottom line of a cost/benefit analysis of the Year 2000 problem is that compliance is necessary for survival, IT-related opportunities do exist and should be incorporated into a comprehensive Year 2000 strategy.

2.6 Call to Action: Why Expedite Implementation?

If you are realizing for the first time that your organization has a Year 2000 problem and nothing has been done about it, your organization is way behind the curve in terms of meeting required event horizons. This also means that a trial-and-error approach, if started at this time, is the worst path to pursue. Early Year 2000 migration teams that have already completed Year 2000 projects applied a "learn as you go" approach. This approach was fine because they had fairly long lead times to complete these projects. Pursuing the same approach now, however, is a very high risk proposition for medium-to-large shops. There just is not enough time left to treat the Year 2000 upgrade as anything other than a tightly managed, high-priority project.

Having said this, the risks of procrastinating further are devastating. The lead times and event horizons are too short. Putting the sheer cost aside for a minute, companies can use a simple formula to get management on board. Take the number of work days left between today's date and December 31, 1998 (the standard industry target date), and divide that number of days into the total number of source programs in your portfolio. This is the number of programs that must be converted and tested daily for your project.

If this statistic does not motivate IT leaders in your company to take action, calculate the number of weekends and divide this number into the number of source programs and the total number of systems. This is the number of programs and systems that must be moved into production each weekend over the life of the project. To refine this number, subtract the number of weekends that fall on a holiday and at the end of a quarter. Couple these statistics with the number of reorganizations anticipated over the next three years, other large projects slated between now and then, and the internal resources needed to fulfill these requirements. If IT management still does not view the Year 2000 issue with an extreme sense of urgency, they probably do not plan to be around when 2000 arrives.

There will be a lack of qualified personnel to perform Year 2000 work between now and the end of the century. There is already a shortage of qualified COBOL mainframe talent in the market, and the shortage will worsen. Offshore migration work, which must be closely coordinated with on-site efforts, will be a necessity as organizations set up the mechanisms for 24-hour projects. At some point, management must ask how many people can work on this problem at the same time and still meet project goals. The answer to this question serves as another motivating factor.

Cost curve increases are given in the Year 2000 market as a shortage of personnel, knowledgeable in the Year 2000 area, drive up consulting rates for skilled resources. The year 2000 is a seller's market and this means that, to get the best people, companies must pay top dollar. Costs will be driven up further by the need for more teams, more concentrated production turnover, and more testing in a condensed period of time. This, coupled with storage and hardware requirements that could peak at 20 to 25 percent above current levels, means that organizations that delay Year 2000 projects will see costs increase two-fold or more.

Building awareness and urgency is a requirement at the executive level and at the business unit level in every organization. These goals can be addressed concurrently by having the CIO commission a business risk assessment. The risk assessment identifies key business areas, related products or services, systems supporting each business area, projected system failure dates, and corporate exposure in terms of lost revenue or legal risks. The risk assessment is derived from the same basic activities performed during the enterprise planning stage of a Year 2000 project. Figure 2.3 depicts an example of a business risk assessment that highlights risk factors for a large financial institution.

Year 2000—Business Risk Assessment Report

Business Area	Key Product or Service	Related Systems	Projected Failure Date	Required Start Date	Projected Risks
International Trading	Monetary Funds Transfer	Worldwide Funds Process	12/01/98	2/01/98	$2 million per week

Business risk assessment links business area risks to the demise of one or more computer systems.

Figure 2.3   Example of Business Risk Assessment

This type of business-based analysis establishes an executive communication vehicle and addresses the number one roadblock to full-scale

Year 2000 deployment—lack of CEO and CFO sponsorship and commitment. In order to sustain executive commitment—a task critical to maintaining project funding levels—this report must be scrutinized quarterly until full compliance is achieved. Motivating executives to take action depends on the execution of each of the following tasks.

1. *Communicate business risk assessment results in a calm and concise manner.*

2. *Discuss resource requirements, shortages, and costs as event horizons move closer.*

3. *Bring the internal and external audit team into the discussion as a means of communicating risk to the organization.*

4. *Once executives are educated about the problem, have the internal legal team conduct a briefing on the legal risks of the year 2000.*

5. *Establish alliances with senior business executives as a means of getting senior management on board.*

6. *Share insights on what other companies are doing in similar industries and business areas—this may be what it takes to sell senior management if the competition is way ahead.*

If none of these approaches work, continue internal awareness efforts by using in-house personnel and existing budget dollars to refine your business case. Sooner or later the people running every computerized organization in the world will have to confront the Year 2000 challenge.

Issues and Strategies

$\mathbf{T}$he next few chapters expose readers to the myriad of issues that must be addressed when an IT organization undertakes a century-date compliance initiative. Chapter 3 provides an overview of the topics discussed in Chapters 4 through 8. Readers wanting a high-level understanding of century migration issues may want to read only Chapter 3, using the remaining chapters in Part 2 to reference topics of interest. Those charged with implementing a century-date compliance effort should read the subsequent chapters to gain a more thorough understanding of these topics. The strategies and techniques described in Chapters 4 through 8 are the foundation for the project-implementation approaches described in Part 3 of the book.

Year 2000 initiatives involve a wide range of issues that encompass much more than simply changing code. The failure of organizations to quickly address Year 2000 issues stems, in part, from a lack of realization of the full extent of these issues. The scope of a Year 2000-compliance project is broader than most application-specific projects because it involves virtually all programs, data, and technology that exist in an organization. It may force an organization to finally confront and resolve many thorny issues—such as obsolete technologies and inconsistent platforms—that had previously been ignored. It will require coordinated efforts among the programming staff as well as the system, operations, and user support staffs. When the enormity of the project is realized, most organizations regret the fact that they did not start their compliance efforts earlier.

There are numerous methodical approaches to resolving Year 2000 issues, some of which are obvious, some of which are not. To the uninitiated, a Year 2000 strategy is simply deciding whether to expand year fields from two digits to four digits or to interpret the century from a two-digit year. As the topics discussed in Part 2 illustrate, the strategies needed for a successful Year 2000 effort are far more numerous and complex.

IT organizations must consider their full range of options before launching their implementation effort. Different strategies are available for each issue, and each strategy has its own impact and implications. Selecting one strategy early in the project may preclude the use of other, more desirable strategies later in the project. Selecting the right set of strategies to fit organizational needs reduces project time and effort and provides an opportunity to gain additional, valuable, and long-term benefits from the completion of the project.

Chapters 4 through 8 deal with the full range of issues that an organization is likely to encounter in its compliance efforts, and discusses strategies for addressing those issues. In addition to discussing the obvious problems and their solutions, these chapters explore the subtle issues that may go unnoticed until they are encountered during the project. Understanding these issues and solutions in advance saves valuable time and resources.

chapter 3

Overviews of Issues and Solutions

$\mathbf{T}$his chapter provides an overview of the issues and solutions presented in Chapters 4 through 8. It is divided into five sections: asset management issues, migration issues, environmental issues, relationship and organizational issues, and management issues. Each section corresponds to a subsequent chapter in Part 2.

3.1 Asset Management Issues

Corporations entrust their IT organizations with an extremely valuable asset—their portfolio of critical business applications. These applications reside on a myriad of platforms, are supported by a variety of internal and external organizations, and operate within a complex environment of system software. The challenge of Year 2000 initiatives is to assure century-date compliance for this entire range of software.

At a high level, all IT managers understand that their software needs to be modified to achieve century-date compliance, but they may not fully realize the meaning and implications of compliance when brought to the implementation level. These issues include:

- Finding all of the software components that require modification

- Selecting conversion strategies that align with long- and short-term corporate goals and budgets

- Assuring compliance of software that is managed outside of IT

- Resolving dependencies among categories of software

- Finding methods to handle obsolete or poorly supported technologies

To understand the scope of the effort, the IT organization must fully understand the assets that it is managing and how best to make each asset century-date compliant. These assets consist of a variety of categories of software, including mainframe systems, client/server technologies, software packages, system software and utilities, end-user software, and PC software packages. While these categories share many of the same century-date compliance issues, each category presents its own specific compliance challenges.

Chapter 4 addresses asset management issues by considering the challenges of developing a detailed inventory, describing high-level conversion strategies, addressing the effect of Year 2000 on new development, and discussing the implications of the compliance effort on each category of software. These areas are highlighted below.

3.1.1 Creating an Inventory

While most IT managers are acutely aware of the most important applications in the corporate portfolio, they are shocked to find that their organizations have tremendous difficulty assembling a complete inventory of the components of those systems. This difficulty increases for lower-profile systems, and the task becomes virtually impossible for end-user software. Somehow, the director of a Year 2000 project must be able to ensure compliance for a portfolio, whose size is not accurately determinable and whose components are not all locatable. Without accurate information, the project director cannot develop a reasonable project estimate, determine which strategies will be most effective, select the tools required to complete the project, or even determine if the portfolio is truly compliant at the close of the project.

The only solution to this challenge is to develop a complete and accurate inventory of the corporate portfolio at the beginning of the Year 2000 initiative. An inventory is more than a list of programs and applications. It should contain information about where those assets reside, the type of system and its compliance status, the age and expected life span of the system, its technical and functional quality, date dependence, platform, and business volatility. This information is used to size the overall effort, divide the project into independent sub-projects, devise the optimal strategy for each sub-project, and determine the sub-project's priority within the overall project. Knowing the types and quantities of each technology represented in the portfolio enables the selection of appropriate software tools and consulting services.

The inventory will also expose potential problem areas such as the use of obsolete technologies, nonstandard technologies, and duplicate, missing, and conflicting versions of software. The final inventory adds value to the enterprise that goes beyond the Year 2000 effort; it is the basis by which the IT organization can proactively manage its assets for the future. This use of the inventory for application management is discussed in Chapter 18.

3.1.2 High-Level Conversion Strategies

Before investing in the conversion of an existing application to handle century dates, IT organizations must consider the high-level conversion strategies at their disposal. For example, can an application be replaced by a new, compliant package, thereby gaining additional features and avoiding the cost and effort of a conversion project?

Many different migration strategies are available to an IT organization, and they can be applied at the level of applications or major system software components. Developing the optimal set of migration strategies depends on many of the factors discovered during the inventory process, such as the technical and functional quality of the systems to be converted and their business value. Strategy development is also influenced by factors such as staffing and time remaining before century-date problems will surface.

No strategy fits all applications. As the century draws to a close, IT organizations may have to ruthlessly select, through a "software triage" strategy, which applications survive. Software triage is used when there is insufficient time left to convert all applications. It involves eliminating nonessential applications entirely or allowing them to fail, fixing them as time and resources permit. A typical large portfolio will use all of the strategies listed below. These strategies are described in detail in Chapter 4.

- **Software replacement.** Replacing an application requires that the IT organization either develop a new application or purchase a package. This option is time critical: the new system must be completely operational before problems occur and must contain all of the functionality of the old system.

- **Full conversion.** Fully converting an application requires expanding all of its dates, in both the source code and file data, to include century information. This strategy requires greater effort than some others to implement but eases future maintenance by producing the least complex software. It provides a permanent fix compared to the temporary fix of minimal conversion.

- **Minimal conversion.** Minimally converting an application involves the correction of only those calculation and comparison routines that will definitely fail. The conversion uses logic to infer the century from context rather than by expanding dates. It should be used as a contingency in case replacement projects fail, an unexpected need arises, or if time or resource constraints do not permit full conversion. It is also a useful strategy for those systems that are relatively stable, are infrequently maintained, and do not interface to external systems or routines.

- **Discard.** A discard strategy is an option for nonvital systems that are either no longer needed or are easily replaced with a package or through other sources.

3.1.3 New Development Projects

IT organizations must also address newly developed systems and systems that are under development. Although these systems are the most likely to be compliant because of the heightened awareness of Year 2000 issues, problems may still arise. Many of these new systems clone code from existing systems, which may be noncompliant. Newly developed applications also share interfaces with existing systems that may be noncompliant and that may exchange noncompliant data. In addition, although new developers may be sensitive to century-compliance issues, years of programming in a noncompliant environment can lead to inadvertent introductions of noncompliant code in new systems.

3.1.4 Software Categories and Related Migration Issues

Although legacy applications receive the most attention in the trade press, century-date compliance issues affect all types of software. Each category of software has its own unique set of compliance challenges.

- Mainframe systems, the bulk of most corporate business applications, are apt to be legacy systems and, as such, are most likely to be noncompliant. Their poor documentation and low technical quality increase the difficulty of their conversion, but their use of common languages and central location means that they will often use the same systematic approach to conversion. On the positive side, conversion efforts for this category of software are most widely supported by commercial tools.

- Client/server technologies face the opposite challenges of mainframe software. Because these applications are newer, they are more likely to be century compliant. Despite the odds, compliance cannot be assumed without verification. Client/server systems often receive noncompliant data from legacy and mainframe applications and can contain noncompliant source code salvaged from those applications. Furthermore, because these systems use newer languages, there are fewer tools supporting their conversion. Client/server systems are highly distributed and typically contain components from many vendors. Finding and coordinating the conversion of the distributed components of a client/server system will require greater effort than that for their mainframe counterpart. Overall compliance depends on the compliance of all vendor components.

- Software packages purchased from external vendors present a variety of challenges. In most cases, the package vendor requires the IT organization to migrate to the latest release of the package to obtain century-date compliance. This requirement presents difficulties for IT organizations that have heavily modified their package or that are using an old release of that package. Those organizations have to convert the older release themselves or take the time to apply their modifications to the new release. Interfaces will have to be coordinated between the package and application systems written in-house. The package vendor may select a strategy that does not match the strategy selected by the IT organization. The timing of a compliant release is a critical factor. If a vendor fails to provide a compliant release in time, the IT organization will have to either assume maintenance for the package, replace the package with another package, or hire vendor personnel to convert the package.

- System software and utilities are typically provided by hardware vendors. Fortunately, most major hardware vendors have committed to supporting their customers' century-compliance efforts. To obtain compliant software, IT organizations will need to migrate to the latest releases of system software, confronting some of the problems outlined above for packages. Upgrading system software often requires changes to application software. These changes may require their own migration efforts, thereby extending the time and resource requirements for application migration efforts.

- End-user software includes those small applications built and maintained by business areas themselves. These applications are not immune from the same compliance issues that affect their mainframe brethren. They may reside on the mainframe or on PCs, use less common languages, and rely on a myriad of PC tools. Although IT may not support these systems, help desks and other support areas will be directly impacted if these systems are not century compliant. These systems may also support important business functions for an organization. IT organizations will confront unique challenges in ensuring the compliance of end-user applications. Business areas will need IT assistance to identify and correct their century-date problems, as they do not have the awareness nor the infrastructure to correct those issues themselves.

- PC software includes off-the-shelf packages and in-house developed code found throughout an enterprise. Century-date compliance within these systems varies widely. Purchasing new releases or replacing in-house systems is the most likely means of ensuring compliance.

3.2 Year 2000 Conversion Issues

Once a systems inventory has been created and high-level decisions have been made on the disposition of each system, IT organizations face a number of choices that determine how to implement century-date compliance at the program and data level. These conversion options affect the details of implementation, including the number of staff resources, expertise requirements, specific tool requirements, infrastructure improvement requirements, and overall time requirements.

One of the most important decisions in any Year 2000 project is the determination of the basic set of conversion approaches that will be used throughout the enterprise. An enterprise migration strategy selects multiple approaches to handle the range of situations within the organization's portfolio. For example, a very different strategy may be applied to a legacy application on the verge of retirement than to a newly developed strategic application. Creating a global set of "default" choices allows the implementation team for each sub-project to select the optimal strategy for their application while avoiding anarchy. Without guidance, sub-project teams can easily select incompatible strategies, causing the Year 2000 project to fail at the enterprise level.

The issues and choices for determining the detailed conversion options are discussed in Chapter 5. These issues include defining compliance standards, selecting detailed strategies, and handling application interfaces.

3.2.1 Defining Compliance Standards

A key to ensuring Year 2000 project success is the definition of compliance standards and guidelines. Compliance standards describe the criteria that will be used to determine if an application is century-date compliant. At the highest level, the criterion is simple: the application must correctly handle century dates. Upon reflection, however, the criteria become more complex. Do all year fields have to be in four-digit formats in all reports, on computer screens, and in all files? If the century is determined by interpreting a two-digit year, do all applications use the same century-cutoff date? Should applications with short life expectancies meet the same standards as high-value applications with a long future? These, and other questions, are answered within the compliance standards and guidelines that are used to conduct all the sub-projects within an enterprise-level Year 2000 project.

Ideally, an IT organization should define a baseline standard as a target. This standard applies to all high-value software within the portfolio. From this baseline, standards are defined to handle specific situations. These variations are based on clearly identifiable system characteristics, including life expectancy, change volatility, business value, level of date dependence, ability to determine century from context, and available time and resources. For example, the baseline standard may require year data within files to be expanded to include century digits. A second standard allows applications with a short life expectancy to use shortcuts to avoid the expense of field expansion.

Compliance definitions will also vary for different categories of software and other century-date dependent materials. Standards are required for new development, current systems, outsourcing, legal contracts, system software, and packages. Not all of these standards are technical. For example, legal standards define basic contract clauses to protect the organization from failures on the part of its vendors.

3.2.2 Year 2000 Century Representation Issues

Selecting how to recognize century data is a fundamental decision in any century-compliance sub-project. There are two principal approaches: converting date formats to include century data (data-based approaches) and following context rules to interpret the century from two-digit years (process-based approaches). Within each category, there are numerous variations. Each approach has its own strengths and weaknesses and affects the level of effort and time required to implement the project.

Most IT organizations will use strategies from both categories within their portfolio. The approach for a given application should be based upon the extent that the application is dependent on dates for operations such as sorting, providing access to end-users, performing high-volume transactions, or handling complicated date calculations and comparisons. IT organizations should select as few methods of representation as possible, and those methods selected should follow common industry standards. The compliance standards should define when a given approach should be used.

- **Data-based methods of representing century dates.** Data-based methods represent the century within the application data by expanding the year to four digits, using a flag, or compressing the date to fit into existing date fields. Data-based approaches handle all century-date situations. They are not restricted by year ranges and sort in correct sequence. They require the fewest changes to program code but require file conversions.

- **Process-based methods of representing century dates.** A process-based approach to representing century dates avoids the need to modify data by using rules to interpret century by context. This approach retains the original two-digit years. An arbitrary cutoff year is established, with years falling below the cutoff belonging in the 21st century and years falling above the cutoff belonging in the 20th century. For example, if the cutoff year is 50, the two-digit year of 11 would be interpreted as 2011, and the two-digit year of 67 would be interpreted as 1967.

  The process-based approach (also called a procedural workaround) is often faster to implement than a data-based approach; however, it has several key disadvantages. It requires more logic changes, increases the likelihood of introducing errors, does not function within sorts, and permits no more than a 100-year range for its dates.

Given their advantages and disadvantages, data-based approaches are the best choice for most situations. This method reduces future maintenance and provides the greatest long-term flexibility for its data. The process-based method should be limited to time- and cost-critical situations typically involving applications with low business value, short life expectancy, and low maintenance requirements. It is also a viable option for applications with limited date processing, high likelihood of replacement, situations where century is easily determined by context, or where there is low sharing and reuse of file data with other applications.

3.2.3 Interfaces Between Applications

Applications are interconnected through many interfaces, typically through shared files or databases. Resolving these interfaces presents difficult technical and project management challenges for Year 2000 efforts. Any changes made to an interface affect all applications sharing that interface. If a file is expanded to include century dates, it cannot be read by any noncompliant applications. The extent of this problem becomes clear with the realization that a typical IT organization has thousands of interfaces between internal and external applications. Figure 3.1 illustrates the number of different interfaces to a single application (DNK). Each of the applications connected to DNK has its own set of interfaces to other applications.

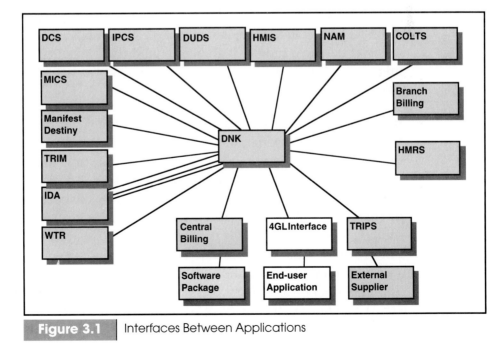

Figure 3.1 | Interfaces Between Applications

An IT organization can use three basic methods to handle interface issues: avoidance, simultaneous conversion, and bridging. The decision about which strategy to use is determined by upgrade units. Upgrade units are a method for partitioning application migration sub-projects to minimize the number of interfaces to other sub-projects. Upgrade units can consist of a single application, several related applications, or even a partial application. In many cases, the natural boundaries of an application are also the boundaries of an upgrade unit. All of the programs within an upgrade unit are converted simultaneously, avoiding the need to be concerned with interfaces within the upgrade unit. Interfaces between upgrade units are handled by using one of the three interface strategies.

- **Avoidance.** This method uses process-based conversion strategies to avoid the need to expand file data. Since the interface remains unchanged, noncompliant applications are not affected by the compliance sub-project. This approach cannot be used for files that are sorted by date, situations where a date range exceeds 100 years, or when a subsequent application requires data in a four-digit format.

- **Simultaneous conversion.** In this method, all affected upgrade units are converted independently but simultaneously. They are tested at the same time, using migrated test data. Production data is migrated when the upgrade units are concurrently moved into production.

- **Bridging.** Interface technology is required whenever data migration is necessary and simultaneous conversion of all applications that use the data is not possible. Batch bridges are utilities that read data in one format and write it in another. Application program interfaces (API), on the other hand, allow concurrent access to shared or online data stores via modifications to application source programs. Interfaces enable compliant programs to access unconverted data or, conversely, a noncompliant program to access converted data. Another bridging strategy is to produce duplicate data files, one for compliant applications and another for noncompliant applications. Figure 3.2 illustrates three interfacing strategies.

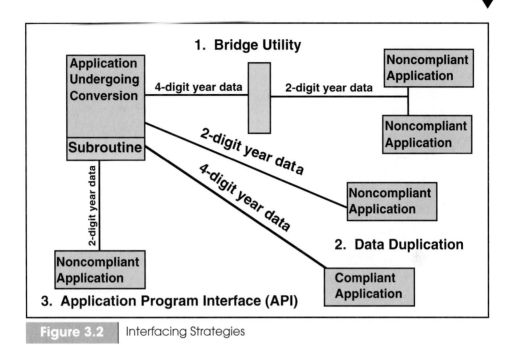

Figure 3.2 | Interfacing Strategies

3.3 Environmental Issues and Support Technologies

The environments that support the operation, maintenance, and migration of production systems are critical to successful Year 2000 migrations. These environments must themselves be century compliant for the applications they support to operate correctly. They must also support the tools required to facilitate the migration. Century-date compliance projects can use the tools and support environments already in place for standard maintenance tasks but may require additional tools or more robust environments for a full-scale migration. Fortunately, most effort spent on improving the support environment for century-date projects yields long-term benefits for future maintenance and support.

Chapter 6 explores the issues that many IT organizations will confront when upgrading their support environments to handle century-date compliance projects. These include requirements for upgrading and removing obsolete tools and environments, shared date routines, configuration management, migration tools, testing and validation facilities, and migration work environments.

3.3.1 Obsolete Tools and Environments

Software tools and environments are not immune to the same century-date issues affecting s other software and must be certified as century compliant. This certification process provides two valuable side benefits. Obsolete tools can be discovered and eliminated, thereby saving the cost of future maintenance fees on unused products. Second, "orphan" technologies, those technologies that are still supported but no longer strategic to an IT organization, can be identified and eliminated.

3.3.2 Change Control and Configuration Management

Century-date compliance projects involve source code modifications on a massive scale. Often, an application migration project must coexist with ongoing support efforts as well as emergency fixes, requiring the end results to be merged. "Freezing" production code during a century-date compliance project reduces the effort and risk of the conversion process. Freezing occurs when program libraries are locked from all normal production modifications until migration is completed. Several less drastic strategies can be employed when a complete freeze is not feasible. In any case, change control tools and processes to manage multiple versions of source code are a core requirement for any century-date project.

Configuration management, also known as library management or version control, consists of the tools and processes that administer the source code and object libraries containing the components of business applications. The most important function of configuration management is to keep track of all the versions of all the source code components that compose an application. This task becomes increasingly complex as the number of components and versions grow and when several versions of a component are modified simultaneously. Strong version and release controls are essential in a century-date compliance project because almost every component of every application will be modified to some extent. Application releases will not function properly if date formats are incompatible among application components or if dates are widely shared among components. The configuration management environment should be robust enough to facilitate these large-scale changes.

Change control and configuration management requirements become that much more critical if any conversion work is to be performed offsite.

3.3.3 Shared Date Routines

The massive cost and effort of a century date compliance project is dramatic proof of the value of common subroutines. Most of the programming effort needed to achieve century-compliance would be eliminated by simply installing a standard set of date subroutines. Unfortunately, rather than implement common date routines, most business applications reimplement date processing logic each time that it is needed. Handling century dates requires finding, understanding, and correcting every instance of date-processing logic throughout the corporate portfolio. Lack of standardization in naming and implementation exacerbates the difficulty of this task.

It is recommended that, as part of the migration process, IT organizations create or purchase a set of standardized date routines. Standardizing date routines reduces future maintenance effort by reducing the size and complexity of application source code and enabling all future changes to be made in one location. It ensures that date calculations are performed identically throughout the organization and reduces the level of testing of date processing.

3.3.4 Migration Tools

The large volume of work effort and tight time constraints of the century-date compliance project make automation a necessity. Automated tools reduce elapsed time requirements and ensure accurate and consistent results. Century-compliance efforts will employ software tools from a wide range of functional tool categories, including project management tools, repository technology, analysis tools, migration tools, redevelopment tools, and testing tools.

Some of these tools are Year 2000 specific, while others can be reused for future maintenance projects. When considering the acquisition of any tool, IT organizations should evaluate the following options: using an off-site conversion service in lieu of purchasing tools (while still ensuring that the vendor uses quality tools), purchasing Year 2000-specific tools that are optimized to handle date identification and conversion tasks but are not useful for other kinds of maintenance, or purchasing a maintenance tool that can not only handle century compliance efforts but can be used to perform routine maintenance. This last category provides the greatest long-term value to the IT organization.

It is important to remember that while tools may eliminate many rote and time-consuming tasks, they do not eliminate the human efforts to coordinate the century-date project, nor do they adequately address every facet of the project. Despite vendor claims to the contrary, there will be no "silver bullets" that eliminate the majority of human resources needed for the project.

3.3.5 Testing and Validation Facilities

Validating the results of century-date migration efforts is the most critical and greatest technological challenge of a Year 2000 project. Applications are tested for compliance, and interfaces between applications are verified. Good testing requires sufficient and proper test data and sufficient hardware resources necessary to support large-scale testing. Individual components must be unit tested; programs, subroutines files, and multiple applications must be integration tested; and the entire application must be system tested for century compliance. System tests should include regression testing of current application functionality, testing with "future" dates to ensure that the application will perform correctly in the 21st century, boundary testing to ensure that the application will handle certain unique or infrequent events, and certification testing for those applications that are believed to be compliant without any modifications.

Test environments have four basic components: test data beds (including files and databases to test a single application), test scripts and scenarios (describing the actions needed to perform the test, set up the environment, and verify the results), test environments (simulating the production environment), and software testing tools (to generate test data, provide test coverage monitoring, environment simulation, and verification of results).

Building a test environment is time consuming and costly. IT organizations should begin by performing a "gap" analysis on the current testing environment to determine what components are missing, which existing components can be extended or reused, and what scripts or test data are insufficient. Next, they must determine whether the current hardware resources are sufficient to support the testing or whether additional resources will have to be purchased or outsourced. IT organizations should acquire testing tools early in the process so that programmers will be well versed in their use prior to the start of the Year 2000 project. Begin collecting and creating test data, using a test coverage monitor. Create test scripts and scenarios by asking programmers to document the steps that they use to perform routine testing activities.

3.3.6 Migration Work Environments

A migration work environment integrates the software tools, processes, and methodology used by the Year 2000 project into a single environment. This integration is accomplished by incorporating a common interface to provide a similar "look and feel" for using tools within the workbench, a repository to store the project information to be shared by the tools within the workbench, a process manager to automate the processes used to accomplish the migration tasks, and a methodology that specifies the processes that are needed to complete the migration. The workbench should be able to perform the functions of project management, analysis, migration, and verification.

Workbench environments can be implemented on the mainframe or workstation. Or, the environment can use both the mainframe and workstation: the mainframe to access production jobs, manage source code versions, and run resource intensive, noninteractive tasks and the workstation to perform interactive analysis and testing.

3.4 Relationships, External Entities, and Related Responsibilities

Year 2000 projects are not just an IT issue. To implement the project, the IT organization must interact with individuals and organizations throughout their corporation as well as with entities external to their corporation. Many of these individuals and organizations have their own stake in the project and are critical to its success. Internal stakeholders include senior management, business areas owning or using the affected software, business areas that rely on external organizations, and auditors. External stakeholders include customers, stockholders, government agencies, business partners, suppliers, IT tool, hardware and software providers, and Year 2000 solution partners.

Chapter 7 explores the issues and needs of these diverse stakeholders in detail. The following sections discuss internal and external stakeholders.

3.4.1 Internal Stakeholders

Widespread sharing of data and computer services among business areas ensures that any Year 2000 initiative will affect virtually every corporate organization. This level of interaction requires a monumental level of interorganization coordination if the Year 2000 effort is to be successful. Methods must be devised to avoid the organizational politics that will otherwise cause significant project delays. This level of interorganization cooperation is impossible to achieve without the strong support and commitment of executive management. Executives play a crucial role in Year 2000 projects by ensuring proper funding, creating urgency among business areas, and resolving conflicts among business areas. In addition, senior executives are well positioned to determine the proper balance between Year 2000 issues and other business concerns. If application triage becomes necessary, executive support is critical to define priorities among the applications from business areas.

The business areas that own and use applications are the organizations most highly affected by the Year 2000 project. It forces them to defer desired application enhancements, may cause changes in application operations, affects their end-user applications, and potentially affects their relationships with customers and suppliers. Business area owners must aid the Year 2000 project by helping to define priorities among applications, approve the selected migration strategy, and assist in testing. They must free resources for migration initiatives by willingly deferring noncritical modifications.

In addition to the applications supported by the IT organization, business areas have Year 2000 issues specific to their organization. They may need to establish their own Year 2000 task forces to obtain and monitor funding, handle interactions among business areas, develop strategies and determine priorities, resolve the impact on application enhancements, assist in testing and verification, develop end-user application compliance efforts, and determine and resolve impacts with external organization interfaces.

Even business areas that do not rely on IT-managed applications are impacted by Year 2000 efforts. They have end-user applications, have the same issues with customers and suppliers, and depend on other business areas for internal goods, services, and information. These areas will also need to be educated about Year 2000 issues and will need to establish, in varying degrees, task forces to deal with some or all of the issues outlined above.

Centralized corporate purchasing departments play a major role in Year 2000 projects inasmuch as they are responsible for all vendor contracts. These contracts cover all software and hardware purchases, outsourcing, and consulting relationships, as well as purchases of supplies and materials. This department, in negotiating these contracts, has considerable leverage over vendors and is an important checkpoint in the compliance process. The purchasing department should review existing contracts to determine whether Year 2000 issues are covered by the contract and who bears responsibility for correcting them. If existing terms are unsatisfactory, then at the time of contract renewal, the purchasing department should assist in efforts to implement proper terms. The purchasing department should also ensure that any new contracts contain standard clauses about compliance. In addition, the purchasing department should assist in resolving contract performance issues by monitoring and updating the status of a vendor's compliance efforts.

Audit departments are responsible for understanding and mitigating financial and legal risks to a corporation. In this capacity they can be significant allies of the Year 2000 project. They can help to assess the full extent of organizational risk, assist in building support and awareness among senior managers, and provide compliance enforcement pressure. Once the project is underway, internal auditors can assist in monitoring ongoing migration efforts by reviewing changes to production applications to ensure that those changes followed verification and security procedures.

3.4.2 External Stakeholders

Century-date compliance efforts affect external business arrangements on two levels. The most obvious impact occurs among organizations that exchange date-based data. Any modifications to that data require the cooperation and coordination of all affected organizations. The less obvious impact occurs when the corporation depends on goods and services of an external organization that has its own Year 2000 risks. If the external organization is unable to meet its delivery commitments because of a Year 2000 failure, the corporation is impacted as directly as if its own systems failed. Corporations must be prepared to mitigate the risk that one of these external organizations either does not recognize and correct the problem or proposes an unsatisfactory solution. The best method of resolving these situations is to quickly identify which relationships are at risk. Doing so provides time to negotiate a mutually satisfactory solution or to implement a contingency approach. These arrangements can be formal—performance and responsibility can be specified in a contract—or informal.

The strategy employed by an IT organization to reduce the risk of Year 2000 problems will depend on the type of relationship.

- Data suppliers are companies that provide information in electronic format. Because these services are typically contract based, IT will have greater leverage in negotiating an acceptable solution.

- Multicompany data interchange occurs when many companies share the same type of data. To avoid chaos in these large-scale data interchanges, standard formats are often defined by industry groups or by agreement among multiple vendors. Involvement in these groups will permit the IT organization to influence the solutions adopted for Year 2000 issues.

- Suppliers provide goods and services to the corporation and can also share data. A corporation is at risk if these suppliers do not address their own internal Year 2000 problems. Vendor relationships and data interfaces must be assessed to determine the level of risk. Where possible, supplier contracts should contain compliance clauses.

- Customers rely on the corporation for goods and services. A corporation must avoid disrupting these relationships by insulating the customer from any Year 2000 issues the corporation may be experiencing. When the "goods" consumed by the customer are data, date interface issues will arise and their resolution must be negotiated among the parties.

- Government agencies share and receive data from the corporation. These agencies have their own century-date compliance issues that mirror those found in the private sector, but on a much larger scale. IT organizations should identify all interfaces to government agencies and contact those agencies to determine what types of changes are required and when.

- Vendors such as outsourcing vendors and package software vendors present their own significant business challenges to a Year 2000 project. Although outsourcing and package replacement are two possible solutions for noncompliant legacy applications, existing packages and outsourcing projects can be a project risk.

  — Outsourcers can assist in a Year 2000 project by performing the century-compliance migration and assuming support for the application. In some cases, the contract with the outsourcer will explicitly state the responsibility and costs for century-date compliance efforts. Older outsourcing contracts may not directly address century-date compliance. Responsibility for funding and performing the migration effort may be ambiguous or may default to the outsourcing vendor if the vendor has contractually agreed to guarantee the correct, continuous operation of the application in production. In either case, an IT organization must face the risk that an outsourcer will fail in its commitment and should reduce that risk through contract penalty clauses or a thorough contingency plan.

— The business relationship between an IT organization and a software package vendor is specified in the purchase contract. It is important to understand the terms of these contracts to handle situations where the maintenance contract for a package has lapsed, a package software vendor offers an inadequate solution, or the vendor fails to meet contractual obligations or goes out of business. Examine contracts for specific vendor obligations to supply century-compliant code, limitations of liability, support for older releases and custom versions, and access to source code.

3.5 Management Issues

A century-date compliance project presents almost every conceivable type of project management challenge. Its size, scope, and execution requirements significantly exceed even the largest system-development project. It requires a monumental level of coordination among organizational entities and the solution to a wide variety of technical issues, all at a time when there are severe resource constraints. There are four categories of challenges faced by Year 2000 project managers: project management skills, project ownership, organizational readiness, and staffing issues. These issues, highlighted below, are explored in detail in Chapter 8.

3.5.1 Project Management

Most of the challenges in implementing a Year 2000 project involve project management. Despite the need for specialized skills to solve a variety of technical issues, the bulk of the implementation tasks require the same skills and activities normally used to maintain an application. These projects do not rely on risky technologies or unproven methodologies. Project success is defined as the ability to perform a myriad of small tasks before an immovable completion date. In short, the Year 2000 effort is primarily an exercise in large-scale project management.

Unfortunately, this exercise presents a huge challenge to IT organizations. Studies have shown that IT has a historically poor record in delivering projects on time and within budget with all originally specified features and functions. Given this track record, achieving even minimal compliance, on time and with constrained resources, will require a significant improvement in project management capabilities. Although many IT organizations have maintenance project managers, they often lack experience in large-scale project management most typically found in new development projects.

Century-compliance projects present unique management issues caused by project size and time constraints. Size and time constraints will cause any shortcomings in the IT infrastructure, such as weaknesses in training, skills, tools, control processes, and training, to become very apparent during the project. In addition, personnel issues will arise because most century-compliance work is simple and repetitive, thereby causing this effort to be viewed as undesirable by most programmers.

These challenges can be overcome through strong project management skills backed by executive management support. The overall project seems unmanageable until it is broken into small sub-projects. The role of the Year 2000 project manager is to oversee this breakup process and assign the individual sub-projects to internal or consulting teams for detailed specification and execution. The manager creates an overall project plan encompassing the individual efforts and is responsible for monitoring the performance of that plan and its sub-pieces. During the execution phase, challenges arise in ensuring that all identified tasks are tracked and completed on time and in coordinating tasks that are shared among separate organizations.

A significant part of the Year 2000 project charter will be to reduce and manage risk. Nontrivial risk factors must be identified; in most cases, these risks will be obvious. Once identified, mitigation strategies for handling these risks are incorporated into the correct level of the project plan. This assimilation requires documenting the early warning symptoms of the risk to enable its timely detection. The best way of handling these risks is to appoint a Risk Officer, an individual whose role is to ensure the identification of all appropriate risks, the monitoring of those risks, and the development and employment of mitigation strategies when necessary.

Identifying and monitoring risks is not enough. Contingency plans are required for risks that cannot be prevented. Contingency plans will identify key checkpoints for assessing the current level of risk to ensure the timely triggering of correction efforts.

3.5.2 Project Ownership

Key to the success of a Year 2000 initiative is central project control. A good indication of a corporation's progress in its compliance effort is the level of management that owns the project. The higher the level, the more successful the effort. As tempting as it originally seems, empowering each area within the company to manage its own migration effort will lead to failure. Each unit will have its own concept of compliance, will place its own priority on the project, and will schedule and complete projects without regard to other areas. These factors will eventually cause conflicts between areas that are dependent on each other for data or resource sharing. In addition, effort is wasted as each area reinvents methods and techniques used by other areas to handle the conversion effort.

Outsourcing can be used for almost any project task, but it cannot be used to offload project ownership from the IT organization. Although outsourcing project ownership may seem like an attractive alternative to many companies because of the consultant firm's experience in managing large-scale projects, consultants do not have the organizational knowledge, relationships, or clout needed to fully manage all aspects of the project. They cannot take responsibility for all project management tasks, such as reviewing contracts, negotiating with customers, and resolving political issues among business areas. In the end, corporate management will be ultimately held accountable for the success or failure of the project.

The solution for managing an enterprise century-date compliance project is to use a central Year 2000 Project Office. This group is responsible for coordinating project activities across the entire enterprise. By assuming high-level responsibility for the project management, this group ensures the integrity of the overall century-compliance effort. Under this model, individual sub-projects will continue to be executed by separate areas throughout the corporation or outsourced according to project needs. The Year 2000 Project Office tracks those sub-projects and provides a central point of contact for the outside world. It is also important to empower the Year 2000 Project Office to make and enforce strategy decisions.

3.5.3 Organizational Maturity and Readiness

In many corporations, IT processes have not been subjected to the same intense competitive pressures that force core business processes to be effective. The scale and complexity of century-date compliance projects makes the inefficiencies inherent in these processes intolerable. First, valuable resources and time are lost through ineffective processes. There will simply not be enough resources available to support this extra level of unnecessary effort. Second, the size of the project will place inordinate levels of stress on all IT practices and processes. It is unrealistic to expect IT organizations to invest the time and energy needed to improve their processes before embarking on a century-compliance project. The best compromise is to focus on improving the efficiency of those processes that are most affected by century-compliance efforts. Key processes include analysis, programming, configuration management, quality assurance, testing, and production turnover.

IT organizations can shortcut their process improvements for century-date compliance by doing the following:

- Assign the responsibility of organizing and managing the process improvement activity to the Year 2000 Project Office.

- Define the century-date migration process by mapping every step and organization involved from the start of the assessment phase to the final delivery of the completed application, identifying the work products consumed and produced at each stage of the process.

- Examine the mapped process steps and query why a given step is needed. Identify unnecessary or redundant steps and reduce these to the maximum extent possible.

- Automate process steps wherever possible and practical.

- Reduce the number of separate organizational units involved in completing a given process. Many process inefficiencies result during handoffs between organizational units.

- Package project deliverables into release packages that are extended through the migration process for eventual production turnover.

- Ensure that the process captures at least rudimentary metrics that can be used to evaluate the effectiveness of the process, including time per step, cost per deliverable, and number of reworks.

3.5.4 Year 2000 Staffing Issues

Project staffing presents another significant challenge to IT management. This challenge increases daily, as procrastination in starting migration efforts will require greater numbers of programmers to complete the same project in a shorter time frame. It is anticipated that there will be a shortfall of programmers able to address century-date compliance issues. This shortfall will be intensified by global competition from other IT organizations and service providers for the same resources.

Because compliance problems will be concentrated in legacy applications, the skills required to address compliance issues will be those traditionally used to work with COBOL programs in mainframe environments. These skills have been slowly dying off over the past decade as client/server systems have grown and as universities have changed the emphasis of their computer curriculums to newer languages. In addition, testing and quality assurance knowledge are two highly valuable skills that will increase in importance over the life of the compliance project. Besides these skilled delivery personnel, the most pressing need is for strong project managers.

The best method for overcoming resource shortages is through advance planning. The sooner an IT organization understands its resource requirements and implementation strategies, the sooner it can obtain the resources that it needs and the less it will pay for them. There are two primary methods for obtaining project resources: shifting existing staff to century-compliance projects or obtaining additional resources from a consulting firm or outsourcer. If consultants will be used, the IT organization should contract with consulting firms to reserve any necessary consulting resources as early as possible to ensure availability. In either case, IT organizations should develop Year 2000 incentive plans for their internal staff and should watch carefully for turnover.

Chapter 4

Asset Management Issues

Many organizations mistakenly view the Year 2000 problem as an issue primarily for older, mainframe, "legacy" applications. They perceive these legacy applications as antiquated candidates for replacement that, regrettably, must be modified to handle century compliance. Newly developed applications are thought to be century compliant, and other categories of software, such as application packages and end-user programs, are excluded as the responsibility of others.

This viewpoint is dangerously incorrect. In fact:

- Application software no longer exists solely on large, central computer systems.

- Newly developed applications are not necessarily compliant.

- Many additional categories of software are impacted by century compliance.

- Business applications depend upon the compliance of these other categories of software to operate.

- The Information Technology organization is ultimately responsible for the corporation's ability to process information in the year 2000 regardless of the source of the software that fails.

The focus on legacy applications as the source of Year 2000 issues underestimates the impact and effort requirements of century-compliance projects, lulling corporate executives into a false sense of security about the compliance of their organization. This lack of awareness directly increases the difficulty of raising sufficient funds to fully address compliance. Moreover, because many IT managers have spent years convincing senior corporate management that legacy applications have limited value, recommending new development or replacement by software packages instead, it is not surprising that these same senior corporate managers now see little value in the Year 2000 migration effort.

Successfully addressing century-date compliance on an enterprise level requires IT executives to step out of their roles as developers of applications to focus on a more global role as managers of a varied and complex portfolio of business and system software, as shown in Figure 4.1. This portfolio includes:

- Mainframe applications of varying ages, quality, languages, and technologies

- Client/server environments that combine application code with a mixture of middleware, distributed databases, and communication software across multiple platforms

- Software packages from multiple vendors, each with their own strategy and timing for century-date compliance

- System software and utilities for mainframe and workstation platforms

- End-user software employing many different tools to extract and manipulate the data from production applications

- A seemingly infinite array of PC software programs

Each of these categories of software presents its own unique set of challenges for a century-date compliance effort. This software is the primary asset managed by the IT organization, and it is the responsibility of IT management to optimize the performance of their software portfolio in support of corporate business objectives. The Year 2000 issue has a silver lining in that it forces IT organizations to become active managers of their corporation's software assets.

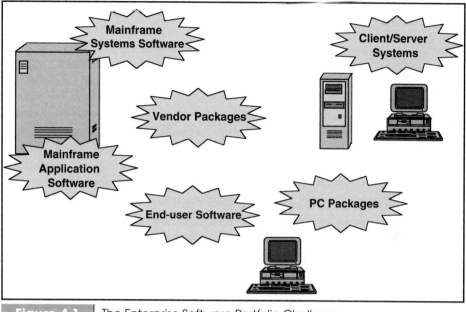

Figure 4.1 | The Enterprise Software Portfolio Challenge

This chapter describes the issues that IT organizations will face as they examine and assess their complete portfolio of software. These issues will be described globally and by specific software categories. It is essential to understand the issues and their ramifications to develop the optimal set of strategies for achieving century compliance.

4.1 Assessment Challenges

The first step of any Year 2000 compliance project is to develop an accurate inventory of all categories of software within an enterprise. The inventory will include more than just a list of application and program names; it will have information about the location, type, and current status of the software. Different issues arise based on the characteristics of system type, age, technical and functional quality, technology, platform, and business volatility. For example, the tools and approaches used to achieve century compliance in a mainframe COBOL application are radically different from those used in a Visual Basic application in a client/server environment. These same assessment characteristics are used to determine the optimal, individualized, century-compliance strategy for each unit of software within the enterprise. A newly developed application may merit a more complete century migration effort than a nonstrategic application with a short life expectancy.

4.1.1 Obtaining an Accurate Portfolio Inventory

Few IT organizations have a complete and accurate inventory of the software that they manage. This inventory is essential for ensuring that all software components within the enterprise have been tested and, if necessary, modified for century compliance. The inventory process ensures the identification of all software systems and applications and of all necessary components within each application. Unless this process is completed, IT organizations risk missing smaller, rarely modified applications or components of even well-known applications. Conversely, an accurate inventory prevents organizations from spending precious time converting programs that are no longer used, yet are stored alongside active programs within application libraries.

Without an excellent configuration management process, an IT organization will find that obtaining this inventory is often far more difficult than anticipated. Even individual application teams have difficulty estimating the size of their own applications in terms of programs, subroutines, files, and other components. In our experience, "guesstimates" of application size are frequently off by as much as a factor of four. This difference is significant when estimating a project that may cost millions of dollars to complete.

The difficulties encountered when creating the inventory foreshadow the level of difficulty of the actual century migration effort. It will expose weaknesses in each organization's asset management processes. IT organizations with tight controls will be able to quickly gather the information needed to produce the inventory, while less rigorous organizations will spend significant effort simply finding the libraries that contain application components. In the latter case, once the components are found, it may be impossible to determine which components are actually active. One large IT organization reported that it spent almost two weeks simply to find all components of a single, large application. Although expending this level of effort to find all system components may seem excessive at first, remember that if a single, date-dependent component is forgotten, the application will not process dates correctly in all cases.

Each major category of software requires its own separate inventory process. The first issue is finding the software. The computer operations area is responsible for maintaining the inventory of mainframe system software (operating systems, database, teleprocessing monitors, utilities, etc.) for most large installations. Mainframe application software is usually contained, through library management software, in a single location, although the rigor of this practice varies widely from organization to organization. Production versions of code may reside in the libraries of individual programmers, and almost every organization is executing one or more programs for which the source code has been lost. Application software from non-mainframe and client/server platforms is often spread across multiple locations and is rarely subjected to more than minimal configuration controls. End-user and PC software is often managed by noncomputer professionals and has no controls at all.

Determining the boundaries of an application (or software package, etc.) is often the next major challenge. Applications regularly share components such as copymembers and subroutines. Libraries may contain many obsolete members that were kept "just in case." Even the definition of an application varies from organization to organization. For example, one IT organization may define Accounting as a single application composed of subapplications such as General Ledger, Accounts Receivable, and Accounts Payable. Another organization may define each of the subapplications as a single application. This distinction becomes important when dividing applications into separate projects for implementation and testing.

Finally, since the inventory process gathers information about the characteristics of each software component, it will uncover a variety of potential conversion problems. These problems include obsolete technologies, nonstandard technology, and duplicate, missing, and conflicting versions of components.

The activities involved in gathering a complete inventory are described in detail in Chapter 11.

4.1.2 Determining System Life Span

The age and expected longevity of a software application are important factors to be assessed during the inventory. Software applications live far longer than anyone anticipated. Many organizations are still using production applications that are older than members of their programming staffs. Studies conducted in the 1980s predicted that the average life of a business application would be approximately 7 years. This misconception led many development organizations to cut corners, expecting their applications to be replaced long before the shortcuts became an issue. Century-date compliance is a good example of the results of one of these shortcuts.

This tendency for old applications to live for long periods of time has several important ramifications for century-date conversion projects.

- The life-cycle stage of a given piece of software is an important factor in deciding the optimal century migration strategy. Applications nearing the end of their useful life will not justify the same level of effort as for newer applications.

- IT organizations cannot assume that an existing application will be replaced before the year 2000 unless a *total* replacement project has been budgeted and scheduled.

- The Year 2000 project team must assume that existing applications will continue to operate well into the 21st century. Thus, shortcuts in the migration effort are still likely to lead to high, long-term maintenance costs.

- One method for adding business value to a century-date conversion effort is to identify and combine the remaining functionality from old applications with their "replacement" application. This effort is justified by avoiding the century-date migration for the old application and through continued operational savings from eliminating the old application.

4.1.3 Assessing Technical Quality

The technical quality of a piece of software is an important indicator of the effort required for the century-date conversion of all software maintained through source code. Technical quality measures the maintainability and testability of a given unit of source code. Technical quality is ideally assessed by using metrics analyzers, such as McCabe's Cyclomatic and Essential Complexity, that capture objective software metrics. These metrics can serve as a particularly good indicator of system testability.

Small differences in technical quality can result in large differences in the cost of modifying and testing a line of code. The magnitude of this relationship is shown in Figure 4.2, taken from the research of one of the authors[1]. It illustrates the relationship between technical quality and maintenance cost for four applications within one IT organization. In this graph, maintenance cost is measured using cost per line of code (LOC) changed. This metric is obtained by dividing total maintenance cost for each application by the number of LOC changed over one year. Technical quality was measured by using a composite of software quality metrics yielding data on a scale of 0 (unacceptable quality) to 100 (excellent quality). This study selected those applications that permitted the elimination of factors other than technical quality from the correlation.

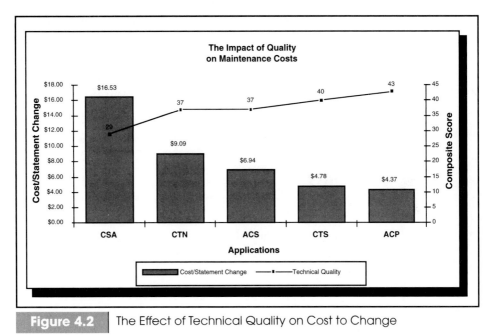

Figure 4.2   The Effect of Technical Quality on Cost to Change

The differences in effort between high- and low-quality code are sufficiently large, thus IT organizations must incorporate the technical quality of their software as a factor in developing migration strategies and in estimating the overall size of the project.

4.1.4 Assessing Functional Quality and Strategic Value

When viewed in terms of importance to the enterprise, not all applications are equal. Some applications are absolutely critical for the operation of the business, whereas others could cease operation with little, if any, impact on the enterprise. The importance and value of a unit of software to an enterprise is measured by functional quality and strategic value. Functional quality is defined as the degree to which a piece of software meets the business requirements of the organization that it supports. Strategic value is defined as the importance of the software's functionality to the enterprise. Although the functional quality and strategic value of an application have no impact on the level of effort required for a century-date migration, they are critical determinants of conversion strategy and priority and must be considered in any Year 2000 project plan.

IT organizations should prioritize their conversion efforts and resources in descending order, from the most critical applications to the least critical. If the entire century-date migration project cannot be completed on time, the least critical applications should be dropped. An understanding of functional quality will also help to determine the value of a particular conversion strategy for a particular application. Figure 4.3 shows a simplified version of the relationship between functional quality and strategic value, and century-date compliance strategy.

Functional Quality	Strategic Value	
	High	Low
High	High-priority migration candidate	Lower-priority migration candidate
Low	Replacement candidate	Discard candidate

Figure 4.3 The Effect of Functional Quality and Strategic Value on Migration Priority

Gathering accurate information about the importance of a unit of software to the enterprise often presents considerable political and psychological challenges. Generally, few application project leaders are able to objectively rate the importance of their application. Similarly, business area managers may be able to rank the various applications that support their area, but they are often unable to compare and prioritize those rankings with other business areas. Nevertheless, all ratings of functional quality are necessarily subjective, but unlike technical quality ratings, there are no automatic and objective methods of measuring software value. The best method of capturing this information is through the use of surveys and interviews. Actual rankings of applications must be performed at the level of management that has responsibility for all applications to be ranked. For example, the manager of the accounting area can rank all accounting applications, while the company's CEO may be required to rank the relative importance of accounting versus manufacturing.

It is best to perform the functional and strategic ranking as part of the inventory process. Doing so ensures that the most important software is identified and migrated early in the century-date project, and it establishes ground rules for allocating scarce resources over the life of the project. It is far easier to establish those ground rules before resource constraints force contention among the company's business areas.

Adding functional quality and strategic value ratings to the corporate software inventory creates value beyond the Year 2000 effort. Organizations can use the inventory to proactively manage corporate software assets. By monitoring changes in functional quality, IT managers can plan in advance for application replacement. This strategy and other future benefits are discussed in Part 4 of this book.

4.1.5 Identifying Obsolete Technology

Many IT organizations continue to operate applications that rely on obsolete hardware and software environments. These environments are no longer supported by their original vendors, and many are unlikely to function after the year 2000. Common types of obsolete environments include back releases of language compilers and other system software, technology obtained from vendors that no longer exist, and technology that has been superseded by more advanced technology. These obsolete technologies increase the elapsed time and effort required to achieve century-date compliance. Unless organizations can discard the applications that rely on obsolete environments, they must move them to a new environment or migrate them to newer releases. Depending on the situation, this work may be considerable and is in addition to any other work needed to make the software century-date compliant. In some cases, the combined effort will exceed the cost of simply replacing the application.

The best strategy for addressing obsolete technologies is to identify any problematic environments as quickly as possible. Early identification enables the IT organization to understand the full scope of the issue, while still leaving enough time to explore and implement the optimal migration strategy. For example, an IT organization can apply a replacement strategy if there is enough time to build or acquire a new version of the existing application. In contrast, tardy identification of obsolete technology may not allow enough time to complete the needed conversions.

4.1.6 *Identifying Nonstandard Technology*

Nonstandard, or "orphan," technologies exist in almost every IT organization. These technologies are those languages, data management systems, and other technical environments and tools that are still supported in the market but are no longer strategic for the given IT organization. In many cases, only a small number of applications use these technologies. For example, COBOL legacy applications may predominate in an IT organization, but legacy applications may also include small pockets of PL/I and/or fourth generation languages. Typically, these orphan applications are late in their life cycle and are rarely maintained, causing some organizations to forget about their existence. These applications present several problems for century-date migration efforts:

- The expertise needed to modify these applications may no longer exist within the organization.

- Tool and consulting support for date migrations of less common technologies is sparse.

- Companies receive little long-term value from investing additional capital in applications utilizing a "dead end" language or technology.

The most appropriate strategy for handling an orphan technology depends on the technology and the business value of the affected applications. If the applications have considerable business value and enough time is available, the best option may be to migrate the applications to a more strategic technology. This approach offers several benefits:

- Internal personnel can maintain the application, using commonly available (and generally less costly) skills.

- The support environment (tools, compilers, etc.) for the orphan technology can be eliminated, reducing support costs.

- Century-date compliance costs can be reduced through the automation that is available for common technologies.

If the applications have value but will be infrequently modified in the future, the best option may be to outsource their century-date conversion to a consulting vendor or conversion factory that specializes in that technology. This approach is especially valuable when the technology in question has little tool support and internal expertise is low.

4.1.7 Identifying Duplicate and Missing Components

The quality of the contents of an IT organization's software libraries presents another challenge when developing an accurate corporate inventory. Even IT organizations that have implemented firm controls of their software libraries are often surprised at the level of duplication of programs and other application components. Programmers often create special-purpose versions of programs for testing and other one-time purposes and fail to remove the code from the libraries when it is no longer needed. These programs are not executed in production and no longer provide any value to the organization. Hence, these programs should be discarded rather than converted to handle century dates. Failure to do so can significantly increase the cost of the century-date compliance effort.

Identifying which library components are truly functional can be a time-consuming challenge involving the examination of job scheduling systems, job control language, system cross-references, and other production job execution records. It is especially important to ensure that the source code components that are modified match the load modules used in production. This process often uncovers situations where the source code for an operational component is missing, a fairly common result for production applications that have remained stable for long periods of time. When source code has been lost, there is no method for converting or even re-creating the load module. There are only three solutions for this situation: abandoning the functionality represented by the existing code, attempting to create a new program that duplicates the functionality, or engaging a source recovery service (see Appendix A). Each of these choices has its own drawbacks. Abandonment is feasible only for noncritical code. Creating a new program is difficult or even impossible without adequate documentation. Source code recovery is a costly option but may be the only solution for a critical, missing source component.

4.2 Conversion Strategies

Once the issues are understood, IT organizations can begin to select their century-date compliance strategies. At the asset management level, these strategies are applied by application or major system software component. These strategies include discarding the software, replacing the software, full conversion, and minimal conversion. Lower-level conversion options such as field expansion from two-digit years to four-digit years are applied within these larger strategies and are described elsewhere in this book.

Selecting the most appropriate strategy is determined by the many factors described earlier in this chapter. The functional quality, strategic value, and anticipated life span of each software component will determine the justifiable level of migration effort for that component. Factors such as the software's technology, date dependence, and technical quality determine the level of effort needed to achieve compliance. The optimal strategy balances the business value against the cost of conversion. Once again, the time remaining before the software is affected by the year 2000 is crucial. The options for addressing a valuable business application narrow from replacement to full conversion to minimal conversion as the available conversion time decreases. If IT organizations run out of time or resources, the ultimate solution is, effectively, discarding the application, because it will no longer operate correctly. IT organizations facing insufficient time and resources to complete their century-date conversion for all of their affected software must exercise software triage to select only the most critical components for conversion within the remaining time window. Each of these strategies and the factors used to select them are described in the following text.

4.2.1 Replacement

Replacement appears to be an attractive option for the older legacy applications within the portfolio. Rather than investing effort in converting these applications, why not simply replace them with new applications that, in addition to being century-date compliant, utilize more modern technology and contain additional business functionality? The costs saved by not converting the original application could partially fund this replacement. Unfortunately, replacement becomes a less and less viable option as the year 2000 draws near.

To be successful, a replacement strategy must:

- Be completely implemented before the original application experiences century-date problems

- Totally replace *all* required functionality in the original applications

Although these two points seem obvious, history has shown that they present problems in many IT organizations. A study by the Standish Group[2] found that only 9 percent of the projects in large IT organizations were implemented on time, within budget, and with all specified functionality. Approximately 30 percent of all projects were canceled outright. Small IT organizations fared slightly better; their percentages were 28 percent and 22 percent, respectively. In either case, most projects arrived either late or without all promised functionality. If a replacement project misses the Year 2000 window by even a few days, the original application must be converted, or the company must be able to operate without the application until the replacement is available.

Missing functionality also presents a problem to a successful replacement strategy. Most IT organizations have partially replaced applications in their portfolio. These new applications replaced most, but not all, of the original applications. While the new application handles most of the business functionality, the old application continues to operate to handle the remaining functionality. The organization usually intends to phase out the old application, but unless the operating costs of the old application are high, there is little impetus to complete the project. If the original application continues to operate in production, it must be made century-date compliant. A century-date compliance effort can provide added value by facilitating the final migration of functionality from a legacy application into its replacement. This benefit is only feasible, however, if there are sufficient time and resources.

There are two major approaches for replacing an existing application: developing a new application or purchasing a software package. Both approaches require significant lead times for gathering requirements, developing or selecting the solution, testing the results, and retiring the old application. As a result, any replacement project that is not fully underway today is not likely to complete in time to avoid the need for converting the original application. Even if the project is in progress, the IT organization must have contingency plans to handle any slippage. Otherwise, enough time may not remain to convert the original application after problems are identified. Contingency planning is discussed in detail in Chapter 8.

Replacing the original application with a software package may require less time than developing a new application, but it presents its own challenges. The package must meet functional requirements or accommodate modifications within the time constraints; it must already be century compliant, and its compliance strategy must fit within corporate requirements.

4.2.2 Full Conversion

Although a given piece of software must be able to handle century dates in all aspects of its processing, the required level of the compliance can vary. For example, one strategy is to convert all files and internal calculation variables to four-digit years while leaving printed dates on reports in a two-digit format. Similarly, the decision about whether to use a procedural conversion approach or a data expansion approach depends on the level of compliance desired. Full compliance for all aspects of a unit of software requires the greatest level of effort, but it ensures that the software is absolutely maintainable. Lesser levels of compliance need fewer resources for conversion but require a greater level of resources for future maintenance.

Later sections of this book will discuss the issues and selection criteria for determining which levels of century-date compliance are optimal for a given business application. Briefly, full compliance addresses the manner by which data is stored and manipulated, how the data is displayed, and the type of internal representation.

- **Data storage and manipulation.**
  How data is stored and manipulated within the application software has great bearing on the complexity of the software and its ease of future maintenance. Expending additional effort to achieve century compliance at this level provides no apparent benefits to the users of the application but provides long-term value in terms of reduced support costs, greater extensibility, and lower error rates. Full compliance includes:

    — Expanding all existing year data from two-digits to four-digits. This simplifies sorting and other file operations and reduces the number of logic changes within the application's source code.

    — Expanding all internal variables used for calculations, comparisons and date storage to four-digit years. This simplifies comparisons and avoids the need to add logic to handle century identification.

- **Data display.**
  Humans are better than computers at determining the century from the context of the data. This provides IT organizations with flexibility in determining whether to expand the year fields displayed in reports and on computer screens. If a user can easily determine the correct century, the year can remain in two-digit format for display fields. Because screens and reports are often carefully designed to display the maximum amount of data, expanding the year can involve considerable reformatting. In this case, ease of programming has to be weighed against the potential for confusing application operators. Display data, if ignored during a conversion project, could be expanded after 2000 if users concur with this "delay" strategy.

- **Quality of internal representation.**
  Part of the difficulty of achieving century-compliance is related to poor programming practices. Date variables are not consistently named or formatted, and multiple versions exist for common date calculations. The quality of these internal representations of year data affect the cost of achieving century compliance as well as the cost of future maintenance. The century-date compliance project provides an opportunity to improve these internal representations through the following activities:

  — Standardizing date formats

  — Rationalizing date field names

  — Employing standardized date subroutines

In an ideal world, all business applications would be made fully compliant. In reality, tight time frames and resource constraints will force many organizations to compromise. The cost and effort needed to achieve full compliance are not justified for some applications. There are a number of factors to consider when selecting the level of compliance for an individual application, including the following:

- **The life expectancy of the application.**
  The longer the life of the application, the greater the benefit of a full-compliance strategy. Conversely, the costs of full compliance are not justified for short-lived applications.

- **Application volatility.**
  Application volatility refers to the frequency of maintenance changes to the application. Very stable applications gain less benefit from a full-compliance strategy than do frequently maintained applications.

- **Business value.**
  The strategic value and functional quality of an application determine its business value, which in turn determines the level of investment that is justified for that application. Applications of low business value may not justify the investment required to reach full compliance.

- **Level of date dependence.**
  Applications that are heavily date dependent and perform many date operations should be made fully compliant whenever possible to avoid compounding the complexity of application logic and

increasing the testing effort. Applications that simply display date information can use lesser approaches.

- **Ability to determine century from context.**
  If the century cannot be determined by context, a full compliance approach will be required.

- **Available time and resources.**
  Full compliance requires more resources than less compliant approaches. If resources are constrained, an organization may be forced to make greater use of less compliant approaches.

4.2.3 Minimal Conversion

The opposite of full compliance is a minimal conversion strategy. This approach performs the fewest possible number of changes to reach century compliance. File data is not converted, display fields are not changed, and only those calculations and comparisons that will fail are converted within programs. Although this approach is suboptimal from both application maintenance and end-user perspectives, it has the shortest implementation time frame and is useful for emergency situations. Typical scenarios for a minimal conversion include:

- Contingency, in case a replacement project does not complete in time

- Unexpected need to convert an application quickly; this includes applications that have a very short window before experiencing century-date problems

- Software triage situations (detailed in the following text) in which resource constraints prevent more optimal conversion strategies

- Applications that are very stable, have little date dependence, and share few interfaces with other applications

Minimal conversion can also be performed as a first step to buy time for future, more complete migration efforts. Performing a minimal conversion guarantees that the application will not fail when processing century dates but increases future maintenance effort and decreases application usability. This two-step approach increases the cost of final compliance and carries the risk that the IT organization will never complete the second step. It is a necessary option when resources are tightly constrained.

4.2.4 Discard

The cost of century-date compliance will encourage corporations to identify and eliminate low-value applications rather than to invest in their conversion. The business value of the application has to be weighed against the direct cost of conversion and, in triage situations, against the opportunity cost of expending conversion resources elsewhere. For PC packages and end-user applications, a discard strategy will often make more sense because any business functionality contained therein can more easily be replaced through other methods. Conversely, few organizations operate production applications that can simply be discarded. A more likely scenario for those applications is to identify the ones whose functionality can be covered through other methods. For example, if a new application replaced most of the functionality within a legacy application, the cost of migrating the remaining functionality to the new application may be more cost and time effective than retaining and modifying the legacy application to handle century dates.

4.2.5 Software Triage

A common IT strategy when experimenting with new technologies or embarking on a new implementation approach is to test the technology on a nonstrategic application. This strategy is thought to lower overall risk—if the approach fails, nothing valuable is harmed. Century-date compliance projects require exactly the opposite strategy—convert nonstrategic applications last. That way, if the organization fails to complete its century-date compliance project on schedule, only the least strategic applications will fail. Deciding which applications can be allowed to fail is the concept of software triage.

Triage developed on the battlefield when scarce medical resources were allocated to those seriously injured patients that were given the highest chance of surviving. Minimal attention was allocated to patients whose injuries were not life-threatening, and little effort (aside from reducing pain) was devoted to patients that were expected to die. This same concept must be applied to the century-date compliance effort in many IT organizations. As the year 2000 draws closer, many organizations will discover that they don't have time to completely migrate their entire portfolio. These organizations will face the difficult challenge of deciding which software to allow to fail. The organizational cost of failing to complete a total Year 2000 effort on time is significantly higher if triage decisions are made by default rather than through advance planning. Each corporation's high-level project plan should incorporate a triage strategy. Given the potential business impact of allowing business applications to fail and the political ramifications of deciding which business units will bear the consequences, the ultimate decisions about triage are best left in the CEO's hands. Less senior managers are unlikely to have the necessary objectivity to concede that their software is less strategic and less essential to the business than others.

The triage strategy requires that the elements of the software portfolio be ranked by their value and importance to the business. The cost of failure or inoperability of each application must also be considered. Some applications are truly mission critical—the corporation would fail without them—whereas the failure of others may result in a tolerable level of pain. Pain has both direct and indirect costs. Indirect costs include public embarrassment and the effect on the operations of other companies. Once all the costs are considered, the CEO can determine which applications must be compliant and which applications can be bypassed if resources become too tight. This evaluation and development of a triage strategy can proceed in parallel with other assessment and estimation activities. The triage strategy is then joined with the estimates to determine if and when triage will be necessary. This strategy can then drive the decision to engage outside resources to complete the migration or to pull internal resources from other projects to ensure that the most critical applications are covered. It is important to recognize that the longer an IT organization procrastinates over its century-date project, the more important the triage strategy and the more likely that it will be used.

4.3 New Development

Recently developed software or software currently under development is not immune to century-date compliance issues. Surprisingly, many new applications are not century compliant. Even applications that were designed for compliance often contain code that will cause problems when handling century dates. One company designed and built a new application with century-compliance as a requirement. They were shocked when the application failed compliance testing. The errors were traced to six instances (out of hundreds of date references) where a programmer hardcoded "19" in the century portion of the year field rather than spend the effort to invoke an operating system subroutine for the actual date.

New applications are often not century compliant for several key reasons:

- These applications are usually built by the same developers who previously built noncompliant applications. These developers may unintentionally fall back into old patterns when coding year fields.

- Code is often cloned from existing applications when building new applications. Unlike official reuse strategies, where code is carefully selected to ensure its quality, code cloning simply replicates existing code, thereby incorporating any century-date compliance issues into the new application.

- New applications frequently share data interfaces with noncompliant applications. These interfaces pass years in two-digit formats. Unless specific code is incorporated into the new application to convert those dates into compliant formats for internal use, the new application may not completely handle century dates. Further, these shared interfaces will have to be converted when the noncompliant applications are migrated.

To ensure the integrity of their century-compliance efforts, IT organizations cannot assume that any new application is compliant unless it has been specifically tested. Even after an application is certified as compliant, all future modifications should be reviewed to ensure that noncompliant code is not introduced during maintenance.

All compliant applications are at risk from bad data provided from noncompliant applications. Although the quality of the data is ultimately the responsibility of the application creating the data, developers of new applications can incorporate defensive techniques if the risk of receiving bad data is deemed to be high. These techniques may include checking dates and date-dependent calculation results for reasonableness, producing warning messages or error reports when in doubt.

Finally, as discussed above under replacement strategies, there is always the risk that new development projects designed to replace noncompliant applications may not complete in time to handle the turn of the century.

4.4 Software Categories

Each category of software within the IT organization's portfolio has its own set of century-compliance issues.

4.4.1 Mainframe Systems

Legacy mainframe applications are the most likely to be noncompliant but also have the greatest level of support for the migration process. These applications tend to be written in a common language, such as COBOL, and by in-house staff. Like their mainframe platforms, they tend to be centrally located and controlled. This centralization greatly eases the task of inventorying application components and simplifies the challenge of configuration management throughout the project. The mainframe's operating software is normally purchased from the same hardware vendor, decreasing the complexity of ensuring the compliance of the operating environment. IT organizations already own many of the software tools needed to support the migration and testing of mainframe applications. On the negative side, these applications are often poorly documented and very low in technical quality, increasing the difficulty of their conversion. This category constitutes the bulk of most corporate business applications; its issues will be covered intensively throughout this book.

4.4.2 Client/Server Technologies

Applications built to utilize client/server architectures have been gaining wide acceptance over the past several years. Client/server architectures distribute an application's processing across workstations (clients) and one or more layers of servers and networks. Application servers may even include the corporate mainframe. Client/server applications face the opposite challenges of the mainframe software category. These applications are newer and therefore more likely to be century-compliant. However, they tend to employ newer languages, such as Visual BASIC, C, and C++, which have considerably less tool support than mainframe languages. Their operating environment is considerably more complex, as it is composed of hardware and software from many different vendors. In order to operate successfully, all of these disparate components must be century compliant, utilize compatible approaches, and be available within coordinated time frames. Unlike mainframes, hardware compliance will be an issue, particularly for the PC clients.

Because client/server architectures are relatively new, the support structures are not as evolved as those available for mainframes. Obtaining an accurate inventory of system components and locations is often very difficult and time consuming. Version control is often weak, resulting in multiple versions of the same software in operation at the same time. This greatly increases the effort required for century-date project management.

The best strategy for client/server applications is to test them for compliance as quickly as possible. If compliance issues are uncovered, the IT organization must devote the necessary effort to develop a complete inventory and identify the noncompliant components.

4.4.3 Software Packages

Application software packages purchased from external vendors present a variety of challenges. Software packages are commonly found throughout most IT organizations because of their ability to decrease programming and support costs. In most cases, actual compliance of the source code is the responsibility of the package vendor; however, achieving true century compliance will usually require more cost and effort than simply installing the package. Further, even when a vendor is contractually bound to provide the necessary levels of support, the stability and reliability of the vendor determines whether compliance will be achieved. Some vendors may well be driven out of business by their century-compliance obligations.

At the time of this writing, many package software vendors had not released definitive information about their compliance strategies, timing, and specific release numbers for the compliant versions. Most, if not all, package vendors will expect their clients to migrate to the latest release of the package in order to reach century-date compliance. This strategy has several important ramifications to IT organizations.

- Many IT organizations use application packages that are several releases behind the current release. Moving to the latest release requires its own conversion and introduces other changes in functionality beyond century compliance. If the IT organization does not want the new functionality, it may have to convert the existing version of the package on its own. If the IT organization has not purchased maintenance on the package, the software vendor may require payment of all back maintenance before shipping the compliant release.

- Few IT organizations install packages without modification. In some cases, these modifications are extensive, requiring considerable effort to merge the organization's changes with those provided by the vendor. This effort is greater for the century-compliant version of the package, as century compliance will affect virtually all components of the package. IT organizations must weigh the time and effort of merging their changes against the effort required to perform their own century compliance on the earlier release.

- The vendor's timing of the new release may not match the needs of the IT organization. For example, if the software vendor does not ship the compliant version of the package until 1999, the IT organization may not have enough time to make the modifications needed to install the package.

- Software packages typically share files and data with internal applications. If these interfaces contain dates, it is essential that the vendor and the IT organization employ the same century-date format strategies. If the vendor selects a different strategy, the complexity and effort required for internal applications will be increased.

The best strategy for an IT organization is to develop a full inventory of their current portfolio of application package software. This inventory must include vendor contact information, current release, the availability of source code, and the level of internal modifications for each package in the portfolio. Concurrently, all software vendor contracts should be reviewed to understand the vendor's obligations and the rights of the customer if the vendor fails to meet those obligations. Most contracts are renewed yearly, and this renewal period offers the best opportunity to renegotiate contract clauses.

If package review and vendor negotiations indicate that a particular package is at risk, the IT organization has several choices. It can:

- **Assume maintenance for the package.**
  In this case, the IT organization takes responsibility for performing century-date migration. This option is possible only if the IT organization already has access to the source code. If not, the organization should negotiate a contract specifying access to the source code if the vendor does not meet agreed-upon delivery criteria. It is essential that the negotiated delivery dates allow enough time for the IT organization to perform all necessary conversion activities.

- **Replace the package with another package.**
  If the troubled package is relatively generic, it may be possible to replace it with another vendor's compliant package. This option is limited by available time and the level of effort required to implement company-specific modifications.

- **Hire vendor personnel to convert the package.**
  When the vendor is unable to perform the necessary compliance work for financial reasons, it is often in the best interest of the IT organization to fund the vendor's efforts. This is especially true for

small vendors that may otherwise be driven out of business by Year 2000 problems. Given their knowledge of the application, vendors can often perform the conversion more quickly and reliably than internal IT staff. This approach may seem burdensome to those who point to the vendor's contractual obligation to fund the effort themselves, but it is likely to be cheaper in the long run than driving the vendor out of business.

4.4.4 System Software and Utilities

Application software compliance is irrelevant if the operating system software and utilities that support those applications are not compliant. More than one IT organization using date simulators to test the compliance of their applications have been chagrined to find that their database software failed before even reaching the application code. Most mainframe and minicomputer system software is provided by the hardware vendor. These vendors are responsible for the compliance of this software. Unlike dealing with application packages, IT organizations usually have little recourse if the vendor fails to meet compliance commitments. Fortunately, the major hardware vendors are committed to supporting their customer efforts. IBM has been in the forefront of the major vendors, publishing its first set of guidelines in October 1995. Other vendors will follow, but without customer pressure, many are loath to publicly publish the names and release information of their noncompliant software. Smaller system software vendors (sorts, backup and recovery, configuration management, etc.) will have to be contacted individually to determine the level of exposure and actions needed to achieve compliance. In most cases, software vendors are using century-date compliance as a method of coercing their customers into using the latest releases of their software; older releases will not be upgraded to support century dates.

Gathering a full inventory of system software tends to be easier than obtaining an inventory of other types of software because of the central control imposed on mainframe and minicomputer operations. Software auditing technology (see Appendix A) is available for IBM environments to find and list all versions of all system software. This inventory, along with vendor names and software release levels, will determine the actions required for century compliance. Although the software vendors are responsible for compliance, the project plan must account for the timing and installation of those releases.

Upgrading system software versions can sometimes require changes to the application source code. The effort required to implement these changes and the time needed to test them must be factored into the application's migration effort. Obsolete system software will not be supported in the year 2000, necessitating a migration of the application software from an old technology to a newer version or even to another platform or environment. This scenario is discussed in section 4.1.5, *Identifying Obsolete Technology*.

It is not uncommon to find system software that is no longer in use, but is still installed. Systems personnel should undertake a concerted effort to identify and eliminate this software from the inventory results. This holds true for all platforms.

Some IT organizations have written their own system utilities or have significantly modified software provided by major vendors. These utilities must be made compliant, following the same approaches described for application software.

4.4.5 End-user Software

End-user software, that is, small software applications built and maintained by the business areas themselves, is one of the largest risk areas within a century-compliance project. End-user applications face the same Year 2000 considerations as the production applications managed by the IT organization. Many end-user applications rely on dates for sorting and calculations. Further, these applications usually draw their raw data from production files and databases. Data changes implemented as part of century-date compliance will affect all end-user applications that rely on the modified production data.

End-user applications may execute on a mainframe, using a fourth generation language such as SAS™ or Focus™, or they may use one of a myriad of PC tools. The number of end-user applications expanded exponentially with the availability of inexpensive personal computers. As a result, few IT organizations know which end-user applications operate against their production data. Obtaining an inventory of these applications ranges from difficult to virtually impossible. These applications are scattered throughout the enterprise, and new programs are created daily. Although IT may not be directly responsible for the support of end-user applications, help desks and other support areas will be impacted as end-users seek assistance.

A number of specific challenges will affect the IT organization as it attempts to cope with end-user applications.

- **Geographic diversity.**
  Many organizations have users residing in a wide range of geographic locations. In one example, a corporate coordinator was responsible for software running in over 25 countries around the world. The inventory process itself was a nightmare. Surveys and a good awareness program can help blunt this challenge.

- **Low awareness of century-date issues.**
  End-user applications are built and operated by business people rather than computer programmers. Such business people may have little awareness of century-compliance requirements or how those requirements can affect their applications. The application operators may be even less computer-literate and unable to recognize whether an application is malfunctioning from century dates or whether it ceases to function because of an interface change.

- **Wide range of technologies.**
  Because end-user applications have evolved with little, if any, centralized direction, they may utilize a very wide range of platforms and technologies. Besides not having an inventory of all end-user applications, IT organizations may not even be able to inventory the technology used by those applications. Worse still, these platforms may be running multiple versions and releases of the same software. The first challenge facing end-users is to identify which purchased software is affected and which release is required to be compliant.

- **Strong need for assistance in identifying and correcting the problem.**
  Help desks and other resources will be deluged by requests for support as these applications begin to fail. Many end-users will need programmer assistance to implement the fixes needed to accommodate century dates. Corporations have become very dependent on key end-user applications, and these applications may have high visibility with senior corporate management, so IT organizations will have little choice when asked to assist on the conversion of these applications.

- **Lack of centralized support functions for quality assurance and configuration management.**
  Unlike the tightly managed mainframe environments, end-user platforms have few controls. They rarely have test data for verifying the correctness of their applications or configuration management to ensure that they are using the correct versions. In many cases, they may not even back up their systems regularly, increasing the difficulty of recovering from a century-date problem.

IT organizations have few good options for handling century-date compliance issues in end-user applications. The best initial approach is to build awareness of the issues and their ramifications. This can be accomplished through training classes and newsletters. The first goal is to ensure that all new applications will be compliant. Since end-user applications typically have a short life span, beginning compliance now will reduce the number of applications that will fail. The second goal is to encourage end-users to seek help as soon as possible. If the IT organization waits until the applications begin to fail, they will face their biggest demand from end-users at the same time their resources are fully occupied with production application failures. Planned changes to production application files and databases have to be communicated to end-users before they are implemented to allow the end-users time to modify their applications to use the new file structures.

4.4.6 PC Software

The final category of software is purchased PC packages. These are the off-the-shelf programs purchased at computer stores or through catalogs. These packages are found throughout the enterprise. These packages are used as stand-alone programs, or they may be incorporated within end-user applications or even production applications. The century-date compliance of PC software packages is highly variable. Many have little or no date dependence, whereas others make heavy use of dates. Compliance efforts, timings, and strategies are completely in the control of the software vendors. In many cases, compliance will be achieved by purchase of the latest version. In other cases, to reach compliance, the package may have to be replaced by another with similar functionality. The best strategy for IT organizations is to contact the vendors providing the packages most commonly used within their company. Through corporate newsletters or other means, the IT organization can disseminate information on vendor compliance and necessary version levels.

References

[1] Hayes, Ian, "Software Metrics: What Do They Really Mean?," *Systems Development Management*, 35-10-10, Auerbach Publications, October 1995.

[2] Johnson, Jim, "Chaos: The Dollar Drain of IT Project Failures," *Application Development Trends*, Volume 2, Number 1, pp.41–47, January 1995.

Year 2000 Migration Issues

$\mathbf{H}$ow should an IT organization implement century compliance at the program and data level? Technicians endlessly speculate on the issues and merits of every approach that has ever been proposed. The fear of changing files and interfaces between applications leads them to recommend complicated programming changes rather than to modify existing data. Nontechnicians point to the simple solution of "just expanding the year field by two digits." The simpler the proposed solution, the less likely the proposer understands the Year 2000 issue and the less likely its chance of success across an entire IT portfolio.

It is very easy to succumb to "analysis paralysis" and lose valuable time arguing about implementation approaches and wallowing in the myriad of decisions that need to be made before beginning conversion. And yet, defaulting on those decisions will quickly result in pandemonium and gridlock during implementation. Mundane decisions about when and how to expand a year field to handle century dates in a single application can have enormous impact on the cost and time requirements for migration projects across the entire enterprise.

If IT organizations could begin from scratch rather than by modifying their current environments to achieve century compliance, they could take a very simple approach to century compliance. All date data would contain four-digit year fields and all software would perform its calculations and comparisons using this format. This method is the most straightforward and least effort-intensive to implement when developing new programs, and its date format is easily understood by the people who will use and maintain the data.

Unfortunately, few, if any, IT organizations will be able to start from scratch for a significant number of their software applications. Existing applications impose a variety of constraints on how century data can be represented and how that representation is retrofitted into existing code, as well as greatly increasing the complexity of the conversion effort. Yet, each corporation depends on and operates with this software; it cannot be turned off or frozen until century compliance is achieved. As Eric Bush once described in an article on software redevelopment, modifying a production application is "a lot like trying to rebuild boats on the open sea... If we try to change too much too suddenly, we sink."[1] In the world of production software, any solution that forces massive, simultaneous change is simply not feasible.

The need for multiple implementation solutions to facilitate "rebuilding the boat at sea" becomes apparent during the portfolio inventory process. Some applications have the business value and anticipated life span to justify perfect conversion, other applications may require the fastest possible conversion to recover from an existing failure, and yet another application's strategy may be determined by the external systems that provide its data. Each of these solutions has its own ramifications. Selecting a given solution seems only to expand the number of new choices and decisions that have to be made. It is clear that Year 2000 compliance does not mean the same thing for each software category.

Assembling the right set of strategies that fit within organizational constraints is not as difficult as it may appear. Once the initial decisions are made, most of the subsequent strategies fall into place. For this reason, the main strategies employed by the organization must be chosen carefully and embodied in project guidelines. Failure to do so allows individual projects to make default selections that will impose major consequences on future project activities.

This chapter describes the range of choices for implementing century-date compliance within business software. Chapter 4 described the major strategies at the portfolio level. This chapter describes the more detailed strategies applied *within* the individual applications. It describes the major strategy decisions, along with their benefits, consequences, and effect on other strategies. The variety of strategies described in this chapter reflects the creativity of IT professionals faced with a complex problem.

The chapter is divided into three sections:

- **Compliance Definition.**

  Lack of standards and development guidelines during the development and maintenance of the corporate software portfolio is responsible for much of the difficulty of the Year 2000 effort. Thus, defining compliance standards and guidelines is key to Year 2000 project success. Many small decisions can be delegated to the discretion of the implementation teams, provided that they make those decisions within the context of the standards. Adherence to standards prevents clashes between the objectives and implementation approaches selected by individual teams.

- **Century Representation.**

  There are two principal methods for recognizing century dates. One method is based on data—expanding existing dates from two-digits to four-digits. The other method is through process—using an approach to interpret dates without modifying the format of the year field. Between these two extremes, there are a variety of choices. This section describes the most common choices along with their pros and cons.

- **Interface Resolution.**

  Unless an IT organization can implement process-based approaches for recognizing centuries across its entire portfolio and can impose its implementation strategy on all external data interchanges, strategies are needed to handle application interfaces. Bridge routines, application program interfaces, and other approaches enable organizations to isolate separate "work units" for conversion. Noncompliant software operates on noncompliant views of the data, while compliant software uses the compliant view. Effective bridging of application interfaces is essential to reduce and control the level of simultaneous change and to avoid "sinking the boat."

Although software changes receive the greatest share of attention, data migration is required whenever date formats are modified. Data migration can range from trivial for simple flat files that are shared between two programs to extremely complex for highly used databases. Issues include determining how and when to best migrate the data. Data migration approaches are closely related to the strategies used for application interfaces. Interface bridges become necessary whenever the software does not match the format of its production data. Often, the same code used to create the interface bridges can be used to facilitate data migration.

This chapter describes how to incorporate the critical implementation decisions described above into project standards and guidelines. Although these issues have a technical basis, the strategies to address these issues are selected to handle project management challenges. Each strategy has its own risks, benefits, and costs that must be balanced against project management considerations of timing, tools, and resource constraints. Most IT organizations will apply multiple strategies during the conversion effort. The selection of each strategy will be based upon the requirements of each business application and tempered by its impact on its surrounding applications. Before selecting *any* century-data implementation strategy, the IT organization must carefully consider the short- and long-term ramifications of that strategy and its implications throughout the conversion project.

5.1 Defining Standards and Guidelines For Year 2000 Compliance

What does year 2000 really mean? Does compliance mean that all dates used throughout a software application are in four-digit format, or is it sufficient to calculate dates correctly and leave the interpretation of the format to the application's users? Is a software package compliance project "underway" once the vendor commits to providing a compliant release by a certain date?

The first challenge facing Year 2000 project planners is the development of a compliance definition. The compliance definition offers guidance for all Year 2000 sub-projects and specifies which approach or approaches are recommended by that IT installation.

On the surface, this task is disconcertingly simple. A system is deemed Year 2000 compliant if it functions properly across multiple centuries. This definition becomes more complex upon greater examination. The compliance definition will be different for different applications and different categories of software. Variations on this high-level definition can and should be specified within a given IT organization.

At one end of the compliance spectrum is minimal compliance as defined in Chapter 4. This level of compliance implements the fewest possible number of changes and expends the least amount of effort to ensure that a given application functions correctly for century dates. This level of compliance leaves dates in their original formats, while adjusting procedural logic to keep a system working.

At the other end of the spectrum is full compliance. Full compliance states that *all* dates be expanded to eight digits. Between these two extremes are a variety of choices: files can be expanded while display fields remain two digits, files can remain unchanged while internal dates can be expanded, and so forth.

Ideally, an organization should define a target standard applicable to all high-value software. This standard becomes the default used by all sub-projects unless circumstances require otherwise. One such circumstance is the existence of a very short window before Year 2000 failure for a critical application. In this case, a minimal conversion is permitted (at least, for the short term) to ensure that the application remains operational. Changes to the default compliance standard usually affect more than one application. For this reason, the decision of when to vary the compliance standard is made for each upgrade unit (applications grouped into logical units of work).

Compliance standards address more than the default formats of dates in application software. It is important to define compliance guidelines for new development, current systems, outsourcing of selected upgrade units, legal contracts, systems software, packages, and audit certification. These compliance guidelines must be documented for distribution to the appropriate areas within the enterprise. Once defined, the guidelines can be incorporated within standard quality assurance practices. For example, a new application is not accepted as production ready unless it is fully century compliant, or a contract cannot be released unless it contains standard clauses to cover potential Year 2000 issues. Broad communication of these standards greatly reduces project coordination issues and significantly enhances the likelihood of project success.

5.1.1 New Development

The Year 2000 compliance standard for software that is currently in development or is planned to be developed before the year 2000 should meet the organization's ideal standards. In most cases, this standard should be full compliance. Newly developed software should, in theory, have the longest potential future life span. Full compliance ensures the lowest future maintenance costs by using the simplest possible implementation for century dates. Aside from a marginal increase in disk storage requirements, full compliance requires no additional costs or programming effort when implemented during application development.

This compliance definition becomes more complex when the new software must share data with noncompliant applications. In this case, the compliance definition should specify organizational standards for these interfaces. For example, all existing applications passing data to the new application must convert that data to a four-digit format even if the rest of the application follows a limited compliance strategy.

5.1.2 Existing Applications

Existing applications will require most of the century-date compliance programming effort for most IT organizations. The diversity of these applications increases the difficulty of defining effective compliance guidelines. Simply stating that all date fields must be expanded to four-digit formats is not always feasible, cost effective, or even desirable. The best solution is to define separate compliance requirements that are selected according to clearly identifiable application characteristics. This approach can be documented in a set of guidelines that enable individual application support teams to select the approach that is most appropriate for their application while still ensuring that the selected approaches are consistent and compatible for all applications within the enterprise.

The characteristics affecting existing application compliance decisions are discussed in detail in Chapter 4. These characteristics include:

- Life expectancy of the application

- Application change volatility

- Business value

- Level of date dependence

- Ability to determine century from context

- Available time and resources

A further consideration is the number of interfaces between a given application and other internal and external applications. Factors affecting interfaces include the overall number of interfaces, the number of applications sharing a given interface, and the relationship between the applications sharing the interface. A procedural approach for handling dates may be the most cost effective method when an interface is shared between only two applications. In this case, the coding effort may be significantly less than the data migration effort. Conversely, if the interface is shared by many applications, the coding effort is multiplied, and a data expansion approach becomes the most cost effective. The relationship between the applications determines the conversion approach for that interface. For instance, if the interface is between an external organization such as the federal government, the compliance definition for that interface may be dictated by the external organization. Interface resolution issues are discussed in Section 5.3.

Guidelines for existing applications should be defined by first stating a compliance standard ideal. This ideal reflects the "organizational default" for century compliance and should be based upon the strategy to be used for applications with a high business value and a long life expectancy. This default would, theoretically, be applied to all applications. Practical considerations will require individual conversion projects to diverge from the ideal. Accordingly, rules for permissible exceptions are required. Failure to clearly define and enforce the rules for permissible exceptions will result in project chaos as project teams create their own rules and approaches for handling difficult situations. The goal of creating rules is to ensure order and to limit the number of century-compliance approaches used within each organization. For example, an IT organization may define field expansion as the ideal standard for high value, long-life applications but may allow a sliding window-based approach for applications that have few interfaces and a short life expectancy. Table 5.1 shows an example of a compliance standard for existing applications.

Table 5.1 Compliance Definition

Application Type	Current Date Format	Migration Strategy	New Date Format Standards				
			File/Database	Internal Fields	Report Fields	Data Entry	Data Display
1. High value, COBOL, mainframe, long life	MM/DD/YY	Date Expansion	MM/DD/CCYY	MM/DD/CCYY	MM/DD/YY* unless year cannot be inferred by context	MM/DD/CCYY	MM/DD/YY* unless year cannot be inferred by context
	YYXXX	(Julian)Date Expansion	CCYYXXX	CCYYXXX	NA	NA	NA
2. Low value, COBOL, mainframe, short life	MM/DD/YY	Sliding Window 01-49 = 2000 50-99 = 1900	MM/DD/YY* Except for SORT keys MM/DD/CCYY* SORT Key fields only	MM/DD/YY Add processing logic to interpret dates in compares Expand date calculation fields	MM/DD/YY	MM/DD/YY	MM/DD/YY
3. Etc.							

5.1.3 Vendor Package Contracts

Compliance takes on a different meaning when applied to software obtained and maintained from external sources. As described in Chapter 4, compliance for purchased application software packages is generally the responsibility of the software package vendor. Unless the IT organization wields considerable power over the software vendor, corporate compliance definitions have little meaning in software packages. In most cases, vendors set their own compliance standards and select their own timing and release strategies.

This does not relieve IT from responsibility for those packages. Even when the vendor provides software upgrades as part of its maintenance fees, internal IT project teams install the releases, report and correct errors during operation, and apply any company-specific modifications. These internal teams are responsible for the compliance of each software package that they support. If the vendor fails to supply an acceptable, compliant version in a timely manner, these teams will have to respond by converting or replacing the package themselves.

In the case of software packages, the definition of acceptable compliance shifts as the year 2000 approaches and the compliance rules become increasingly more stringent. Although migration is not complete until all packages achieve level-four compliance, this layered approach enables a Year 2000 project team to set regular, defined targets for the internal IT project teams.

- Level one: The vendor contract includes language specifying responsibility for Year 2000 compliance, setting a target date for that compliance and specifying penalties and remedies if that target date is missed.

- Level two: The vendor has committed to, and documented, a compliance strategy specifying the approach to be used to implement century dates, a specific product release number for the compliant version, and an actual date for that version.

- Level three: The internal project support team certifies the vendor's strategy and commitments. This includes certification of the acceptability of the vendor's solution and delivery timing; the team's assessment of whether the package will be delivered and installed on time to meet overall corporate requirements; and a contingency plan in case the vendor fails to meet commitments.

- Level four: The compliant version of the package has been delivered, installed and tested.

The Year 2000 project team should set target dates for reaching each level of compliance. For example, all packages must reach level-one compliance by September 1997, level two by December 1997, etc.

5.1.4 System Software

System software compliance is essential to ensure the continued execution of the application software that operates within it. System software includes operating systems, databases, teleprocessing monitors, utilities (such as sorts), and tools (such as compilers). In mainframe and minicomputer environments, the majority of systems software is provided by the hardware vendor, although utilities and other support software may be developed internally or purchased from third-party suppliers. Software supplied by a hardware vendor is covered by standard software maintenance agreements, and few IT organizations have sufficient leverage to force compliance requirements on these vendors. Fortunately, all major vendors are committed to compliance. The major issues are timing of the compliant release and the level of impact that the installation of that release will have on existing application software.

The compliance of internally developed system software should generally be treated in the same manner as existing application software. The exception to that rule is when certain system software has a far-reaching impact on a number of software applications. For example, several large insurance companies developed their own precompiler extensions for COBOL. The use of these precompilers presents a number of challenges beyond century-date compliance. Their use limits the ability of the company to use Year 2000 automation tools for COBOL because of precompiler language constructs. In this case, the compliance definition may specify eliminating the use of the precompiler.

As with packaged software, four levels of compliance can be defined for systems software. These levels should have target dates and become increasingly more stringent as the Year 2000 deadline approaches.

- Level one: The vendor has been contacted and has provided a date and release number for the compliant version of the system software. The IT systems programming area has determined the impact of the new release on application software and has communicated any change requirements to the application programming areas.

- Level two: A schedule has been devised to ensure that any required application program changes will be completed in time for the target installation date of the compliant release of system software.

- Level three: The application environment is prepared, and the compliant release of the system software has been received and is undergoing testing. The production installation of the compliant release of system software has been scheduled.

- Level four: The compliant version of the system software is fully operational.

5.1.5 Outsourcing Agreements

Many IT organizations use outsourcers to handle portions of their operations. The outsourcing contract will specify the degree of the outsourcer's responsibility for century-date compliance. Unless it is clearly specified within the agreement, the IT organization should not assume that the outsourcer will bear the cost of the conversion effort. The first step of developing a compliance definition is establishing both parts of this responsibility: who will perform the migration and who bears the cost of that effort.

Early outsourcing agreements may not include specific references to Year 2000 compliance but may require the vendor to provide all support necessary to ensure continued operations. Year 2000 compliance may be considered within this requirement; unless compliance is reached, the applications will fail to operate. The vendor may argue that compliance is a change in application specifications and is therefore a separately funded activity. It is essential not to let the disagreements over funding delay the project or lead to foolish shortcuts—the most important task is to ensure that the application operates in the next century. Forcing the outsourcing vendor into an unfair situation will ultimately cost the IT organization more than it gains.

Financial situations notwithstanding, the outsourcers generally will perform the work needed to achieve compliance for the applications they support. Although the outsourcer will usually handle testing, final certification of compliance remains the responsibility of the IT organization. The outsourcer should follow the same compliance definitions used for internally supported applications of the same type. Compliance requirements and specific task responsibilities should be specified contractually to avoid misinterpretation. If the IT organization has any doubts about the vendor's ability to achieve compliance in a timely manner, a contingency plan should be developed to meet initial compliance standards.

As with packaged software, four levels of compliance can be defined for outsourced applications. These levels should have target dates and become increasingly more stringent as the Year 2000 deadline approaches.

- Level one: The vendor contract includes language specifying responsibility for Year 2000 compliance, setting a target date for that compliance, and specifying penalties and remedies if that target date is missed.

- Level two: The vendor has committed to, and documented, a compliance strategy specifying the approach that will be used to implement century dates and the actual delivery date for that version. This approach has been certified by the IT manager responsible for the application(s) and the Year 2000 Project Office. (This is the central team responsible for managing the Year 2000 effort for an enterprise. It is described in Chapter 11.) This includes acceptance of the vendor's solution and delivery timing and an assessment of whether the conversion will be completed and installed in time to meet overall corporate requirements. If necessary, the internal team will create a contingency plan in the event of vendor nonperformance.

- Level three: The vendor has completed and tested the necessary changes to achieve compliance.

- Level four: The completed application has been certified as Year 2000 compliant by the IT manager responsible for the application and by the Year 2000 Project Office, and the compliant version is in production operation.

5.1.6 Interfaces to External Organizations

Even if a given business application is compliant internally, it is at risk if it shares interfaces with external organizations. These interfaces range from tape files to real-time Electronic Data Interchange (EDI) transmissions. An additional challenge imposed by interface sharing among organizations is determining responsibility for selecting the compliance strategy, determining the conversion timing, and converting the interface data. Each of these three activities can be assigned differently, depending on the nature of the interface and the relationships among the organizations. For example, a governmental agency may require using the data expansion strategy and mandate a compliance date but leave the responsibility for performing the conversion to the IT organization. If responsibility is not clear, it should be quickly negotiated by the affected parties. This negotiation should produce a compliance definition for the shared interface. If multiple peer organizations share the same interface, this negotiation process can quickly become difficult and time consuming. In this situation, we advise all organizations to adopt a default standard of full four-digit years. This standard eliminates many negotiations and puts the data in a format that satisfies most requirements.

A variation of the four-level compliance strategy can be applied to each interface to an external organization. If the interface relationship is governed by a contract, that contract contains the compliance definition for that interface.

- Level one: The external organization(s) for each external interface in an application have been identified and contacted. If a contract is in place, it includes language specifying responsibility for Year 2000 compliance, setting a target date for that compliance and designating penalties and remedies if that target date is missed.

- Level two: Organizational responsibility for the interface has been determined. The responsible organization has committed to, and documented, a compliance strategy specifying the approach that they will use to implement century dates and has set an actual date for conversion.

- Level three: One organization (either internal or external) has completed the conversion of its side of the interface. If necessary, a bridging strategy is in place and operational until the other organization completes its conversion.

- Level four: Both organizations have completed conversion, the interface has been tested and any bridges have been removed. The interface is fully compliant and operational.

5.1.7 Noncomputer Interfaces to External Organizations

Although the compliance definitions described above focus on data processing issues, corporations are exposed to Year 2000 issues in external organizations even when there are no direct system interfaces. For example, if a corporation depends on a supplier for delivery of key manufacturing components, the supplier's inability to deliver those components because of Year 2000 problems with its internal systems will cause problems for the corporation. To avoid potential problems, corporate purchasing offices should set compliance certification standards as part of their contracts with key suppliers. These standards should require the supplier to show reasonable progress toward Year 2000 compliance and, ultimately, to provide certification documentation that the supplier will provide uninterrupted service through the Year 2000 transition.

5.2 Year 2000 Century Representation Issues

At the lowest level, Year 2000 compliance is achieved by implementing some method for recognizing the difference in century in a given date. This recognition can be achieved either by adding century data to the format of each date representation or by following defined rules for interpreting the century by context while still using two-digit dates. A secondary, but equally important, issue is the extent of the date conversion effort. Will all year fields be updated to reflect century data, or only those fields that absolutely require conversion?

As simple as these choices seem, they have tremendous implications for how the Year 2000 migration is implemented at the application and enterprise levels. The selection of a century-representation approach drives a number of requirements for events that occur downstream in the conversion project. For example, selecting a data-expansion approach requires a physical migration of an application's data. This data migration requires the use of bridging techniques and the coordination of conversion efforts for the applications that share the data.

Specific factors influenced by the choice of century representation and conversion extent are:

- **Implementation effort.**

  The wider the extent of the conversion and the greater the intrusiveness of the approach, the larger the implementation effort. Complete conversion of all dates to full, four-digit year representation requires the greatest implementation effort.

- **Testing effort.**

  Testing effort increases in proportion to the number of changes made to program logic. All logic changes must be carefully exercised to ensure correctness. The greater the number of logic changes, the greater the likelihood of introducing errors in the migration process.

- **Time requirements.**

  Elapsed time requirements are affected by the number of tasks required to implement a given approach. As the Year 2000 deadline approaches, minimal approaches will have to be selected to ensure timely project completion.

- **Coordination requirements.**

  Changes to application data require careful coordination among separate application projects during the conversion process. This coordination is not required for process-only approaches.

- **Future usefulness of application data.**

  The overall value of application data depends on its ability to be easily accessed and interpreted. Full data expansion offers the greatest flexibility, while compression approaches may greatly limit the usefulness of file data to ad hoc query programs.

  Unfortunately, there is no such thing as a perfect approach to be applied to all situations. Yet, the separate approaches are incompatible by nature (e.g., one application cannot write compressed year data for an interface with another application that expects expanded years). Despite the obvious attractiveness of selecting and enforcing a single strategy, it is unrealistic to expect that it will be effective across an entire enterprise. External factors, such as resource and time constraints, will force the selection of shortcut approaches in certain instances.

  While it is tempting for IT organizations always to select the strategy that requires the least effort during conversion, all shortcuts have to be balanced against their long-term implications on application support and future data value. For example, if an application uses date fields only for printed report headings, two-digit year formats are perfectly acceptable. This format is not acceptable if the same application relies on multiyear transactions sorted by date. Similarly, applications that perform high volumes of date transactions will not benefit from a shortcut migration strategy. Full date expansion facilitates all possible operations and should be the default selection for all new applications. Approaches for existing applications should be selected on the basis of the extent to which each application depends on dates for the following operations:

- **Sorting and key field sequencing.**

  Although some sort utilities accept parameters to change the sort order of two-digit years, we *strongly* recommend using a data-driven approach for applications relying on sorts or sequencing by key fields that contain date values.

- **Access by end-user applications.**

  Simpler is better for data likely to be used by end-user applications. Dates should be expanded.

- **High transaction volumes.**

  Applications with high transaction volumes should limit the number of operations required for date manipulation by storing fully expanded dates.

- **Complicated date calculations and comparisons.**

  Process-based approaches increase the complexity of date logic within programs and should be avoided whenever date processing is already highly complex.

IT organizations must also resist the temptation to create their own company-specific methods for representing centuries because doing so could lead to mismatched data formats among interacting applications. The implications of this problem are compounded when data is shared among external organizations such as suppliers and governmental entities.

For the above reasons, we strongly recommend that IT organizations select as few methods of representing centuries as possible and that those methods follow common industry standards.

IT organizations must select their set of default century-date representation approaches carefully to ensure that they meet long-term organizational requirements. Once selected, these approaches are documented and included in the century-date compliance standards followed by all Year 2000 project teams. Management enforcement is required to ensure that only the standard approaches are used and that each approach is used only in the appropriate circumstances.

5.2.1 Methods for Representing Century Dates

As shown in Table 5.2, there are two principal methods for handling century dates: data-based approaches and process-based approaches. Each method has dozens of variations. The following discussion does not attempt to cover all known variations; rather, it highlights the advantages and disadvantages of some of the most common formats.

Table 5.2   Two Approaches for Handling Century Dates

	Data-based	**Process-based**
Date process logic	Minor changes	Logic changed to interpret century from context
Date fields	Expanded to include centuries	Mostly unchanged
File data	Migrated to new format	Unchanged
Date sorts	Handled	Will not handle
Interfaces	Bridges to noncompliant applications needed	Not necessary
Limits	No range limits	100-year range

5.2.1.1 Data-based Approaches

Data-based approaches represent the century within the application data. Year data is fully expanded to four digits, expressed through flags, or compressed into existing date fields. Data-based approaches have the following advantages:

- Guarantee correctness of century information
- Least costly for long-term maintenance (four-digit approaches)
- Least costly option when a date-dependent file is shared by many applications
- Most widely accepted standard (four-digit approach)
- Decreased need for process logic changes
- Highest data usage value
- Directly handle all common operations such as sorts, comparisons, and calculations

The disadvantages of data-based approaches include:

- Require data migration
- Most costly option for simple interfaces
- Increase conversion project complexity by requiring coordination among applications sharing data files

- Increase direct access storage device (DASD) requirements (expansion approaches only)

- Require screen or report redesign when applied to user views

There are many variations of the data-based approach. These variations differ in their DASD requirements, processing logic requirements, and data flexibility. Full expansion approaches require the greatest increase in storage requirements in exchange for fewer process logic changes and the greatest data flexibility. In contrast, compression approaches require no additional DASD storage at the cost of increased processing logic and decreased data flexibility. Because all data-based approaches change the format of existing data, they require a physical file conversion to use the new date formats and coordination among the internal and external applications sharing that data. Once the data is converted, applications using the old format cannot use the new data. This also presents an issue for applications saving and using historical files. Methods for coordinating file interfaces are described in the next section of this chapter.

There are four principal data-based approaches:

- Ordered dates

- Standard expansion (CCYY)

- Flag bytes

- Date compression

Each of these approaches is described in detail in the ensuing pages.

- **Ordered dates.**

  This is the most common variation on the standard two-to-four digit expansion approach. This approach, illustrated in Figure 5.1 uses eight-digit dates and reorders the commonly used DD/MM/YY approach to CCYY/MM/DD for all data stored in files or used for internal calculations and comparisons. Report and display representations are usually maintained in "standard" format. As shown in the illustration, this format simplifies the process of sorting and reduces the logic required to compare two dates by relying on mathematical methods of comparison.

```
01    ORDERED-DATE-1.                      01    STANDARD-DATE-1.
      05    CC-1      PIC 99.                    05    MM-1      PIC 99.
      05    YY-1      PIC 99.                    05    DD-1      PIC 99.
      05    MM-1      PIC 99.                    05    CC-1      PIC 99.
      05    DD-1      PIC 99.                    05    YY-1      PIC 99.
01    ORDERED-DATE-2.                      01    STANDARD-DATE-2.
      05    CC-2      PIC 99.                    05    MM-2      PIC 99.
      05    YY-2      PIC 99.                    05    DD-2      PIC 99.
      05    MM-2      PIC 99.                    05    CC-2      PIC 99.
      05    DD-2      PIC 99.                    05    YY-2      PIC 99.


* 7/26/1996                               * 7/26/1996
MOVE 19960726 TO ORDERED-DATE-1.          MOVE 07261996 TO STANDARD-DATE-1.
* 8/07/1994                               * 08/07/1994
MOVE 19940807 TO ORDERED-DATE-2.          MOVE 08071994 TO STANDARD-DATE-2.

IF ORDERED-DATE-1 > ORDERED-DATE-2        *** This test required to produce the
    DISPLAY 'CORRECT!'                    *** correct result
ELSE  DISPLAY 'INCORRECT'.                IF YY-1 > YY-2
                                              DISPLAY 'CORRECT'
                                          ELSE IF YY-1 = YY-2
                                              IF MM-1 > MM-2
                                                  DISPLAY 'CORRECT'
                                              ELSE IF MM-1 = MM-2
                                                  IF DD-1 > DD-2
                                                      DISPLAY 'CORRECT'
                                                  ELSE DISPLAY 'INCORRECT'.

Ordered dates with compare logic          Standard dates with equivalent compare logic
```

Figure 5.1   Ordered Date Format

The advantages of the ordered date approach are:

— Provides the greatest reduction in the size and complexity of program logic

— Reduces long-term maintenance effort

The disadvantages of this approach over other data-based approaches are:

— Requires additional programming effort to retrofit the new format in existing programs

— Requires data migration

— Increases the cost and effort of the conversion effort

— Increases likelihood of introducing defects

— Lengthens the conversion window

— Must be used consistently (Mixing CCYY/MM/DD formats with MM/DD/CCYY formats will cause confusion and may introduce errors if dates are accidentally mixed.)

Recommendation: The ordered date is unlikely to gain wide acceptance in Year 2000 projects. The programming effort required to simplify the processing logic to make use of the new format limits its usefulness for existing applications. It is an ideal strategy for new application development, where the simplicity of its process logic greatly reduces initial programming time as well as future maintenance.

- **Standard Expansion (CCYY).**

Expanding two-digit year fields (YY) to four digits (CCYY) to accommodate century data (CC) is the most straightforward method of achieving century compliance at the code level. This approach is the most widely used standard and is the announced standard for applications interfacing with the federal government programs.

The advantages of the standard date approach are:

— Requires relatively few program logic changes

— Reduces long-term maintenance effort

— Handles all date operations

— Avoids extraneous logic to determine century or expand and compress dates

— Offers excellent data flexibility

— Is the most common industry standard

The disadvantages of this approach are:

— Requires the greatest amount of additional DASD (requires two additional bytes for every date field)

— Requires data migration

Recommendation: This is the most common approach for all newly developed software and, in the perfect world, the best approach for existing applications. In the real world, this approach is not recommended for applications where data migration is not feasible owing to size or interface considerations. Although the expansion approach increases project complexity because of bridging and coordination efforts, its long-term maintainability and data flexibility compensate for the extra effort on high-value projects. This approach should not be used for minimal conversion efforts or for short-lived applications.

- **Flag bytes.**

  Flag bytes are a shorthand approach for gaining many of the advantages of a field expansion approach without the full increase in DASD storage. This approach uses a one-byte field to contain a flag indicating the century. This flag byte may be incorporated with each date field, or it may be stored separately. If all the date fields within a single record occur in the same century, a single flag byte can be used for the entire record. In certain cases, flag bytes can be used to avoid data migrations and interface coordination efforts. Some older applications maintain "filler" fields at the end of records for later expansion. If the flag(s) can be placed within this section of the record, DASD size does not need to increase, file migration can occur with the application that creates the data, and other applications can access the flag(s) as they are converted, eliminating the need for bridges. Incorporating flags into sort keys ensures that date-dependent records sort correctly.

  The advantages of the flag byte approach are:

  — Provides accurate century data

  — Saves DASD storage (requires no more than one byte per date)

  — Can eliminate data expansion issues in certain cases

  — Handles all date operations

  The disadvantages of this approach are:

  — Is typically application and file specific

  — Decreases data flexibility (data requires interpretation)

  — Increases processing logic complexity

  — Is less straightforward to maintain

  Recommendation: This compromise approach may be attractive for specialized situations, such as short-lived applications, or applications that are not date dependent for calculations but that sort transactions by date. This approach is most attractive if existing storage is available for flag bytes. If file expansion is required and overall

DASD requirements are not an issue, the CCYY is a better choice. With rare exceptions, this approach will not be feasible for interfaces shared with external organizations.

- **Date Compression.**

  Date compression packs the century representation within the same bytes used for current date storage, thereby avoiding file expansion. While file conversion is still required to implement the new format, DASD requirements won't change. These DASD storage savings are gained at the cost of additional processing logic to pack and unpack the year data. Date compression requires "tricky programming." There are almost as many compression schemes as there are inventive programmers. Figure 5.2 shows several variations on the theme. Example 1 uses a binary format to store up to 65,535 years with the use of the sign bit. Example 2 uses a signed, fixed decimal (COMP-3) field to store a three-digit year in two bytes. The high-order digit is used to store 0, for 1800, 1 for 1900, 2 for 2000, etc. Although the year is not in a traditional format, Example 2 handles all operations, including sorts and year calculations. Example 3 uses all six existing date characters to compress a complete date in CCYY/MM/DD format, using fixed decimal. In its Year 2000 guide, IBM describes another method that substitutes characters and digits to extend the number of years contained in each byte from 10 (0–9) to 36 (0–35). This allows up to 1,295 years to be represented in two bytes. Using 1900 as a base year, this approach will work until 3195[2].

  Compressed dates sort and compare correctly without expansion; however, not all compression schemes enable calculations without expansion. Expansion is also required to display year data. This expansion has to be performed for each year stored in a record and can be quite costly in terms of computer resources. Date compression and expansion is best performed through the use of subroutines. This method saves the addition of numerous lines of process logic whenever dates are used.

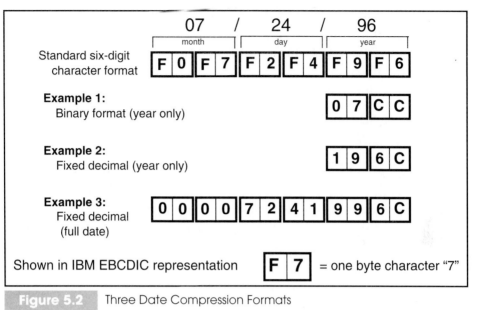

Figure 5.2 Three Date Compression Formats

The advantages of the date compression approach are:

— Provides accurate century data

— Saves DASD storage (requires no extra storage)

— Handles all date operations

The disadvantages of this approach are:

— Requires data migration

— Tends to be application-specific; few common compression standards

— Requires the most programming of any data-based approach

— Increases the complexity of program logic

— Increases future maintenance effort

— Offers lowest data flexibility; data is not human readable

Recommendation: Because of its limitations, data compression is useful only for applications that are highly date driven, have severe DASD constraints, and are not CPU constrained. It is not recommended for other types of applications. Certain vendors may promote tools and solutions that could reduce programming changes and increase the viability of this option.

5.2.1.2 Process-based Approaches

Process-based approaches avoid the need to modify database and file data by using rules to interpret the century by context from two-digit years. Based on the characteristics of an application's use of dates, an arbitrary cutoff year is determined. The century to be used for years above the cutoff is 1900, and years that fall below the cutoff are interpreted as occurring in the 21st century. Century interpretation is implemented through process logic in the application software. Although these applications do not store expanded dates in their files, year data can be expanded as needed within programs for use in calculations or comparisons. This limits coding changes for century interpretation to only those situations where it is required. Process-based approaches allow applications to handle century-dependent processing over a hundred year range of dates.

For example, selecting 50 as the cutoff year results in the following interpretations:

Two-digit Year	Fully Interpreted Year
67	1967
01	2001
50	1950
49	2049

IT organizations can use multiple cutoff years to fix their processing needs. For example, a forecasting application will require a different set of rules for interpreting centuries than an application maintaining birth records. Although different sets of rules can be used, all applications sharing the same set of files must follow the same interpretation rules. Failure to follow standards will result in processing errors if one application interprets 37 as 1937 while another interprets it as 2037.

The primary advantage of process-based approaches is avoiding the need to modify data. Eliminating modifications in file formats leaves the interfaces between applications sharing files unchanged, so that individual application migration projects can be completed independently without the need for bridging techniques. This reduces the complexity of project coordination and often lowers the cost and effort needed to implement compliance. Process-based approaches offer these advantages:

- Eliminate data migrations; only option if file size prevents migration

- No impact on file storage (DASD) size requirements

- Simplify Year 2000 project coordination

- Limit coding changes to instances where century context is needed

- Least costly alternative in many situations

Although the advantages of process-based approaches are very attractive, they are offset by serious limitations. Process-based approaches sacrifice data usability and long-term maintenance costs to achieve short-term savings during the Year 2000 migration effort. Unlike data-based approaches, process-based approaches cannot be applied in all situations. Direct file operations, such as sorting records by year, are not easily supported. Situations such as year comparisons and calculations require the addition of complex processing logic. This logic can be extensive in highly date-dependent applications. Moreover, this logic must be replicated through all applications accessing the unexpanded files. Insidious interpretation errors occur when data falls outside of the 100-year range supported by two-digit years. These limitations increase future maintenance and support costs of applications using process-based approaches. Disadvantages of process-based approaches include:

- No common industry standard for sharing external files

- Can be used only when years remain within a 100-year range

- Provide incorrect results for data that falls out of its range

- All applications sharing the same file *must* use the same century cutoff year

- Require additional logic to handle common operations such as sorts, comparisons, and calculations

- Impact application performance by increasing date processing overhead

- Increase program complexity

- Higher likelihood of introducing coding errors during conversion

- Lowest long-term data usage value

Given their disadvantages, the use of process-based approaches should be limited to time- and cost-critical situations. Applications with low business value, short expected life spans, and low maintenance requirements are the safest candidates. These approaches can be used for applications with:

- Limited date processing

- High likelihood of replacement in the short-term

- Year data where century is easily determined by context

- Low sharing and reuse of file data by other applications

    Process-based approaches should be avoided for situations where:

- Files are sorted by key fields with dates

- Ability to determine century by context cannot be guaranteed

- The application or the file has long-term value

- Processing logic is frequently maintained

    Process-based approaches differ by whether their hundred-year interpretation "window" is fixed or sliding. Although either approach can be coded directly wherever year processing logic occurs in a program, it is far better to implement them through shared subroutines to reduce complexity and decrease coding effort.

- **Fixed window.**

    The fixed window approach uses a static century cutoff year to define its 100-year interval. This cutoff year is determined during conversion and, unless manually updated, remains constant for the life of the application. This affects the number of years that an application can look forward or backward in its century processing. In 1997, using 50 as the century cutoff allows the application to look forward 53 years until 2049 and backward 47 years until 1950. In 2003, the same century cutoff limits the ability to look forward to 46 years and increases the ability to look backward to 54 years.

    The advantages of the fixed window approach are:

    — Requires the simplest logic

    — Easily defined and enforced as a standard

    The disadvantages of this approach are:

    — Century interpretation range does not change, creating an issue if processing requirements ever exceed the defined range

    — All applications sharing a file *must* use the same century cutoff year

— Very confusing if multiple fixed dates are used across an enterprise

— Requires intensive effort to update

Recommendation: The fixed window approach is most useful for applications that have limited life expectancy and that maintain a limited range of year data. For example, an application that retains records over only a 5-year range could operate safely within a fixed window for up to 95 years. This approach is not recommended for applications maintaining records over a wide range of years.

- **Sliding window.**

  Rather than fixing the century cutoff year, the sliding window approach uses a self-advancing base. Unlike the fixed window approach, this method allows an application to look forward and backward the same number of years throughout the life of the application. This eliminates the need to update the century cutoff year if century processing requirements change. This approach is implemented by defining the number of years forward and backward relative to a base year (typically the current year). For instance, an application can sets its sliding window starting from 50 years before the base year. This allows the application to look backward 50 years and forward 49 years from the base year. In this case, the range in 1997 is 1947 through 2046. In 2003, the range moves to 1953 and 2052.

  The advantages of the sliding window approach over the fixed window approach are:

  — Greater flexibility

  — No need to reprogram over time

  The disadvantages of this approach are:

  — More complex processing logic

  — All applications sharing the same files must use the same assumptions for base year and relative years backward and forward

  Recommendation: Given its increased flexibility, the sliding window approach is recommended over the fixed window approach for most projects whenever a process-based approach is required. Although the differences between approaches are not significant for applications with a short life expectancy or that maintain a narrow range of years in their files, using a sliding window approach reduces the need to monitor and modify the application code if assumptions ever change.

5.2.2 Conversion Extent

Once the century representation approach has been selected for a given application, the next strategy decision is to select the extent of the conversion. Dates are used in a variety of contexts throughout an application. They appear in file records, in work fields, in calculations, and on reports and display screens. In certain cases, such as calculations and comparisons, dates must be modified to handle centuries in order to produce correct results. The decision to convert dates becomes more difficult for dates displayed on reports. If the context of these dates is easily determined by the user of the report, converting the date fields may be unnecessary. This topic was introduced in a larger context in Chapter 4 in Section 4.2, *Conversion Strategies*.

The extent of date conversion is directly influenced by short-term considerations—the overall conversion effort—and long-term considerations—the application's usability and maintainability. Deciding upon the extent of the conversion requires balancing these considerations. Updating all program code and data to reflect full years maximizes application value. Conversely, restricting the extent of the conversion to only those fields needed to ensure correct application operation minimizes conversion time and effort but increases the difficulty of future maintenance.

The method selected for century representation within files is an important factor in the extent of the conversion. This topic has been discussed extensively in thepreceding text. The following discussion covers conversion considerations for the other types of date fields found within application programs.

- **Dates within reports.**

  Since fields with printed reports are carefully formatted and spaced, expanding year fields within printed reports is expensive and time consuming. Significant reformatting of other data may be necessary on crowded report pages. Unless century data cannot be determined by context, report dates should not be expanded as part of a typical conversion project.

- **Dates on display screens.**

  Operator ease of use is a critical consideration when selecting the date conversion approach for data entry screens. Conversion shortcuts that save programming time can be very costly in long-term operator time for transaction-bound applications with thousands of users. In most cases, date fields displayed in read-only mode can be treated in the same manner as report fields and expanded only when necessary. Data entry fields present a greater challenge. If expansion is difficult owing to screen space and century can be determined from context, the entry field can remain two digits. The year field can be expanded in the background for use in calculations or storage in four-digit format. For simplicity or if context cannot be determined, four-digit year expansion is the method of choice.

- **Dates within sort and file or database keys.**

In almost every case, dates within sort keys must be expanded. This is also true for file or database key fields used to access data in date sequence. Although not encouraged, this rule can be violated for situations where the ramifications of incorrect sorting or sequencing are minimal. For example, a program that produces a printed report containing sorted data from the previous week will process incorrectly only during the first week of the year 2000. During this week, report users can easily compensate for the sorting problem through manual methods.

- **Work fields.**

Work fields contain dates used for calculations and comparisons within programs. If a program receives its year data in four-digit format, it is best to use this format for work fields throughout the program. This simplifies calculations and comparisons by avoiding the need to add logic to handle century identification. If dates are received in a two-digit format, they can be expanded on receipt and used in four-digit format throughout the program or they can be expanded only when needed. The former approach is recommended for maintainability and should be used in any program that performs significant date processing. The latter approach can be used for minimal conversion efforts if the program performs little date manipulation.

5.3 Interfaces Between Applications

Perhaps the most difficult challenge in century-date compliance projects is resolving the data interfaces between programs and applications. These interfaces consist of files, databases, EDI transactions, parameter passing, and other methods of sharing data between two programs. Any changes made to the data formats passed through these interfaces affect all programs that access that interface, regardless of their application or location.

Data format changes are especially troublesome for widely shared files and databases. For instance, a customer information database may be accessed throughout an enterprise by dozens of separate production applications as well as countless small end-user applications. In theory, any change to the size or format of year fields within this database requires simultaneous modification of all of these applications. Even if it is feasible, this presents an enormous coordination and testing nightmare. Figure 5.3 illustrates an example.

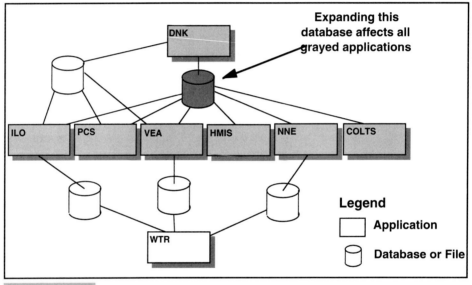

Figure 5.3 Interfaces Among Applications

Fortunately, there are numerous methods for reducing the effort and mitigating the risk of changes to application interfaces. The Year 2000 Project Office is responsible for selecting the appropriate methods and coordinating their implementation across multiple organizations. Project Office responsibilities include selecting the century-representation approach for that interface, specifying the timing and responsibility of the data migration, and providing bridging solutions when needed.

5.3.1 Upgrade Units

The best method for reducing the number and complexity of interface issues is to minimize the number of interfaces that require coordination.

Three types of interfaces require attention: those that cross organizational boundaries, those that cross century-compliance sub-project boundaries, and those that are used within a century-date compliance sub-project. Cross-organizational interfaces are fixed in number and must be resolved individually. Interfaces that occur *within* a sub-project are converted and tested simultaneously during the sub-project. Simultaneous conversion eliminates most interface conversion issues. Cross-project interfaces generally present more complex issues. The number of interfaces between sub-projects depends on how those sub-project boundaries are determined. As shown in Figure 5.4, sub-project boundaries can be drawn in a manner that increases or decreases the number of cross-project interfaces. Boundary 1 encompasses three applications but requires interfaces for four files. Boundary 2 encompasses five applications and lowers the interface requirements to two files. The goal of the century-date compliance effort is to contain as many interfaces as feasible within each free-standing conversion project. This grouping of application components for a sub-project is called an "upgrade unit."

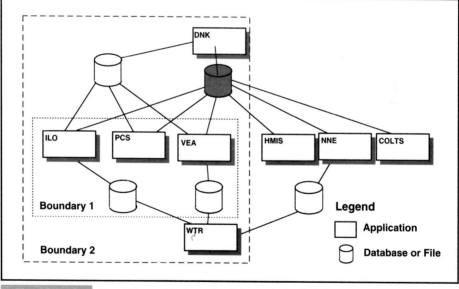

Figure 5.4   The Effect of Sub-project Boundaries in Interfaces

When planning a century-date compliance project at the enterprise level, the Year 2000 Project Office, working with application personnel, divides the overall application portfolio into upgrade units to be assigned as separate sub-projects. Through the use of the data migration techniques described in Section 5.3.2, these sub-projects can be implemented in parallel or in series. This permits the Year 2000 Project Office to assign upgrade units to internal staff, consultants, conversion factories, or to offshore resources as needed. Selecting upgrade unit boundaries to minimize the number of shared interfaces between sub-projects reduces overall conversion effort.

Depending on the characteristics of the portfolio, an upgrade unit can consist of a single application, several related applications, or even a partial application. This division reduces overall project effort by minimizing interface conversion effort. The composition of an upgrade unit is determined by functionality, data usage, and number of interfaces. Functions can be represented by separate jobs that share files extensively internally. In this case, upgrade units are defined by job. Functionally related applications share the greatest level of data, resulting in numerous interfaces between them. A set of applications can revolve around a central database or file. Grouping these applications into a single upgrade unit reduces conversion effort by eliminating many coordination issues.

The best starting point for determining ideal upgrade units is a complete system inventory. This inventory contains the information needed to identify all interfaces between applications. In many cases, the natural boundaries of an application are also the natural boundaries of an upgrade unit. This can be verified by using the system inventory to examine the application's interfaces. Experiment with different upgrade unit groupings until a balance is achieved between minimal interfaces and overall size of the sub-project. Sub-project size should be limited to a scope that can be quickly implemented by a small project team. In COBOL, this usually results in 500,000 to 1 million lines of code per upgrade unit.

5.3.2 Data Migration Approaches

Once upgrade units have been assigned to sub-project teams, the process of coordinating interface conversions among those units can begin. The process involves assigning the responsibility for determining the migration approach, implementing that approach, and selecting its timing. Although these decisions can be determined by consensus among the individual upgrade unit teams or can be dictated by the Year 2000 Project Office, for expedience we recommend that responsibility for all data migration issues rests with the upgrade unit that *creates* the data used in the interface. Following this convention reduces the need for negotiation among projects over the best approach. If data is created in multiple upgrade units, consensus-based negotiation is the only alternative.

There are five principal strategies for migrating data: avoidance, simultaneous, phased, first, and last.

- **Avoidance.**

  Interface issues can be avoided if data formats are not modified. The process-based century representation approaches previously described enable organizations to achieve date compliance without resorting to data modifications. At best, process-based approaches will provide only partial relief. Further, if the interface is controlled by an external organization, such as a major customer or the federal government, data format changes may be imposed on the IT organization. Accordingly, the implementation teams for all significant century-compliance efforts must have a working knowledge of methods for resolving interface issues even if their default compliance standard is the use of a process-based approach.

- **Simultaneous.**

  In this strategy, the upgrade units that share an interface prepare for conversion independently but simultaneously. Fixed conversion dates are selected for interface testing and production cutover. All affected upgrade units must complete their conversion efforts in time to meet these dates. Data migration for test purposes only occurs on the first date, and migration of production data occurs for the cutover date. The biggest advantage of this approach is eliminating the overhead and effort of employing bridging technology. Its disadvantage is the increased interdependence of the affected upgrade units.

- **Phased.**

  The phased data migration approach is used when two or more upgrade units share a number of common interfaces. In this approach, the physical data for each interface is migrated when the code upgrades relating to that interface are completed for each upgrade unit. In effect, this approach is simply a series of simultaneous conversions. The phased approach requires a greater level of coordination among upgrade unit projects. Like the simultaneous approach, it avoids the need and overhead of bridging technology.

- **First.**

  When multiple upgrade units share the same interface, coordination among projects becomes overwhelming. In this case, data migration is separated from the internal conversion effort for each upgrade unit. Data is migrated at the beginning of the project as part of the conversion of the upgrade unit that produces the data. Bridges or application program interfaces (APIs) are required so that unconverted upgrade units can process the converted data; these bridges must be put in place as part of the data conversion. As subsequent upgrade units complete their conversions, they simply remove their API or bridge to access the compliant data. The advantage of this approach is that it uncouples separate upgrade unit projects and simplifies access to compliant data. The disadvantage of this approach is the need and overhead for multiple bridges until all upgrade units reach compliance. Further, this approach cannot be used if multiple upgrade units create or update data.

- **Last.**

    This strategy is similar to the First strategy defined above, except that physical data migration occurs after the final upgrade unit is converted. As each upgrade unit is converted, a bridge or API connects it to the unconverted data. When all conversions are complete, the data is migrated and all of the bridges are removed. Unlike the First strategy, this approach can be used when multiple upgrade units create or update data. This approach allows greater independence of separate upgrade unit projects. Project coordination from the Year 2000 Project Office is necessary to ensure that the final data conversion is performed and that all bridges and APIs are removed.

5.3.3 Interfacing Strategies

Whenever data migration is necessary and simultaneous conversion is not possible, some method is needed to provide compliant data to compliant programs while providing the original format to noncompliant programs. These methods are commonly referred to as bridging technologies.

There are a variety of interfacing strategies to handle a wide range of phased date migration requirements. There are no perfect strategies that can be applied universally, but the breadth of options will provide a reasonable solution for almost every requirement. Interface technologies can be applied intrusively or nonintrusively. Nonintrusive approaches use utilities external to the upgrade unit to handle data translation. They can be activated or deactivated without changing the source code within the upgrade unit. Intrusive approaches handle data migrations at least in part within the upgrade unit source code. These approaches can be activated or deactivated only by source code changes.

The most common categories are data duplication, bridge utilities, APIs, and phased coding.

- **Data Duplication.**

  Data duplication creates and stores a compliant and a noncompliant version of data passed through an interface. It can be implemented intrusively by modifying the program(s) that create the data to produce two versions; it can be implemented nonintrusively by using a bridge utility to create a noncompliant version of a file from a compliant version. If an intrusive approach is used, the code used to implement the duplicate file must be removed at the end of the conversion process.

  The advantages of the data duplication approach are:

  — Simple to implement

  — Provides data in both compliant and noncompliant formats

  — Does not require finding all end-user applications that access noncompliant data

  The disadvantages of this approach are:

  — Doubles disk storage requirements

  — Adds overhead (double I/O) to produce

  — If implemented intrusively, requires later coding changes

  Recommendation: This approach is best suited for small volumes of critical data accessed by numerous upgrade units. It is also useful for situations where an unknown number of end-user applications access the data and the consequences of interrupting those applications may be high. The end-user applications can continue to use the duplicate data until they are found, upgraded, or eliminated. This approach is not feasible for large volumes of data.

- **Bridge Utilities.**

  Bridge utilities are programs that read data in one format and write it in another format. They are typically used for batch applications. Bridge utilities can be a program written specifically for a given application or a generalized utility that is customized through parameters to identify and reformat the correct data. Generalized utilities are the easiest to use and require the least effort to implement; however, they do not handle all data formats, and the generalization often adds overhead. Custom programs offer greater flexibility, and they can be reused for other conversion activities, such as selecting and modifying test data.

Bridge utilities are implemented as a separate step between the upgrade unit that produces the compliant data and the upgrade unit(s) that need to access the data in its original format. Temporary data storage can be used if the interface is shared between only two entities. Otherwise, the bridge utility should be used as part of a data duplication strategy. When a bridge utility is no longer needed, it is deactivated by deleting the job step. No coding changes are required.

The advantages of the bridge utility approach are:

— Simple to activate and deactivate

— Requires the least effort to implement

— Nonintrusive

— Utility can be used for final data migration

— Custom programs can be used to select and modify test data

The disadvantages of this approach are:

— Doubles disk storage requirements (at least temporarily)

— Requires double I/O to produce

— Removal must be monitored

Recommendation: This approach is ideal when performance and storage requirements allow the additional processing overhead. It requires the minimal level of project coordination. This simplicity of implementation causes bridges to be forgotten; care must be taken to remember to remove the bridge once all conversions are complete. Bridging is not appropriate for high volumes of data or when performance is an issue.

• **Application Program Interfaces.**

APIs are an intrusive approach that implements a data conversion layer within the application programs creating or accessing an interface. APIs are associated with I/O activities such as READs, WRITEs, GETs, CALLs, etc. APIs are required for on-line programs that pass data through communications areas, shared databases, parameters, and other nonfile methods. APIs are equally applicable to on-line files and batch programs, sharing databases with other upgrade units.

APIs can be used by either compliant or noncompliant programs. A compliant program may implement an API for a READ by calling a routine that requests and expands a noncompliant record. The program receives what appears to be a compliant record from the API. A noncompliant program uses the API to request and reformat compliant data to its original noncompliant format.

APIs can be implemented as a section of code within the program itself or as a call to a linked external routine that mimics the desired I/O activity. Once conversion is complete for all upgrade units sharing the interface, the application source code must be modified to remove the API.

The advantages of the API approach are:

— Avoids data duplication

— Does not require duplicate I/O

— Only method for on-line programs

— Well suited for high volumes of data

The disadvantages of this approach are:

— Requires greater effort to implement

— Requires changes to the code after the conversion is completed

— Requires greater coordination among upgrade units

Recommendation: This approach is required for nonfile/database situations. It is especially valuable in high-volume transaction situations because it introduces only minimal overhead. Its primary disadvantage is the need for later coding, which adds effort and opens the door for potential errors.

- **Phased Coding.**

This method uses partial code conversions to eliminate the need for the overhead or intrusiveness of other approaches. For example, a noncompliant application that accesses converted data as read-only may redefine the date fields to match its required noncompliant format. The compliant application is able to produce compliant data, while the noncompliant application can continue to operate until it is converted.

The process becomes more complicated if the noncompliant application creates the data or if data creation is shared. If carefully planned, most of the required coding effort is reused in the later application conversion effort. Highly complex file structures are not suitable for this approach.

The advantages of the phased coding approach are:

— Introduces little overhead

— Avoids duplicate I/O

— Requires little additional programming

The disadvantages of this approach are:

— Requires additional coordination among applications

— Difficult to implement for complex or shared data creation

— Requires two separate projects for the noncompliant application

Recommendation: This approach is useful no matter the volume of data or performance requirements. Although it requires additional coordination and planning, it is easily implemented for simple file structures. This approach is recommended for applications that will be converted by internal staff members who are used to working closely together. It is not recommended for outsourced applications.

References

[1] Bush, Eric, "A CASE For Existing Systems," white paper produced for Language Technology, Inc., 1988.

[2] IBM, "The Year 2000 and 2-Digit Dates: A Guide for Planning and Implementation," Publication GC28-1251-00, first edition, October 1995.

Environmental Issues and Support Technologies

Century-date compliance projects provide challenges and opportunities for the application support environments used within most IT organizations. These projects are impossible to accomplish without strong tool support, adequate configuration management, and excellent test environments. To a large degree, century-date compliance projects use the tools and support environments that exist to support standard maintenance tasks. However, existing application support environments often lack the robustness needed for projects of the scale of century-compliance efforts. Gaps exist in tool coverage and integration, usage skills, version control processes, and test data availability. Although IT organizations can make effective use of existing tools, many of these tools are poorly deployed. Further, these tools may not be century-date compliant themselves.

Fortunately, with the exception of some century-date, project-specific tools, any effort spent on improving the support environment provides long-term benefit for future maintenance and support. Investing effort in defining, obtaining, and implementing an excellent application support environment will immediately benefit the century-date compliance project. This same environment can be used concurrently to reduce cost and improve support for existing maintenance projects.

Different levels of support environments are needed, depending on the overall strategy selected by the IT organization to implement its century-compliance project. For example, organizations that choose to implement compliance with internal staff or by employing supplemental staffing consultants will need to implement the most robust environments. Conversely, organizations that plan to outsource the project to conversion factories or off-site consultants require fewer tools for analysis and conversion. In all cases, IT organizations must have strong configuration management to handle version control and change merging and must be able to support compliance testing activities. IT organizations cannot delegate responsibility for system and acceptance testing or final production integration. Rather than cutting corners on tools, it benefits IT organizations to make the necessary investments to bring as much of their support environment up to an adequate level as is feasible. The cost of the improvements is a minor investment given the overall cost of the project, and as just discussed, it is one of the few century-date compliance activities that provides direct payback.

This chapter discusses the major issues and the strategy choices available to IT organizations upgrading their support environments to handle century-date compliance projects. The next six subsections cover obsolete tools and environments, configuration management, use of standardized date subroutines, software tool requirements, test environment requirements, and the migration work environment.

6.1 Obsolete Tools and Environments

Software tools and environments are not immune from the same century-date issues as other software that must be certified as century compliant. Even software that does not appear to be date dependent may use date processing in surprising locations. Many tools use dates as part of their security routines. In this case, the software ceases operation when the date is exceeded. It is important to ensure that all software tools relied upon for routine support will remain operational after the year 2000. The compliance definition for system software is described in Chapter 5.

An additional benefit of tool compliance certification is the elimination of unused tools. Many IT organizations have software tools that are no longer used ("shelfware"), yet the organization continues to pay maintenance support fees. These tools can be eliminated and their maintenance contracts terminated, saving the cost of future fees. Obvious candidates for elimination are tools that support environments, such as old versions of COBOL or macro CICS, that will not be supported in the year 2000. Additional savings are achieved by eliminating "orphan" technologies and their support environments. Orphan technologies include languages, data management systems, and other technical environments that are still supported in the market but are no longer strategic for the given IT organization. Converting applications that rely on those technologies to more common or strategic technologies adds value to the century-compliance effort by reducing century-conversion costs, allowing the elimination of the support environment for the technology, and increasing the life and usefulness of the application. The elimination of these nonstandard technologies is discussed in additional detail in Chapter 4.

6.2 Configuration Management

Configuration management, also known as library management or version control, is the "Achilles heel" of many IT organizations and presents one of the greatest environmental challenges to century-date compliance projects. Configuration management is the set of tools and processes that administer the source code and object libraries containing the components of business applications. Although meticulous and time consuming, configuration management is necessary to ensure the operational integrity of business applications. Strong control procedures, automated tools, and management enforcement are needed to build an effective configuration management environment. Unfortunately, many IT organizations operate with minimal configuration management. Century-date compliance projects quickly and painfully expose deficiencies in configuration management practices. Two early problem indicators are missing source code and inability to quickly create a complete application inventory. Poor configuration management practices add significant risk and difficulty to the implementation and testing tasks in century-date compliance projects. To avoid these issues, it is necessary to understand configuration management in more detail.

6.2.1 The Function of Configuration Management

The most important function of configuration management is to ensure that business applications are composed of the correct versions of their building block components. Most applications contain hundreds of components, and large applications often contain thousands of separate components. Components are also shared among applications. Many versions can exist for each component. Some components may not have been revised since their creation, whereas others have undergone dozens of revisions over their existence. Separate versions of components also exist for different stages in the change life cycle. One version operates in production, while other versions are stored in development and test libraries. Similarly, the application as a whole exists in multiple versions or releases. Each release is a complete set of an application's components. Releases usually contain a mixture of component versions (see Figure 6.1). For example, a group of five programs was modified to add a new function (change I), while another group of programs was modified to correct a bug (change II). Program E was modified twice: once for each change. In this example, the baseline source code is version 1, the programs modified for either change are version 2, and Program E is version 3. The application will operate correctly only if the right sets of versions are combined to make the new release. If version 1 of program E is used within the release rather than version 3, neither change will work. If version 2 of program E is used, the new function (change I) will work, but not the bug fix (change II).

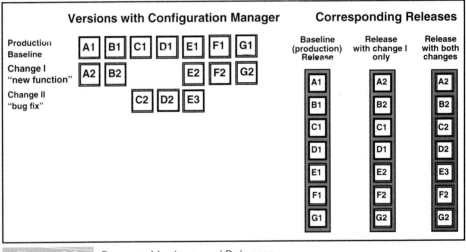

Figure 6.1   Program Versions and Releases

The complexity of assembling and reconciling release components is evident even in this simple example. This complexity increases by orders of magnitude as the number of components and versions grow. Further complexity is added when several versions of a component are modified simultaneously. Most business applications are supported by multiple programmers working independently and collectively on a variety of overlapping projects. The components that compose each project must be carefully managed to ensure their individual integrity and to prevent projects from overlaying each other's changes. Finally, changes from these separate projects must ultimately be merged into a completed release.

The scale and complexity of century-date compliance projects increases the difficulty of this already challenging process. A strong configuration management environment is an essential component of a successful century-date compliance project. Application releases cannot function if date formats are incompatible among application components and dates are widely shared among components. Further, interface and component sharing among applications requires careful management of multiple component versions to ensure that the compliance effort for one application does not cause the failure of another application.

6.2.2 Century-Compliance Configuration Management Requirements

To successfully support a century-date compliance project, IT organizations must take a critical look at their current tools and processes for configuration management. Many organizations have adequate tools to support their mainframe environments, but tool support is often limited for non-mainframe environments and is nonexistent for PC environments. Very few end-user applications are subject to any configuration management controls. Even when tools are available, their implementation and use may be limited or their supporting processes may be weak and not consistently followed. These deficiencies must be identified and corrected before the implementation phase of a century-compliance project is undertaken.

To provide the level of support necessary for century-date compliance projects, configuration management environments require the following capabilities:

- **Ability to manage large volumes of programming changes.**

  Virtually all components in virtually every application may be changed during a century-compliance project. The sheer magnitude and frequency of these changes will strain many configuration management tools and the efficiency of the supporting processes. For example, procedures that require each module to be checked in individually are too slow and cumbersome to support mass check-ins of thousands of modules.

- **Ability to handle multiple, simultaneous projects.**

  In most cases, the century-date migration for a given application has to coexist with ongoing application support efforts. Few application teams have the luxury of completely freezing their normal project work during a century-date migration effort. At a minimum, emergency fixes and high priority changes will have to proceed in parallel. The configuration management environment must allow these efforts to proceed independently but provide the tools to enable the merging of their end results.

- **Ability to support off-site conversions.**

  The greatest difficulty encountered during off-site conversions is often finding and packaging all necessary components for shipment to the conversion site. This process frequently requires multiple iterations to resolve missing components. An adequate configuration management facility avoids this wasted time and effort by having knowledge of all system components and the capability for mass retrieval. When the converted components are returned, the facility must support mass check-in and merging of results with ongoing project work.

- **Simple to use.**

  Configuration management environments must be simple to use for two key reasons: to ensure the use of the procedures and to facilitate access to the valuable data within the environment. If the procedures are overly cumbersome, programmers will circumvent them, compromising the integrity of the environment. Many configuration management tools offer facilities for creating custom reports of their contents. If easily accessible, these reports provide invaluable status information, listings of code changes, last modification dates, and lists of who is currently working on a given module.

- **Audit support.**

  Most companies will have rigorous audit requirements for their Year 2000 efforts. Auditors will need access to a variety of reports to understand who was responsible for making which changes at what point in time. The stronger the reporting capabilities of the configuration management environment, the less effort will be needed to support the auditors.

- **Ability to handle multiple environments.**

   Ideally, the configuration management facilities consistently handle application components from all platform environments supported by the IT organization. Where this is not possible, the organization must ensure that separate environments are available to handle PCs, midrange computers, and end-user applications. One method used by several large IT organizations is to upload all application components from all environments into their mainframe configuration management facility.

- **Ability to control future integrity.**

   Once an application reaches compliance, the configuration management system functions as the gatekeeper to prevent programmers from implementing noncompliant changes. Amazingly, according to companies participating in Year 2000 seminars, this is a common occurrence. Without strong configuration management controls, these changes may go unnoticed until the supposedly compliant application fails in production.

6.2.3 Implementing Configuration Management

Most large IT organizations already have some form of configuration management in place. These organizations should evaluate the adequacy of their environments according to the criteria defined in the foregoing paragraph and perform any necessary upgrades. Organizations without strict configuration management will need to implement the required facilities. This effort must be performed quickly to avoid impact on Year 2000 time schedules. IT organizations must avoid the temptation to overanalyze configuration management decisions. Little time is available for full-scale evaluations or pilot projects. Instead, the organization should focus on only those upgrades needed to support Year 2000 activities.

The details of designing and implementing a configuration management environment is beyond the scope of this book, but we strongly suggest the following steps as part of the implementation process.

- **Step 1. Access the Environment.**
   Evaluate the existing environment for adequacy. Are all functional requirements covered? Are all platform environments adequately covered? Who currently uses or performs the configuration management function? Are staff members adequately trained in the use

of the configuration manager? Identify the weaknesses and develop improvement requirements.

- **Step 2. Implement improvements.**
  Implement all identified improvements. Implementation includes the purchase of new or additional tools, the development or rewriting of current processes, and the creation of training materials.

- **Step 3. Set up libraries for century-compliance projects.**
  Unless century compliance is performed as part of a standard maintenance cycle, additional libraries are necessary to support the change life-cycle methods used for the compliance project. Separate libraries are needed for compliant and noncompliant code.

  For example, the original, noncompliant code is contained within the production library. Code undergoing migration is contained in a Year 2000 development library. Components used during ongoing maintenance efforts are kept in a separate development environment. When Year 2000 code changes are complete, the components are promoted to a Year 2000 test library. When Year 2000 testing is complete, the code is merged with maintenance changes and placed in a system test library. Promotion from the system test library to the production library completes the cycle.

- **Step 4. Set up custom reports.**
  In addition to setting up libraries, customization for century-compliance projects involves defining project-specific reports. Many configuration management tools support the addition of user-defined fields within their libraries. Define fields to contain status information about project stage, assessment results, and other component-specific project management information. The standard reports provided with the tool are a good starting point, but consider creating Year 2000-specific reports to eliminate extraneous information and include status information. Separate reports can be created for project team members, auditors, and managers. This process should be closely coordinated with repository tracking tools referenced later in this chapter.

- **Step 5. Load libraries.**
  It is essential to begin the century-date compliance process with a complete and intact set of components for each application. The integrity of the overall migration process is only as strong as the integrity of its starting components. Shortfalls will be uncovered

during the inventory/assessment phase of the century-compliance project. In some cases, the correct version of application source code may be in a programmer's private library or it may be missing and require re-creation. Ideally, move all source code for a given application into the Year 2000 development environment and recompile, relink, and test the code to ensure that the complete application is in place and that the versions of each component match. This step is especially important if the code will be shipped to an off-site facility for conversion.

- **Step 6. Ensure process integrity.**
  Before modifying any application components, test the configuration management procedures for that application to ensure that all necessary controls are in place and are safe from circumvention. Produce and examine configuration management reports to check the integrity of library components and to test the value of the reports. Make sure that the procedures will identify and prevent future addition of noncompliant code.

6.2.4 Code Freezing

When it is possible, "freezing" production code during a century-date compliance project greatly reduces the effort and risk of the conversion process. Freezing occurs when program libraries are locked from all normal production modifications. During the freeze period, only century-date compliance changes are allowed. There are four possible freezing strategies.

- **Total Library Freeze.**

  This strategy does not allow *any* modifications during the freeze period. All other changes are deferred until the century-date compliance project is completed and the freeze is lifted. This approach is the simplest to implement, avoids the need for separate Year 2000 libraries, and guarantees the integrity of century-compliance changes. This approach is most suitable for short-duration migration efforts, thereby limiting the freeze period. Its greatest disadvantage is that it is an option only for those highly stable applications that are unlikely to suffer an application failure that requires an emergency change during the freeze period.

- **Partial Library Freeze.**

  The partial freeze strategy limits modifications to high-priority changes, such as emergency fixes, during the freeze period. All remaining changes are deferred. The high-priority changes are implemented in separate libraries and are either implemented simultaneously in both versions (small changes) or merged with the completed century-compliant code prior to final testing (larger changes). This is the most commonly used approach, representing a compromise between the ease of century-compliance changes and the need to support the production application. This approach facilitates larger conversion efforts by allowing longer freeze periods. The primary disadvantage of this approach is the need to duplicate or merge changes. Careful coordination and additional libraries are needed to implement a partial freeze strategy.

- **Parallel Libraries.**

  This approach does not freeze production application components. Instead, changes are performed simultaneously in separate libraries. Normal application support activities continue while the base version of the application is migrated to century compliance. The changes are merged after the compliant code has been fully tested. This approach requires separate libraries and entails additional conversion effort after merger to ensure that all new code is compliant and does not adversely affect other century code changes. While feasible, this approach is not recommended because of its increased cost and risk. This approach is most commonly used in conjunction with off-site conversion strategies.

- **Concurrent Changes.**

  This strategy mixes century-compliance changes along with normal application changes in the same libraries. The advantages of this approach are avoiding the need to duplicate changes and eliminating the need for duplicate libraries. While it eliminates the need to coordinate changes, this approach increases the difficulty and risk of testing. Further, it prevents parallel testing of compliant and noncompliant versions of the application. This approach is best suited for applications that require minimal changes to reach century compliance. It is not appropriate when century-compliance efforts must be merged with significant functional changes.

6.3 Common Date Routines

The massive cost and effort of a century-date compliance project is dramatic proof of the value of common subroutines. Imagine that all business software used the same standard set of subroutines to handle common date manipulations. Most of the programming effort needed to achieve century-compliance would be eliminated by simply installing upgraded versions of those subroutines. Testing effort would be greatly reduced, and there would be little need for this book.

Unfortunately, rather than implement common date routines, most business applications reimplement date processing logic each time that it is needed. This practice allows programmers broad latitude for implementing creative versions of even simple date routines. As a result, two routines ostensibly performing the same function can return slightly different results. Even IT organizations that have attempted to achieve some level of common date routines are not immune from the issue. One company reported finding over 250 different "common" date routines to handle approximately 15 different date calculation requirements.

Handling century dates requires finding, understanding, and correcting every instance of date-processing logic throughout the corporate portfolio. Lack of standardization in naming and implementation exacerbates the difficulty of this task. Although there are many possible types of date manipulations, most applications require only a small handful of routines for the majority of their processing requirements.

These routines fall into these basic categories:

- **Date verification.**

    Check a given date to see if it is valid. For example, are the date fields within range (13 is not a valid number for a month)? Is the format correct? Does the day actually exist (February 29, 2001 is not a valid date)?

- **Date characteristics.**

    Determine the characteristics of a given date. Is it a leap year, which day of the week, is it a holiday, or is it a valid business day?

- **Distance between two dates.**

    Calculate the number of days, months, years between two dates, or conversely, calculate a future or past date, using distance and a base date. These routines have to handle calendar date calculations, as well as specialized calculations for 360-day years and differences between business dates.

- **Conversion between two date formats.**

  Convert dates from one format to another, such as Julian dates to calendar dates, two-digit years to four-digit years, or compressed dates to expanded dates.

Although there may be many ways to code the algorithm for a particular calculation, there is no reason for an IT organization to have more than one version of any given date routine. Century-date compliance projects offer the opportunity to standardize date routines as part of the conversion process. Although standardizing date routines will require some additional effort during conversion, it offers a variety of benefits.

- It reduces future maintenance effort by eliminating redundant date logic, thereby reducing the size and complexity of application source code, and enabling all future changes to be made in one location.

- It ensures that each date calculation is performed in the same manner throughout the organization.

- It reduces the level of testing needed to prove the correctness of date processing.

The first step in implementing common date routines is obtaining a good set of common date routines. Even if they are not regularly used, many IT organizations already own date routine libraries that they have purchased or developed internally. The Year 2000 Project Office should review these routines to ensure that all required functions are covered. When duplicates exist, the Project Office should select one version as standard. This is often the most difficult task in the process, as programmers endlessly champion their favorite version. In reality, there is usually little difference, and the primary benefit is gained by standardization.

Organizations without standard common date routines can build their own library or they can purchase a date subroutine package from a software vendor. We recommend purchasing an existing package over internal development. Purchasing a package saves significant development time and is usually less costly, and the subroutines are already thoroughly tested. Vendors also provide thorough documentation and other implementation assistance. At the time of this writing, at least one vendor offers a facility for generating code and testing the parameters needed to call the appropriate subroutines from its libraries. Several software vendors offering date subroutine packages are listed in Appendix A.

6.4 Migration Tool Requirements

All century-date compliance projects require a wide range of software tools to be successful. The large volume of work effort and tight time constraints make automation a necessity rather than a luxury. There are simply not enough programmers available in any organization to accomplish all of the migration tasks manually within the remaining conversion window. Automation must be applied wherever possible to reduce project costs, decrease elapsed time requirements, and increase the quality and reliability of the converted applications.

Automated tools perform many tasks in a fraction of the time and effort required for manual efforts. This reduces the elapsed time requirements of the project and frees people for tasks that cannot be effectively automated. An even greater benefit is the accuracy and consistency of automated tools. Programmers are human and prone to errors. The number of errors quickly increases as programmers perform by rote the highly repetitive tasks that typify a century-compliance project. While a programmer manually performing hundreds of modifications to a program can easily overlook an occasional change, a software tool will never make that mistake.

Software tools are required throughout all phases of the compliance project. For example, century-date impact assessments are virtually impossible without the assistance of tools. The sheer number of project tasks, deliverables, and resource assignments are beyond human capacity to track and coordinate without project management tools. Test results cannot be accurately verified without the use of tools to find and compare tedious details.

Given the importance of tools, it is essential that IT organizations carefully select the tools they plan to use throughout the project. Even when code migration is outsourced to off-site factories, it is essential to understand the quality and completeness of the tools used by the consultants at those factories. A project cannot be more accurate and effective than its tools allow. The size of the Year 2000 market attracts many new tool vendors, with more vendors appearing daily. Unfortunately, their tools are not all equal in quality, performance, and level of support. These factors must all be considered as part of any tool purchase decision. Despite their costs, tools account for only a small percentage of Year 2000 project budgets. When properly selected and used, these tools will repay this investment many times over in effort and risk reductions. Tool-selection criteria are discussed in detail in Chapter 15.

Despite the benefits, software automation is not the panacea that will eliminate Year 2000 migration effort. Tools may eliminate many rote and time consuming tasks, but many project activities cannot be automated. For example, coordinating interface strategies among internal and external organizations is resource intensive and can be performed only by people. Further, even those activities supported by automation contain gaps in tool support. Testing, which accounts for over 50 percent of the effort in most projects, contains many gaps in coverage. Tool coverage is strongest for the most common languages and environments. It decreases rapidly as the environments become less common. Some environments have no tool support at all, necessitating strictly manual analysis and migration efforts. While tool support will continue to evolve and improve over the next few years, IT organizations holding out for "silver bullet" solutions will be sorely disappointed.

6.4.1 Tool Strategy

Aside from their scale, the activities performed for Year 2000 migration projects are fundamentally the same as those performed for routine software maintenance. Thus the tools used for maintenance can be applied to migration projects. New software tools have been created specifically to support century-compliance projects. These tools are not reusable for routine maintenance tasks but are optimized for century migration tasks. Other century migration tools are owned by conversion vendors and are installed within their off-site conversion facilities. IT organizations do not use these tools directly, but they receive their benefits when they outsource their applications to the conversion vendor. As IT organizations plan their Year 2000 projects, this range of tool categories offers three distinct tool strategies: off-site conversions, Year 2000-specific tools, and maintenance tools.

- **Off-site conversions.**

  The first tool strategy leaves the majority of the tool selection process in the hands of the conversion vendor. Numerous vendors offer off-site conversion services at regional conversion centers or off-shore in countries such as India and the Philippines. IT organizations outsourcing their conversions to these companies should consider the tools used by the vendors as part of their selection criteria. The quality of the tools strongly affects the quality and reliability of the converted application. Off-site facilities can use less robust analysis and conversion tools, counting on their consultants to fill gaps in tool capabilities. Vendors that do not begin with adequate tools cannot totally compensate for their deficiencies through their programming staff. Human accuracy will always be less than tool accuracy. Further, even if the vendor's programmers are paid significantly less than their U.S. counterparts, insufficient automation raises the overall cost of the conversion effort. The ideal conversion facility uses the best tools available on the market. If the tools were developed by the vendor, part of the vendor evaluation should include observing the tools in action to ascertain their quality and accuracy. Selecting off-site conversion does not provide the IT organization with any tools that can be used for future maintenance activities.

Testing, change control, and inventory tools are all standard requirements even when conversion work is performed off-site. These tools support various tasks that tend to remain onsite, even when conversion work is performed off-site.

The next two approaches apply to IT organizations that will perform their century-date compliance project at their own location. Either approach is usable whether the conversion is performed by consultants or by internal staff. If tools are brought to the project by consultants, the IT organization should determine if the tools will be left for future use after the conversion effort is completed.

- **Year 2000-specific tools.**

Year 2000-specific tools are one of the fastest growing segments of the software tool market. These tools are optimized to handle date identification and conversion tasks. One common example is Year 2000 project estimation tools. These tools contain a repository of knowledge about common date formats and naming conventions and can quickly analyze a large volume of programs to estimate the overall size and impact of the century-conversion effort. Use of a Year 2000-specific tool saves considerable setup and tuning effort during the century-compliance project. The trade-off is that these tools are discarded after the conversion effort. Vendors find that Year 2000-specific tools are faster to build than fuller-featured tools. This enables vendors to quickly build tools for technologies that would not otherwise be supported. These tools have the greatest value for performing one-time tasks or for supporting nonstandard technologies. Common technologies should use more generalized tools whenever possible to gain the future value of those tools. The exceptions to these rules are Year 2000-specific tools that provide a large measure of enhanced performance over generalized tools handling the same function. In this case, the savings obtained from the Year 2000-specific tool will easily cover the later purchase of the generalized tool.

- **Maintenance tools.**

  The fact that Year 2000 projects can use the same tools as standard maintenance offers a double benefit to IT organizations. They can reduce the tool costs for the century-compliance effort by reusing existing tools, and they can supplement their collection of maintenance tools to support century compliance, thereby enhancing future maintenance productivity. Since IT organizations are historically weak in their maintenance tool support, they gain significant long-term value from a century-compliance effort. The first step in this strategy is to collect an inventory of the software tools already owned by the organization. This inventory is compared with the tool requirements for century-date projects to identify gaps in tool coverage. Outdated tools are replaced or brought to the current release. New tools are obtained to fill in gaps or to replace existing tools with stronger functionality. Since tools are a relatively insignificant portion of the cost of a Year 2000 project and they provide benefits that greatly exceed their costs, organizations should not be afraid to obtain the best tool in a category and then replace that tool if a stronger tool appears at a later point. This strategy ensures that the conversion is always operating at peak efficiency.

6.4.2 Technology Requirements by Functional Category

Century-compliance efforts employ software tools from a wide range of functional tool categories. While these support requirements appear significant, many IT organizations already use tools from each category. Organizations performing their conversion projects onsite will need to supplement their existing tools to cover gaps in required tool functionality. Unfortunately, software tools are language and platform dependent, requiring additional tools to be purchased to cover functionality for each major environment supported by the IT organization.

The list below covers the major functional categories of tools required for a Year 2000 project. This section provides an overview of tool requirements; Chapter 15 covers the tool selection criteria and describes specific tools in greater detail.

- **Project management tools.**

  Most century-date compliance projects are too large and complex to manage without strong project management tools. These tools must be able to support a large number of individual analysis and migration projects. These individual projects must roll up into a master plan that can cover the entire enterprise. This master plan must coordinate individual efforts and provide senior management with accurate information about project status. Project management tools must be able to accurately assess the high-level impact of the century-date projects for budgeting purposes. Project estimation capabilities and "what if" analysis are needed by the Year 2000 Project Office to evaluate and select the optimal analysis and conversion strategies.

- **Repository technology.**

  Although the word "repository" has negative connotations to many IT organizations, Year 2000 projects can leverage the technology to manage the myriad of details associated with an enterprise-level, century-compliance project. The repository contains information about application "objects" and the relationships between those objects, forming a complete application inventory that includes file interfaces between programs, applications, and external organizations. The repository is essential to ensure coordination among entities sharing interfaces and acts as the global checklist of objects that require conversion. The status of each object is updated as it is converted, enabling the Year 2000 Project Office to monitor the progress of the actual conversion.

- **Analysis tools.**

  Analysis tools are critical components of the Project Planning and Enterprise Assessment Phases of Year 2000 projects. At the highest level, enterprise inventory tools are required to build a complete inventory of the entire portfolio of applications and their components. Once the inventory is known, system-level impact analysis tools can assess the level of date usage and sharing across multiple programs and multiple applications. This information determines the extent of the conversion effort and identifies which programs and files require conversion. Detailed analysis tools examine individual programs to identify the specific data items and lines of source code that need to be modified. Information from these tools is valuable for selecting optimal conversion strategies, planning test scenarios, and auditing project activities.

- **Migration tools.**

Migration tools are used in the Implementation and Deployment Phase of the Year 2000 project. This category contains the greatest coverage by programming tools and offers the highest potential for efficiency from automation. These tools handle the updating of application source code, data conversion, unit testing, and data bridging activities. The application source code tools required for migration activities range from standard programming tools, such as compilers and editors, to mass change tools for automatically converting large volumes of source code. These tools must support the changes required for both data expansion and process-based conversion approaches. Unit testing tools ensure the quality of individual components; thorough unit testing reduces the time and cost of system-level testing. Data migration tools are required whenever conversion efforts affect application data. These tools can be written by internal staff to handle a specific file or database, or generalized tools can be purchased to handle multiple types of files. Data bridging tools are essential for date expansion approaches to allow applications sharing an interface to be converted separately.

- **Redevelopment tools.**

Redevelopment tools offer a means of adding value to the implementation phase of the migration effort. While not required for most projects, these tools simplify programs by structuring their logic, rationalizing their data names, and breaking large programs into smaller and more manageable modules. These technologies are best applied to the most highly maintained programs within an application to provide the greatest return on the investment in them.

- **Testing tools.**

Testing and validation of newly migrated applications is the most costly and difficult phase of a century-compliance effort. Unfortunately, despite the opportunity for automation, there are notably fewer software tools covering this category. Testing requirements fall into three categories: the ability to create test data, the ability to execute system level tests, and the ability to verify the results of those tests. The first category requires tools to identify testing requirements, generate test data, and monitor the coverage of that data. These requirements are simple for mainframe batch applications but become very complex for client/server applications. The second category requires tools to simulate various operational environments, including the ability to set system dates into the next century. The final category requires data comparison programs to enable programmers to verify that tests completed successfully when run over large volumes of data.

6.5 Testing and Validation Facilities

Validating the results of century-date migration efforts is by far the greatest technical challenge faced by Year 2000 project teams. Multiple levels of tests are required for virtually every application within the enterprise portfolio. At a minimum, these tests certify the compliance of applications that already (or don't need to) handle century dates. Testing requirements grow for migrated applications. Century dates can appear in virtually all components of an application, necessitating full integration and system testing to ensure the correctness of those changes. Testing does not stop at the application's boundaries; interfaces between applications also require verification. Testing of this scale is rarely performed for a single application within an IT organization, yet century-compliance efforts require it to be performed across the entire enterprise.

6.5.1 Testing Issues

Testing is a meticulous process, requiring careful planning, excellent test data, and tedious review of large volumes of test results. The stakes of failure are high: a single incorrect date calculation within an otherwise compliant application can cause that application to fail or corrupt its database with incorrect data. The key to successful century-compliance testing is thoroughness and attention to detail. Unfortunately, few IT organizations have the skills, tools, or proper test environments to handle large-scale testing. Most application changes are perfunctorily tested at best. Test data is typically created by simply taking a subset of production data. This type of data does not guarantee full coverage of application functionality, nor can it support century-date compliance requirements. Testing remains a primarily manual activity, due in part to lack of IT investment in test support tools and in part to the relatively few tools available on the market.

The hardware resources to support large-scale testing are an issue in many organizations. The creation and retention of adequate test data requires large volumes of disk storage, and the execution of test jobs uses considerable machine resources. Care is required to ensure that testing does not impact production applications. Care must be taken when performing future date testing to ensure that current production applications and system software are not accidentally corrupted. Ideally, testing is performed in an environment separate from that used for production.

6.5.2 Test Requirements

All levels of tests are required to ensure correct century compliance. Unit testing of individual components ensures that date processing occurs correctly within each program. Because dates are widely shared among application components, thorough integration testing ensures that there are no mismatches between programs, subroutines, include files, and other application components as they are combined to form the application. Finally, system testing proves that the entire application is century compliant. Four distinct types of system tests are required for a century-compliance project:

- **Regression testing.**

    Regression testing ensures that century-compliance changes did not adversely affect current application functionality. Aside from potential differences in data formats in files, reports, and visual displays, the original version of the application and the compliant version must produce the same results. The ideal regression test environment requires test data that covers *all* application functionality. Intelligent data comparison tools reduce the verification effort by enabling direct comparison of test results from the original and compliant versions of the application. Adjustments in date formats are specified through parameters to avoid false positives when searching for differences in the data. Test coverage monitors must ensure that all critical process and data flows have been tested.

- **Future testing.**

    The next level of system test ensures that the application performs correctly within the 21st century. This test requires executing the application in an environment that simulates future processing. This environment must produce future system dates and include compliant versions of all system software. New test data is necessary to create future dates. One method of creating this data is to duplicate the regression test data while incrementing all dates within the data to the next century. Care is required when incrementing the date to ensure the integrity of the information between records. For example, incrementing current years by 10 to produce dates in the next century will result in test data that falls on different days of the week than the original program. This may cause transactions to be rejected or posted differently, resulting in unexpected data variations. In this case, incrementing the current year by 28 maintains the integrity of weekly data by ensuring that the newly incremented dates fall on the same day of the week as the originals.

Using a full set of incremented regression test data eases the task of verifying test results. Aside from variations in the date formats and the actual dates, all other test results from the compliant application should match the results of the original application using the original regression test data.

- **Boundary testing.**

  This level of system testing verifies that each application correctly handles boundary conditions. These conditions include calculations that cross century boundaries, transactions that occur at exactly midnight on January 1, 2000, and other situations that push the limits of date calculations and sorting capabilities. Boundary testing requires the generation of its own test data to ensure that all boundary conditions are covered. Unless a test data generator is available, this process must be performed manually. A test coverage monitor must ensure that all necessary test cases have been created. Boundary testing is executed in the same environment as future testing, since it requires future system dates. Multiple test runs using different system dates may be required to ensure complete testing. Manual verification of test results is required, as boundary testing cannot be performed on the original version of the application, which prevents the creation of comparison data.

- **Certification testing.**

  This type of system testing verifies that applications are century compliant. Certification tests are performed by using the same approach and environment described above for future testing. In this case, the original application and the compliant version are the same; only the data used for testing varies. If the cost of application failure is high, boundary testing should also be considered.

6.5.3 Components of a Test Environment

Although century-date compliance projects may have more stringent requirements than typical application support projects, their test environments are composed of the same components. If the existing test environment is sufficiently robust, it can easily be extended for handling century-date verification. Conversely, any improvements made to existing test environments remain useful for testing future maintenance and enhancement projects.

Test environments are composed of four basic components:

- **Test data beds.**

  Test data is the foundation of all test environments. Multiple test files and databases may be required to support a single application. This combination of test data is called a test bed. Ideally, each application's test bed contains enough test cases to cover all valid execution paths within that application. Subsets of production data rarely accomplish this goal, as they typically exercise only a small percentage of the possible paths. For example, high-quality production data will not trigger any error condition processing. Building a complete test bed is time consuming and effort intensive. The test data must not only cover all paths, but it must fit with dates in the test bed. For instance, testing a particular transaction may require matching records from three different files. Once the test bed is created, subsets of its data can be used to cover a wide variety of tests. Regression tests use the entire test bed, whereas various extracts are used for unit and integration testing.

- **Test scripts and scenarios.**

  Test scripts describe the actions needed to perform a particular type of test. They describe the test data requirements, the setup of the test environment, the steps needed to execute the test, and the methods for verifying the results of the test. Within these scripts are test scenarios. These scenarios cover specific situations to be tested. For example, one scenario may test an on-line application for the time period between 11:00 PM December 31, 1999, and 1:00 AM January 1, 2000. Large-scale system tests can be quite complex, requiring multiple scenarios, job executions, and verification steps. Test scripts guide programmers through these activities, ensuring that all steps are properly performed in the correct order. Test scripts are fully reusable for future testing activities.

- **Test environments.**

  Test environments simulate the environment used to execute the production version of the application being tested. The test environment must match the production environment as closely as possible, using (or mimicking) the same type of hardware environment and system software. Different test environments can be created to handle a variety of testing needs. For example, end-user applications can be tested on a separate workstation set up specifically to operate with a future date. Mainframe applications can execute on a different mainframe or within a test partition. Simulation software enables testing activities that cannot be performed in production environments. Date simulators for artificially setting the system date into the future are an example of this software. Other examples include CICS emulators that enable unit testing of mainframe programs on PCs.

- **Software testing tools.**

  A proper testing environment is supported by as much automation as possible. Software testing tools significantly reduce the effort required for testing and enhance the accuracy and quality of the verification activities. Tools cover all activities from test data generation, coverage monitoring, and environment simulation to providing verification support. Specific testing tools are discussed in Chapter 15.

6.5.4 Building a Test Environment

Building a proper test environment is a costly, long-term project. Fortunately, all components of this environment are reusable for future testing activities. This offers another value-added benefit from Year 2000 projects. Aside from supporting the century-date conversion, the test environment will reduce future testing costs and enhance the quality and reliability of the applications it supports.

Given the effort required to create the necessary test environments, it is imperative that IT organizations start immediately, so that the test environment for an application can be created in parallel with the application's assessment and migration activities. Failure to start now will either delay application testing until the test environment can be completed or will force testing to occur within an incomplete environment. While few organizations will devote the resources necessary to create the perfect test environment, all deviations from this target must be assessed against the risk and cost of failure. The following steps describe the high-level process for building a test environment. The construction of test environments merits a more complete discussion than is possible in this book. We recommend that interested readers consult one of the numerous books available on software testing.

1. *Perform a gap analysis on current testing environment.*

   Examine the test components currently available for each application. Extend or reuse existing components wherever possible to reduce the cost and time required to create the complete environment. Assess the coverage of the test data and estimate the level of disk and computer resources that will be needed to perform full testing. Note tool and script shortfalls in the existing environment. Use this information to create a test environment improvement plan.

2. *Determine if current system resources are sufficient.*

   Hardware acquisitions typically require long lead times. Determine if additional disk space or CPU resources are needed to support the anticipated level of testing. Another alternative is to lease additional resources from a computer service bureau. Several vendors offer dedicated Year 2000 test environments for organizations that do not want to acquire additional hardware. The vendor handles the creation and support of this environment and often offers testing tools and consulting support.

3. *Acquire testing tools.*

   Acquire testing tools as quickly as possible to allow application programmers to gain experience with those tools during their normal testing activities. This practicing eliminates the learning curve at the time of century-date testing and increases programmer efficiency at using the tools before attempting large-volume testing.

4. *Begin collecting or creating test data.*

   Test data creation is the most lengthy and tedious task in building a test environment. A subset of production data can be used as a starting point, but it will have to be extended to ensure more complete coverage. Use a test coverage monitor to determine the current level of coverage and to establish requirements for additional test cases. Once a baseline is established, test data can be added over time to increase coverage. Test data can be created manually, generated by a test data generator, or collected by a capture/playback tool. It may not be feasible to build (or retain) a complete test bed for applications that require very large amounts of data or utilize very complex environments. In this case, develop an alternate testing strategy. One approach is to build a set of job tasks to generate and delete the appropriate test data as needed.

5. *Begin documenting test scripts and scenarios.*

Test scripts often exist solely in the heads of the application's programmers, who must document the scenarios for use by others. The documentation process can be performed incrementally by asking each programmer to note the steps they use as they perform their routine testing activities. Once captured, these scripts and scenarios can be extended to cover Year 2000 requirements.

6.6 Migration Work Environment

The efficiency and effectiveness of assessment, migration, and testing efforts can be greatly enhanced by the design of the work environments used to support those activities. One of the many lessons that IT organizations can learn from the consulting firms offering Year 2000 services is the value of an integrated migration work environment. This concept is the basis of the conversion factory approach. Traditionally, IT organizations treat their work environment as a collection of unrelated, single-task software tools that are applied at the discretion of the programmer. This approach is only as effective as the programmer applying it. Further, it does not take advantage of synergies between tools nor implement the efficiencies that are possible when performing highly repetitive tasks. Amazingly, most IT organizations have yet to learn the value of assembly-line processes. This concept has been applied by manufacturing organizations for decades, and it is the basis for the conversion factory approach used by consultants.

Conversion factories define the optimal steps needed to perform an effective Year 2000 migration process. These steps are codified into a methodology, supported by integrated tools, and executed in a standard fashion for all projects. The standardization enforced by this approach offers many benefits. First, each process can be designed for maximum effectiveness. As experience is gained during operation, those processes can be tuned to further enhance their efficiency, thus producing benefits for all subsequent projects. The second benefit is optimal application of technology. This approach clearly illustrates where and how tools fit within the process and maximizes synergies between the tools. Finally, this approach guarantees consistent, high-quality results. It codifies "best practices" and

ensures that all programmers operate to its standards of quality and productivity.

6.6.1 Components of a Migration Work Environment

A migration work environment integrates software tools, processes,
and a methodology into an environment that supports the tasks associated
with a Year 2000 project. An idealized example of such a work environment is shown in Figure 6.2.

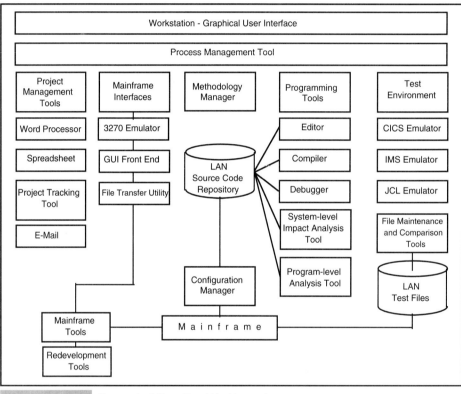

Figure 6.2 Example Migration Workbench

The level of integration is the key to the workbench concept. A fully
integrated environment organizes its tools in a task-based workbench structure that enables programmers to work within this environment unencum-
bered by concerns over tool boundaries. Programmers spend less time
trying to understand the tools and more time using them for specific tasks.
Integration enables additional productivity gains by exploiting synergies
between tools. In addition, instead of having to be trained on each specific

tool, programmers can learn to use all tools contained within the workbench at the same time.

This level of integration is achieved through four structural components: a common interface to provide similar "look and feel" to the tools within the workbench, a methodology describing the techniques for performing the processes supported by the workbench, process management software to integrate those processes with workbench tools, and repositories to track and share work products among tools.

- **Common interface.**

   The common interface hides unnecessary differences between tools and organizes those tools in a manner that encourages the use of the correct tools at the correct point in the migration process. Tool features that are not needed for the migration effort can be hidden, and especially valuable features can be highlighted. Workstation-based workbenches can take advantage of graphical user interfaces (GUI) to further simplify ease of use. Mainframe workbenches can utilize commonly used programming environments such as IBM's ISPF™ to provide a common look and feel. The common interface also combines the Help facilities from the separate tools into one location.

- **Repositories and central tracking facilities.**

   A central repository provides a common way of storing project information to be shared by all software tools within the workbench. The advantage of using repository technology is central storage of important information. This information is easily tracked, allowing completion of important work products to be monitored. While a single, all-encompassing repository maximizes the level of possible integration, most IT organizations will prefer several smaller repositories. The configuration manager provides repository capabilities for source code management. Several vendors offer repository capabilities that recognize relationships between the various entities that compose software applications. Other work products, such as documentation, specifications, and test cases, can also be stored within a repository. To be successful, repositories must be kept up-to-date. A workbench environment includes the necessary repository load and update tools to support repository maintenance. The workbench structure supports hooks to automatically trigger the appropriate repository maintenance tool to ensure that all repositories remain up-to-date.

- **Process management.**

  Process management tools automate the processes used to accomplish century-compliance migration tasks. These tools follow the methodology specified for the project, assign and track the completion of work products, and trigger the use of the optimal software tools at the appropriate time. They eliminate many tedious project management tasks by automatically capturing and reporting the necessary cost and status information. The best process managers provide their own repository for managing the work products created during the migration process. When a process manager is used within a workbench, it assumes the role of the common interface.

- **Methodology.**

  Every integrated work environment must have an underlying methodology that specifies the processes needed to complete the conversion. Each process contains a series of tasks that have input requirements, resource requirements, and associated tools and techniques and that produce work products. The project methodology can be delivered through the process manager, its own methodology manager, or it can be integrated within the workbench's Help facilities. Methodology selection and requirements are described in Chapter 15.

  The functional capabilities of the workbench are provided through its software tools. These software tools are organized by function: project management, analysis, migration, and verification. These categories are described below. Supporting tools, such as the configuration manager, are shared among functional categories rather than having their own separate interface. Depending on the organizational requirements of the Year 2000 Project Office, these functions can be combined into one global workbench, or they can be supported as separate workbenches. The combined workbench approach is recommended when individual application support teams are responsible for their own conversions: separate workbenches are recommended for "swat" team approaches. IT organizations that are outsourcing their conversion activities will require workbench capabilities only for project management and verification activities.

- **Project management.**

  Including project management capabilities within a workbench environment reduces the management overhead of the project.

Tools in this category include a word processor, a spreadsheet package, a time accounting/chargeback system, and a project tracker.

- **Analysis.**

  The analysis category contains the tools used for enterprise assessment, estimation, and detailed assessment activities. Example tools include system-level analyzers, static and graphical analyzers, and metrics analysis tools.

- **Migration.**

  A migration workbench includes most of the tools used for normal maintenance activities, such as editors, compilers, and debuggers, as well as Year 2000-specific tools, such as mass change tools and date subroutine interface generators. This workbench must cover capabilities for program and data migration and support unit testing activities. Tools used in the analysis workbench will reappear within this category to handle impact assessments and debugging activities.

- **Verification.**

  The verification workbench contains the tools needed to create test data, set up the test environment, execute tests, and verify their results. This workbench supports integration and system-level testing requirements.

6.6.2 Mainframe versus PC Workbenches

Workbench environments can be implemented in either mainframe or workstation environments. Despite the attention paid to workstation solutions, many IT organizations still rely on mainframe environments for most of their production software. As a result, most mature software tools remain on the mainframe. While a pure mainframe environment limits graphics use and inhibits certain interactive tasks, almost any tool capability can be obtained for a mainframe environment. Mainframe-based work environments are the most familiar to programmers supporting the legacy applications that form the bulk of century-compliance project work. By working within a mainframe environment, those programmers do not need to upload and download program source code to perform their work. Mainframe tools involve mainframe pricing, which can be prohibitive for small IT shops. They may be the least expensive alternative in large shops where the cost is spread over many programmers.

Conversely, workstation-based migration workbenches free programmers from their ties to the mainframe, allowing them the flexibility to work from home or other remote locations. Many programming tasks can be off-loaded from the mainframe to the workstation, decreasing mainframe costs and improving the responsiveness of interactive tasks by performing those tasks on the desktop microprocessor.

Advances in workstation computing capabilities helped create truly powerful workstation-based maintenance workbenches. The GUI capabilities available under Microsoft® Windows™ and OS/2® allow the creation of very intuitive workbench front ends. In fact, several vendors equip their tools with simple scripts that enable users to add tools to their menus. Advanced workstation tools make full use of graphics, colors, and the workstation's interactive strengths to create powerful analysis features that offer new levels of productivity enhancement.

Although workbenches provide many benefits, they are not a panacea for all programming environments. Corporate mainframe use may drive the platform decision. If mainframe resources are scarce and expensive, workstations become more attractive. Conversely, if mainframe cycles are plentiful and cheap, workstations may not be an attractive alternative.

For most IT organizations, mixing mainframe and workstation platforms is likely to be the best option. This approach relies on the mainframe as a server for accessing production jobs, managing source code versions, and for running resource intensive, noninteractive tasks. The workstation is used for more interactive analysis and testing tasks. For a mixed platform to be successful, source code version control must be tight, and data between the mainframe and workstation must be transmitted quickly. Tools can reside on either platform as long as they can be easily accessed from the workstation. This approach allows the company to retain its investment in mainframe tools while incorporating the capabilities offered only within workstation environments.

6.6.3 Implementing the Workbench Environment

Successfully implementing a migration workbench involves more than simply selecting its platform and tools. Its real benefits are achieved only through effective use. Unless properly trained and motivated, programmers may not gain the full advantage of the workbench. Proper attention to the right details will go a long way to ensure that the workbench achieves its desired benefits.

Keys to success in implementing a workbench:

- **Do not "overanalyze" purchases.**

  IT organizations often commit the cardinal sin of overanalyzing their tool purchases. Most available tools are competently built and will provide much-needed productivity gains. Successfully implementing an initial workbench and deriving its benefits is more important than spending months evaluating slight differences between competing tools. Spending the time saved from tool evaluation on creating a truly competent rollout plan will more than compensate for any tool differences.

- **Change the standards, not the tools.**

  Another common error is trying to force tools to conform to archaic in-house standards. Unless years of research have proven the value of the in-house standard, eliminating unnecessary, company-specific nuances in the application code will broaden the spectrum and value of available tools.

- **Train thoroughly.**

  A workbench is only as powerful as the features that are actually used. Train users to accomplish typical migration tasks rather than focusing on extraneous tool options.

- **Work out operational details.**

  Sort out issues such as file backups and data security before releasing the workbench for general use. Processes will need tuning, and tool parameters will need adjustment. Use the new workbench(es) for analysis and migration pilot projects. Use the experience to adjust the workbench before general rollout.

- **Build a strong deployment plan.**

  Create a well-documented deployment plan featuring training, operational responsibilities, and support. This plan must fit within the constraints of the Year 2000 Project Office's overall master plan and should contain a schedule with defined milestones and regular reviews to ensure that all phases of the rollout proceed successfully. Full management support is critical to ensure that workbench use receives a high priority.

Relationships, External Entities, and Related Responsibilities

Managers chartered with the task of achieving century-date compliance cannot underestimate the impact of organizational issues on their migration efforts. Year 2000 projects do not occur in isolation. The sheer magnitude of the project directly and indirectly affects numerous entities inside and outside of each corporation. Many of the decisions that affect budgeting, implementation strategy, timing, and contingency planning involve negotiations between IT and other organizational entities. Each of these entities has its own set of priorities and requirements for the century-date compliance effort, and somehow these differing agendas must be aligned to allow the project to move forward. Although considerable time and effort will be spent performing actual migration work, much of the elapsed time and most of the project management effort will be devoted to coordinating the large number of disparate stakeholders in the migration process. This negotiation and coordination effort can never be automated. To a large degree, the success of a century migration project depends on the people and negotiation skills of the project's managers. These skills ensure that issues between the various entities are identified and resolved quickly and reasonably to avoid project delays, solution incompatibilities, and wasted work effort. The fixed deadline of a Year 2000 project does not allow time for potential inefficient interactions between organizations.

Numerous internal and external organizations are stakeholders in the century-compliance project. The Year 2000 Project Office must understand the roles and motivations of these diverse organizations in order to devise effective working relationships. In some cases, the Year 2000 Project Office will be in a position to mandate its requirements, whereas in other cases, it will be at the receiving end of mandates. Many external relationships involve negotiated contracts. In many situations, however, neither side of the relationship is in a position to mandate requirements. These types of relationships require excellent communication and the willingness of both parties to arrive quickly at an acceptable solution. Figure 7.1 illustrates the principal Year 2000 stakeholders.

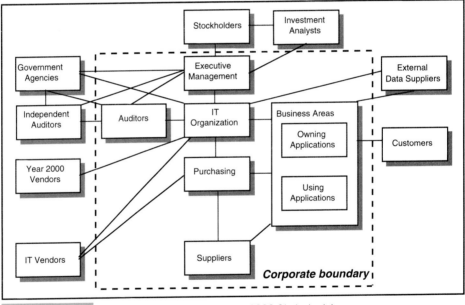

Figure 7.1 Relationships Among Year 2000 Stakeholders

Internal stakeholders include:

- Senior management
- Business areas owning or using the affected software
- Business areas that rely on external organizations that have a potential Year 2000 impact
- Internal audit department

The external stakeholders include:

- Customers

- Stockholders

- Government and regulatory agencies

- Business partners that share computer data with the affected software

- Suppliers

- IT tool, hardware, and service providers

- Year 2000 solution partners

This chapter focuses on the impact of the century-date compliance project on these stakeholders, and vice versa. It describes strategies for negotiating with internal entities and assessing and mitigating the risks associated with external organizations.

7.1 The Impact on Organizations within an Enterprise

The century-date compliance project impacts almost every area within an organization. Virtually every area uses some form of computer system and relies on data provided by other areas within a company. Although century-date compliance is of major importance to the Year 2000 Project Office, other internal groups have their own priorities and resource and budget constraints. Unless they fully understand the potential impact of Year 2000 failures on their operations, they will not place high priority on compliance activities. They are even less happy when they have to fund compliance activities that draw resources away from projects that they consider strategic to their business interests.

Century-compliance projects need the cooperation of functional business areas for more than just funding. The business owners of application systems must help to define priorities among applications, approve the selected migration strategy, and in many cases, assist in testing the migrated application. The business owner must agree to defer desired enhancements and accept an application modification freeze during the implementation period. Further, interconnections between applications cause interactions between different business areas. This requires cooperation between business areas for strategy selection and migration timing.

Organizational politics among areas is a major risk factor. Political games waste tremendous amounts of management resources and can cause significant project delays. A powerful manager who does not understand the Year 2000 issue may have tremendous influence on his/her peers' ability to initiate their own migration efforts. Politics will become a greater factor when project resources become constrained and application triage strategies become necessary. Infighting over which systems will receive resources will cause unnecessary and costly delays. To avoid these negative organizational issues, the Year 2000 Project Office needs the active support of senior management. The CEO must set organizational priorities to ensure that Year 2000 compliance efforts receive their proper level of funding and attention. Although senior management cannot eliminate organizational politics, the CEO can step in to resolve serious conflicts among business areas.

7.1.1 Senior Management

The support and commitment of the senior management team is the most critical success factor for a century-date compliance project. Without the support of the CEO, CFO, and other executives to properly fund the project, create sufficient urgency among business areas, and resolve conflicts among business areas, the century-compliance project will have great difficulty succeeding. The best method to determine the stage of maturity of a century-compliance effort is to find its highest-ranking sponsor. If this sponsor does not report directly to the CEO on the progress of the project, the company is not devoting sufficient attention to the issue and is likely to have underfunded the project and undercommitted to it.

Senior executive awareness is increasing at a rapid pace. The Year 2000 issue is widely reported in the popular press and is being addressed by financial analysts, the legal community, and corporate auditors. The CEO is likely to confront questions about corporate exposure to Year 2000 issues and to have concerns about its impact on business operations. For this reason, it is critical to keep the CEO and other executives informed about project progress and issues. The CEO must balance Year 2000 requirements against a myriad of other business concerns and can set the right priorities only if provided with the best and most accurate information. Despite the importance of the Year 2000 issue, other priorities may still take precedence (for example, fending off a hostile takeover).

Executive support is especially critical if application triage is necessary. Triage issues are discussed in Chapter 4. Few business area managers are sufficiently objective to determine their organization's relative importance within the corporation. The most mission-critical systems must be selected and converted to ensure corporate survival. An application that is important to one department may not be essential compared to other applications. The CEO and other executives are in the best position to determine which areas of the company have the greatest strategic importance and what levels of risk through conversion shortcuts are acceptable.

7.1.2 Business Areas—Application Owners

Almost all functional business areas are highly affected by Year 2000 projects. The project defers desired application enhancements, may cause changes in application operation, affects their end-user applications, and potentially affects their relationships with customers and suppliers. In most corporations, the business applications are owned by the business areas that they support rather than by IT. These business areas set the budget, decide on enhancement priorities, and make business decisions based upon the operation of the application. Unlike IT, the business area's focus is on using the application rather than modifying it. It is important to understand this motivation when approaching a business manager about supporting a century-compliance project.

Devoting resources to century-date compliance can be painful to a business manager whose business plan depended upon marketing a new financial product. Introducing this product may require extensive application changes that will be delayed by the century-compliance project. Delayed introduction of the product will result in decreased revenues and may result in the loss of departmental bonuses.

Sensitivity to these issues is invaluable to ensure proper support for the project. Before approaching business area management to support and fund a century-compliance project, the Year 2000 Project Office and the application's support team must do their homework. From an application standpoint, this includes determining the likely business impact of the year 2000 on the business area's application, developing a reasonably accurate estimate of the cost and effort to correct the application, assessing the project's impact on other application priorities, and determining what level of support and assistance will be required from the business area. Supplement this information with an assessment of nonapplication business impacts and risks, such as the effects of outside relationships and legal/contractual issues. Balance this information against the priorities and pressures faced by the business area manager. Senior management assistance and support in determining relative priorities is especially useful at this stage.

Initial meetings with business area management should educate key individuals about the Year 2000 issues. Business area managers must understand why the project is important and why their assistance is required. It is often valuable to involve internal auditors and representatives from the legal department to provide credibility and raise awareness of Year 2000 issues outside the corporate IT organization. Part of the education process must be to assist business area personnel in identifying and developing solutions for these non-IT issues. For example, do forms have 19 preprinted in the year field? Are they at risk if a supplier has Year 2000 problems? Are there business benefits to being century-date compliant before the competition?

Once the seriousness of the Year 2000 issue and its impact have been established, it is easier to receive funding and support for resolution efforts. Each business area should create its own Year 2000 task force to address area-specific concerns and to assist the efforts of the IT organization. This task force is the day-to-day contact between the business area managers, the Year 2000 Project Office, and the team performing the migration project. The task force also has responsibility for non-IT Year 2000 issues within their business area. The major responsibilities of the task force are listed below.

- **Obtaining and monitoring funding.**

  Unless the migration project is funded out of a central Year 2000 fund, each business area will have to identify funding for its own projects. The task force assists in funding decisions and monitors the migration project for its area.

- **Handling interactions among different functional areas.**

  Few applications are used solely by one business area. Application priority and funding issues often require balancing the objectives of multiple business areas. The Year 2000 Project Office can avoid political turf battles by deferring these decisions to business area task force members from each of the affected business areas. For example, if an application is shared among multiple business areas, representatives from each area's task force determine the funding allocation from their areas. Disputes between business areas that cannot be resolved on the task force level are referred to the senior management team.

- **Developing strategy and determining priorities.**

  The primary responsibility of the task force is to assist IT in developing application migration strategies that balance business priorities against IT needs. There are numerous additional strategy issues that are best resolved with the assistance of the task force. For example, expending less effort on application migration will free resources for other tasks. These tasks may include implementing critical application enhancements or supporting migration projects elsewhere in the company. Conversely, cutting corners during the conversion will impact future application support and can lead to significant extra costs at a future date. Involving the task force in these decisions will result in a smoother project than if the decisions are made arbitrarily by the Year 2000 Project Office.

Many business areas own more than one application. These applications may have differing migration priorities. It is the responsibility of the task force to ensure that applications with the greatest business impact are migrated first. When time or resource pressures force shortcuts, the task force determines if and where the business area can live with minor century-compliance problems such as mis-sorted reports or odd-looking date fields.

- **Resolving impact on application enhancements.**

Year 2000 projects affect the priority and delivery dates for new enhancements and problem fixes. Aside from drawing resources away from desired application enhancements, the century-date migration effort presents a logistical challenge for merging changes, planned enhancements, and problem fixes that occur during century-date migration. Ideally, all business changes are deferred and the application code is frozen for the duration of the migration, but this is not an option for highly volatile applications. In all cases, as many changes as possible should be deferred to decrease project risk and effort. Decisions on the length of an acceptable freeze period and the changes that can be deferred are made by the business area task force.

- **Assisting in testing and verification.**

Although parallel test runs and data comparisons are used to verify some applications, most others will require user assistance in final testing and in the verification of test results. This is especially true for difficult-to-test interactive mainframe and client/server applications. The individuals that use an application daily are in the best position to detect incorrect results and date format anomalies. The task force members can directly assist in testing efforts or they can obtain resources as needed from within their business area.

- **Directing end-user application compliance efforts.**

  End-user applications exist in most business areas. These applications are rarely owned by and inventoried through a central area. As a result, compliance efforts must begin with education. The task force is responsible for building awareness among end users. Their initial goal is to ensure that all new end-user applications are constructed to be date compliant. Some end-user applications take data from the mainframe applications supported by IT. End users must be informed in advance about any changes in date formats to prevent disruptions in their operations. The task force can also serve as a clearing house for information about Year 2000 issues and methods for resolving those issues. The task force should also work with IT PC specialists to distribute upgrade information and to set up testing facilities.

- **Determining and resolving impact with external organization interfaces.**

  The task force works with the purchasing, legal, and audit areas to review their contracts and external relationships for Year 2000 issues. For example, a marketing department may depend on outside data sources for its market research data. The vendors for this data must be contacted and the Year 2000 compliance strategy and timing determined. If the vendor is at risk for noncompliance, a contingency plan may be required. Wherever possible, contracts should specify commitments. The task force must also evaluate the risk of other types of nonperformance. For instance, if the business area depends on a supplier for essential manufacturing components, it must be concerned with that supplier's ability to operate without interruption into the year 2000. The task force should work with the purchasing area to contact the most critical vendors to receive certification of compliance. This should be documented and contractually specified. Customers of the business area will expect the same assurances about the goods and services that they purchase. The task force is responsible for developing the strategy for responding to these requests, including determining the level of contractual commitments that their organization is prepared to make.

7.1.3 Other Business Areas

Even business areas that do not directly rely on IT-managed applications are impacted by Year 2000 efforts. These business areas have the same issues with customers and external sources of supplies and data as the other business areas have. They also have end-user applications. Further, all business areas depend on each other for internal goods, services, and information. For these types of business areas, the greatest issue is creating awareness and building urgency. Many of these areas will not perceive that century-date compliance is an important issue for their organization. The teams within the IT organization will be preoccupied with century-compliance projects for the applications that they manage. The initial responsibility for contacting these business areas will reside with the Year 2000 Project Office. Senior executives need to create a sufficient level of urgency to attract the attention of the business area's management. Members of the Year 2000 Project Office offer the same form of educational assistance as described in the previous section. The business area is then responsible for creating and supporting its own task force to address internal and external Year 2000 issues. This task force operates in the same manner as the task forces in the business areas that own applications. Business area task forces should share information with each other and work with the Year 2000 Project Office to ensure that all compliance efforts are coordinated and are directed toward the best interests of the company as a whole.

7.1.4 Purchasing Departments

Central corporate purchasing (or procurement) departments play a major role in Year 2000 projects. In most companies, the purchasing department is responsible for all vendor contracts. These contracts cover all software and hardware purchases, outsourcing and consulting relationships, as well as purchases of supplies and other materials. The purchasing department is responsible for the initial negotiation of new contracts, review and extension of existing contracts, and resolution of performance issues with vendors. In this role, the purchasing department works closely with the corporate legal department or external corporate counsel to create and refine contracts. Given its role, this department has considerable leverage over vendors and is an important checkpoint in the compliance process. The Year 2000 Project Office makes use of the purchasing department's talents and relationships to review existing IT contracts to establish whether Year 2000 issues are covered by the contract and to determine who bears responsibility for performing necessary corrections. If existing contract terms are not satisfactory, the purchasing department assists efforts to negotiate the proper terms at time of contract renewal. This assistance is not limited to software contracts and services. Other business areas will use the same type of assistance to ensure protection against century-compliance issues on the part of their suppliers.

In the context of a Year 2000 project, the purchasing department supports the following tasks.

- **Reviewing current contracts.**

  The process for current contracts is to review the contract for century-date compliance related clauses, contact vendors about those findings, and resolve issues that may arise. All software, hardware, and outsourcing contracts require immediate review to establish responsibility for century-compliance efforts. Most older contracts will not contain any direct references to century-date compliance but may contain clauses that can imply responsibility. For example, an outsourcing contract might specify that the outsourcer is responsible for the correct and uninterrupted operation of a given software application. Conversely, the contract might contain clauses that specifically exclude liability unless certain conditions are met. Because contract clauses are often open to interpretation, the purchasing and legal departments must analyze critical contracts for enforceability and level of vendor liability. If the vendor is not clearly responsible for migration effort or unlikely to perform those efforts even if responsible, the IT organization has to assume responsibility for the effort or negotiate with the vendor to provide the necessary services. The earlier that responsibility is established and the sooner that performance risk is assessed, the more time is available for alternative approaches.

  Many contracts have yearly renewals. Contacting the vendor before renewing the contract offers the purchasing department the greatest leverage for gaining concessions. New terms can be added to the contract as a condition for renewal, and assurances can be demanded for compliance with existing terms. The Year 2000 Project Office must assist the purchasing department by defining the desired contract terms. These terms specify the actions required from the vendor, the timing of those actions, and the penalties for failing to perform those actions. Contingency clauses are established in case of nonperformance. For instance, a software package vendor may be required to provide application source code and the rights to modify that code if the vendor does not provide a compliant version by a specified date. In all cases, for the corporation, the vendor should be contacted to state its interpretation of the contract and to understand the vendor's position. Negotiations are required to resolve issues if both sides cannot come to a successful agreement. The goal should be to prevent future legal battles by clearly delineating responsibility through the contract.

- **Adding language to future contracts.**

    All new contracts for goods and services that may be affected by Year 2000 compliance issues should contain standard clauses about compliance. The content of these "boilerplate" clauses is determined by a combination of purchasing, the Year 2000 Project Office, and the legal department. Increasingly, customers and vendors will have their own Year 2000 clauses in their contracts. Standard responses for common clauses can be established to decrease future contract negotiation efforts.

- **Resolving contract performance issues.**

    Most parties that enter into contractual arrangements want their relationships to be successful. Contract terms are meant to protect the company from unnecessary risk. Risk exists even when a vendor has the intention of fulfilling its obligations. For example, a package software vendor may promise, and intend to deliver, a compliant version of its packaged application by a certain date. Development problems may cause this date to slip, causing serious problems for the IT organization. If the date slips long enough, the IT organization will not be able to install the new release in time to avoid a failure. Contractual obligations must be monitored throughout the century-date compliance project to quickly detect performance problems and to identify potentially risky situations. If problems are noted, the purchasing department works with the Year 2000 Project Office to resolve the issues. It is important to understand what recourse is available and balance those possibilities against the desired action. For example, suing the delinquent package software vendor, while allowed by the contract, will not speed up delivery of the version nor buy time for the IT organization. A better option may be to cancel the contract and invoke a contingency plan to replace the application with another package. The best recourse is to require frequent status updates for all performance-critical products, allowing potential problems to be identified early enough to enable an acceptable alternative resolution.

7.1.5 Internal Audit Department

The internal audit department is another important constituent in a Year 2000 project. The role of auditors is to understand and mitigate financial and legal risks to their corporation. Once they understand the potential ramifications of Year 2000 issues, corporate auditors can be significant allies of the Year 2000 Project Office. They can help assess the full extent of organizational risk, assist in building support and awareness among senior managers, and provide compliance enforcement pressure.

- **Assessing organizational risk.**

  Auditors are in a good position to assess organizational risk across the entire enterprise. They analyze the ramifications of system failures in financial and legal terms and often fully understand the risk of losing any given application. This knowledge is very useful for building the necessary level of corporate awareness about the problem. Knowledge about specific application risks becomes important for prioritizing individual migration projects and for triage decisions.

- **Gaining senior management support.**

  Auditors typically report to high-level executives within a corporation and are often responsible to the Board of Directors. They can use this access to build executive awareness of the risks and liabilities associated with the failure to address the Year 2000 issue. It is important for the Year 2000 Project Office to work closely with the auditors in this effort to ensure that a consistent message is presented at all levels of the organization.

- **Providing enforcement pressure.**

  Because of their role, auditors wield considerable influence in many organizations. Pressure from corporate auditors is often far more effective than pressure from the IT organization for gaining the support of business areas. The auditors will formulate their own compliance requirements and audit individual departments to ensure that they are following these audit standards. It is essential that the Year 2000 Project Office work closely with the auditors to develop reasonable and enforceable standards.

Independent auditing firms offer another level of risk assessment and compliance assistance. These firms must certify that all financial statements fairly present the condition of the organization and that all important risks have been disclosed. At the time of this writing, many of the major auditing firms have begun or are considering including an assessment of Year 2000 risk as part of their auditing requirements. The Securities and Exchange Commission is currently pondering its involvement in formulating Year 2000-specific auditing requirements. These audit requirements will increase the awareness and pressure on senior corporate managers to address century-date compliance.

Another role of internal auditors is monitoring the results of ongoing migration efforts. Auditors typically review changes to production applications to ensure that those changes follow verification and security procedures. Auditors accustomed to examining typical maintenance changes may be overwhelmed by the scale and complexity of Year 2000 compliance projects. Organizations, such as financial institutions and government agencies, that make heavy use of auditors should involve the audit department early in Year 2000 project planning. This enables the auditors to review planned procedures and point out methods for mitigating risks and reducing later audit pressures. For example, auditors may not allow off-site conversions unless the conversion vendor has passed certain security and audit tests. It is better to understand audit requirements before negotiating with vendors for these services. The auditors may also require specific tests for verification and certification of century-date compliance. The rules associated with these certification procedures can be included in application compliance definitions if they are identified early in the project.

7.2 The Impact on Business Relationships

Business thrives on relationships. Organizations have hundreds or thousands of relationships with other external organizations where they exchange goods, services, and information. These relationships involve customers, business partners, and suppliers. Century-date compliance efforts affect external business arrangements on two levels. The first, and most obvious, impact occurs between organizations that exchange date-based data. This list includes government agencies as well as other business organizations. The second level, less obvious but equally important, is between organizations that depend on goods and services produced by companies that have their own Year 2000 risk. For example, a car manufacturer may be century-compliant for all of its own systems and processes but still suffer losses if a major supplier is unable to provide the necessary parts because of its own century-date failures. This type of risk is two-way. Almost every organization that depends on its own suppliers has customers that depend on it as the supplier.

Organizations must ask themselves if the third parties that they depend upon are prepared to handle century-compliance issues. In most cases, customers and suppliers will have their own century-compliance initiatives. Problems arise when the external organization doesn't recognize the problem or refuses to cooperate in developing a solution, a solution proposed by a supplier or customer is not satisfactory, or it is unclear that the external organization can meet its obligations. IT organizations must be prepared to devise solutions to each of these issues.

Resolving Year 2000 issues with external organizations will require serious negotiation combined with flexibility. Each organization has its own strategies and agendas. Their priorities and migration timings will be different. In most cases, neither side is in the position to mandate a specific solution. The best method of resolving these issues is to identify the relationships that are at risk as quickly as possible. This allows both sides enough time to negotiate a mutually satisfactory solution. It also provides time to implement a contingency approach. Resolving relationship issues is easier when they are contractually defined. In this case, responsibility is easily assigned and performance clauses and penalties can be assigned in the contract. Less formal arrangements or those involving many companies will be more difficult to resolve. The best approach in these cases may be defensive, i.e., assume the worst and implement "firewall" barriers to protect against bad data or loss of services. Each type of relationship has its own strategies. These are highlighted by type in the sections that follow.

7.2.1 Data Suppliers

Data suppliers are those companies that provide information in electronic formats. This data may be transmitted or shipped on tapes or diskettes. Examples of the data offered by these types of suppliers include market research, mailing lists, and financial information. Because these services are typically provided on a contract basis, the corporation normally has greater leverage in negotiating an acceptable solution. Contact the vendor to understand its Year 2000 strategy, when the strategy will be applied, and which types of format changes may be necessary.

7.2.2 Multicompany Data Interchange

Standard interchange formats are used when many companies share the same type of data. For instance, financial institutions such as credit card processors receive data from hundreds or thousands of separate customers. Point-of-sale terminals used by merchandisers have to exchange data with large numbers of suppliers. To avoid chaos in these large-scale data interchanges, standard formats are often defined by industry groups or by agreement among multiple vendors. One common example is the Electronic Data Interchange (EDI) standard. Because these standards affect many companies, changing formats is extremely difficult. It requires gaining agreement from the member companies and coordinating large, multicompany conversion efforts. Thus, format changes are avoided whenever possible. Involvement in the standards committees or associated user groups is the best method for receiving advance warning about format changes and for influencing the strategies that will be used to support century compliance.

7.2.3 Product and Services Suppliers

Suppliers are the vendors that each corporation depends upon for receiving goods and services. Nowadays, many of these suppliers have direct computer links with their customers to support "just in time" ordering of supplies and materials. Billing and payment between large companies occur through system interfaces, and the suppliers may provide data on ordering and usage patterns for their client's planning and forecasting applications. Many of these data interchanges involve dates or information that was calculated with dates. Corporate risk exposure arises from ordering mistakes, receiving incorrect data, or failure of the supplier to provide goods on a timely basis. One example of this exposure was reported by a speaker at a Year 2000 conference. A manufacturer's assembly line was shut down when its computer system received what it thought were expired materials from a supplier. The expiration date was calculated incorrectly due to the century-date problem. The shutdown caused significant losses for the manufacturer and is now the subject of a lawsuit.

To mitigate the risk of similar problems, companies should identify all data interchanges with their suppliers and assess these interfaces to see if they depend upon the results of date-based calculations or use dates directly. Aside from expiration dates, other examples of potential problems include supplies with future shipment dates, date-based payment calculations, and date-based inventory strategies such as FIFO (first in, first out) and LIFO (last in, first out). Care must be taken to identify situations, such as the aforementioned example, that will be triggered before the turn of the century is reached. Although this task is ultimately the responsibility of the corporate purchasing department, it will require assistance from the individual business areas and the Year 2000 Project Office. Whenever a potential problem is identified, the supplier should be contacted immediately to verify the issue and determine a correction strategy. In the meantime, the vendor's contract should be reviewed to determine who bears liability for any losses caused by the supplier's problems, responsibility for correcting those problems, and the degree of leverage over the supplier. A major corporation can exert a great deal of pressure on a smaller supplier to meet its requirements. Smaller organizations have little control over their larger suppliers. These organizations should devise their own contingency plans to protect them against failures from suppliers. Whenever possible, commitments from the supplier should be added to the existing contract. This provides strong incentives to the supplier to meet its obligations and offers ammunition to the supplier's IT organization in its quest to gain support for its own century-date compliance efforts.

As discussed previously, corporations are at risk even when data is not exchanged with the supplier. If failures in the supplier's application systems cause delays in the shipment of key components, significant losses may still occur. Corporate business units must work closely with their purchasing department to evaluate the risks associated with their strategic suppliers. When risks are identified, they should be resolved in the same manner described above for data interchanges.

7.2.4 Customers

An organization's customers are its most important asset. Without customers, the corporation cannot survive. Century-date compliance issues directly affect the company's customers. Year 2000 failures or problems can affect customer service or cause damage to customer operations. This can cause the customer to leave for a competitor or can even lead to a lawsuit.

The best method for handling customer issues is prevention. Correcting century-date issues before they affect the customer provides the corporation with a strategic advantage over less prepared competitors. The ability to certify century-date compliance and guarantee uninterrupted operation into the next century offers a tremendous advantage when seeking new customers. Amazingly, some companies are still naively considering approaches that involve fixing problems as they arise.

Whenever data is shared with customers, date interface issues arise. It is extremely critical to ensure that bad data is *never* passed to the customer's application systems. When date expansions are required, changes in the interfaces must be timed and negotiated with the customers. This situation is the reverse of the situation first described for suppliers; business areas must determine which of their customers are receiving data and what the impact of century-date issues is on this data. Proactively approaching customers with a recommended solution is a far better strategy than waiting until the customer contractually forces a strategy. Select strategies that limit the level of impact as much as possible. If customers will be required to convert their interfaces, provide bridging routines to allow customers to select their own conversion timing.

Some corporations, such as Chubb & Son Inc., have taken the proactive approach to the next level. Aside from beginning their own century-compliance efforts well ahead of most companies, Chubb actively shares information and assistance with its customers to help them avoid their own Year 2000 losses. This approach makes excellent business sense. It enhances the customer's perception of Chubb as a business partner and helps Chubb mitigate potential claims for business interruption policy losses.

While the discussion above focused on the effect of the corporation on its customers, data received from customers can cause century-date issues with internal applications. This is a risk whenever data containing dates is shared, but it is especially an issue for organizations such as banks and other financial clearing houses that receive data from hundreds of customers. While the best approach is to help their customers avoid creating bad data in the first place, these organizations must be prepared to handle bad data from at least a few of their customers as the year 2000 approaches. This data must be identified and trapped before it can affect other customers or interrupt internal processing. One method is to anticipate the types of errors that can occur and develop specialized programs to recognize these errors in incoming data. Unrealistic transactions, such as credit cards with balances that are overdue by ninety-nine years, can be rejected before entering the application. The customer is notified immediately of this bad data to trigger correction efforts.

7.2.5 Government Agencies

Almost every organization of any significant size shares data with one or more government agencies on the federal, state, or local level. These government agencies have their own century-date compliance issues that mirror those found in the private sector. The scale of their interface issues is monumental compared to private industry. For example, virtually every company sends electronic wage information to the Internal Revenue Service (IRS). The type and format of the data passed through these interfaces is usually regulated, and failure to provide the right data at the right time can result in fines or other penalties. Government agencies can mandate changes to these interfaces as needed, and corporations are at the mercy of these agencies over the timing of these changes. The federal government has already established a standard mandating four-digit years in the data that is passed to it and has set a target date for companies to meet that standard.

While IT organizations can do little to affect the type and timing of interface changes, they can lessen the impact of those changes through proactive efforts. The first step in this process is to identify and catalog all interfaces to government agencies. These agencies can then be contacted to determine which types of changes will be required and when those changes must be in place. This information can then be factored into project schedules. If the agency has not yet established a century-date compliance strategy, the IT organization can either anticipate the strategy or closely monitor the situation. Anticipating the strategy involves implementing the required changes and placing a bridge to provide the old format data to the agency. If the anticipated strategy is selected, compliance is simply a matter of removing the bridge. If anticipating the strategy is too risky, contact the agency regularly to ensure immediate notification of the new requirement. This provides the maximum possible time to implement the required change. This approach is also risky. If the agency defines its requirements too close to the year 2000, the IT organization will have to pull resources from other critical projects in order to meet the date.

Companies that receive data from government agencies must devise their own strategies to determine their risk of receiving bad data and the steps needed to mitigate that risk. The century-compliance efforts at many agencies are underfunded, increasing the likelihood of century-date issues occurring within their applications.

7.3 The Impact on IT Vendor Relationships

IT organizations work with many external organizations that will be affected by century-date compliance efforts. Organizations that assist in implementing century-compliance solutions, such as software tool vendors, service bureaus, and consulting firms, are covered elsewhere in this book. Two vendor categories, outsourcers and package software vendors, can present significant business challenges to Year 2000 projects. Inasmuch as outsourcing and packaged software are two possible sources of solutions for noncompliant legacy applications, existing outsourcing projects and packages can be a project risk.

7.3.1 Outsourcing Vendors

Outsourcing as a method of achieving century-date compliance has been rapidly gaining favor among IT organizations. In these projects, the outsourcer performs the century-compliance migration and then assumes support responsibility for the application. The contracts for these projects explicitly state the responsibility and costs for century-compliance activities. The situation may be very different for older outsourcing contracts. IT organizations face two challenges with existing contracts that do not directly address century compliance: determining the responsibility for the century compliance effort and developing contingency plans if the vendor fails to meet conversion requirements.

- **Responsibility for migration efforts.**

    Corporations that have outsourced portions of their application support activities in the past must review their contracts with the outsourcing vendors to establish responsibility for the century migration efforts. Outsourcing contracts negotiated over the last few years usually contain clauses that clarify the responsibility for making and funding the changes. In these contracts, the outsourcer typically performs the migration effort but bills the IT organization for the additional effort. Older outsourcing contracts will not explicitly account for century migration activities.

    Responsibility for funding and performing the migration effort may be ambiguous or may default to the outsourcing vendor. For example, if the vendor contractually guarantees the correct, continuous operation of the application in production, by default they are responsible for the century migration effort. Before assuming that the vendor is responsible, however, subject the contract to careful legal review for responsibility, liability, and contract cancellation clauses. In the best case, the vendor will accept the responsibility and perform the necessary changes in a timely manner. If the contract is ambiguous and the potential costs of the effort are high, a legal battle may ensue. In another scenario, the vendor may deem the costs and liabilities too high and seek to cancel the contract and return the application.

    Before embarking on a battle with their outsourcer, the IT organization must consider its objectives. A protracted legal battle will delay the application migration, potentially triggering century-compliance problems. If the vendor chooses to abandon the contract, the IT organization may find themselves ill-prepared to handle the unexpected effort of migrating the application. The best approach may be to treat the outsourcer's application in the same manner as other applications—either allow them to reduce other support activities to perform the migration effort or separately fund the project.

- **Contingency planning.**

  Risk management issues arise for applications supported by out-sourcers. If an outsourcer fails in its commitments, the IT organization will have to take responsibility for completing the conversion. This risk must be reduced through contract penalty clauses and through a contingency management plan. The contingency management plan establishes a series of checkpoints that allow the IT organization to identify performance problems early enough to correct them. This enables the IT organization to assume responsibility for the application while sufficient time remains to perform the century migration.

7.3.2 Software Package Vendors

The business relationship between the IT organization and a software package vendor is specified in the package purchase contract. This contract defines the obligations of the vendor for continued support and the rights of the IT organization if that support is not provided. The contract also specifies the fees, terms, and coverage for the ongoing support. As discussed in Chapter 4, it is essential for the Year 2000 Project Office to understand the terms of each software package contract when developing compliance strategies. This understanding is essential in handling the following situations.

- **The maintenance contract for a package was allowed to lapsed.**

  IT organizations sometimes allow the maintenance contract to lapse for older, heavily modified packages. The vendor usually has no obligation to provide any level of support in this situation. Depending on the terms of the contract, an IT organization must restore the maintenance contract in order to receive the latest compliant version of the application. This may require payment of all back maintenance fees or even the repurchase of the package.

- **The software package vendor offers an inadequate solution.**

  The software vendor may meet its obligations as defined by the contract but offer a solution that is deemed inadequate by the IT organization. For example, the vendor may provide the compliant release too late for the IT organization to install, merge internal changes, and adequately test the release before having century-date compliance problems, or the release may implement a strategy that does not fit organizational standards. The contract defines the IT organization's ability to implement its own solution or to terminate the contract and proceed with another vendor.

- **The vendor fails to meet contractual obligations or goes out of business.**

  Although many vendors are contractually bound to provide the necessary levels of support, the ability to sue for noncompliance has little value when a critical application is not functioning. Further, all of the vendor's customers will face the same predicament, greatly limiting the likely rewards of litigation. The largest software package vendors have the highest likelihood of successfully supplying compliant versions of their packages in a timely manner. Smaller package vendors may be driven out of business by the demands of century compliance. Some vendors will simply drop support for some of their package software lines. The organizational risk of a vendor failing is especially high if the IT organization does not have access to the source code. Without access and rights to modify a package's source code, the IT organization has little recourse in case of vendor failure.

To mitigate its risks, the Year 2000 Project Office must work with the purchasing department and the affected business areas to review the current status of all software package contracts. Concurrently, all software vendors must be contacted so the Project Office can understand their compliance strategy and timing and assess their ability to meet their contractual obligations. The initial information for this activity is taken from the application inventory created at the start of the century-compliance effort. This inventory must include vendor contact information, current release, the availability of source code, and the level of internal modifications for each package in the portfolio.

The best time to contact and negotiate with software package vendors is at the time of contract renewal. Most contracts are renewed yearly, and this renewal period offers the best opportunity to renegotiate contract clauses. Check the contracts for the following:

- **Specific vendor obligations to supply century-compliant code.**

  This obligation may be implied but not directly stated. If possible, negotiate a clause that specifically states which release will be compliant and when that release will be available. The clause should define penalties and remedies, such as providing source code, if the obligation is not met.

- **Limitations of liability.**

  Many contracts have clauses that limit the vendor's liability for problems caused by their software. Given the potential magnitude of century-date related failures, IT organizations must carefully evaluate the level of the vendor's liability when considering their strategy for a given software package. On one hand, vendors with unlimited liability may shut down operations rather than accept the risk. Conversely, vendors with no liability have inadequate incentives to ensure the quality of their century-date compliance effort. The best approach is to devise an equitable sharing of project risk between both organizations.

- **Support for older releases and custom versions.**

  Most software package vendors provide support only for the current release, or perhaps one or two previous releases. Many IT organizations are intentionally several releases behind the current release. Unless the contract specifies rights to updates for older releases, these IT organizations must migrate to the latest release to implement the century-compliant code. Often, custom extensions to a base package are not covered by standard package maintenance fees. The vendor may charge extra for any modifications to these extensions, or these modifications may be the responsibility of the IT organization. If the vendor will implement the necessary changes, make sure that those changes will be performed in a timely manner after the availability of the release.

- **Access to source code.**

  Access to the package source code is essential if the vendor goes out of business or fails to deliver the compliant version in a timely manner. Many packages are sold with their source code to allow purchasers to customize the package to meet their needs. In this case, ensure that the contract allows the IT organization to perform any changes necessary to reach century-compliance. Verify that application libraries contain all source code. Vendors sometimes provide only load modules for proprietary subroutines; other times the entire package is sold only in executable format. If the vendor does not supply all source code, make sure that the necessary source code is escrowed with access if the vendor fails to meet contractual obligations. If the vendor does not normally supply source code, this tactic places an additional burden on them to ensure the quality of their migration effort.

Chapter 8

Management Issues

$\mathbf{A}$chieving century-date compliance across the entire enterprise is the single, largest project that most senior IT managers will face in their careers. Its size, scope, and execution requirements significantly exceed even the largest system development project. It contains every conceivable project management challenge, requiring a monumental level of coordination among organizational entities, solving a wide variety of technical issues, and facing crippling resource constraints. It exposes all shortcomings in the IT infrastructure. Tools are inadequate, existing processes are weak, and necessary skills are in short supply. Studies have shown that most IT organizations are notoriously poor at meeting deadlines and budget commitments. Unless these weaknesses are corrected, they will prove fatal, as century-date projects have no latitude in project scope or delivery dates.

From an IT manager's perspective, assuming responsibility for a century-date project can be terrifying; the career upside seems limited, but its downside is enormous. IT managers will have to deflect criticism from all quarters by people who wonder how the problem was ever allowed to reach this point. Yet through all of these challenges, the century-date compliance issue offers a tremendous opportunity to hone management skills and build an infrastructure for the future. Managers can use their century-compliance efforts to increase the effectiveness of their organization and to position themselves to better handle the application management tasks of the future.

This chapter explores project management issues that must be overcome to ensure the success of a century-date change project. It discusses four categories of Year 2000 management issues: project management, project ownership, organizational maturity, and staffing.

8.1 Project Management

Century-date compliance projects are primarily an exercise in large-scale project management. Unlike new development projects, century-date compliance efforts do not utilize risky technologies or unfamiliar methodologies. The bulk of its tasks require the same skills and activities normally used to maintain the application. Project success is defined by an IT organization's ability to complete a myriad of small tasks before an immovable completion date. Strong, effective project management is the foundation for this success. While many project management techniques are clearly based on common sense, it is surprising that they are frequently ignored or forgotten. While smaller application support projects may be managed on an ad hoc basis, formal project management skills and processes are required to manage enterprise-level projects.

The first task faced by Year 2000 project managers is obtaining executive management support. Without this support, the project cannot succeed, despite the best efforts of its project managers and staff. The greatest project risk is obtaining enough resources and support to complete the project within the required time frames. Strong executive management support is the only way to ensure that the project gets the necessary resources in a timely manner.

The project management challenge is planning. Planning is required to ensure that the focus of project management is execution rather than disaster recovery. The tight time and resource constraints of a century-compliance project leave little room to recover from major surprises during project implementation. It is essential that project managers resist all temptation to shortchange the planning process if they wish to have a controllable project. Careful planning avoids problems by ensuring that all critical project tasks are identified and potential problems are uncovered.

When viewed as a whole, the century-date compliance project appears overwhelming; when broken into smaller component projects, it quickly becomes manageable. Breaking the Year 2000 effort into separately assigned sub-projects allows the overall effort to be managed at two levels: at the sub-project layer where multiple project managers execute component projects, and at the project layer where the Year 2000 Project Office manages and coordinates the completion of those component sub-projects. At the conclusion of the planning process, the Year 2000 project managers should have a comprehensive checklist of all of the tasks and sub-projects that must be completed, an understanding of task time lines and dependencies, and a thorough grasp of resource requirements.

Once planning is complete, the project is ready for execution. During execution, project management challenges arise on three fronts: ensuring that all identified tasks are tracked, ensuring that those tasks complete on time, and coordinating tasks that are shared among separate organizations. While each of these activities is relatively mundane, the sheer numbers of tasks make the management process complex. A high-quality, project tracking tool is an absolute requirement. Executive management pressure is needed to ensure that all sub-project managers religiously report upon their progress. Given the level of dependencies between tasks, slippage in any project task must be quickly identified and corrected before its ramifications spread throughout the project. The effort required to coordinate tasks shared among separate organizations cannot be underestimated. This effort greatly increases when the coordination involves outside organizations.

Despite the best efforts of the Year 2000 project managers, problems will arise and tough decisions will be required. While risks cannot be avoided, they can be identified and managed. The symptoms of serious risks can be described, and project checkpoints can be set to recognize those symptoms when they first appear. By developing contingency plans, managers can quickly respond to project problems while there is still enough time to keep the project on track.

8.1.1 Project Management Concerns

While century-date compliance projects follow basic project management principles, there are some very real concerns about the ability of IT organizations to complete the project within the required constraints. Unlike any other project, the final completion date cannot be delayed. Although the degree of compliance can be reduced to some extent, a minimal level of compliance must be met to avoid failures. Even if the corporation has an infinite budget, the number of available resources within the company and on the market is strictly limited. These constraints are more ominous when viewed against the IT track record for project delivery. Perhaps the best study of IT project failures was published by Jim Johnson of the Standish Group[1]. This study found that only 16 percent of all development projects surveyed completed successfully. Success was defined as on time and on budget with all originally specified features and functions. Projects that completed but failed to meet the success criteria accounted for 53 percent of the total, and 31 percent of the projects were outright canceled. This sad track record is worse for large IT organizations. Only 9 percent of their projects met the success criteria.

Getting beyond these statistics requires IT organizations to understand and overcome their limitations. The Standish Group Study identified ten key success factors for development projects: user involvement, executive management support, clear statement of requirements, proper planning, realistic expectations, smaller project milestones, competent staff, ownership, clear visions and objectives, and hardworking, focused staff. These success criteria are equally important for century-compliance projects. Once again, these factors appear to be obvious, but evaluation of any project failure will find that they are not universally applied.

In addition to the success factors described above, a number of issues are unique to century-compliance projects. These issues include project size, lack of large-scale maintenance management experience, shortcomings in IT infrastructures, and personnel issues.

- **Project size.**

  The scale of century-compliance projects tests the upper bounds of all IT practices. The very size of the effort will overwhelm and demotivate staff members. Control processes and project management practices that work for small projects will be inadequate to handle the rigors of a large-scale project. Breaking the project into many smaller projects is the only method to handle project scale. Even with this method, there will be many volume-related problems. For example, one large IT organization allows major production updates to occur only on weekends. A quick calculation by the Year 2000 project manager revealed that there are not enough weekend days before the year 2000 to accommodate all of the updated applications.

- **Lack of large-scale maintenance management skills.**

  The actual tasks within a century-date compliance project bear closer resemblance to maintenance projects than to new development projects. Changes to existing applications have side effects and ramifications on other applications, documentation, and interfaces that do not exist in new development projects. While many organizations have experience in managing large development projects, they lack similar experience in large-scale maintenance. Most maintenance efforts are usually small, independent projects, and they are rarely managed with formal project management tools and techniques. As a result, the existing maintenance practices do not scale up adequately to handle century-compliance projects. For example, maintainers typically coordinate issues that cross projects by building consensus through multiple, face-to-face meetings. The tight time constraints and volume of cross-project issues preclude using this method for century-compliance projects.

- **Shortcomings in the IT infrastructure.**

  Shortcuts from the past and weaknesses in skills, tools, and processes will become very apparent during the century-compliance project. Year 2000 project managers will often have to overcome these limitations before they can successfully tackle century-compliance tasks. Some obvious examples include poor training, weak control processes, and lack of adequate test environments. Owning to lack of training, many maintenance programmers use very little automation to perform their routine tasks. They will need considerable training before they can effectively apply the automation that is required for a century-date compliance project. Control processes will have to be tightened to prevent clashes between simultaneous projects. Few IT organizations have the required quality and volume of test data to verify the results of their migration efforts. The time and effort needed to create the necessary test environments must be included in project plans.

- **Personnel issues.**

  Year 2000 project managers will face many personnel issues throughout the century-date project. Of course, personnel issues occur on any large project, but several issues are unique to this project. Few programmers will want to volunteer for Year 2000 assignments. At the implementation level, most of the tasks are simple and repetitive. Programmers will resent being taken off more interesting projects. Balancing the boredom will be increased salaries offered by consulting vendors and other companies seeking skilled Year 2000 resources. Once the salaries reach a high enough level, retaining existing employees will be difficult. This will be especially true for IT organizations that will not have completed their conversion by Year 2000. Programmers will have little incentive to stay and face the inevitable date problems.

8.1.2 Risk Management

Most IT organizations do not devote much energy to understanding and specifically managing project risk. This omission is not fatal on the smaller-scale projects typically used for the maintenance and enhancement of production systems; however, as Edward Yourdon states in his book *Rise and Resurrection of the American Programmer,*

"But on large projects, a healthy respect for significant risks is often the difference between success and failure; and on the large projects, the financial consequences—as well as the legal, social, and political consequences—can be devastating."[2]

Century-date compliance projects are fraught with potential risks. Examining the characteristics of these projects identifies a laundry list of high-risk factors: very large scope, tight time frames, involvement of many internal and external organizational entities, a great variety of technologies and platforms, and tremendous project complexity. Without adequate project management, any of these risks can cause the project to spin out of control. Given the project's fixed completion date, the results *can* be devastating.

Certainly, risks are not insurmountable, but their reduction requires advanced planning. The first step of this process is identifying all nontrivial risk factors. This exercise does not have to be extended and time consuming. Instead, it should concentrate on identifying the obvious risks. For instance, at the level of the Year 2000 Project Office, the major risks are straightforward: does the project have strong senior management commitment, is it adequately staffed and funded, are its objectives reasonable? Individual application migration projects have more risk factors. For example, an application based on a software package is at the mercy of the package vendor. It is at risk for late delivery, inadequate quality control, and even the failure of the vendor's business.

Once the risks have been identified, they are incorporated into the correct level of the project plan. This incorporation requires documenting the early warning symptoms of each risk to enable its timely detection. For package software vendors, the symptom may be failure to provide an adequate plan for supporting century-date compliance by a fixed date. The team members charged with risk identification are responsible for determining methods for avoiding or at least mitigating each risk and developing contingency plans in case that risk materializes. Specific risk factors along with strategies for mitigating those factors are discussed throughout this book.

Implementing effective risk management requires resources. If the corporation already has a risk management function, it should be involved throughout the process. If not, the Year 2000 Project Office should appoint an individual to be the project Risk Officer. The Risk Officer ensures the identification and monitoring of all appropriate risks. The Risk Officer also reviews the development, updating, and employment of mitigation strategies. Every project plan should contain contingency reserves. These reserves include time, funds, and key resources. The contingency reserves are determined by weighing the costs of each contingency against its probability of occurring.

8.1.3 Contingency Planning

Simply identifying and monitoring risk situations is not enough. Problems require time and resources to correct. Uncovering a problem too late offers no chance to correct that problem before it impacts the organization. The greatest challenge faced in risk management is knowing when to invoke contingency efforts. In the case of century-date compliance projects, the limiting factor is often time. Contingency plans identify key checkpoints for assessing the current level of risk to ensure the timely triggering of correction efforts. Depending on the level of risk and the consequences of failure, a correction effort may be triggered as an insurance policy. If the problem occurs, the results of the correction effort are available for use; if the problem doesn't occur, those results are discarded.

The discussion below illustrates the process for creating a contingency plan, using a replacement project as an example. This process is useful for many other contingency scenarios, including software package installations and outsourcer-performed conversions.

Example 1:

Project XYZ is developing a century-compliant replacement application for legacy application ABC. Project XYZ is scheduled to complete in September 1999. ABC will not have century-compliance problems until January 1, 2000. The plan is to fully replace ABC, thereby avoiding the need to migrate the application.

Three major risks are associated with example 1: Project XYZ fails entirely; Project XYZ is late; or Project XYZ completes with less than the specified functionality. The odds of encountering one of these risks is fairly substantial. In any of these situations, the organization will have to forgo its Project XYZ efforts and instead focus on making application ABC century compliant. For instance, if the completion date for XYZ slides to February 2000, the corporation must be prepared to operate without ABC for two months or to make it at least minimally compliant. If achieving century compliance in application ABC requires a 6-month total effort for analysis, migration, and testing, this project cannot begin at the point at which XYZ misses its delivery date.

Similar scenarios exist for package software and migration efforts within outsourcing projects. The compliant release for a software package may be delivered too late to permit its timely installation and testing, or a small outsourcer may fail rather than accept the liability for the applications they support. In either case, the IT organization will inherit the liability for converting the existing version of the application.

Handling the risks described in example 1 requires developing an effective contingency plan that sets the appropriate checkpoints throughout the XYZ development project. These checkpoints are set by the time requirements to implement correction activities. At each checkpoint, the current situation is assessed and a management decision is made to either continue with the project or to trigger the actions specified in the contingency plan. Figure 8.1 shows the time line for the contingency plan for Project XYZ.

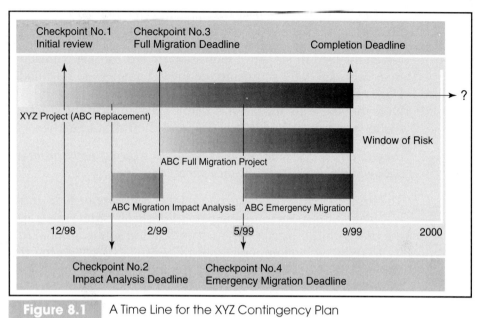

Figure 8.1 A Time Line for the XYZ Contingency Plan

This plan is developed by using the following steps:

1. *Set a fixed end date for project completion.*

   In this example, the fixed date is set at September 1999. This allows up to 3 months of slippage before application ABC fails. Migration project slippage outside of this window is a secondary risk that must also be included in the plan.

2. *Establish the solution(s) for the most critical set of risks.*

   There are two solutions for this example. A full migration is required if Project XYZ fails or if portions of ABC's functionality will continue to operate indefinitely after 2000. An emergency project for minimal migration is used if Project XYZ's delivery date slips past December 31, 1999, and ABC will continue to operate for a short period after 2000. An impact analysis is used to develop an accurate project plan for either solution.

3. *Determine the minimum lead time for each solution.*

   A full conversion of ABC requires 7 months, a minimal conversion requires 4 months, and an impact analysis requires 2 months. Because the impact analysis must be performed before a conversion, the total lead time for a full conversion is 9 months.

4. *Working backward from the fixed end date, determine when each solution must be started in order to complete on schedule.*

Given the lead times, a full migration project for ABC can start no later than February 1999, requiring the impact analysis to start no later than December 1998. An emergency conversion must start by May 1999. Note that these are the latest possible start times. If the risk is triggered earlier, the correction projects can, and should, start earlier.

5. *Set an initial checkpoint to allow some time to correct problems in the project without invoking the contingency plan.*

The first evaluation of Project XYZ is set for October 1998. If the project is at risk at this point, a management decision can be made to mitigate the risk within Project XYZ (such as deleting some optional functionality to reduce development time) rather than by triggering the migration of ABC. Conversely, if the risk is high, an early migration effort is triggered.

This contingency plan is put into practice by performing a management assessment of project risk at each checkpoint. As described above, the first checkpoint is used to get an early assessment of project risk. At the second checkpoint, the manager decides if the risk is high enough to justify performing the impact analysis of ABC. This impact analysis becomes the insurance policy by performing the setup work for either migration alternative. If the later risks fail to materialize, the results of the impact analysis are discarded. If the project has no risk, the analysis is skipped. Checkpoint 3 is the last start date for a full migration. Since this is the most costly option, it is triggered only for substantial risk of project failure or severely truncated functionality. Checkpoint 4 is the final "drop dead" date for achieving century-compliance in application ABC. At that stage, the management decision weighs the remaining risk against the cost of performing the emergency migration as an insurance policy.

8.2 Project Ownership

Century-date compliance projects require an unprecedented level of central project control. Given the project management issues described in the previous section, it is quickly apparent that an enterprise-level, century-date compliance project cannot be run by a part-time manager from the central planning area in IT. A good indication of a corporation's progress in its compliance effort is to examine who owns the project and what type of structure is used to manage the project. Two classic mistakes made by corporations in the earlier stages of the project are to assume that strong central control is not necessary or that project management can be entirely outsourced. These two mistakes are part of an evolutionary process. Typically, a corporation starts by assuming that each area within the company can independently manage its own migration efforts. This approach quickly leads to chaos. At this stage, the corporation turns to consulting firms as a method for gaining control of the entire project and quickly discovers that, despite the best efforts of all parties, this approach leaves critical gaps in the project management structure. Finally, the corporation decides to create an empowered, central Year 2000 Project Office. This evolutionary process can be avoided by understanding why the first two approaches do not work.

8.2.1 Why Each Organization Cannot Manage Its Own Migration

As tempting as it originally seems, empowering each area in the company to manage its own migration efforts is a recipe for failure. Because each initiative operates independently, it is impossible to ensure that the entire corporation will be century-compliant at any given time. Each organizational unit has its own of concept of compliance and places its own priority on the project. These concepts and priorities often conflict with those of other organizations. Internal politics are a major factor. If the manager of one area refuses to believe in the importance of the Year 2000 issue, thereby delaying the start of that area's compliance efforts, that decision impacts the ability of other areas to achieve timely compliance. Further, the widespread sharing of interfaces requires the use of standardized approaches for handling migration strategies. We have witnessed several situations where internal politics have led to incompatible standards between organizations and caused significant project delays.

If the corporation does not have a centralized message internally, it will certainly send mixed messages to its customers, suppliers, and other external organizations. This problem is compounded when these external organizations deal with several areas of the corporation.

Finally, lack of centralized project management wastes significant effort as separate areas reinvent the methods and techniques used to handle the conversion efforts. No opportunity is available for reusing the hard-won experience of other areas; efforts and tool purchases are duplicated. While project autonomy may be a valid strategy for supporting the needs of disparate business areas during standard application development and maintenance, it is a costly and risky strategy for century-compliance efforts.

8.2.2 Why Overall Project Management Cannot Be Outsourced

Outsourcing overall project management to outside consultants, often as part of outsourcing the bulk of conversion activities, offers an attractive alternative to many companies. Consulting firms have significant experience in managing large-scale projects. They bring their own "best practices" and offer an outside perspective on company practices. This experience can be an extremely valuable addition to a century-date compliance effort. Unfortunately, although many of the details of project management can be performed by consultants, ultimate project responsibility cannot be delegated because of several factors.

- **Consultants do not have the organizational knowledge, relationships, or clout needed to fully manage all aspects of the project.**

  All organizations have their own cultures. This culture includes the official method for accomplishing a task and the "underground" method that obtains faster results. Long-term personal relationships with managers throughout the company are important in receiving necessary support and assistance. Even when consultants are hired by executive management, they do not have the power to hire, fire, or even review internal employees. As a result, they lack the internal clout needed to direct those employees.

- **Consultants cannot take responsibility for all project management tasks.**

  Many century-compliance activities fall outside the boundaries of most consulting company services. For example, the consulting company cannot take responsibility for contract reviews or changes in the purchasing process, negotiations with customers and other external organizations over interfaces, or political issues among different areas.

- **Corporate management will be held accountable.**

  Ultimately, the IT organization and senior corporate management will be held accountable for the corporation's ability to function in the next century. This accountability cannot be delegated to external consultants.

  Although high-level project management must remain the responsibility of the corporation, consultants can be used to handle many of the detailed project management tasks. Full responsibility for executing analysis and conversion projects can be outsourced if desired. If consultants are used to manage portions of the project, the IT organization must be prepared to support the consultants with its own staff and expertise to overcome the issues described above.

8.2.3 The Need for a Year 2000 Project Office

The solution for managing an enterprise century-date compliance project is a central Year 2000 Project Office. This group is responsible for coordinating project activities across the entire enterprise. It overcomes the limitations of the previous approaches by providing a means for sharing organizational knowledge and ensuring standards. By assuming high-level responsibility for project management, this group ensures the integrity of the overall century-compliance effort. The individual sub-projects are executed by separate areas throughout the corporation or outsourced according to project needs. The Year 2000 Project Office tracks those sub-projects to ensure that all required activities are completed within the required time frames. It also provides a centralized point of contact for the outside world. As such, it can exchange knowledge with other companies, vendors, and research organizations. By representing the entire corporation, this group has greater leverage in negotiations with vendors or in the purchase of software tools and services. The structure and specific functions of this group are described in Chapter 11.

Although the Project Office can function as an informal clearinghouse that primarily tracks projects and shares information, it is more effective if it is empowered to make and enforce strategy decisions. The tight time constraints of a century-compliance project require faster decision making than is possible through consensus management. If followed throughout the project, centrally defined project standards greatly reduce the amount of time and effort required to coordinate efforts that overlap organizational boundaries.

The Year 2000 Project Office is the central collection point for all project information. This gives its managers the best possible view of overall project status. This information is tracked and reported to executive management. When project issues arise between areas, the Year 2000 Project Office can draw upon its executive management sponsors to resolve the situation.

8.3 Organizational Maturity and Readiness

Most corporations would not be in business if their core business processes functioned at the same level of efficiency as their IT processes. IT processes have not been subjected to the intense competitive pressure that forces core processes to be effective. As a result, most IT organizations are still managing their software support by using processes that have evolved from the days of punchcards. These processes are usually woefully inadequate to handle the complexity of modern application support. However, the small size of most application maintenance and enhancement projects allows process limitations to be overcome by "brute force" on the part of the IT staff. The scale and complexity of century-date compliance projects makes the inefficiencies inherent in these processes intolerable. If an IT organization is currently experiencing infrastructure problems during its routine work, those problems will grow exponentially during the century-compliance project.

Ineffective processes impact century-date compliance projects in two ways. First, valuable resources and time are lost through ineffective practices. There will simply not be enough resources available to support this extra level of unnecessary effort. Second, the size of the project will place inordinate levels of stress on all IT practices and processes. Practices that are adequate for managing two-week enhancement projects with a small team will not necessarily meet the demands of an enterprise-level, century-compliance project. For example, the configuration management process will have to allow multiple applications to check out and check in virtually all of their modules at the same time. Configuration management processes that are highly manual, such as requiring management approvals or audit reviews, will quickly become bottlenecks.

It is unrealistic to expect IT organizations to invest the time and energy needed to improve their processes before embarking on a century-compliance project. However, it is equally unrealistic for IT organizations with poor processes to expect to be successful in their century-compliance efforts. Some key processes include analysis, programming, configuration management, quality assurance and testing, and production turnover. Unlike standard application enhancement efforts, where tasks vary by application, the century-date compliance tasks performed within each of these processes are highly repetitive. This enables IT organizations to derive major increases in efficiency through limited process improvements.

8.3.1 SEI Capability Maturity Model

One commonly accepted method of measuring an IT organization's process maturity is the SEI Capability Maturity Model, shown in Figure 8.2. This model defines five increasing levels of process maturity: Initial, Repeatable, Defined, Managed, and Optimized. Organizations at the *Initial* level perform their work on an "ad hoc" basis, with programmers performing tasks and using tools as they personally choose. There is very little formalization of process, and hence successes are difficult to repeat and failures difficult to avoid. The next level of the process model is *Repeatable*. This level relies heavily on rigorous project management to control its efforts and meet project cost and time commitments. In the third level, *Defined*, processes have been formally defined, documented, and are followed by IT staff. At this level, programmers implement the same task in the same manner. Formal process models establish best practices and illustrate the correct points to employ software tools. Level 4, *Managed*, adds automatic collection of process metrics to manage the operation of the formal processes. Level 5, *Optimized*, implements continuous improvement based on the results of the process metrics to achieve major quality and efficiency enhancements.

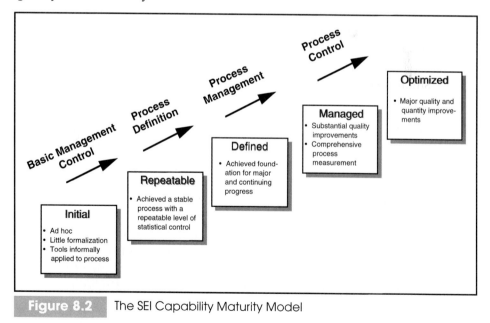

Figure 8.2   The SEI Capability Maturity Model

Using this scale, it is easy to see that an IT organization must perform at least at level two, Repeatable, to have any chance of meeting its century-date project commitments. Given the potential for reducing project risk and achieving significant implementation efficiency, IT organizations should aim to reach level three at least for the processes used for century-date compliance. Unfortunately, according to Edward Yourdon, "...as of late 1994, about 90 percent of U.S. IT organizations were below level 3..."[2]

The level of reworks for a typical program change cycle is indicative of an IT organization's position within this hierarchy. Reworks are situations in which a previously completed task must be repeated because of incorrect implementation, misinterpretation, or other process failures. Examples of reworks include programming changes rejected by QA due to testing failures, specifications returned to analysts for additional explanation, and end user rejection of an implemented change for failure to meet requirements. Although few organizations do so, reworks can be tracked. When they are measured, the IT organization discovers that the cost of reworks in time and effort is enormous. In one company, the combined rework rate through their maintenance process was 230 percent. In essence, this means each change is processed 2.3 times before it is finally accepted in production! A century-date compliance project implemented with that level of rework requires better than twice the level of resources to complete the same effort as a more efficiently managed project.

8.3.2 Implementing Targeted IT Process Improvements

As discussed previously, most IT organizations will not have the luxury of implementing major IT process improvements as a prelude to their century-date compliance projects. IT organizations can shortcut their process improvements for century-date compliance projects by following the steps below. This approach does not replace a true IT process redesign, but it will provide significant efficiency gains for the century-date compliance project.

1. *Assign responsibility.*

   The responsibility to organize and manage the process improvement activity should reside with the Year 2000 Project Office. Part of their responsibility is "time boxing" the process improvement to ensure that the effort does not get bogged down by scope creep or excessive analysis. This effort should not require a large investment of people or time.

2. *Define the century-date migration process.*

   The entire century-date migration process must be defined and understood before meaningful improvements can be implemented. Map every step and every organization involved from the start of the assessment phase to the final delivery of the completed application. Identify the work products consumed and produced at each stage of the process. Ignore organizational boundaries and responsibilities when laying out the process steps. These boundaries will be handled after the processes are optimized.

This effort can be greatly reduced through the use of a Year 2000 methodology or blueprint. These methodologies can be purchased separately or can be provided by a tool vendor or consulting service provider as part of their solution. If an existing methodology is used as a starting point, it needs to be customized only to meet organizational requirements. It is important to note that simply having a methodology does not move an IT organization to the Defined level of the SEI maturity model. The real benefits of process improvement occur when the model is consistently used by all project staff.

3. *Reduce process inefficiencies.*

Once the process steps have been mapped, examine them carefully to identify unnecessary or redundant steps. Ask why each step is needed, and do not keep steps that exist only "because that is the way we do things." Remember that the work performed on a century-date compliance project is highly targeted, so many steps usually needed for standard support projects will be unnecessary. Given the number of times the process will be performed during an enterprise-level Year 2000 project, each step eliminated results in significant time and effort reductions.

4. *Add automation.*

Look for opportunities to add automation wherever possible. If an existing methodology is used as a starting point, the hooks for software tools will already be defined. If a tool vendor methodology is used, it may not include tools for categories that are not supported by the vendor. Be sure to include tools already owned by the IT organization wherever appropriate, especially those tools that enhance productivity. Specify which tools are to be used for each step. Chapter 15 discusses the types of tools that can be applied to century-date compliance efforts.

5. *Reduce organizational overhead.*

When the entire process is examined, it is often astonishing to discover the number of separate organizational units involved. Many process inefficiencies result during handoffs between organizational units. Attempts to fix handoff problems in a piecemeal fashion usually result in increased bureaucracy and further degradation in cycle efficiency. Ruthlessly ask why each organization needs to be involved in the implementation process. Remove every possible organizational hand-off. Each organization's objectives may be performed by a single team for each conversion sub-project by including the necessary steps in the process.

6. *Package your deliverables.*

Century-date compliance sub-projects are highly amenable to release packaging. The major project deliverables are the same for every application subproject. These deliverables should be included in a release package that is extended through the migration process. This package is effectively a virtual folder that is passed from step to step. With this model, the migration process behaves like an assembly line with each step adding its changes to the deliverable package. This practice facilitates quality assurance and ensures that all necessary deliverables have been created. At the end of the process, the release package is used for production turnover. At that point it contains all modified and verified components of the application, including source code, documentation, and so forth. This is the approach used by commercial software vendors for packaging their own software releases.

7. *Measure effectiveness.*

The process should capture at least rudimentary metrics that can be used to evaluate its effectiveness. These metrics should include time per step, cost per deliverable, and number of reworks. Collect the metrics throughout the project. Periodically examine them to uncover process bottlenecks and to identify opportunities for improvement.

8.4 Year 2000 Staffing Issues

Project staffing will be one of the largest challenges faced by IT management. Many articles have predicted massive shortfalls of programmers able to address century-date compliance issues. This challenge is increasing daily because of procrastination and the fixed end-date of the project. Because the volume of effort required to reach compliance does not decrease, each day that an IT organization delays increases the number of programming resources required to complete the effort. Further, the competition for resources will be fierce. IT organizations are competing with service providers and other IT organizations for the same resources. Because the problem is global, competition can come from anywhere.

It is clear that there are not enough programmers available in the world to solve the problem manually. The Gartner Group quotes the global cost of compliance at $400-$600 billion. Even assuming that programmer costs account for only 25 percent of this number, that programmers work 2000 hours per year, and that their average fully burdened cost is $50 per hour, the result is a projected requirement of 800,000 to 1,000,000 programmers *per year* through 2000. Without the use of automated tools, the programmer requirement would be much higher. Although increasing levels of automation will offer some relief, their effects on yearly programmer requirements will be negated by the effect of procrastination.

Given numbers of this magnitude, it is clear that IT organizations will need outside assistance in addition to devoting the bulk of their programming staff to Year 2000 projects as the close of the century draws near. Extra resources can be obtained from consulting firms and offshore outsourcers, but even these resources are not infinite. IT organizations that need extra resources late in their migration effort will pay top dollar for barely trained programmers.

8.4.1 Skill Requirements

Compounding this issue are the types of skills required for century-date migration efforts. Although date issues can affect any type of software, a disproportionate level of the effort will be concentrated on legacy applications. These applications rely on traditional programming skills in COBOL and mainframe data architectures. These skills have been slowly dying off over the past decade as client/server systems have grown and as universities have changed the emphasis of the computer curriculums to workstation architectures and languages. Many companies have viewed these skills as outdated and have been replacing mainframe programmers with client/server specialists. Before realizing the extent of the Year 2000 issue, several major companies laid off large numbers of the very programmers they now require. Skill shortages become more severe in the less common legacy environments. IT organizations that use assembly language or older fourth generation languages like RAMIS or MARK IV, will have an especially hard time finding programmers with the appropriate skill sets. To an extent, there are some "hidden reserves" of programmers who have experience in these older skill sets, although these skills are not included on resumes (a tactic used by programmers to avoid dead end assignments). Once the price for these skills starts to rise to astronomical numbers, many of these programmers will suddenly remember their experience.

Within the programming process, specific skill areas will be in high demand. Chapter 11 discusses the skills and job positions for the Year 2000 Project Office. Testing and Quality Assurance are two highly valuable skills that will increase in importance over the life of the project. These functions require specialized skills and are very manual. These functions will suffer shortages of qualified resources, although several consulting firms will specialize in providing Year 2000 testing support.

While shortages will exist for skilled delivery personnel, the most pressing need is for strong project managers. Project management skills are a crucial requirement for any century-date compliance project, and those skills are especially prized by consulting companies. Lack of project managers will be the biggest limiting factor for the growth of many IT consulting firms. IT organizations that start century-date compliance projects late will desperately seek experienced managers to launch their efforts. Salaries for Year 2000 project managers are already outpacing standard salary levels and will increase dramatically over the next few years as consulting firms and laggard IT organizations fight for experienced managers.

8.4.2 Overcoming Shortages

The best method for overcoming resource shortages is through advance planning. The sooner an IT organization understands its resource requirements and implementation strategies, the sooner it can obtain the resources that it needs and the less it will pay for those resources. The number of additional resources required depends heavily on the migration strategy selected by the company. Although code migration appears at first to have the greatest resource requirements, it is not likely to be a constraint in most projects. Code conversion work is easily outsourced to consultants, conversion factories, or offshore facilities. As it is relatively mundane, low-skill work, it will be significantly automated over the next few years. Testing will require the greatest number of resources. This function represents approximately 50 percent of the cost and time requirements of the century-date project. This activity will be primarily performed on site and, even if consulting support is used, will require heavy involvement from the IT organization and business areas.

Although there are many variations on the theme, IT organizations have two primary methods for obtaining project resources: shifting existing staff to century-compliance projects or obtaining resources from a consulting firm or outsourcer. External staffing issues and options are discussed in

Chapter 17. Most companies will use a combination of both approaches. In either case, IT organizations must pay attention to the following rules.

- **Reserve consulting resources early.**

  Even the largest consulting companies cannot adequately support a full migration project for more than a fraction of their existing customers. These organizations are quickly being booked by their key customers. At the time of this writing, several consulting firms have stopped actively marketing their services, as they have already signed up as many customers as they can handle. The demand is the highest for the best consulting firms. These firms will be fully booked first, leaving only lower-tier firms for the laggards. Following the laws of supply and demand, those laggards will pay top dollar for their inexperienced resources. These issues can be avoided by quickly determining the level of resources required and signing up the appropriate consulting company. Be sure to select a company that can commit to staffing all phases of the project. These rules apply equally to local consulting firms and offshore providers.

- **Develop Year 2000 incentive plans for IT staff.**

  Many employees will not find Year 2000 work attractive. Those that do will quickly discover their rising market value. The IT organization will have to develop creative methods for retaining their critical Year 2000 resources. Bonus and recognition programs, based on project success, are a good method for rewarding loyalty and commitment to the project. If the bonuses are sufficient, they will draw employees that would otherwise avoid the project.

- **Watch carefully for turnover.**

  High outside salaries will cause programmers to leave for greener pastures, as will severe project problems. High staff turnover can mortally wound a century-compliance effort. Once a project gets into trouble, turnover leaves the remaining staff members with an increasingly hopeless situation. Few programmers will want to remain on a disastrous project as it crosses into the next century. These issues can be addressed by carefully watching salaries and bonus plans and by careful project management. Project crises must be addressed as quickly as possible to prevent the start of a self-fulfilling turnover cycle.

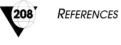

References

[1] Johnson, Jim, "Chaos: The Dollar Drain of IT Project Failures," *Application Development Trends*, Volume 2, Number 1, pp41–47, January 1995.

[2] Yourdon, Edward. *Rise & Resurrection of the American Programmer.* (Upper Saddle River, NJ: Prentice Hall 1996)

Part 3

Assembling a Year 2000 Solution

Now that we have presented the implications of the year 2000 and have exposed the numerous issues that make this dilemma the most perplexing in the history of the IT field, it is time to focus on solutions. Chapters 9 through 17 discuss various options for addressing the Year 2000 problem. Chapter 9 emphasizes several basic principles that serve as the foundation for an enterprisewide initiative. Topics include common pitfalls, sponsorship, executive role definition, a planning summary, requirement for a central coordination capability, and a software technology overview. Chapter 9 also discusses the need for a formal, solution-oriented process to plan and implement Year 2000 projects.

Chapter 10 describes the process of developing a budget for a Year 2000 initiative. The size of the problem makes accurate "one-shot" budgeting impossible. We therefore describe a strategy for developing an evolving budget to support the implementation of accurate, yet obtainable, objectives.

Chapter 11 describes project mobilization for a Year 2000 effort. Topics include Project Office Setup, preplanning activities, work task and work product definition, resource planning, and summary of a Year 2000 strategy.

Chapter 12 describes the importance of and techniques for performing a Year 2000, enterprisewide assessment. This chapter covers inventory requirements, project segmentation, infrastructure assessment, and deployment planning.

Chapter 13 describes the execution of the implementation phase of a Year 2000 project, including the detailed analysis and actual system upgrade process. This chapter describes implementation tasks and deliverables and a summary of the techniques required to execute Year 2000 projects.

Chapter 14 discusses the validation setup and execution process necessary to guarantee that upgraded systems work properly when encountering events beyond 2000. Because Year 2000 validation consumes up to 50 percent of the Year 2000 conversion budget, the topics covered in Chapter 14 are vital to all Year 2000 projects.

Chapter 15 describes how to select the right tools for Year 2000 compliance projects. Topics include tools that support project management, inventory and cross-systems analysis, impact analysis, system upgrades, data migration, interface development, and validation. The chapter also discusses blueprints and methods, selection and categorization criteria, technology environments, technology categorization, and long-term tool utilization.

Chapter 16 is aimed at small IT organizations that may not have the budget or the resources necessary to establish a Year 2000 delivery capability. With these resource limitations in mind, this chapter outlines various alternatives so that these companies can maintain a viable information processing capability in the face of the Year 2000 challenge.

Chapter 17 discusses various alternatives for obtaining third-party assistance for Year 2000 projects. It describes the kind of support functions that third parties can provide, including in-house consulting support, use of software conversion factories, and project outsourcing. Chapter 17 also discusses the pros and cons of each service option and describes how to develop a valid request for proposal (RFP) as a means of identifying and procuring third-party services.

Chapter 9

Enterprise Strategy for Year 2000

Starting down the right path toward a solution is one of the most important aspects of a Year 2000 project. Sustaining an initiative of this size and scope is just as critical. This chapter deals with obtaining project sponsorship, defining the role of the senior executive, developing a high-level budget strategy, and using a formal process to plan, manage, and implement a project.

Discussion of the use of formal methodologies to define Year 2000 solutions is particularly important for those organizations that are just beginning planning or implementation. The first thing organizations should be aware of, however, are the ten most common mistakes that organizations make during the course of a Year 2000 project. The list of ten common mistakes is based on real-life experiences and can serve as a guide to organizations exploring a multitude of options.

9.1 Ten Common Mistakes in a Year 2000 Project

The wise learn from their mistakes. The truly wise will learn from the mistakes of others. With this as our theme, we have outlined ten of the most common mistakes (see Figure 9.1) that organizations encounter when embarking on a Year 2000 project. Organizations that have become aware of these pitfalls, and that have chosen to ignore them, tend to be largely unsuccessful over the long-term.

---

1. Inadequate project ownership and sponsorship

2. Distributing and diluting central project team responsibility

3. Reinventing solutions and approaches on an ad hoc basis

4. Not defining Year 2000 compliance standards

5. Underestimating the need for an enterprise assessment

6. Wasting time on unnecessary tasks

7. Omitting critical tasks from the project plan

8. Depending too much or too little on software tools

9. Not addressing information infrastructure issues

10. Assuming that current testing processes are adequate

TSG, Inc. - 1996 all rights reserved

Figure 9.1 Top 10 Year 2000 Mistakes

9.1.1 Inadequate Project Ownership and Sponsorship

Upon realizing that date fields no longer support future date processing, management's first instinct is to assign a project manager to the problem. The more these managers learn about the year 2000, the more they discover that the problem reaches functional areas and management levels to which they have little or no access. Historically, most companies have taken at least 6 months to assign an executive ultimate responsibility for the Year 2000 problem. This low level or total lack of ownership significantly hinders project startup and is a clear symptom of inadequate sponsorship.

Executive-level sponsorship takes time to obtain unless the project was commissioned by the CIO, CEO, or CFO. Proper sponsorship means that senior executives actively participate in advisory sessions and take an aggressive stance in preventing politics from standing in the way of progress. Even with proper sponsorship, distributed organizational structures can encounter political gamesmanship that must be reconciled by senior management. If management functions are highly distributed, the CIO may need to take an even more active role in the project. When sponsorship is either weak or nonexistent, a project is destined to be bogged down by internal politics or the recurring reorganization efforts that are so common within IT environments.

9.1.2 Distributing and Diluting Central Project Team Responsibility

IT management may initially assign two people to create a high-level, Year 2000 approach and then let each application area individually deal with the issue. Unfortunately, time frames do not accommodate this approach. An enterprisewide initiative, requiring the coordination of hundreds of projects and interfaces, must be controlled centrally to avoid chaos. A central team must set the agenda for the Year 2000 project based on collective knowledge of the problem and available solutions. Isolated approaches for dealing with numerous aspects of a Year 2000 problem, such as system software, hardware, tools, configuration management, change control, and validation, will result in a repetitive, costly, and haphazard approach.

The Year 2000 team, or Project Office, focuses on communication, skills transfer, tool management, central infrastructure issues, and third-party relationships. Multilevel representation from the data center, data administration, business areas, audit, and legal is important. Early formalization of team assignments and empowerment of the Project Office to help plan and monitor compliance efforts are critical success factors for any Year 2000 project. Once the team is assembled, it must remain intact. If the team is tampered with or disbanded because of a reorganization or similar upheaval, the project will ultimately fail.

9.1.3 Reinventing Solutions and Approaches Ad Hoc

With thousands of companies and IT professionals working on the Year 2000 problem, it seems ridiculous to reinvent the planning and implementation process again and again. IT organizations pursue this route partly because early success stories from companies that began work in the early 1990s indicated that this is the approach these companies used. However, with time running out and with blueprints available from various vendors, reinventing a process from scratch no longer makes sense.

Standard blueprints provide detailed, yet flexible, guidelines to planning, budgeting, implementation, interface development, data migration, validation, and status tracking. When a standard process is used, several problems are alleviated. For example, tool selection is simplified under a formal assessment and implementation process. Blueprints also provide cost models, tool guidelines, forms, and sample reports. In spite of the availability of sophisticated Year 2000 methods and blueprints, many IT professionals continue to attempt to build processes from scratch. This attempt flies in the face of common logic and will severely delay project implementation unless management steps in and curtails this fruitless activity.

9.1.4 Not Defining Year 2000 Compliance Standards

Standards and guidelines are a key component of the Year 2000 solution. Year 2000 compliance, defined in Chapters 1 and 5, is summarized as an ability to accurately process dates and related events that span multiple centuries. Expanded or modified compliance language should be included in development standards, system upgrade plans, vendor contracts, outsourcing agreements, validation criteria, and auditor certification plans. All standards should be communicated broadly to ensure project success.

While it seems logical that compliance standards should be established at the onset of a Year 2000 project, in order to solidify project goals, many organizations delay this step. The lack of Year 2000 compliance standards means that goals for each of the many aspects of a Year 2000 problem remain unclear to the numerous individuals that must set project objectives based on those goals. This misstep should be avoided by establishing compliance definitions early in the project.

9.1.5 Underestimating the Need for an Enterprise Assessment

A number of organizations have initiated individual Year 2000 migration projects without the benefit of an enterprisewide view of the problem. The results of this misstep have been less than positive, to say the least. For example, before the CIO at an insurance company would assign central coordination responsibility, managers there were forced to *repeatedly* demonstrate that the Year 2000 project was in trouble because of divisional infighting. This problem was linked to the lack of perceived need for a cross-enterprise view of the Year 2000 problem. The enterprise assessment and planning process, once centralized, allowed the insurance company to proactively address inter- and intradivisional issues.

The enterprise assessment inventories systems, segments a portfolio into reasonably sized projects, reviews business strategies, sets priorities, and establishes a cohesive plan that benefits the enterprise as a whole. An enterprise can be defined as an individual division or an entire organization. In a government, individual agencies make up an enterprise. An enterprise should minimally encompass an entire business unit to accommodate the Year 2000 learning curve within constrained planning windows. Underestimating the need for a Year 2000 enterprise assessment is a huge mistake that must be avoided.

9.1.6 Wasting Time on Unnecessary Tasks

There is precious little time to complete a Year 2000 upgrade, and organizations can ill afford to waste this time on extraneous activities. For example, some companies believe that step one of a project is to count all of their date fields. These "impact studies" create massive amounts of data that becomes outdated before it can be assimilated. Another misdirected activity is the software product "bake-off." Defining a solid implementation approach that accommodates a mix of tools is more critical. Software tools, which can be identified by using blueprints or through consulting help, can then be selected on the basis of the tasks that they support.

Assessing service firms has tremendous value but sending the same "pilot" system to multiple firms is a waste of time. Assigning a different system to each firm, along with strict specification criteria, facilitates third-party evaluation and results in converted production systems. Another potential waste of time is the request for proposal (RFP). The RFP process is time consuming and draws responses only from second-rate firms as consulting resources grow scarce. An exception to this situation is a legal requirement for the RFP.

Clearly, one of the biggest and most expensive failings involves unnecessarily upgrading systems that are going to be eliminated or replaced. This wasted activity stems from IT professionals pursuing Year 2000 conversion projects with little or no input from the business analysts or managers that these systems support. There is no excuse for spending large sums of money on converting a system for a business unit that is being phased out, sold, or consolidated.

Finally, attempts to roll unrelated tasks into a Year 2000 project will result in failure of both projects. Extraneous tasks that can intrude upon the planning and infrastructure setup phases of a Year 2000 project include data warehouse development, enterprise repository creation, or other broad initiatives that may forestall the momentum of a Year 2000 project. Extraneous tasks that could creep into a Year 2000 migration project include functional changes to upgraded but untested source code and nonessential code improvements. As it is now, organizations may barely make the December 31, 1998, deadline, and scope creep is the last thing that a Year 2000 project can afford.

Authors' Note: We are in no way trying to discourage the collateral benefits that can be derived from a Year 2000 project, as described in Chapters 18 and 19.

9.1.7 Omitting Critical Tasks from the Project Plan

Many Year 2000 teams, in an effort to avoid scope creep, may defer certain tasks or responsibilities that are important to the overall compliance project. Omission occurs when teams limit scope to mainframes or systems under their direct control. Systems that could be erroneously excluded from an inventory effort include user-developed systems, system software, application packages, or noninformation systems such as process control systems. Omission also occurs when teams exclude areas such as legal or internal audit from representation in the project. Sponsors must ensure that all systems and topic areas are addressed by the planning team and coordinated throughout the project.

Furthermore, Year 2000 teams must retain control of vital areas of responsibility, including the inventory process, budgeting, planning, coordination, portfolio segmentation, interface management, and system certification. If any of these areas are ignored, the project could face real trouble. Finally, some application or support areas may be secretive or uncooperative with the central coordinating team, causing the team to ignore the needs of that area. If that situation is allowed to develop, all other areas of the organization may suffer as a result.

9.1.8 Depending Too Much or Too Little on Software Tools

Software tools help automate many Year 2000 assessment and migration tasks, but tools are not the centerpiece of these projects. In other words, tools add value to a project as long as that project does not become tool-driven. For example, planning teams may rely on software tools to define the scope of the tasks that need to be performed. This misplaced reliance could result in the omission of key tasks, organizational issues, and unsupported platforms from the planning process because a given tool does not support that task. This is particularly true if software tool vendors assist in the planning phase of the project. Care must also be taken so that tool research does not become a drawn-out academic exercise.

Conversely, useful tools may be erroneously omitted from a Year 2000 project. Some companies have avoided the use of tools to shorten the systems inventory process. Others have leaned away from obtaining technology to support the application upgrade, data conversion, or testing tasks. Tool omission in these specific cases can result in reduced productivity and less than adequate results. Tools clearly have a place within Year 2000 projects, but their role must be managed and tempered by skilled analysts and a well-defined process.

9.1.9 Not Addressing Information Infrastructure Issues

Dealing with surrounding information infrastructures is vital to successful Year 2000 projects. Key infrastructure categories to be reviewed include system volatility, change control, configuration management, production turnover policy, and testing capabilities. A second category involves reviewing the compliance status of mainframes, workstations, controllers, and system software. Storage and hardware capacity must also be reviewed and adjusted to support peak project-processing loads.

It may also be worthwhile, or necessary, to create a project support infrastructure for the Year 2000 initiative itself. This involves the acquisition and integration of tools to support planning, implementation, communication, and project management for all environments. It may also include establishing project teams, communication facilities, and reporting structures. Each infrastructure category requires analysis for potential risks and correction of weaknesses in key areas.

9.1.10 Assuming that Current Testing Processes Are Adequate

The Year 2000 involves complex testing cycles. The first validation phase maximizes logic coverage (70 percent or more) and minimizes data volume. If this is not the case, a project must be launched to correct it. The second phase runs original and upgraded system outputs through automated comparison tools (this requires expanded data where date expansion was used) to verify that no errors occurred during

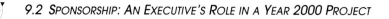

the upgrade effort. An upgrade unit could be returned to production at this point.

The last step is Year 2000 compliance certification, using modified test data to reflect future events. Certain tools support baseline-data-to-future-data analysis to assist with compliance certification. Where these tools are unavailable, standard testing techniques apply. Finally, all of this must be coupled with system acceptance testing as defined by in-house standards.

9.2 Sponsorship: An Executive's Role in a Year 2000 Project

Executives are under scrutiny from board members, stockholders, and other governing bodies who, having heard about the year 2000, question the viability of information infrastructures. With the potential liability high, senior executives must be knowledgeable about the Year 2000 problem and exactly what their organization is doing to address it. Senior executives play a vitally important role in shaping an organization's response to the problem by assessing levels of risk, approving strategy, and establishing communication policies. Most importantly, executives must create an overall environment under which a Year 2000 project can succeed (see Figure 9.2).

---

1. Requesting and approving overall strategy

2. Establishing Year 2000 Project Office

3. Establishing and working with advisory counsel

4. Raising awareness

5. Commissioning risk analysis

6. Performing contingency planning

7. Approving budget allocation

8. Setting communication policy

Figure 9.2   Executive Year 2000 Responsibilities

9.2.1 Establishing Overall Strategy

Senior executives must commission and approve an executive Year 2000 strategy. This strategy serves as a high-level guide to the project and as a vehicle for reporting progress. Clarifying the objectives listed in Figure 9.2 with business executives is a key part of obtaining the sponsorship needed to move the organization toward Year 2000 compliance. If the executive team is not driving the solution, the organization is at severe risk of not achieving Year 2000 compliance.

9.2.2 Setting Up a Year 2000 Project Office and Advisory Counsel

The Year 2000 Project Office is the cornerstone for planning and implementing a Year 2000 project. The Project Office, which remains intact for the life of the effort, oversees project execution and direction. The advisory counsel, on the other hand, is an executive oversight committee that meets either quarterly, or as needed, to set strategy, review progress, and report back to senior executives with recommended policy changes. Creation of these organizational bodies is discussed further in Chapter 11.

9.2.3 Raising Awareness

Raising Year 2000 awareness is a goal that has been linked to obtaining executive sponsorship. If executive sponsorship is in place, however, awareness should focus on communicating the issue and high-level strategy to the board, business units, internal IT personnel, and business partners. An individual with solid communication skills should be assigned to speak with these diverse factions so that they can understand the implications of the year 2000 for their job functions.

9.2.4 Analyzing Risk

If the risk factors that an organization faces regarding the year 2000 are unclear, senior executives must commission a business risk assessment. The risk assessment, introduced in Chapter 2, identifies risks in terms of potential lost revenue or legal exposure by business unit. Once the risk analysis is in place, the results are used as input to defining the Year 2000 strategy and annual budget requirements for various business units.

9.2.5 Planning for Contingencies

Part of the process of establishing a project approach and related milestones is to create contingency plans for each business area. Contingency planning requires active executive participation, because a broad knowledge of issues is needed to weigh a multimillion dollar system upgrade against other alternatives. This decision is based on the criticality of a system and the business area that it supports. For example, could a system be discarded in favor of a similar application in a related business area? This solution would likely require sacrifices in selected business areas that only an executive could order.

9.2.6 Allocating Budget

The enterprise assessment and the resulting deployment plan form the basis for the Year 2000 budgeting process. The CFO uses the results of the analysis to build Year 2000 funding requirements into multiyear budget cycles. This process requires an executive mandate to gather and assimilate data in an orderly fashion.

A major problem with large IT organizations is that many executives do not understand the Year 2000 issue and related budget allocation process. If executives do not take budget allocation into consideration quickly, they will find themselves in a reactive budgeting mode, which will be their undoing when the board demands an explanation for inaction—around 1998 or sooner.

9.2.7 Communicating Policy

Senior executives must work with the CIO and advisory board to articulate a clear solution to the board of directors, corporate shareholders, and financial analysts. This communication includes a description of the problem, the chosen solution, budgetary requirements, and contingency plans. How much of this information is communicated to external sources is up to the senior executives to define as part of the overall strategy.

Sponsorship implies solid leadership and good common sense. It is, therefore, important that senior executives not assume that the year 2000 can be addressed through last-minute heroics, acquisition of third-party software, or a massive outsourcing effort. Proper sponsorship and ultimate ownership of the Year 2000 project centers around shared accountability for the problem. This concept must be communicated from the top of the organization in order to succeed.

9.3 Year 2000: An Evolutionary Planning Process

The Year 2000 planning process requires iterative refinement of the information that is gathered, it can be compared to peeling an onion one layer at a time. The planning process is based on the multiple levels of analysis required to determine the breadth and depth of the problem. For example, it may take several attempts to discover which systems are currently running in production and how these systems interrelate. Until all systems, platforms, and interfaces are identified, which takes a great deal of detective work, the breadth of the problem is unknown. Gathering 70 to 80 percent of this information, however, can provide enough of a baseline to draft an initial plan that can be refined later.

Similarly, the complexity of the problem is not fully revealed until each system is assessed in detail—a process that is deferred until the system upgrade process actually begins. This detailed analysis is not completed during early enterprise planning for two reasons. First, it takes an inordinate amount of time to gather and assimilate system-level date utilization at an enterprise level. Second, this detailed level of information becomes outdated soon after it is collected because it may not be required until a year or more down the road when upgrade work on a given system actually begins. Even the enterprise assessment, covered in depth in Chapter 12, is typically performed in phases if system upgrade efforts cannot wait for a complete enterprise analysis.

Once IT-related information has been gathered, business planners review business strategies to help refine Year 2000 deployment plans. For example, a system that appears to be an obvious candidate for date field expansion may be deferred, based on input from business planning specialists. It is common for these planning specialists to provide input later in the project that differs from that provided during initial analysis. This reinforces the truism that, in an IT environment, the only constant is change. This volatile situation, coupled with a layered discovery and analysis process, requires iterative and evolutionary planning.

Evolutionary planning tends to stymie management's need to know exactly how big the Year 2000 problem is, how long it will take to fix it, and how much it will cost. Of course, management must have this budgetary analysis immediately. This is one of the most difficult challenges in the evolutionary Year 2000 planning process. It also has a direct effect on the budgeting process. (Budgeting and assessment techniques are discussed in great detail in Chapters 10 and 12.) During the sponsorship procurement phase of the project, however, it is important to set management's expectations as to how the plan, the budget, and the implementation process evolve throughout the Year 2000 initiative.

9.3.1 Budgeting—The Rolling Accuracy Concept

Budgeting for Year 2000 projects is an evolutionary process. The industry has established a cost-per-line figure as a way of estimating gross budget requirements for addressing the problem. These numbers, which range between $1 to $2 per line of code, are useful for establishing general estimates during the early budgeting process. Lines of code figures reflect total lines for all programs, database definitions, control languages, screen definitions, and related components. The problem with using these numbers is that each organization is unique in terms of system types and supporting infrastructures, which causes a given organization to fluctuate dramatically from standard industry estimates.

For example, actual historic costs for a Year 2000 project range between $.60 to $4 per line of code. Again, differences may be based on services or tools used, in-house process maturity levels, learning curves, system complexity, and infrastructure quality. Ranges can vary by even greater margins. The United States Department of Defense (DOD), for example, estimates that command and control systems will cost from $1 to $8.52 per line of code. This leaves organizations with little recourse to use any figures other than the $1 to $2 per line of code metric for initial budget analysis.

Even these figures are too broad for accurate planning purposes. Imagine telling a CFO to set aside between $40 million and $80 million for this project over the next 3 years. This may be a good estimate on day 1 of the project, but is not a good number going forward. The good news is that these wide cost variations exist only until the situation is examined in more depth. We call this the rolling accuracy budget concept because organizations do not know what they must fix, or how they will fix it, until they look more closely at the problem.

9.3.2 Multiphased Budgeting Strategy

Gross budget estimates, based on lines of code, suffice as a way to gain executive awareness. Organizations using these statistics beyond the early planning stage run a risk of measuring the project against unrealistic numbers. Actual Year 2000 costs must evolve through various stages of the enterprise planning cycle. Actual costs fall into two categories: the enterprise budget and the migration budget. Enterprise costs are linked to project mobilization, cross-enterprise analysis, and asset acquisitions that span system ownership boundaries. Migration costs are directly linked to converting various upgrade units (segmented units of work) over the life of the project.

Enterprise costs include project definition and mobilization, methods deployment, enterprise assessment, the inventory process, planning, tool management, ongoing coordination, budget evolution, system software upgrades, and hardware appropriation. Enterprise costs, contrary to popular belief, must be spread across the life of a Year 2000 project and are not just expenditures linked to the startup phase of the project. Many of these costs, which include conferences, meetings, phone research, vendor sessions, and executive discussions on awareness, are not stated in bottom-line budgets. This may be a politically astute maneuver but does not reflect actual expenditures for the project. The bottom line on enterprise costing is that a separate set of budget line items should be allocated to plan, control, and manage Year 2000 projects.

Upgrade unit costs are determined by using metrics captured during the inventory process and are refined over time. Migration approaches for upgrade units include the procedural workaround, partial or full date field expansion, a package upgrade, data migration, integration, and deactivation projects. Each project involves unique tasks and a distinct set of activity-based cost models. These models represent project planning templates that allow project managers to assign hours for each activity, based on quantitative and qualitative metrics collected from each unit of work to be upgraded. These metrics can be adjusted as needed, based on resource constraints and other environmental factors.

Initial enterprise and migration cost models reflect early approximations. These models, once established, can be refined as more information is collected about the systems and supporting infrastructures. These cost models provide project managers with realistic project planning templates and work estimates against which projects can be managed. These templates are not available when one applies the line of code metrics that are typically used to establish initial budget figures. It is unrealistic to believe that a line of code, or a date metric for that matter, could ever approximate such a complex set of project planning requirements.

9.3.3 Selection of Strategies by System

As alluded to in section 9.3.2, *Multiphased Budgeting Strategy*, every system may need to be positioned under a unique strategy within the scope of an overall Year 2000 project. Management cannot assume that the preferred or approved approach will suffice for every system in a shop. Many systems may need to undergo date field expansion, if this is the established standard, but certain systems may require a procedural workaround because of resource constraints. Even within a system, multiple approaches may apply.

Other strategies, such as eliminating duplicate systems and transferring users to other in-house applications, could save millions in unnecessary conversion costs. Packages and system software also require unique approaches. Once a system is identified, IT and business analysts must review that system to determine the exact approach, resources, budget, and time frames required to accommodate the year 2000. Only in this way can organizations be reasonably sure that expenditures are maximized and that the project will be a success.

9.4 Formal Process to Address Year 2000

It is too late for organizations to use trial-and-error approaches in defining a process for addressing the Year 2000 problem. Clear-headed planning and the use of a formal method facilitates the creation of cost-effective and readily implementable solutions. Inventing solutions, either centrally or project by project, is too time consuming for a project with such a near-term and unforgiving due date. Because virtually all solution providers, consulting firms, and outsourcing companies claim that they have a Year 2000 methodology, we discuss the differences between the various types of methods available by describing what components should be included in a Year 2000 methodology and how those components apply to a given project. Although the market uses many terms to describe a process to guide the performance of Year 2000-related work, we selected the term "methodology" to refer to all types of "methods," "blueprints" or "processes." These terms are used interchangeably throughout this text.

The attributes that constitute a given methodology or that are noticeably absent tell quite a bit about the usefulness of that methodology. Figure 9.3 depicts various attributes that a methodology would necessarily need in order to support Year 2000 projects. It also lists the different project types, or scenarios, that fall under a Year 2000 initiative. To position the use of formal methods within this text, we discuss these attributes, the project scenarios that a Year 2000 methodology must support, and the types of methodologies available in the market.

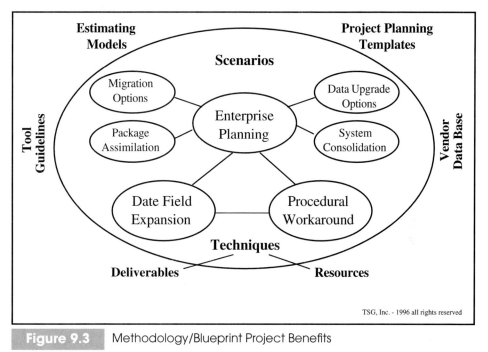

Figure 9.3   Methodology/Blueprint Project Benefits

9.4.1 Methodological Components

Those familiar with formal methodologies will recognize the various attributes listed in Figure 9.3. Techniques are the detailed guidelines that define what a given task is to accomplish and how it does so. Most methodologies have a myriad of techniques organized into individual tasks. Various levels of decomposition, depending on the type and maturity of the method, group these tasks. Each task has associated deliverables and resource requirements that constrain the scope of that task and help define who should perform it. Lack of deliverable definitions for each task is a clear sign of an immature methodology.

Other components of a commercially available methodology include tool guidelines, to augment the generic techniques, and a vendor database that analysts can use to identify and procure the tools that support the method. Estimating models are critical to any method that is to be used on high-volume projects. Other attributes of a mature methodology include metric definitions, forms, meta-model definitions, and project planning templates. Project planning templates combine estimating guidelines, by task, within the framework of a given project type, also called a scenario. A template is essentially a starting point for project planners. In a Year 2000 project, where literally hundreds of project plans can be required over a multiyear period, prepackaged project plans could save hundreds of hours in research and menial planning tasks. Templates are derived directly from a given scenario.

9.4.2 Scenarios

Scenarios facilitate rapid analysis and implementation of Year 2000-related requirements. A scenario identifies a unique path through a methodology to accommodate project-specific objectives. By grouping individual tasks drawn from a generic methodological framework, scenarios deliver initial project planning templates that can be customized as needed for a given environment and project.

Prepackaged planning templates make a methodology applicable to a variety of situations while limiting overall training requirements. Learning curves are shortened because a scenario allows a project manager to construct a project plan directly from the template. The steps in the project plan then provide the implementation team direct references to the detailed techniques needed to guide implementation work. Each template, which includes detailed task guidelines, deliverables, estimating models, tool references, and resource requirements, forms the foundation for a detailed project plan and implementation guide. Figure 9.3 lists several types of scenarios that are used within the context of a Year 2000 initiative.

The enterprise assessment scenario includes guidelines for project mobilization, preplanning setup, inventory, portfolio segmentation, project prioritization, and deployment plan development. Central control and coordination, along with infrastructure setup guidelines, are also incorporated into this scenario. Implementation scenarios include date field expansion and procedural workaround templates. Each of these scenarios includes detailed analysis, system upgrade, and validation guidelines for conversion projects for individual upgrade units. Related scenarios support alternative migration options, standalone data store upgrades, package assimilation efforts, and system consolidation projects.

9.4.3 The Role of a Methodology in Year 2000 Projects

Some organizations have misconceptions about the value and role of a methodology in a Year 2000 effort. One misconception is assuming that an outsourcing vendor should have a method in place for conversion work but not recognizing that there should also be a method for the in-house project work connected with testing and implementation. Another mistake is assuming that a method is required for the implementation phase of the project but not for the enterprise planning phase. The planning component requires a methodological approach as much as the implementation phases require one.

Another misconception is that only consultants require a method and that in-house personnel should just go along with whatever is suggested. This is a very serious mistake; the client does not have the understanding of the process used by the consultant and is unable to determine if steps are being skipped, if deliverables are being missed, or if the right approach is being used. Having access to the consultant's methodology also allows in-house personnel to work independently from consultants on projects—an ability that will become a requirement as projects progress.

Inventing a Year 2000 solution within such a limited time frame makes very little sense. Jumpstarting a project by using a well-defined set of guidelines is a much more effective way of using the skills of in-house personnel. As tool research continues, organizations should look to the methods on the market that contain tool guidelines and vendor databases as a way to shorten the tool analysis cycle in which many find themselves.

9.4.4 Available Year 2000 Methodologies

Various types of methodologies are available containing many different features. If a methodology is sold as a commercial off-the-shelf (COTS) product, as opposed to a consultant's handbook, the likelihood is that it will be more robust, more complete, and more useful for Year 2000 projects. Off-the-shelf methodologies are packaged in a way that facilitates quick access to information. These products typically include graphics and hypertext access to guidelines, spreadsheet forms, and other components. A COTS product should also include solid documentation and use of process management technology.

Process management tools provide a way to bridge methodological tasks and planning templates to project management tools. They also provide a vehicle for estimating project level of effort and for tracking activity by various team members throughout the life of a project. Chapter 15, which discusses supporting tools and technologies, provides more detailed information on process management tools.

The consultant's handbook concept assumes that consultants can figure out how to use a methodology—but few others can. Surprisingly, few organizations actually check a consulting company's claim to having a Year 2000 methodology and instead fall victim to a good marketing presentation. The true test of knowing how good a method is, and if it really exists, is to ask to see it. If one cannot be produced or consists of a binder full of paper, then assume it will not serve the needs of the project team. If, on the other hand, the methodology is a fully packaged on-line product, it is more likely to meet an organization's needs.

Historically, few organizations have actually used methodologies as an integral part of the education, planning, and implementation process. Those that wish to expedite Year 2000 project implementation, however, should consider reversing this trend.

9.5 Getting Started on the Right Foot

As discussed in this chapter, successful Year 2000 projects must get started properly and stay on track. Solid sponsorship, defining the executive's role early in a project, recognizing the need for evolving a budget through several steps, and using a formal process all contribute to launching and sustaining a successful Year 2000 project. Chapter 10, *The Year 2000 Budget*, and Chapter 11, *Year 2000 Project Mobilization*, continue to expand the discussion of ways to ensure that projects are successfully launched with the proper foundation in place.

Chapter 10

The Year 2000 Budget

This chapter describes the process of creating a budget for an enterprisewide, Year 2000 initiative. The size and generally nebulous scope of the problem make the process of creating an accurate budget in a single pass impossible. We therefore describe a strategy of building a budget that can be refined over time as more information is obtained about the systems that are at risk. This strategy allows an organization to continue refining each phase of the Year 2000 process, while adjusting funding requirements at well-defined checkpoints. As stated in earlier chapters, this process may appear somewhat foreign to many executives, but is necessary when planning an enterprise-level Year 2000 initiative.

This chapter introduces various Year 2000 budget models, compares and contrasts the value of each approach, outlines how to build an evolving budget model, and provides details on how to finalize a Year 2000 budget by means of a concept called the activity-based cost model. Finally, the chapter closes with a discussion on how to validate and refine budget figures through pilot projects and early project results.

10.1 Year 2000 Budget Models and Costing Techniques

Several methods can be used to develop a Year 2000 budget. The first and most commonly used budgeting technique is the line of code estimating approach. The second approach uses tools to scan for date occurrences and calculate estimated level of effort based on date and system component metrics. The last approach, which is typically applied once upgrade units have been identified, uses activity-based costing techniques. Each of these three approaches provides varying degrees of value within certain phases of the budgeting process. These approaches, however, can also be counterproductive when positioned incorrectly in the budget cycle.

10.1.1 Cost Per Line Budget Model

The industry has settled on a high-level approach for determining Year 2000 costs. This approach is based on estimates that relate to a line of code metric. As stated in prior chapters, the industry believes that it will cost an organization between $1 to $2 per line of source code to upgrade systems to Year 2000 compliance. This is an aggregate number and not scientifically based when viewed in light of the wide variety of migration strategies available. Nevertheless, this approach is a default budgeting tactic for the many companies that have not performed a detailed assessment on their systems. The line of code estimating technique is particularly useful in scenarios that are similar to the following example.

Senior management wants an IT planning team to assess the level of exposure and the related cost to correct the Year 2000 problem. The team reviews industry literature and discovers the line of code estimating approach. Intuition tells the IT management team analyzing the issue that more detailed analysis is needed to create a true estimate for fixing the problem. Executive management, however, wants to obtain these numbers quickly to begin setting aside budget dollars across several years. To accommodate this short-term demand, the IT planning team performs a cursory inventory of applications and determines that they have roughly 50 million lines of production code. Further analysis suggests that there may be another 2 million lines of user-developed software. The team puts together a recommendation that includes an initial estimate of Year 2000 related costs as follows:

1. *Fifty million lines of code are identified in a very preliminary survey of applications.*

2. *Two million additional lines of code are estimated to exist in the user domain.*

3. *IT team builds assumptions that only 85 percent of portfolio requires date adjustments.*

4. *Thus, 44,200,000 lines belong to programs that will require correction.*

5. *From preliminary survey results, the IT team determines that standard languages and hardware platforms should keep costs at the low end of standard scale.*

6. *IT team assigns a $1 to $1.50 per line estimate to 85 percent of portfolio.*

7. *Executive management receives a report stating that it will require between $44 million to $66 million to correct the Year 2000 problem.*

8. *IT team requests initial funding of $1 million to perform an accurate survey of portfolio, refine an economic model, and proceed with two or three pilot projects.*

The scenario described above is fairly common within a majority of large IT environments. Executive management needs a rough budget estimate in order to establish a Year 2000 fund or to determine how much of the current budget can be reallocated to accommodate at least some of the planning and conversion work that is required in the near term. This may not be considered ideal in terms of meeting accurate budget goals, but it is a starting point that organizations can use to initiate a project.

This budget scenario helps highlight the following strengths of the cost per line budget model:

- Cost per line of code figures are derived from early Year 2000 conversion cost analyses on individual systems that, when extrapolated, provide reasonable costing guidelines.

- Establishing an estimated line of code metric does not require extensive research by the Year 2000 planning teams.

- Calculating a cost per line of code estimate for executives provides them with a simple metric that requires little explanation.

- Line of code cost models are supported by research from the Gartner Group and other consultants and analysts.

- There is no faster way to build a Year 2000 cost estimate than to survey total lines of code and calculate a cost per line range based on industry figures.

The cost per line of code estimating technique also has a downside. Anyone who has managed projects in complex IT environments can attest to the fact that no single metric or overly simplified cost model can be used to manage numerous projects with any degree of certainty. The line of code budget model includes the following flaws or weaknesses:

- Cost per line figures apply a conversion cost model that omits enterprise planning, coordination, management, infrastructure upgrade, and tool acquisition expenditures.

- Each organization, with its unique environment, can expect dramatic fluctuations in cost estimates from standard industry figures on a given project.

- Nonstandard languages or platforms, lack of tools or tool knowledge, personnel issues, in-house versus outsourcing plans, resource limitations, or other issues vary widely.

- Cost per line figures assume a single approach that may not accommodate procedural workarounds, variations on date expansion, package upgrades, system software, duplicate system elimination, or any of a variety of other Year 2000 options.

- Organizational maturity can generate wide cost variations based on project management errors, process maturity, commitment to success, and motivational factors.

- Testing infrastructures, or lack thereof, can have a significant impact on project costs where testing is normally considered half of the effort in a Year 2000 upgrade.

- Public sector restrictions, including RFP requirements, procurement restrictions, or personnel contracting may drive costs up beyond the standard model.

Building and tuning the line of code cost model should take into account the aforementioned strengths and weaknesses. Some of these factors can be accommodated, whereas others cannot. General guidelines for line of code costing include the following items:

- Base the costs on total lines of source code for all components found in an IT systems environment.

- Include the following as components: source programs, copied or included code, macros, screens, database or data file definitions, and control languages.

- Take into account duplicate or missing source code.

- Do not include in the line of code count systems that are not in production.

- Collect line estimates by system, and subsystem if applicable, and then total the estimates to obtain an enterprisewide figure.

- Include mainframe, midrange, client/server, and PC line counts.

- For systems that use screen painters that generate only object code (versus source code), estimate by using the number of lines depicted on the screen.

- Do not attempt to gather exact line of code counts because this is virtually impossible at a cursory level.

- Temper cost per line based on current industry numbers and unique figures associated with specific industries. For example, missile systems cost more than payroll systems.

- Temper cost figures based on in-house weaknesses in testing, process maturity, configuration control or the fact that one is dealing with a government entity.

  Note: Process maturity measures can be derived from the Software Engineering Institute (SEI) Capability Maturity Model (CMM); Chapter 8 discusses a variety of process maturity issues.

- Use different multipliers for line of code cost for different system types if there is a wide degree of diversity in a portfolio.

Table 10.1 depicts a high-level, line of code cost summary for an enterprise, based on lines of code found within the systems portfolio.

Note that budget figures vary according to the type of system. Also note that application packages and system software upgrades are assigned a migration cost figure based on methods other than a line of code count. This level of budget planning requires research into the system itself, support requirements, and future plans for that system. Although time frames may restrict this level of research, it is strongly recommended in order to reflect realistic Year 2000 costs.

Table 10.1 Year 2000—Initial Line of Code Estimate

System Area	Platform	Lines of Code	Cost / Line	Projected Cost
Financial	IBM / 3GL	8 million	$1 / line	$8 million
H/R system	IBM / 3GL	Package/2 million	N/A	$500,000 upgrade
Inventory	IBM / 3GL	3 million	$1 / line	$3 million
Process contro	M/R / 2G	1 million	$3 / line	$3 million
Order entry	IBM / 4GL	2 million	$2.50 / line	$5 million
System software	IBM / 2GL	Packages	N/A	$3 million upgrade
etc............	etc............	etc............	etc............	etc............
All systems	Multiple	25 million	Variable	$32 million
2GL/3GL/4GL = 2nd/3rd/4th generation languages			N/A = not applicable	

Line of code estimates should be applied at an individual level across a systems portfolio.

Enterprise coordination and planning, tools, hardware upgrades, and other factors are not reflected in the line of code figure. In order to attain a reasonably accurate estimate during the early Year 2000 budgeting phase, planning teams should add in these enterprise costs as overhead items. A reasonable approach for estimating overhead costs is to take the total system upgrade estimate for all application software, packages, and system software and increase the estimate by 10 percent. This 10 percent figure includes estimates for enterprise-level project management, software tools, excess computing power and storage facilities, external interface management, infrastructure adjustments, and other overhead costs. From the budget total derived in Table 10.1, the new total estimate, including overhead costs, is derived below.

$32.0 million
+ $3.2 million (10% of $32 million)
$35.2 million

Whether 10 percent or a lower percentage is used as an overhead figure depends on testing infrastructures, process maturity, percentage of hardware utilization at current levels, current level of configuration and change control, and other factors that may even include the internal political climate. The line of code estimate facilitates rapid initial budget planning efforts and becomes more valuable if a degree of reality is overlaid on basic estimating formulae.

10.1.2 Cost Per Date Budget Model

The concept of identifying and applying a per date cost model is another approach to estimating Year 2000 costs. The value of this model is directly linked to the ability to accurately and rapidly collect this information from the systems that are being assessed. Accuracy and efficiency hinge on the use of software tools that can scan or parse source code and provide a concise analysis of the number of dates and how they are used within a system. Many organizations are using this analysis capability as the basis of their Year 2000 cost estimates. While this approach certainly has value, it should not be applied in a vacuum.

The cost per date model is based on a variety of proprietary algorithms that are used by a number of impact analysis software tools. Chapter 15 and Appendix A provide more information on specific software tool categories and tools. These tools vary in terms of commercial availability, platform support, completeness, language support, date field tracing ability, extrapolation techniques, and algorithm flexibility. Table 10.2 lists a subset of some of the system attributes that impact-analysis tools capture and use in building a cost per date cost model.

Table 10.2 Year 2000—Cost Per Date Estimating Model

Component Name / Type	# Procedural Dates	# Nonprocedural Dates	Total Dates Identified	Approach	Projected Cost*
IV0011/PGM	167	787	954	EXPAND	
IV0012/MAP	N/A	7	7	EXPAND	
IV0099/PGM	56	1511	1567	EXPAND	
IV0018/PGM	112	1519	1631	EXPAND	
DB0012/PSB	N/A	11	11	EXPAND	
IV0018/COPY	N/A	7	7	EXPAND	
DB0012/PGM	51	568	619	EXPAND	
ETC......					
TOTALS					

N/A = not applicable   *Adjustable cost formula takes into account approach, lines of code, etc.

This is a generic cost model. Typical tool reports include lines of code, percent date usage, algorithms applied, and other factors gathered from a system.

Planning teams that apply an impact analysis tool to a system or to an entire portfolio must consider the following requirements:

- **Language applicability across a system and the portfolio.** If a tool cannot examine an entire system, it may not be adequate for costing that system.

- **Component coverage analysis.** Tools must look beyond programs and examine screen maps, data store definitions, control languages, and other system components that use dates.

- **Ability to modify cost algorithms to adjust resulting metrics to specific environments.** For example, testing cost has a close relationship to the number of data stores in a system.

- **Completeness in terms of capturing nonobvious date references.** Analysts should not rely on a software tool that cannot trace date field usage and that uses only field names to find date fields.

- **Reliability.** Analysts should consider these two points: how much code has been processed by a tool and vendor's ability to estimate level of effort and related upgrade costs.

Because of widespread disparity in impact tool features, organizations must take care in how these tools are applied. The specific tool selected is less critical than rapid tool selection and, if applicable, rapid selection of third-party assistance to perform the analysis. There are clear pluses and minuses to using a cost per date approach. The cost per date budget model has strengths in the following areas:

- Cost analysis of one or more upgrade units can be greatly expedited through automated scanning technology and cost calculations.

- In theory, costs for similarly sized upgrade units can be estimated by extrapolating costs from other upgrade units that have already been analyzed by the cost per date approach.

- Consistency can be maintained across a large portfolio by applying the same costing algorithms to many systems via automated analysis techniques.

As with any budgeting approach, there are also downsides. The cost per date estimating technique has the following flaws or weaknesses:

- Cost per date models, depending on the product used, may not consider non-conversion-related tasks such as testing, implementation, or project management.

- If a tool cannot analyze all of the components or language types in a given system, the resulting analysis will yield inaccurate or incomplete results.

- The accuracy of the estimate is highly dependent on the amount of customer tuning to tool parameters.

- Estimating algorithms will vary depending on whether they are developed by software vendors or service firms.

- The number of date occurrences do not have an overwhelming impact on project costs because, on average, a fairly predictable and consistent percentage of system components must be analyzed, upgraded, tested, bridged, and returned to production.

A usage scenario for the cost per date cost model includes the following general guidelines:

1. *Inventory and identify individual upgrade units to be migrated.*

2. *Systematically run the impact analyzer against each upgrade unit to assess migration costs.*

3. *Adjust impact analysis estimates to accommodate additional factors, such as testing costs or other items, that the impact analysis tool did not consider in its initial estimate.*

4. *Add the total migration costs, derived for each upgrade unit, to determine the complete migration costs for the enterprise.*

There are some final general guidelines that should be followed in order to avoid the misuse of impact analysis tools and the cost per date estimating model. First, analysts should apply the cost per date model as an estimating technique only where the environment, the tools, and the skills are readily available for the scale of analysis required. For example, companies should not attempt to run a 50-million-line mainframe portfolio through a PC-based impact analyzer.

Second, companies should avoid using the cost per date cost model until actual upgrade units are segmented and a migration approach has been identified. Applying the cost per date cost model in this way follows a logical progression of tasks that determines whether an upgrade unit is a candidate for a Year 2000 upgrade before including that upgrade unit in an estimate. Finally, blind application of an impact analyzer during the inventory phase of a project is a huge waste of time, given that the absolute number of upgrade projects, approaches, infrastructure issues, and other variables are all unknown at that point.

One final note for organizations making exclusive use of the cost per date model. The 10 percent overhead figure used for upwardly adjusting the cost per line budget model should also be applied to the total cost per date migration estimate.

10.1.3 Activity-Based Cost Budget Model

This model is derived from the simple concept that each project has a given set of tasks and that each task can be assigned a given level of effort. Total level of effort, once quantified, is used to ascertain total costs based on in-house or external billing rates. Activity-based costing of a Year 2000 project is the most sophisticated, and therefore least utilized, costing technique available. The activity-based cost model is based on project planning techniques. Tasks associated with a given conversion project are identified, estimated, and totaled to assess the overall cost of migrating a given upgrade unit. These cost models are essentially project planning templates that can be used to manage a project through the implementation phase. These templates reflect what work must actually be performed to complete a project and, therefore, the actual costs for that project.

A reluctance to use these models typically stems from the following factors:

- A lack of knowledge of activity-based costing techniques
- Unavailability of project planning templates from which to derive estimates
- Unclear definition of tasks, deliverables, and resources needed to complete a project
- Indifference to the need for accurate costing based on the tasks to be performed
- Unwillingness to collect the metrics to generate the cost models and related estimates
- Inability to automate the creation and utilization of these templates in process management and project management tools

These concerns, if raised by management team members, are typically a warning sign that the organization may lack the ability to apply proper project management methods to the Year 2000 project. If this is the case, outside consulting help should be retained to help manage implementation projects.

Costing these activities under the activity-based cost model requires an understanding of the projects to be performed in a Year 2000 initiative. These projects minimally include enterprise planning, date field expansion, data migration, procedural workaround, and package upgrade projects. Many organizations may require hybrid versions of these project scenarios. Once these basic scenarios have been defined, planning templates containing tasks, deliverables, estimates, and resource requirements must be established for ongoing use across the enterprise.

These planning templates require certain metrics in order to complete and finalize the estimating models. Metrics are derived from component counts across a portfolio and across each upgrade unit to be migrated. These components include source programs, macros, copy or include members, database definitions, control languages, screen definitions, and other components impacted by the year 2000. Specific estimating models are defined in section 10.3 *Phase II: Year 2000 Enterprise Budget* and section 10.4 *Phase III: Year 2000 Implementation Budget*.

The activity-based cost budget model has strengths in the following areas:

- This approach reflects the actual work to be completed and therefore more accurately reflects the true cost of a project.

- As a Year 2000 upgrade effort progresses across a portfolio, experience can be used to adjust estimates and related costs for upgrade units yet to be converted.

- At the upgrade unit level, these models more readily reflect work to be completed. For example, a line of code cost model cannot be used to estimate a vendor package upgrade.

- A given cost model can be adjusted to fit unique circumstances of an upgrade unit. For example, if special date conversion requirements exist, these can be added as tasks in the work plan.

- A wide variety of planning templates can be included in the budget plan that would not be available under other cost models. These include special migration projects, retirement or consolidation projects, or other options that arise as part of an overall solution.

The activity-based cost budget model has the following flaws or weaknesses:

- The effort to collect the metrics and customize planning templates could exceed time frames associated with other cost models.

- Implementation costing requires a solid understanding of the systems portfolio and the strategies selected for each of the systems included in various upgrade units.

- Managers could apply project planning templates at face value and not spend the time to customize the task structure according to the approach being applied to a given upgrade unit.

- Companies with limited experience in following formal processes may not see the value of, or may not properly apply, project planning templates and related cost models.

- Because every organization is unique, project planning templates themselves must be customized to fit a given IT group's approach.

- The learning curve associated with acquiring and learning how to use process and project management tools could delay project startup by a few days.

A usage scenario for the activity-based cost budget model includes the following general guidelines.

1. *Identify and, if needed, obtain commercially available process management and project management tools.*

2. *Examine requirements to either build or obtain a process to perform Year 2000 planning and implementation work. Refer to section 9.4,* Formal Process to Address Year 2000 *for more information on this topic.*

3. *Build an enterprise planning budget based on work tasks required to assess the Year 2000 problem and to build a plan to address it. Appendix A lists commercially available methodologies.*

4. *Capture relevant system metrics as input to creating the implementation cost model. Techniques used to define the enterprise plan guide analysts through this process.*

5. *Examine each upgrade unit to determine the approach required to make it Year 2000 compliant.*

6. *Create or customize a project planning template to support the approaches selected in point 5. This may include date field expansion, procedural*

workaround, package upgrade, system consolidation, database migration, or other project types.

7. *Review each upgrade unit to verify that the information gathered during the enterprise assessment is complete enough to build an activity-based cost model for that unit.*

8. *Adjust task list and estimating formulae in the project planning templates being used to create the cost models for various upgrade units.*

9. *Calculate work effort, by task, for each upgrade unit and multiply total hours by the average rate per hour for the organization.*

10. *Total all upgrade unit estimates across the enterprise to obtain aggregate Year 2000 implementation costs.*

Activity-based costing seems to work best for organizations that are more mature in the area of process utilization. If the practice of project management is a well-defined discipline and process management is an accepted concept, an organization has a much better chance of succeeding with this approach. If, on the other hand, these concepts are foreign or intimidating, it may be better to let third-party service providers develop this portion of the budget model, or to use the budget models introduced earlier in this chapter.

10.1.4 Applying Various Year 2000 Cost Models

Because each of the three Year 2000 cost models discussed thus far have degrees of merit depending on circumstances, it is important to distinguish where and when to apply each of them. These cost models can be used independently or in conjunction with each other at various phases of the Year 2000 budget cycle. Shifting from one model to another as one progresses through this cycle is common and, in most cases, necessary. Including all relevant tasks and supporting expense items, attaching a reasonably derived estimate to each of these items, and allocating costs appropriately across functional areas are key factors in building a successful Year 2000 budget.

The following sections outline how to use the Year 2000 cost models at each phase of an evolving budget cycle. These phases include the Year 2000 mobilization budget, the enterprise-level budget, and the implementation budget. It is important that planning teams carefully manage each phase of the budgeting process to avoid omitting key budget items or dealing with those budget items inappropriately.

10.2 Phase I: Year 2000 Mobilization Budget

Project mobilization is a gray area of the budgeting process where organizations tend to omit certain front-end tasks that should be included as an enterprise cost. Typically, this omission occurs because management has not bought into the Year 2000 problem or the need to establish a comprehensive solution. Managers may find themselves performing many unbudgeted tasks in order to gather statistics, assess scope, obtain free advice, build a business case, and sell this business case to the executive team. These setup activities, which may take up to a year or more to complete and consume hundreds of thousands of dollars of unallocated funds, can become an exercise in futility without proper sponsorship.

When those chartered with Year 2000 analysis determine that a project startup phase is mired in a seemingly endless justification loop, they must communicate the need to establish a mobilization project and related budget. The mobilization budget is typically funded by money that has been reallocated from existing budget categories to enable a team to put an actual budget in place.

The mobilization tasks that must be budgeted for include the following items:

- Assembling a working team of three to four people for a 1 to 2 month mobilization project

- Performing a quick inventory to develop a rough estimate of portfolio size

- Creating a risk analysis for mission-critical systems

- Developing a per line cost estimate for the portfolio as a way of creating a rough total projected budget

- Establishing an enterprise assessment plan, time frame, and related budget

- Meeting with service providers to review options for performing an enterprise assessment

- Reviewing tools (and related costs) that may be used by in-house or consulting personnel to perform the enterprise assessment

- Communicating the Year 2000 issue and proposed solution options to the Year 2000 advisory committee

The deliverables from the Year 2000 mobilization project, which should be completed no more than 2 months after the project start, include the following:

- A summary of the high-level inventory effort, including total systems, a total line of code estimate, and a general platform summary

- A high-level risk assessment of mission-critical systems identifying a worst case scenario for the organization if these systems fail

- Projected total cost range for a Year 2000 upgrade, using the cost per line budget model

- An enterprise assessment work plan and related cost estimate

- The enterprise assessment infrastructure, including analysis tools, process and project management tools, a methodology, forms, communication tools, and workstations

- Recommendations for staffing and empowering a Year 2000 Project Office and advisory board

- A high-level summary of the recommended Year 2000 implementation strategy

The total cost of mobilization varies but must minimally include the equivalent of 4-6 person months of time and the cost of supporting components. These components include a methodology, as a guide to building an enterprise plan and proposed implementation strategy, and the enterprise assessment work environment. This environment includes an electronic mail capability, repository or database to store assessment data, spreadsheet, word processor, and presentation technology. Analysts should assume that mobilization costs will total roughly $100,000 to $200,000 if no tools exist. If these tools are in place and people are already trained in the use of these tools, the costs are likely to be lower.

Another factor that drives up mobilization costs is the level of risk assessment performed. Risk analysis, to determine maximum exposure of mission-critical systems, is generally performed during the enterprise assessment. It is common, however, for management to request a summary of the financial and legal risks as a means of justifying a Year 2000 project. If this is the case, the guidelines for enterprise assessment risk analysis (found in Chapter 12) should be applied to the top 5 to 10 percent of mission-critical systems. This should include systems used to obtain revenue or retain customers or that have a direct link to corporate survival. Extra analysis time and funding should be allocated as needed.

RFPs are not listed as deliverables because we contend that formal RFP creation should be avoided wherever possible. Year 2000 delivery time frames preclude the addition of extraneous tasks to the project time line. We consider RFP development a waste of precious time that organizations can ill afford. If RFP development is unavoidable, the RFP should be added to the deliverable list, budgeted as one extra person for 2–3 months, and completed by following a formal methodology. The RFP, in this case, focuses on the enterprise assessment project itself. If one or more pilot projects are to be started during the same general time frame as the enterprise assessment, these pilots should be identified as separate line items in the RFP. Running a pilot project in parallel with an enterprise assessment may be necessary for large shops that are behind schedule with a Year 2000 initiative.

The mobilization budget is a critical element of the Year 2000 startup process and a phase during which many organizations tend to struggle. This struggle can be alleviated by formalizing the mobilization process, budgeting for it appropriately, and establishing a basic framework for the team to move forward. The Year 2000 team itself can be expanded or adjusted as needed during the early phases of the enterprise planning process. There is some flexibility for management to defer some of the costs of the mobilization process to the enterprise planning phase, as long as project mobilization is viewed as a formal line item in the overall budgeting process.

10.3 Phase II: Year 2000 Enterprise Budget

The enterprise budget defines funding requirements needed to scope, plan, and coordinate a Year 2000 project across system and functional boundaries. The items to be included in the enterprise budget are startup costs (includes mobilization budget), infrastructure setup, method and tool acquisition and deployment, training, enterprise assessment, third-party coordination, central project management and tracking, budget management, and hardware appropriation. These costs must be spread across the life of a Year 2000 project.

One major line item in the enterprise budget is enterprise assessment. The assessment project is required to derive a realistic implementation plan. Table 10.3 depicts a sample project plan, using an activity-based cost model, for an enterprisewide Year 2000 assessment. In a large IT organization (more than 50 million lines of code), with highly distributed functions, this assessment may consume six to eight people for up to 4 months.

A portion of these costs reflects funding for the core project team; while remaining costs reflect time needed for subject matter experts from various support areas.

Table 10.3   Enterprise Planning Estimating Guidelines

Year 2000: Enterprise Planning Tasks	General Estimating Guidelines*
Build enterprise Year 2000 analysis plan Perform enterprisewide Year 2000 analysis	1 week for medium-sized shop 2 weeks for large shop
Categorize systems inventory Categorize systems inventory Summarize technological attributes Inventory enterprise physical systems Update technical summary legacy model	2-4 weeks for medium-sized shop with no prior inventory in place 4-8 weeks for large shop with no prior inventory in place
Analyze physical data architecture Detail enterprisewide physical data usage Load data usage into open repository	1-2 weeks for medium-sized shop 2-4 weeks for large shop
Establish Year 2000 upgrade units Analyze current business architecture Assess current IT project activities Create enterprise segmentation strategy	1-2 weeks for medium-sized shop 2-3 weeks for large shop
Finalize enterprise Year 2000 strategy Assess enterprise IT infrastructure issues Build enterprise project recommendations Finalize enterprise Year 2000 strategy	2-3 weeks for medium-sized shop 3-4 weeks for large shop *Assumes 4-6 person team for duration of project*

This high-end cost range is unique to large IT shops with systems, functions, and management distributed across multiple geographic regions. In extremely large and complex situations, trimming the breadth and the depth of deliverables allows an organization to reduce the duration and the cost of an enterprise assessment. Analysts should carefully assess requirements during the mobilization phase of the Year 2000 project in order to establish an acceptable time frame and an accurate budget for the enterprise assessment.

In addition to Year 2000 mobilization and the enterprise assessment project, other cost items must be included in the enterprise budget. A separate line item should be included for methods and tools, excess hardware requirements, infrastructure upgrades, and project coordination activities through the life of the project. Table 10.4 highlights these items in a sample enterprise budget summary for a medium-to-large IT organization.

As Table 10.4 suggests, the identification of individual budget items is critical in order to accurately reflect enterprise budget projections over a 3-year period. Method and tool costs are allocated to the enterprise budget because individual systems areas will be using these tools and techniques across functional boundaries. Excess hardware requirements are determined during the enterprise assessment, based on the deployment schedule, but can represent as much as a 10 to 20 percent increase over existing CPU and direct access storage device requirements. These costs represent peak numbers that tend to occur during the middle or later portions of the implementation and validation effort.

Table 10.4 Example: Year 2000 Enterprise Budget Summary

Year 2000: Enterprise Budget Items	Allocated Cost	Year
Mobilization effort	$ 100,000	1
Enterprise assessment project	650,000	1
Method and tool acquisition	350,000	1–2
Excess hardware expenditures	1,200,000	1–3
Infrastructure upgrade costs	1,600,000	1–3
Long-term coordination costs	1,000,000	2–4
Total enterprise expenditures	$4,900,000	1–4

Infrastructure costs vary dramatically, depending on the maturity of the configuration control, change control, and testing processes in a given area. If these items are found to be deficient during the enterprise assessment, special cleanup projects may be required to address these matters during the course of the project. Other infrastructure-related costs may be tied directly to updating old, yet critical, technologies. For example, an old teleprocessing monitor, compiler, database, or operating system may have to be eliminated or replaced if the systems are to survive the millennium. Initial estimates for these costs should be established and should be based on how well management believes the current support environment can function past 2000. Real costs may be finalized during the enterprise assessment effort.

Finally, long-term coordination of the Year 2000 project requires central control and management. This task includes project and interface tracking, internal communication, third-party coordination of vendors and service providers, external business entity coordination, and ongoing identification of non-IT based systems. Other centrally assigned activities include skills transfer in the areas of method and tool utilization, system upgrade activity, and validation tasks. The level of centrally assigned skills transfer varies by organization and project structure and must be finalized during the enterprise assessment.

It should be clear by now that the enterprise assessment, covered in depth in Chapter 12, provides much of the input into the Year 2000 enterprise budget. Organizations should strive, however, to establish the basic framework for the enterprise budget prior to the onset of actual enterprise assessment. Initial estimates can then be adjusted as analysis results become available. Once the enterprise assessment is completed, the enterprise-level budget can be integrated with the overall Year 2000 implementation budget for the organization.

10.4 Phase III: Year 2000 Implementation Budget

The implementation phase is the most costly component of a Year 2000 project. Every implementation project includes a project finalization step, detailed upgrade unit analysis, system upgrade activities, data migration, validation, and implementation. Project management costs are included as an overhead percentage for individual work tasks.

Any one of the three budget models can be applied to the creation of the implementation budget. The per line of code cost model becomes less valuable as more detail about a given upgrade unit is uncovered. The cost per date model has some merit, depending on the impact tool employed but has limits when the tool or supporting process omits estimates for various implementation tasks. The preferred choice is the activity-based cost model.

The activity-based cost model provides a direct link between initial budget analysis, project management, and project tracking. We have, therefore, applied the activity-based cost model as a means of defining implementation budget requirements. Secondary references to the cost per date model are included when applicable and as a means of validating activity-based cost models.

The implementation budget consists of a project plan and related cost summary for each upgrade unit. The enterprise assessment identifies individual upgrade units and estimates the effort and the cost required to make those upgrade units Year 2000 compliant. A sample budget summary appears in Table 10.5. For reference, assume that each system in Table 10.5 equates to an upgrade unit. This implementation budget summary applies a combination of estimating techniques and budget models. For example, systems under direct IT control, where automated analysis tools provide a wealth of system-related metrics, use an activity-based cost model. User-controlled systems, in this example, have optionally applied a line of code budget model.

In addition to identifying the activity-based cost model used to estimate a given upgrade unit, it is equally important to identify the scenario (refer to section 9.4.2 for more on scenarios) that defines the tasks within that model. In Table 10.5, for example, the activity-based cost model used to estimate upgrade costs for the Financial system applies the date field expansion scenario. The activity-based cost model for the Inventory system, however, applies the procedural workaround scenario. The H/R system uses a third type of activity-based costing scenario, the package upgrade, to derive the cost of making that system Year 2000 compliant. All of these systems use an activity-based cost model but differ in terms of the tasks defined within that cost model.

Table 10.5 Year 2000—Implementation Budget Summary

System Area	System Type	Costing Model	Scenario	Projected Cost
Financial	In-house	Activity Based	Date Expansion	$8 million
H/R system	Package	Activity Based	Package upgrade	$500,000 upgrade
Inventory	In-house	Activity Based	Workaround	$3 million
Process control	Real time	Activity Based	Workaround	$3 million
Order entry	In-house	Activity Based	Date expansion	$5 million
IMS database	System software	Activity Based	Data migration	$3 million upgrade
Collection	User controlled	Line of code	Rewrite	$150,000
etc............	etc............	etc............	etc............	etc............
All systems	Multiple	Multiple	Variable	$32 million

Candidate scenarios that can be applied under the activity-based cost model include:

- Date field expansion

- Procedural workaround

- Standalone validation

- Data store expansion project

- Package upgrade and assimilation

- Duplicate system elimination

This example demonstrates the flexibility of the activity-based cost model—it can be used to estimate many different approaches, depending on the type of system and the related compliance requirement. The estimating strategy for each upgrade unit is based on unique requirements for that systems area and is finalized during the enterprise assessment. This allows each application area leeway with respect to the approach and the cost of making a system Year 2000 compliant. Because of the variety of projects and challenges encountered in most organizations, it rarely makes sense to apply a single cost model or scenario to an entire enterprise.

Regardless of the cost model or the scenario being applied, certain metrics must be captured during the inventory process. Once baseline metrics have been extracted, they can be input to the various cost models to develop estimates for each upgrade unit. The enterprise assessment, upgrade unit derivation, metrics to be captured, and related planning activities are explained in more depth in subsequent chapters. At this point in time, however, it is useful for the reader to gain a high-level understanding of the tasks on which these cost models are based and against which these metrics are to be applied. Table 10.6 shows a high-level task summary for the date field expansion and procedural workaround scenarios. These tasks decompose into more detailed steps that serve as the project planning template and the activity-based cost model for a given upgrade unit. Detailed project planning guidelines are included in subsequent implementation chapters.

| **Table 10.6** | High Level Task Summary—Year 2000 Scenario Templates |

Data Field Expansion	Procedural Workaround

1. Finalize upgrade unit analysis plan
2. Derive upgrade unit detailed design
  • Finalize systems inventory
  • Perform data definition analysis
  • Perform physical data analysis
  • Analyze interface requirements
3. Finalize upgrade unit migration plan
4. Perform upgrade unit expansion
  • Expand record groups & source code
  • Expand related system components
5. Expand & migrate data stores
6. Build & activate/deactivate interfaces
7. Perform validation testing activities
8. Certify Year 2000 compliant
9. Implement upgrade unit
	1. Finalize upgrade unit analysis plan
	2. Derive upgrade unit detailed design
	  • Finalize systems inventory
	  • Perform data definition analysis
	  • Analyze interface requirements
	3. Finalize upgrade unit migration plan
	4. Perform upgrade unit compliance change
	  • Create date handling routines
	  • Propagate date handling logic
	5. Adjust / expand special cases
	6. Perform validation testing activities
	7. Certify Year 2000 compliant
	8. Implement upgrade unit

The best advice that planning teams can follow when building an implementation budget is to create or obtain standard scenario templates, adhere to solid project management principles and, when activity-based costing is not an option, revert to a cost per date or cost per line budget model for a given upgrade unit.

10.5 Multiphased Budgeting: Putting it All Together

The budget models and phasing introduced thus far serve as a basic framework from which to evolve a comprehensive Year 2000 budget. This means that an overall budget must contain a mobilization phase, an itemized enterprise section, and an implementation section for each upgrade unit. The mobilization phase is estimated by using general guidelines introduced in this chapter. A key deliverable from this analysis is an interim, cost per line estimate to make the organization Year 2000 compliant. This working budget figure must suffice until the enterprise assessment project is completed.

The enterprise planning guidelines in Table 10.3 can be used to develop an assessment plan. This plan, coupled with the remaining items in Table 10.4, should be used to create a final enterprise budget. The bulk of the enterprise budget relies on completion of the enterprise assessment.

The enterprise assessment also produces the implementation budget, which identifies costs on a system-by-system (upgrade unit) basis.

The implementation budget relies on a complete systems inventory and careful analysis of the needs of the systems areas involved. Each upgrade unit may rely on a different cost model and scenario. The best approach is to apply activity-based costing to each upgrade unit, where the plan for that upgrade unit reflects the cost of making it Year 2000 compliant. Time constraints or other factors may make this goal difficult to achieve for certain systems. In these situations, a cost per date or cost per line budget model must suffice.

When impact tools are available, using a cost per date budget model as a way of validating or expediting the upgrade unit estimating process is a reasonable course of action. Scanning or parsing tools can analyze systems fairly quickly, and the independent estimate is useful when justifying final budget figures.

Validating numbers through pilot projects is also highly recommended in parallel with the enterprise assessment. Pilot projects allow a planning team to build confidence and accuracy into Year 2000 implementation estimates. It should be clear by now that the project planning and estimating process for the Year 2000 is not wholly scientific. It should be taken a step at a time, relying on the most highly skilled professionals available, and it should not be handed over entirely to third-party consultants.

Once the numbers are in place, the advisory board and Project Office must work with senior financial officers to complete a multiyear budget plan. This means that the budget figures for each phase must be allocated over a 3-year window. Creative budgeting may be required where the bottom-line expense exceeds past budgets by a significant sum. For example, some organizations have investigated obtaining multiyear loans as a way of spreading Year 2000 costs over a period of time that actually exceeds the length of the project itself. However, at this point in time accounting standards mandate that Year 2000 costs be treated as an expense item. Other public sector organizations have looked into raising funds through special tax initiatives. The only way for senior financial officers to complete this level of analysis is for the Year 2000 Project Office to deliver a realistic, multiyear budget based on solid analysis.

Finally, organizations must be prepared to adjust budget allocations over the life of a Year 2000 project. This means that cost allocation in years

2 and 3 will require adjustments based on changes in plans, new systems, mergers, acquisitions, and unforeseen scheduling problems. Historically, slow starts and other factors have forced many IT projects into longer schedules. Because the Year 2000 project has an inflexible deadline, the results of a slow start or poor progress will be to backload much of the cost into 1998 and 1999. All of these changes must be monitored closely by senior management so that the budget can be adjusted proactively along the way.

Chapter 11

Year 2000 Project Mobilization

This chapter describes the Year 2000 project mobilization phase. This critical stage of the life cycle determines the overall pace and the level of aggressiveness that an organization applies to solving the Year 2000 problem. Organizations have, in many cases, wasted precious time on extraneous activities during project startup. A poorly managed startup results from a lack of focus, direction, and commitment from project management and other participants. A bad startup could spell delays that keep mission-critical systems from becoming Year 2000 compliant within required event horizons.

Deliverables produced by the mobilization phase of the Year 2000 project include:

- Requirements for establishing the Year 2000 Project Office and advisory board

- Deployment of Year 2000 standards to applicable IT environments and other areas

- Summary-level inventory of systems and operational environments

- High-level risk analysis of mission-critical systems

- Overall strategy for Year 2000 assessment and implementation phases

- Enterprise assessment project plan, resource requirements, and proposed budget

- Summary of the role third parties are to play in the Year 2000 project

- Preliminary working budget for the Year 2000 enterprise and implementation phases

The following tasks must be performed in order to complete these deliverable requirements:

1. *Define roles and responsibilities needed to finalize the Year 2000 Project Office and advisory board.*

2. *Finalize and distribute Year 2000 guidelines and standards across the enterprise.*

3. *Survey and summarize the operational and systems environment as input to the enterprise assessment and overall strategy.*

4. *Identify, as needed, the business areas and systems at greatest risk of exposure to the Year 2000 problem.*

5. *Establish a proposed strategy for an enterprisewide Year 2000 solution.*

6. *Scope the enterprise assessment project, determine time and resource constraints, create project plan, and finalize assessment budget requirements.*

7. *Determine who is to perform enterprise planning and implementation tasks and finalize recommendations for third parties to support these efforts.*

8. *Based on initial findings, create a preliminary working budget that can be refined during the enterprise assessment phase of the project.*

11.1 Mobilization Project Initiation

Chapter 10 outlined the overall work tasks and budget requirements for a mobilization project. Although management may want to create a detailed project plan for the mobilization phase, the nature of this phase of a Year 2000 project makes it difficult to stay within a formal project plan. Therefore, we recommend that management finalize the tasks, resources, and budget for this effort as defined in the introductory section of this chapter and in section 10.2, *Phase I: Year 2000 Mobilization Budget.*

The three to four team members assigned to complete the mobilization effort should be drawn from internal staff and the management team. Trusted consultants can selectively be added to the group as determined by the management team. The time allotted to this project should be limited to a maximum of 2 months because of limited project time constraints. Once the team is in place, senior management should communicate that the mobilization project is underway and that full cooperation is required from all areas of the IT organization.

The remaining sections of this chapter discuss how to implement the Year 2000 mobilization phase.

11.2 Year 2000 Project Office

The Year 2000 Project Office, introduced in earlier chapters, controls the Year 2000 project. In order to establish and empower the Project Office, executives must finalize the reporting structure that provides sponsorship, management, direction, and control to the Year 2000 project. This requires a structure similar to the one depicted in Figure 11.1. The CIO, or equivalent IT executive, must have the support of other officers, business executives, and the board. The individual chartered with solving the Year 2000 problem must be a director, or equivalent-level manager, with direct reporting responsibility to the CIO. This level of reporting is required to ensure project success.

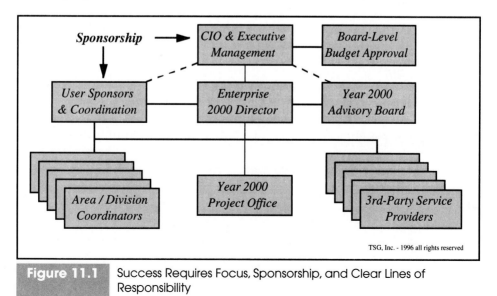

Figure 11.1 Success Requires Focus, Sponsorship, and Clear Lines of Responsibility

If this level of sponsorship is not in place, the entire project is at risk. An organization having difficulty establishing this level of sponsorship can benefit from the sponsorship discussion found in Chapter 9. The project director heads the Year 2000 Project Office but might not be the day-to-day manager. Regardless of the individual selected, the person leading the project must have access to all IT organizational levels so that progress can be sustained throughout the project.

The Project Office is a permanent fixture that must remain in place until an organization is Year 2000 compliant. The following responsibilities should be considered for inclusion in a Year 2000 Project Office. Note that the number of individuals performing these functions is determined by the scope of each role within a given project. For example, third-party coordination may be of limited scope and therefore can be one of several tasks assigned to a project team member, or it may require a full-time person because of the number of relationships to be managed within the context of a given project.

- **Project office manager.**

  — In a large organization, the project office director may assign a full-time manager to control the Year 2000 budget, lead the enterprise assessment, and manage the Project Office team.

  — This individual likely has management communication responsibility and sits on the Year 2000 advisory board.

  — The Project Office manager is typically the person responsible for tracking and adjusting the overall Year 2000 budget throughout the life of the project.

- **Communication coordinator.**

  — Project status, Project Office activity, Year 2000 awareness, budget issues, and other factors must be communicated to multiple organizational levels, either formally or informally, throughout the life of the project.

  — Large or highly political infrastructures may require that one or more individuals be assigned communication responsibilities.

- **Enterprise assessment analysts.**

  — Tackling the enterprise assessment is the most immediate responsibility the Project Office faces.

— This is an area where outside consultants can perform the analysis work.

— The role of internal personnel varies from performing the analysis to monitoring and reviewing assessment results.

— In-house personnel assigned to an assessment can be reassigned to other roles once the assessment is completed.

— These individuals can, for example, be "borrowed" from application areas, participate in the assessment project, be assigned to a skills transfer role, and eventually be rotated back into their application area after 6–9 months.

— This concept of a "rotational analyst" avoids Year 2000 burnout—a common occurrence in dedicated Year 2000 teams.

- **Status tracking and project reporting coordinator.**

  — Once implementation begins, tracking numerous projects, upgrade unit interfaces, and the conversion state of cross-functional data stores evolves into a critical role.

  — This function includes updating central repository data, running status reports on the inventory, feeding information into change and configuration control efforts, providing ad hoc reports to the communication coordinator, and generally tracking the enterprise Year 2000 project.

  — In small- or medium-sized shops, this role may be combined with that of the communication coordinator and change and configuration control manager.

- **Change and configuration control manager.**

  — Accurately managing change and configuration control determines the success or failure of a Year 2000 project.

  — The change and configuration control manager ensures that continuity is maintained across system areas and that systems software and application upgrades are synchronized.

  — This individual verifies that systems moving into and out of production are added to the enterprise plan.

  — This individual also serves as change control reviewer for application areas and plays an active role in interface activation and deactivation strategy.

— The change and configuration control role is critical in complex and highly volatile environments.

• **Third-party business partner and package vendor coordinator.**

— Numerous interfaces to third-party organizations require coordination to determine data compatibility as internal and external systems reach Year 2000 compliance.

— Furthermore, third-party application vendors and system software vendors must be contacted to discuss the Year 2000 issue, compliance requirements, and contract issues.

— The third-party business partner and package vendor coordinator works with contract coordinators and legal counsel to ensure that application and system software areas have the proper level of support regarding third-party issues.

• **Software tools and tool vendor coordinator.**

— Software tools support the analysis, modification, validation, project status tracking, and communication tasks.

— This function, in addition to driving tool research, procurement, implementation, and utilization, also coordinates training in the use of various tools and skills transfer.

— This function typically requires at least three individuals in a medium-to-large IT migration effort.

— The number of individuals assigned depends on the project size, the extent of third-party consulting usage, and the number of tools and environments to be supported.

• **Third-party consulting services liaison.**

— Outside consultants are typically used by medium-to-large IT organizations.

— At least one individual is typically assigned to review and procure consultants to perform assessment and implementation projects.

— Coordination with application areas and contracting teams is a key requirement of this role.

- **Implementation process and methods expert.**

  — Someone in the Project Office must be responsible for selecting and overseeing the process used to perform Year 2000 implementation.

  — This person performs methodology analysis, procurement, customization, and knowledge transfer.

  — Knowledge of the migration process is critical to ensuring that key tasks are not omitted or incorrectly applied—regardless of who performs the work.

  — If the bulk of the work is performed by consultants, this individual is chartered with third-party quality assurance review.

  — If more of the work is performed in-house, multiple individuals must be assigned to knowledge transfer support.

  — These individuals can be external consultants or can be application area rotational analysts assigned over the life of the project.

- **User area and business area liaison.**

  — The Project Office typically does not have direct responsibility for user-owned systems.

  — During the assessment cycle, a number of these systems may be identified.

  — If it appears that a large number of user-developed or commissioned systems exist, a user area liaison should be designated throughout the assessment and implementation phases of the project.

  — This individual must possess multifaceted skills in order to help analyze Year 2000 exposure and migration requirements, assist with budget development, recommend third-party help and software tools, provide guidance to the upgrade effort, recommend that a user system be scrapped or replaced., and assist with business risk assessment.

  — This considerable task could make the difference between true Year 2000 compliance or a series of unpleasant surprises late in the project.

- **Validation and testing expert.**

  — Because validation techniques are always required and are almost exclusively an in-house activity, centralized validation expertise is mandated for a Year 2000 project.

  — This specialized role is responsible for defining and transferring knowledge of testing environment maturity, software tool usage, test bed enhancement, the validation process, and Year 2000 certification.

  — These aspects typically require one individual assigned during enterprise infrastructure assessment and more supporting personnel added as implementation efforts ramp up.

It is important to reiterate that the Year 2000 Project Office should not be disbanded after completion of an enterprise assessment. The role of the Project Office becomes even more critical once implementation begins. Ongoing monitoring, communication, reporting, coordination, knowledge transfer, and, in some cases, budget lobbying are required to ensure successful completion of the Year 2000 initiative. The Project Office is a critical infrastructure component that should be established during the project mobilization phase and staffed as needed during subsequent phases of the Year 2000 life cycle.

11.3 Year 2000 Advisory Board

A Year 2000 advisory board is a management steering or oversight committee that reviews high-level and potentially sensitive issues relating to the Year 2000 project. The Year 2000 advisory board differs from the Year 2000 Project Office in terms of charter, scope of responsibility, and depth of participation. The advisory board embodies the following characteristics:

- Includes a wide range of high-level managers from legal, internal audit, functional areas, senior IT areas, contracting, and senior business operational functions

- Includes senior IT representation from quality assurance, data center, operations, data administration, security, Project Office director and manager, the CIO, and applications

- Views Year 2000 issue as a strategic initiative that requires executive direction in order to succeed

- Has no day-to-day operational responsibility for the Year 2000 project

- Sets and monitors high-level policies to ensure that the Project Office stays on track

- Meets quarterly to receive Project Office status and to direct the Project Office to make adjustments as required

- Has direct link to CEO and CFO as required to recommend policy or budget adjustments

- Works with CIO to manage communication policy, project schedule, and contingency plans

The Year 2000 advisory board takes different forms under different organizational structures. It may, for example, be incorporated into periodic senior staff meetings for the convenience of attendees. Meeting with Project Office personnel should include status reports from the Project Office, legal, contracting, internal audit, and selected operational areas. Discussions of outstanding issues would lead to a series of recommendations that the CIO could either implement or would need to take to the CFO or CEO for further discussion. Issues that could not be directly resolved by the CIO would likely involve budgetary changes or the need for radical contingency action because a mission-critical system was on the brink of failure.

Regardless of the forum or format, it is important for the executive team to appoint some type of steering committee to oversee the Year 2000 project. Regardless of the advisory board's charter, the CIO retains ultimate responsibility for the Year 2000 project. This having been said, the advisory board supports the CIO by providing a sounding board for major decisions and by recommending policy changes as needed to the executive team. Any IT project with such bottom-line implications and an unforgiving due date requires no less from a well-managed IT organization.

11.4 Distribution of Guidelines and Standards

Year 2000 guidelines and standards were discussed in detail in Chapter 5. These standards cover developer guidelines, date formats for interfaces and data stores, user guidelines, Year 2000 migration standards, vendor package contracts, legal issues, third-party business partners, hardware analysis, and standard date routines. Finalizing and communicating these guidelines should be accomplished under the scope of the Year 2000 mobilization phase. This includes the following tasks:

1. *Finalize guidelines for all relevant parties defined in Chapter 5.*

2. *Create a distribution strategy with communication coordinator within the Year 2000 Project Office.*

3. *Determine distribution vehicle, for example, internal electronic mail or similar medium, that facilitates information access and the ability to update these procedures.*

4. *Focus on using the same distribution medium that is being used for survey collection and other Year 2000 communiqués.*

5. *Develop a feedback mechanism for updates and changes to standards as required.*

6. *Verify through face-to-face meetings or via teleconference that individuals chartered with applying these standards have received them and understand them.*

These tasks should be included under the mobilization phase project plan. Early development and distribution of Year 2000 standards and guidelines sets the tone for the entire project and demonstrates that the Project Office has thought through the many issues associated with project deployment.

11.5 System Inventory and Environmental Summary

In order to scope the Year 2000 enterprise assessment project and to create a high-level budget estimate, summary information is required for the portfolio. The summary-level inventory data to be collected includes an estimate of the total number of systems, total lines of code per system, and total programs per system. These figures represent rough estimates that, if not available at the system level, can be summarized at the enterprise level. Enterprise totals can be obtained by summing total programs and lines of code for each system or by using library scanning technology if available. The guidelines used in Chapter 10 for developing a line of code cost estimate for the enterprise can be used to gather this information.

In addition to a basic inventory, identification of major software and hardware platforms is required to determine general levels of difficulty to be expected during the enterprise assessment and implementation phases of the project. For example, if an enterprise is primarily an IBM MVS™ environment and secondarily an IBM RS/6000™ environment, two separate sets of software tools may be minimally required to assess these applications. If the environment is highly nonstandard or contains a significant amount of obsolete technology, tools may be harder to find, projects may take longer to complete, and costs may be higher than average. Difficulty in obtaining this preliminary information is a clear indication that the enterprise assessment inventory step will take longer than average to complete.

The information collected during this step of the mobilization phase is used as input to the enterprise staffing and budget analysis process. It is important to gather this environmental data up front to plan and launch the project properly. The enterprise assessment process, discussed in Chapter 12, provides greater detail on how to use repository technology and related techniques to store environmental data and produce project status reports from that data. We recommend that this information be placed into a more permanent facility, such as a repository, to enable long-term data capture, updating, and status reporting.

11.6 Preliminary Risk Assessment

A risk analysis is typically performed during the enterprise assessment phase of a Year 2000 project. Mission-critical systems can, however, be reviewed during the mobilization phase if executives require this analysis to justify subsequent phases of the project. A risk assessment performed at this stage also facilitates the setting of priorities for projects that may need to be started before the enterprise assessment is completed. If, for example, systems have been found to have event horizons that fall within the next 3–6 months, risk analysis of these systems is strongly warranted during project mobilization.

When the preliminary risk assessment is geared to expose financial and legal risks as a way of justifying a Year 2000 project, it should be applied to the top 10 to 20 percent of mission-critical systems. Targets of this analysis ideally include systems that are responsible for procuring or tracking revenue, servicing or retaining customers, or in some way ensuring organizational survival. This limited level of analysis ensures that a risk assessment is completed quickly, while dealing with the top percentage of the systems that manage the bulk of an organization's risk. Examples of these types of systems include income tax, order entry, customer information, billing, and collections systems.

It quickly becomes apparent to senior executives requiring Year 2000 justification that an organization is at risk when its main vehicle for customer tracking or revenue procurement is disabled. If the goal of the risk analysis is to determine the affect on the organization of the failure of systems with near-term event horizons, all systems of this type should be added to the list of mission-critical systems to be analyzed. Including both mission-critical systems and systems subject to near-term failure under the mobilization phase risk assessment allows an organization to target systems that constitute 80 percent of the organization's long-term exposure to the Year 2000 problem.

A sample business risk assessment report, described in Chapter 2, depicts key items that should be included in a comprehensive risk analysis. The risk assessment produced during project mobilization, however, can be streamlined into a brief, one-line summary for each system. Each line should indicate the business function, system, and estimated monetary loss if that system fails. Event horizons should be included for each system for which time to failure is less than 6 months or for which event horizon data is readily available. Chapter 12 provides an expanded discussion of incorporating the risk assessments into the larger enterprise assessment process.

11.7 High-Level Project Strategy

A high-level summary of the recommended Year 2000 implementation strategy will help executives and others understand the long-term implementation plan for the project. A summary of the planned Year 2000 strategy allows all parties to work from the same general planning blueprint during project startup and deployment. Figure 11.2 depicts a high-level strategy that includes generic timelines for the enterprise assessment, infrastructure related projects, enterprise coordination, and a series of upgrade unit implementation projects.

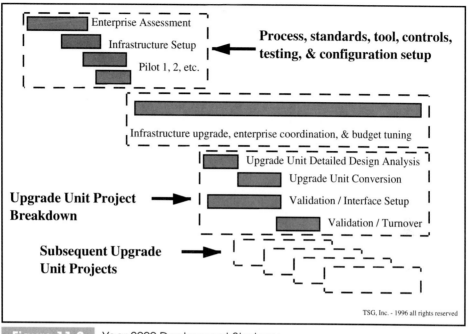

Figure 11.2 Year 2000 Deployment Strategy

In addition to creating a pictorial overview of how the project proceeds out over a multiyear time frame, a brief description of each phase, along with budget recommendations, should be developed during project mobilization. This project overview provides a useful tool for advisory board, executive, and functional area summaries of the approach being taken to address the Year 2000 problem.

11.8 Enterprise Assessment Project Plan

An enterprise assessment project plan, resource requirements, and related cost estimate is required prior to beginning the enterprise assessment project. Table 11.1 depicts a project task and deliverable summary that corresponds to the enterprise assessment budget model shown in Chapter 10. The high-level tasks involved in this assessment include establishing the enterprise plan (described in this section), a technical assessment of the systems environment, a review of the data architecture as it relates to the Year 2000 project, segmentation of the enterprise into upgrade units, and completion of the overall strategy.

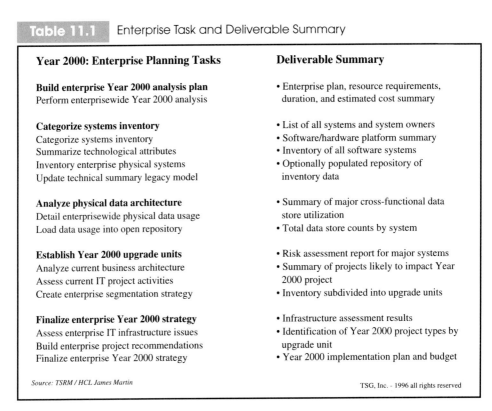

Table 11.1   Enterprise Task and Deliverable Summary

Year 2000: Enterprise Planning Tasks	Deliverable Summary
Build enterprise Year 2000 analysis plan Perform enterprisewide Year 2000 analysis	• Enterprise plan, resource requirements, duration, and estimated cost summary
Categorize systems inventory Categorize systems inventory Summarize technological attributes Inventory enterprise physical systems Update technical summary legacy model	• List of all systems and system owners • Software/hardware platform summary • Inventory of all software systems • Optionally populated repository of inventory data
Analyze physical data architecture Detail enterprisewide physical data usage Load data usage into open repository	• Summary of major cross-functional data store utilization • Total data store counts by system
Establish Year 2000 upgrade units Analyze current business architecture Assess current IT project activities Create enterprise segmentation strategy	• Risk assessment report for major systems • Summary of projects likely to impact Year 2000 project • Inventory subdivided into upgrade units
Finalize enterprise Year 2000 strategy Assess enterprise IT infrastructure issues Build enterprise project recommendations Finalize enterprise Year 2000 strategy	• Infrastructure assessment results • Identification of Year 2000 project types by upgrade unit • Year 2000 implementation plan and budget

Source: TSRM / HCL James Martin

11.8.1 Enterprise Assessment—Resource Staffing

This generic enterprise assessment plan assumes that a minimum of 2 and one-half people would be assigned to analyze a small environment and that up to 6 people would be assigned to assess a large IT environment. Staffing for the enterprise assessment project includes the following resource recommendations:

- Assign one to three analysts to survey systems, produce the inventory, and identify upgrade units. Planners should assign one full-time analyst for the first 15 million lines of code and one full-time analyst for each additional 20 million lines. The number of analysts assigned to this effort should be capped at three so the project does not exceed reasonable parameters. Accuracy may, as a result, be sacrificed in cases where a portfolio exceeds 50–55 million lines of code. Time becomes the driver in many cases and this can dictate the level of accuracy attained during an inventory process.

- Assign one full-time analyst to assess the information infrastructure and perform the business risk assessment. In small- to medium-sized environments, this individual can also help develop the final plan and can also assume management responsibilities.

- Where assessment tools are being used, assign one full-time analyst to run inventory tools and, optionally, load this information into a repository. A second analyst is required for inventories in excess of 25 million lines of code. This individual's assignment should be limited to systems that can be analyzed by automated tools. This position is optional in cases where software tools are not used.

- Assign a full-time manager to plan, track, and communicate progress on the project. This individual also develops the bulk of the final implementation plan and report.

These staffing guidelines should be adjusted as needed to fit the time frame and budget set aside for the enterprise assessment. Organizations should strive to keep the enterprise assessment within a 2 to 4-month window. These time frames and the deliverables listed in the assessment plan in Table 11.1 can be reasonably attained in environments that meet the following criteria:

- Application inventory is stored in easily identifiable source libraries that are under centralized control.

- Naming conventions reliably define which source, load, control, data definition, and data components belong to which systems.

- Missing and duplicate system components are exceptions to the rule.

- Obsolete or inactive systems rarely reside in production libraries.

- All business areas that own systems are easily identifiable.

- System boundaries are generally quantifiable.

- All hardware, remotely installed and centrally controlled, is documented.

- Distributed system locations, types, and owners are in some type of centralized tracking facility.

If it is determined that the environment does not meet the criteria listed above, management has several alternatives:

- Increase the time frames allotted to the assessment project.

- Increase the number of application analysts assigned to the project.

- Decrease the depth of analysis and scope of deliverables.

Increasing time frames may not be an option for organizations already behind with their Year 2000 initiative. Increasing the number of analysts on the project may shorten delivery time frames, as long as individuals do not become conflicted in their efforts to complete their assigned tasks. Finally, decreasing the depth, as opposed to the breadth, of project deliverables is another reasonable option. Many times, management opts to reduce the number of systems being analyzed, which results in an incomplete analysis of Year 2000 requirements. It is more important to include all systems within the inventory, with the exception of selected peripheral systems that are either obsolete or targeted for elimination.

Launching the assessment project is the most important and overriding factor in the face of these challenges. This means that management should not struggle for too long with these issues if they are preventing the project from getting started.

11.8.2 Enterprise Assessment—Infrastructure Support Requirements

Tools and a methodology must be procured and deployed during the mobilization phase to ensure a rapid enterprise assessment launch. Enterprise infrastructure components include a methodology, inventory tools, status tracking facilities, work environments, and communication tools. These items should be reviewed, obtained, and deployed as discussed below.

A methodology is an important tool that guides the development of the enterprise plan and proposed implementation strategy. The importance of methods and processes was discussed in Chapter 9. Methodology utilization should begin during project mobilization and continue throughout the implementation phase. Deployment of a Year 2000-specific methodology is limited to the Year 2000 Project Office during mobilization and the enterprise assessment phases.

Inventory and component cross-reference software tools should be considered for major language types and platforms. These types of tools provide an inventory of software components by parsing and cross-referencing control language statements and system source code. If a tool is unavailable or unobtainable, in-house utilities or configuration management tools can be substituted. Deployment of these tools for an enterprise assessment is limited to Project Office analysts.

Status tracking facilities should be made available to implementation teams via a central repository or database facility. A repository, when used as an information tracking facility in the enterprise assessment phase, puts the required tracking infrastructure in place for the implementation phase of the project. When no repository is available at the time of an enterprise assessment startup, a simple database system must suffice. This facility should be coupled with process and project management tools.

Work environments, including mainframe access and workstations, should be set up in advance of the launch for all project participants.

Communication tools, including internal electronic mail, spreadsheets, a word processor, and a presentation tool, should be in place for forms distribution, data collection, project deliverable packaging, and presentations.

11.8.3 Project Plan Finalization

In order to finalize the enterprise assessment project plan, total staffing costs and total infrastructure costs must be authorized by senior management. The enterprise assessment plan, including the resource and deliverable definitions defined above and the cost estimates defined in section 10.3, *Phase II: Year 2000 Enterprise Budget*, define the personnel costs required to complete this project phase. This cost should be augmented by the additional hardware time used by automated assessment tools, the cost of the tools themselves, and the cost of procuring and deploying a methodology. Hardware utilization during the enterprise assessment tends to be fairly minimal.

Once this information has been assembled, the Project Office director should gain CIO approval to proceed. If third-party consulting support is required to complete the enterprise assessment, analysts should refer to *Mobilization Strategy for External Service Providers*, that follows. Undergoing formal sign-off on this project means considering and approving all internal requirements and procedures as required by current organizational protocol.

11.8.4 Project Orientation

The enterprise assessment requires interviews with dozens of IT personnel, managers, and third-party coordinators. These individuals must be briefed prior to starting an enterprise assessment project. This briefing defines everyone's role, distributes required forms (which can also be distributed via electronic mail), and verifies management's mandate that all players cooperate with the assessment team. Highly distributed organizations can use teleconference facilities to launch the project.

11.9 Mobilization Strategy for External Service Providers

External service providers can be used to plan and implement a Year 2000 project. How these external resources are procured and managed can mean success or failure to a Year 2000 initiative. Specifically, Year 2000 service providers, when contracted to perform work across multiple phases of a Year 2000 project, have a tendency to reanalyze systems and repeat work already performed by another service provider or in-house personnel. The reasons for this are (1) consistent methodologies are not used across various project phases, (2) much of the work performed by contractors during the assessment phase is tool-centric, and (3) clients tend to let third parties drive the analysis rather than establishing concrete requirements and deliverables up front.

The value of consistent methodologies was discussed in Chapter 9. Using a consistent methodology to define requirements and deliverables for each phase of a Year 2000 project addresses each of the major concerns associated with third parties. It allows work products from initial project phases to be integrated with work products from subsequent project phases. A methodology-driven project also avoids the problem of overemphasizing project deliverables provided by a given software tool. Finally, the use of a standard methodology allows the client to dictate work tasks and deliverables to third-party contractors and to drive the project according to their needs rather than what the contractor believes that the organization needs.

Third-party support is most effectively utilized when projects have well-defined parameters and time frames. One use of third parties involves the enterprise assessment, which can be performed in conjunction with outside consultants that have demonstrated skills in the Year 2000 arena. Procurement of services for an enterprise assessment should identify tasks and deliverables listed in this chapter, along with the detailed information found in Chapter 12. The key is to control task and deliverable requirements, avoid a protracted decision process, minimize RFP usage, and not permit the vendor to deliver results that are either tool-centric or that cannot be used during implementation efforts.

Use of third parties is also recommended for the numerous Year 2000 upgrade projects that comprise the implementation phase. It is never too early to secure at least two service providers to perform Year 2000 implementation work on selected upgrade units. This implies that once upgrade units are identified as deliverables from the enterprise assessment, they can be divided among the applicable implementation teams. Selecting service providers is covered in depth in Chapter 17 and should begin during project mobilization in order to secure the required resources through the life of the project.

11.10 Defining a Preliminary Year 2000 Budget

As discussed in Chapter 10, the early stage of Year 2000 project mobilization is typically when executives require a preliminary cost estimate for the entire project. This is expected and is a reasonable request from an executive team facing a massive, multiyear expenditure. However, accurate budget estimates are generally not available until the completion of the enterprise assessment project—which usually involves a significant expenditure in and of itself. The way to meet this requirement is through the use of the per line of code budget model described in Chapter 10.

Developing a per line cost estimate for the portfolio is a rapid way of specifying an implementation cost range for a Year 2000 project, based on a preliminary review of the systems portfolio. The cost per line implementation estimate, when combined with the enterprise assessment planning costs developed during the mobilization phase and projected enterprise costs beyond the initial assessment, provides a fairly complete working budget estimate. The line of code cost model suggests that the total implementation estimate may be increased by a factor of 10 percent to include enterprise planning, coordination, and infrastructure expenditures. This can be used as the final figure, or actual enterprise assessment costs can be factored into the equation to create a more accurate total projection.

One final recommendation when using the cost per line model: present a range that management can use for planning. This cost range is impacted by internal infrastructures, maturity, tool utilization, testability, level of obsolescence, language levels, and hardware environments in use at a given installation. In other words, if all of these factors are working against the smooth implementation of a Year 2000 project, costs will tend to fall at the high end of the $1 to $2 per line of code model. Planners should refer to section 10.1.1, *Cost per Line Budget Model*.

11.11 Mobilization Finalization

Once the items specified in this chapter are in place or have been accommodated, an organization should move rapidly into the enterprise assessment project. When event horizons are extremely tight or organizations have waited too long to launch their Year 2000 initiative, implementation projects can be started in parallel with the enterprise assessment project. This suggestion should be included in the recommendations resulting from the mobilization phase and should refer to the implementation chapters that follow Chapter 12.

Year 2000 Enterprise Assessment

$\mathbf{T}$his chapter describes the process used to perform a Year 2000 enterprise assessment. This project phase gathers the detailed information needed to plan and fully implement the Year 2000 implementation phase. The enterprise assessment budget and work plan were discussed in Chapters 10 and 11, respectively. To gain more insight into prerequisite activities associated with the enterprise assessment, review the enterprise assessment sections in each of these chapters.

The enterprise assessment may, at first glance, seem like unnecessary overhead to those individuals new to the Year 2000 challenge. This mistaken impression stems from the fact that few, if any, prior projects have ever needed to apply a commonly defined set of requirements across the entire IT enterprise. Organizations that choose to bypass the enterprise assessment will be dogged by poor coordination across system areas, redundant efforts to create or acquire similar solutions and tools, uncoordinated business partner and vendor communications, and general management and infrastructure setup inefficiencies. Management can haphazardly struggle with these issues throughout the life of a Year 2000 project and increase the odds of failure, or they can commission the enterprise assessment tasks outlined in this chapter.

Deliverables from the enterprise assessment phase of a Year 2000 project and related activities, all discussed in this chapter, include:

- Deliverable: Summary of enterprise assessment roles and skills
Activity: Finalize role and skill requirements.

- Deliverable: Summary of enterprise assessment technology and infrastructure
Activity: Finalize enterprise assessment technology requirements.

- Deliverable: Enterprisewide systems inventory
Activity: Inventory in-house developed systems, third-party software, and all applicable hardware systems.
Activity: Identify each system by owner, type, platform, size, and related attributes.

- Deliverable: Cross-functional interface requirements
Activity: Examine cross-functional data store utilization and Year 2000 data interface requirements.

- Deliverable: Business area risk assessment
Activity: Identify interfaces to, and requirements for, external business partners.
Activity: Perform business area risk assessment and integrate results into Year 2000 implementation plan.

- Deliverable: Upgrade unit segmentation results
Activity: Segment the enterprise into implementable upgrade units.

- Deliverable: Year 2000 upgrade unit migration plan
Activity: Define upgrade unit migration scenarios and detailed conversion options.

- Deliverable: Package, system software, end-user, and non-IT system plans
Activity: Establish application package and system software upgrade plans.
Activity: Review and create end-user and non-IT system strategy.

- Deliverable: IT infrastructure analysis and recommendations
Activity: Identify infrastructure weaknesses and create plan to correct as required.

- Deliverable: Deployment support technology infrastructure
  Activity: Finalize implementation technology, tracking facility, hardware, and work environments.

- Deliverable: Implementation project plan and deployment strategy
  Activity: Prioritize upgrade units within a multiyear implementation plan.
  Activity: Create project implementation strategy, including in-house and outsourcing options.
  Activity: Establish enterprise monitoring, status tracking, and coordination strategy.

- Deliverable: Refined implementation and deployment budget
  Activity: Draft a Year 2000 implementation budget.

- Deliverable: Pilot project plan and results
  Activity: Complete and execute the first project or a pilot plan.

These enterprise assessment tasks represent an all-inclusive list that can and should be customized according to the scope of analysis, type of organization, time constraints, or budget limitations. The task summary sections included in this chapter outline the benefits derived from these tasks and the potential drawbacks of scaling back on selected activities. Scope definition should include all computer systems in an entire enterprise unless there are overriding political or economic reasons for omitting a given area. We caution against arbitrary omission of systems in an assessment project. Separate companies under a conglomerate or separate agencies within a government hierarchy can legitimately be defined as separate enterprises for purposes of a Year 2000 project.

The following two sections summarize the roles needed to perform an enterprise assessment and the tools required to support it. Subsequent sections discuss the inventory process, business risk assessment, upgrade unit segmentation, migration options, third-party and non-IT system planning, infrastructure assessment, implementation support environments, final implementation strategy and budget, enterprise coordination, and pilot project execution.

12.1 Enterprise Assessment: Roles and Skills Summary

For proper completion of an enterprise assessment project, individuals with a wide variety of skills must become involved in the project. The number of individuals in a given category varies by project size and should be determined according to the enterprise assessment project staffing guidelines found in Chapter 11. The individuals involved in this project are either on the assessment team itself or are supporting participants that provide input or support to the project as needed.

Note that the time and cost allocated to the enterprise assessment reflect the project team itself and do not include application area and specialist participants in the project. The guidelines below should assist in determining the level of support needed from these individuals so that their costs can be reflected accordingly. While this may be irrelevant to some organizations, others may want to control personnel time and cost allocation to a much greater degree.

12.1.1 Assessment Team Roles

The core team of assessment analysts, whether it comprises internal personnel, outside consultants or some combination thereof, requires the following basic skills.

- **Assessment Project Manager.**
    - Builds plan, manages team, interviews subject matter experts, presents findings, develops final report, oversees process.
    - Skills include large-systems project management, analysis skills, and ability to think creatively.
    - This person is likely the Project Office manager.

- **Inventory and upgrade unit analyst.**
    - Customizes interview and survey forms, collects survey data, performs interviews, analyzes inventory data, segments portfolio into upgrade units, builds implementation plan.
    - Optionally surveys third-party suppliers, business partners, and end users unless application personnel retains these roles.
    - Skills include interviewing experience, knowledge of general environment, ability to distill large amounts of data, and some knowledge of Year 2000 assessment process.
    - Normally one to four analysts are assigned per project, depending on the size and distribution of the organization.

- **Software tool analysts.**
    - Provide input on tool selection and platform applicability.
    - Customize, execute, and interpret results produced by inventory/cross-reference tool.

— Implement central tracking facility (database or repository) and incorporate survey and automated tool analysis into that facility.

— Customize communication technology (e.g., electronic mail) and other presentation tools for use on the project.

— Skills include tool knowledge, tool integration experience, strong background with technical work environment, repository (optional if not used) background.

— Typically, one person assigned per small-to-medium project and two assigned to larger projects.

• **End-user and non-IT systems liaison.**

— Responsible for communicating Year 2000 issue to end-user areas and non-IT areas that build or buy systems outside scope of IT organization.

— Skills include Year 2000 knowledge, liaison skills, and ability to guide non-IT people on how to address issues.

— One person assigned per project where end-user and non-IT systems are significant or mission-critical.

12.1.2 Support Roles

A number of individuals must be made available to the assessment team during the course of the project. Project orientation sessions should clearly communicate the requirement for the following support roles during project startup.

• **Application area managers and analysts.**

— Provide input on system ownership, platform, boundaries, whether the system is a package or an in-house application, general system attributes, and short- and long-term plans.

— For application packages, work with vendor to determine compliance time frame and approach, upgrade requirements, and related upgrade costs.

— Time allotted averages roughly 2–4 hours per application area over life of assessment.

• **Systems software or operations analysts.**

— Provide active list of system software and utility inventory, vendor compliance status and time frame, and upgrade requirements.

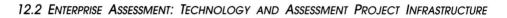

— Time allotted averages 2–10 days over life of assessment, based on level of research and size of inventory.

- **IT directors and managers.**

  — Provide input to support and testing environment and long-term plans for various application areas.

  — Time allotted averages 1 hour per major application area.

- **Third-party interface coordinators.**

  — Contact third-party application package vendors, system software vendors, and third-party business partners to ascertain compliance plans, approaches, and time frames.

  — Time allotted averages 1–2 hours per third party to be contacted.

- **Business analysts and end users.**

  — Provide input on strategic plans for a given business area as input to risk assessment.

  — Identify end-user or non-IT commissioned systems for review and possible correction.

  — Time allotted averages a maximum of 1 hour per major business area for planning input.

  — Time allotted averages 2–4 hours to assess impact on each system commissioned in their area (does not include cost to correct the problem).

All assessment projects vary in terms of skill requirements, and the roles defined in this section should be reviewed closely to ensure that the project is properly managed and staffed.

12.2 Enterprise Assessment: Technology and Assessment Project Infrastructure Summary

Technologies supporting the enterprise assessment project include communication tools, an inventory and cross-reference tool, a tracking facility or repository, an impact analyzer, process and project management tools, and presentation technology. These tools are used to gather and represent information critical to this assessment. In a worst case scenario, an assessment can be performed without the benefit of certain tools, but the results may be highly suspect. Specific recommendations for using these tools in an enterprise assessment are addressed below. These tool categories are discussed in more depth in Chapter 15, and specific vendor tool references can be found in Appendix A.

- **Communication technology.**

  — Communication tools typically include an electronic mail facility and data gathering capability to facilitate information capture via remote access.

  — This capability is particularly important when organizations are highly distributed and direct access to support personnel is limited.

  — Spreadsheets also help to record survey data.

  — One option provides direct access into the facility that actually stores captured information.

  — The repository discussion that follows contains more information on this concept.

- **Inventory and cross-reference tool.**

  — It is difficult to perform a large-scale systems inventory without automated tools.

  — In many mainframe environments, it is time-consuming to gather inventory data across numerous libraries.

  — The inventory tool automates much of the system inventory capture and the information reporting process for the project.

  — Another role for this tool is to populate the applicable repository facility.

- **Tracking facility/repository.**

  — A repository provides the ability to represent relationships between systems and system components to support Year 2000 planning efforts.

  — A recommended meta-model to support this analysis is illustrated in section 12.3.6.

  — The repository provides a summary view of enterprise data and enables subsequent status tracking during the implementation phase of the project.

— This facility is recommended for Year 2000 projects at large, complex, or highly distributed IT organizations.

- **Impact analyzer.**
  - The impact analyzer, or impact analysis tool, finds selected field types—in this case, dates.
  - An impact analyzer is considered optional for an enterprise assessment.
  - Using this tool to find all of the dates across an enterprise wastes valuable time during the assessment because data captured at this level becomes outdated before it is used in the migration phase.
  - Where available, impact analyzers can verify that the systems deemed compliant by application areas truly are compliant and can provide input to the ongoing budgeting process.

- **Process and project management tools.**
  - Basic project management technology is a requirement for creating individual, upgrade unit project plans.
  - Process management technology is optional, although highly recommended, because of the volume of metrics, estimating models, and upgrade unit plans that typically result from an enterprise assessment.

- **Presentation technology.**
  - A plan, summary reports, presentations, and other deliverables normally result from most sizable projects, and the Year 2000 enterprise assessment is no exception.
  - Presentation tools should be designated in advance for the assessment team to use. If these tools are unavailable, the project office director should move quickly to procure them.

12.3 Enterprise Assessment: Inventory Process

The basic building block for the Year 2000 implementation plan is an enterprisewide inventory of all computer systems across all environments. This task is not optional. Survey forms help define an initial inventory of systems and related system attributes. This information is refined by means of automated tools, then loaded into a tracking facility to manage planning, interface deployment, status tracking, and project implementation tasks. Performing each of the tasks listed below will ensure that the data collected reflects a comprehensive systems inventory for purposes of this assessment.

1. *Finalize the exact type of information to collect during the inventory process in the form of a survey.*

2. *Obtain a list of IT and non-IT systems in whatever format is available.*

3. *Target all areas and individuals to survey—include applicable application, system software, operations, data administration, facilities management, and end-user areas.*

4. *Send surveys out through electronic mail or hard-copy format to each survey target.*

5. *Work with teams to complete survey information as needed.*

6. *Where available and applicable, run inventory tool against production libraries to identify active systems.*

7. *Cross-reference information collected via surveys with automated analysis to build inventory.*

8. *Identify and resolve "orphaned," missing, obsolete, and duplicate components and systems.*

9. *Load this information into a tracking facility or repository to facilitate reporting and updating of information throughout the life of the project.*

10. *Review and update results periodically to verify that this facility is a living representation of the systems inventory.*

12.3.1 Establishing System Ownership, Boundary, and Background Information

Occasionally, analysts believe that the first step in the inventory process is to run an analyzer across the portfolio. Automated analysis, particularly in environments with poor naming conventions, may have little documentation value in the absence of certain background data. Although automated analysis can be run concurrently, collection of basic background information via survey forms is a main priority.

This background data creates a framework for organizing information collected through the use of automated tools. It also verifies that systems for which automated analysis is unavailable are not excluded from the inventory process. Standard forms are typically delivered with off-the-shelf methodologies and blueprints. Refer to Appendix A for information about these products.

Basic information required to categorize systems includes the name of the application area or division claiming ownership for the system, a technical contact name, and manager name and location. Additional identification and categorization data includes the name and abbreviated acronym for the system, the type and function of the system, and a list of names and acronyms for all subsystems, where applicable. System type includes in-house, application package, system software, and end-user commissioned systems. System function examples include accounts payable, human resources, tape management, account query, and so on.

If the system or various subsystem components are made up of a third-party application or system software vendor package, several points should be explored. Analysts should determine if the system is under vendor maintenance, if the package is Year 2000 compliant, when the vendor plans to become Year 2000 compliant, and the approach the vendor plans to use. Analysts must also determine if in-house personnel have modified the package source code, the extent of those changes, the level of effort required to retrofit changes into a new release, and the number of releases that the system may lag behind the currently available market version of the product.

Additional background is required in order to define an upgrade strategy for each system. Analysts must determine if there are plans to replace, rewrite, or eliminate a system and, if so, when this is scheduled to occur. Other required data includes determining whether program source code is available, whether the system is managed by configuration technology, and whether diagrammatic documentation is available. Additional information provided by support teams can be useful, but analysts are cautioned against trying to collect extraneous data not directly linked to the Year 2000 project. The extra time required by support personnel to research this data and for planning teams to assess the information may not be warranted.

It should be noted at this point that survey data should be collected on all systems—not just on application software developed in-house. Forms should be distributed to system software managers, application package support teams, operational areas, such as data administration, that may be responsible for utility systems, and end-user organizations that may have commissioned non-IT based systems. Additionally, automated control systems in manufacturing firms, actuarial systems at insurance companies, and building maintenance and security systems should, at a minimum, be inventoried and duly noted in the survey results.

12.3.2 Documenting Operating Environments

A second category of survey data concerns operating environments. Environmental data, gathered during project mobilization, ensured that the required software tools were procured in advance for the assessment project. Gathering data at this level allows analysts to focus the right software tools at selected systems and ensures that systems for which automated tools are not available are also included in the inventory.

Operating data to be collected for each system includes identification of primary programming languages, data files and database management software, operating systems, and hardware platforms. Additional information may include the type of teleprocessing monitor used, type of control languages employed, and any special, home-grown or obsolete technologies associated with a given system. System software release levels for each of these categories can be noted and cross-referenced with system software inventory results when time permits.

12.3.3 Analyzing Portfolio Size and Scope

Automated analysis tools provide significant value in assessing the size and scope of a given system. These tools generate lists of components and related component counts, such as lines of code, that provide valuable input to sizing efforts. Figure 12.1 depicts the tool analysis, repository load, and reporting process that can be established to support the Year 2000 inventory process. The tools additionally can decompose an inventory into source, copy, data file, screen map, database definition, and other component categories that can be manually or automatically summarized into a total count for that system. These component counts provide a source of metrics to upgrade unit cost models and are key to project planning efforts.

Information gathered for each system includes the total number of load modules and source programs, total lines of source code for all components, number of batch reports, number of on-line screens, number of control language members, and the total number of files, database segments, records, and table counts. Automated tools can gather much of this data quickly and efficiently, although support personnel should verify the resulting information to ensure some degree of accuracy. When analysis tools are not available for certain languages or hardware platforms, analysts must manually gather system-related data. This task typically involves a combination of analyzing library management reports and interviewing personnel responsible for those systems. Survey forms are the main source of information in these situations.

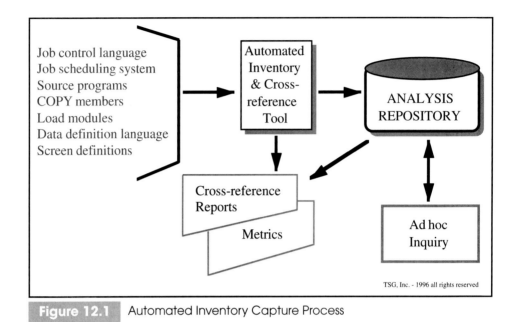

Figure 12.1 Automated Inventory Capture Process

When automated analysis tools are used, analysts must verify system scoping metrics by synchronizing the data provided by the tools and the data gathered via survey forms. This process includes tracking missing components, identified through automated cross-reference analysis, and determining if they are truly missing or just misplaced. Most of the inventory tools provide the ability to depict "where used" information. For example, where-used reports link, a job step to the load module that it executes, a load module to the source programs used to create that load module, and physical data used by a given job step and load module. This level of information is extremely important so that analysts can gain a complete picture of the overall systems environment. Analysts should consult with the software tools coordinator on the assessment project for more information about this topic.

12.3.4 Identifying Date-Related System Issues

Analysts should selectively examine date utilization on a systems-by-systems basis. When assessment time frames are constrained, limit the analysis to mission-critical systems and systems for which event horizons are suspected to be less than 1 year. Date-related analysis includes determining if a system uses two-digit year representations (e.g., "95" for 1995) and, if so, ascertaining if procedural workaround logic was already used on that system. In other words, analysts must determine whether a system is already Year 2000 compliant. If system owners claim that a system is compliant, run an impact analysis tool against that system to verify the accuracy of the claim.

Event horizons can be quantified by asking knowledgeable systems support personnel if the application contains forward date calculations. If this is the case, examine the systems more closely to determine how far into the future these dates actually project. One way to do this is to ask someone close to the application for input. Another approach is to run an impact analyzer to highlight date usage in context. Examining the high-lighted procedural date produced by the impact analysis tool typically provides clues to event horizon timelines.

Another requirement is determining whether standard date rou-tines are implemented across an application. If this is the case, collect a list of the date routines so that the routines can later be reviewed at the enter-prise level. Standardization of date routines is an important step during the infrastructure assessment and Year 2000 upgrade process. If time per-mits or a tool is available, analysts should attempt to find out the three most commonly used date formats. The answer to this question helps ana-lysts uncover special conversion requirements that may affect the upgrade unit migration plan.

Analysts must also examine the level of date-dependent processing within a system. For example, if a system has fewer than 10 procedural calculations and comparisons per source program, date dependence should be considered light. An occurrence of 10–25 date-related calcula-tions and comparisons per source program is considered as medium date utilization. More than 25 of these occurrences per program is considered heavy date utilization. These factors are considered when weighing the level of effort assigned to an update project for a given upgrade unit.

Finally, analysts should find out if a system has ever experienced Year 2000 production problems to date which may have appeared as total system failures, corrupt data, inaccurate reports, or other symptoms. If this is the case, place the system on a tier-one priority list. This means that this system will be included in the business risk assessment and slated for an early conversion date.

12.3.5 Assessing Internal and External Data Interface Impacts

Special application programming interfaces (API) or bridge routines may need to be built to interface data stores that span the boundary of a given upgrade unit. Batch file bridges to and from expanded and unexpanded data stores must be enabled and disabled throughout the migration cycle. Database files and on-line files, shared across multiple on-line or batch systems, similarly require an API to facilitate phased implementation. Batch bridges require the insertion of a data expansion or contraction routine into batch job streams. An API, on the other hand, requires an interface routine to interactively change data formats. This concept of utilizing batch bridges and interactive APIs drives the interface analysis within this stage of the enterprise assessment.

Input to the interface requirements analysis process requires analysis of system data store usage. While systems and upgrade units do not necessarily have a one-to-one correspondence, identifying data stores that cross major system boundaries is a valid starting point for interface identification. The first level of research determines whether a system imports or exports any files or databases to external entities. These entities include government agencies, such as the IRS, creditors, business partners, or other private institutions. If this is the case, all data store names should be identified for each external entity along with a person who has been assigned as the point of contact for that external entity. Any additional documentation regarding regulatory requirements or externally imposed timetables should be included for each impacted system and external entity within that system.

Internal interface impact analysis requires analysts to determine if systems share data stores with other systems. If this is the case, analysts should review automated tool analysis and system documentation, or work with system support personnel, to identify all data stores that extend beyond the bounds of each system, as listed below.

- Identify the number of batch files received from or sent to other systems and the name of each.

- Identify the number of on-line files shared with other systems and the name of each.

- Identify the number of databases shared with other systems and the name of each.

The last level of analysis regarding interfaces is to determine if any API or bridge routines already in place can be used to support Year 2000 interface efforts. This analysis is relatively critical to the project planning effort associated with each upgrade unit and should not be bypassed during enterprise assessment.

12.3.6 Establishing an Assessment and Project Tracking Repository

We recommend the creation of a year 2000 tracking facility in order to establish a vehicle for managing portfolio evolution, interface deployment, Year 2000 project status, and related project activities. This facility can be a repository or a relational database, but it is not the native data storage capability embedded in many of the tools used to capture inventory data during prior assessment steps. Inventory tools use relatively fixed data structures to store physical information extracted from a software portfolio and are not capable of representing the numerous variations of organizational or project data required by a Year 2000 project. The inventory tools also cannot reflect inventory data for systems that they do not directly analyze. In other words, a separate facility is needed to represent the status of a systems inventory during the life of a Year 2000 project.

Formal repositories and relational database structures both can represent relationships among systems, data stores, interfaces, upgrade units, management structures, and related components. Repositories additionally offer powerful loading and reporting capabilities and, in select cases, can import information directly from inventory tool data structures. An enterprise-level tracking facility is a minimum-level requirement for the Year 2000 project; it should be maintained by the Year 2000 Project Office and updated upon periodic reviews from system support areas.

Meta-model definition for this tracking facility tends to have a high degree of commonality across IT environments but should be flexible enough to support unique categorization schemes within a given organization. Categorizing systems based on ownership, boundary, and functionally related information is highly dependent on internal structures. Some hierarchies are flat, with systems randomly assigned. In other cases, systems are placed into well-defined hierarchies that can include financial, marketing, human resources, claims, manufacturing, and so on.

Figure 12.2 depicts a simple meta-model that can be expanded to reflect a more customized organizational model based on unique requirements within a company. Additional entities that may be added include division, business area, and so on. As a rule, volatile or irrelevant information such as a manager name or position should be defined as an attribute, not an entity. An expanded, upgrade unit-specific model is examined in Chapter 13 and more detail is covered in Appendix C.

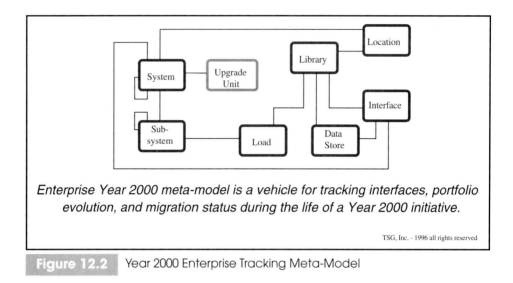

Enterprise Year 2000 meta-model is a vehicle for tracking interfaces, portfolio evolution, and migration status during the life of a Year 2000 initiative.

Figure 12.2   Year 2000 Enterprise Tracking Meta-Model

Physical inventory data, such as program statistics, system scoping metrics, component relationships, and related items, should be refreshed periodically by using the inventory and cross-reference tools applied during the initial analysis effort. Analysts must also update logical data, including compliance status, interface utilization, management changes, new systems, and related "soft" data. Physical updates tend to rely on links that are either provided by vendors or created by in-house support teams. Logical information must be entered by a tracking facility coordinator, typically found in the Year 2000 Project Office.

Although information in this facility should be readily accessible to concerned parties, central control of the data and the reports produced from that data should remain in the hands of the Project Office coordinator for status tracking and project reporting. Initial inventory summaries are a required deliverable from the enterprise assessment and are readily produced from the tracking facility. In some cases, these summaries may require a special reporting tool that can extract data from relational databases. Reporting of inventory updates and project status should be a recurring deliverable from the Year 2000 Project Office.

12.4 Business Area Risk Assessment

The business risk assessment was introduced in Chapter 2 as a way of helping analysts build awareness and reintroduced in Chapter 11 as a means of justifying an enterprise assessment during project mobilization. A complete business risk assessment across the enterprise is difficult to perform in the absence of a well-defined, enterprisewide system inventory.

If a business risk assessment was started during project mobilization, the enterprise assessment phase of the project can be used to refine, extend, or verify the information produced during that project. If no prior work was performed to determine business risks, this phase of the project should minimally produce a risk assessment for mission-critical systems and systems with event horizons of less than one year. Note that end-user commissioned systems should be included in the mission-critical list if they are linked to revenue procurement or if the demise of these systems creates some form of legal exposure for the organization.

Analysts should use the following guidelines when creating a business risk assessment report from scratch for executives and business managers.

1. *Obtain the systems inventory from earlier enterprise assessment steps.*

2. *Work with senior IT management to rank systems in general order of importance to the business.*

3. *Divide the list into mission-critical and non-mission-critical systems.*

4. *Treat all systems with event horizons of less than one year as mission-critical systems.*

5. *Create report template with the following categories: Business area, Key product/service, Related system, Projected failure date, Required start date, Loss exposure.*

6. *For each system on the list, identify the product and/or service that the system supports and the business area (if applicable).*

7. *Add the projected failure date and a projected start date (event horizon) that is at least 6 months prior to the projected failure date.*

8. *Meet with IT analysts and business analysts for that area to determine a weekly estimated monetary loss projection for that business area if the system fails.*

9. *Where legal exposure is high, note this in the Loss exposure column.*

10. *Consider issues such as loss of customers, regulatory violations and subsequent fines, or other business-specific risk factors.*

11. *Continue this process for all mission- and time-critical systems and, when time permits, non-mission-critical systems.*

The business risk assessment should not be a long, drawn-out process. Analysts should move quickly to put a minimal risk analysis in place and provide working copies to management in order to procure or sustain funding for subsequent project phases or to drive implementation project priorities.

12.5 Upgrade Unit Segmentation Strategies

Prioritizing Year 2000 implementation projects requires that all in-house, third-party, and related systems, depending on scope, be categorized into upgrade units. The goal is to quantify the number of Year 2000 projects, define the types of projects to be performed, assign time frames for each project, and determine the resources needed to complete those projects. Assessing and prioritizing the different types of implementation projects are discussed in greater depth later in the chapter.

The segmentation task ensures that systems are not erroneously included or omitted from a given implementation project. This process relies on the expertise of system support analysts and the intuition of Year 2000 assessment analysts. If this latter level of expertise is unavailable in-house, third-party consultants can bring a level of objectivity to the process. The two major objectives of segmentation are to minimize the number of interfaces required between compliant and noncompliant systems and to minimize the time that a system or group of systems is out of production.

Previously discussed interface strategies have a clear bearing on this analysis process. If external files are received by or produced from a batch system, creation of one or more bridge routines may be required. If shared data files or databases are accessed by either a batch or on-line system, API development may be required. Since larger upgrade units tend to reduce interface requirements but also tend to increase migration windows, a balance must be struck between these potentially conflicting objectives.

Because most IT organizations functionally categorize their software systems, this is a reasonable place for segmentation to begin. Examples of functional categorization include human resources, finance, personal line claims, sales and marketing, order entry, and so on. Subsequent segmentation techniques are based on data usage, ownership, size, related plans, and shared platforms. With these concepts in mind, we have outlined a high-level set of guidelines for segmenting a portfolio into Year 2000 upgrade units.

1. *Select a group of functionally related systems or subsystems. An example is accounts payable or all accounting systems.*

2. *Work with knowledgeable analysts or documentation to define boundaries based on function, platform, ownership, and management structure.*

3. *Identify a central "core" system within a functionally bounded group of systems and subsystems.*

4. *Establish the core system as the basis for an upgrade unit.*

5. *Expand this core system upgrade unit by including surrounding system and subsystems that:*

   - Feed data directly into the core system

   - Receive data directly from the core system

   - Are on the same hardware or software platform as the core system

   - Have no, or minimal, interfaces with shared data stores other than those used by the core system

   - Are under the same scope of ownership and systems management as the core system

   - Share a common end-user base and test environment with the core system

   - Are not highly volatile in comparison with other systems and subsystems contained in that upgrade unit

   - Do not require new or significant numbers of APIs or bridge interfaces

   - Are not larger than the core system or do not cause the upgrade unit to increase in scope to the point where implementation time constraints are exceeded

Because size is always an indicator of how long a system may be out of production, it is more significant than some of the other considerations. If, for example, a core system consists of 150 programs and a surrounding subsystem adds another 100–150 programs, this is a reasonable upgrade unit scope. If a third system contains 200 programs, that system should most likely be moved into another upgrade unit.

Batch systems tend to "fan in" and "fan out" to and from a single core system. This concept implies a batch system flow where multiple peripheral systems feed data into a central, core system. That system in turn produces data used by a number of small, downstream systems. Whenever possible, the systems and subsystems that create this fan-in and fan-out view (typically found in diagrammatic documentation showing system job and data set flows) should be included in the upgrade unit with the core system. When testing considerations or size prohibit the inclusion of a given system or subsystem in an upgrade unit, batch interface bridges, which are relatively easy to construct, can be used to keep one or more of these systems or subsystems synchronized during ongoing date field expansion efforts.

Multiple on-line and batch systems that share a central database may need to be grouped into separate upgrade units based on size or other factors. On-line systems are relatively easy to segment because, in many cases, the interfaces to files and databases are fairly limited. In the case of shared on-line files or databases, an API can be inserted into a system if it will be Year 2000 compliant prior to other systems that share that data. Finally, large databases may need to be updated as standalone projects, with APIs added to each upgrade unit that accesses the database.

12.6 Upgrade Unit Migration Strategies

Once a portfolio is segmented into upgrade units, the planning team must establish migration strategies and priorities. Strategies and priorities are based on event horizons, business criticality, upgrade requirements, and related plans. Migration planning requires the selection of upgrade unit compliance approaches, based on analysis completed to this point, and synchronization of these approaches across the enterprise. The ultimate goal is to assign each upgrade unit a migration approach, from which budget numbers can be derived, and a project start date. Ultimately, the final implementation strategy depends on a review of the entire plan and the options required to fund and implement that plan.

Note that the process of segmenting upgrade units and selecting a migration approach for each of them requires a degree of reciprocal analysis; ultimate upgrade unit boundaries are typically not finalized until the final phases of the planning process. Topics covered in this section focus on upgrade unit strategy selection and include the procedural workaround, date field expansion, application package, system software, and non-IT system strategies.

12.6.1 Upgrade Unit Strategy Selection

At this point in the assessment, it is critical to synchronize Year 2000 plans with general IT plans to create a Year 2000 strategy capable of accommodating other IT projects being implemented concurrently. To that end, analysts must review each upgrade unit to determine compliance or noncompliance; see Figure 12.3. If a system is marked compliant, this should be verified with impact analysis tools and slated for validation. Validation project startup must allow enough time for analysts to correct constructs determined to be noncompliant.

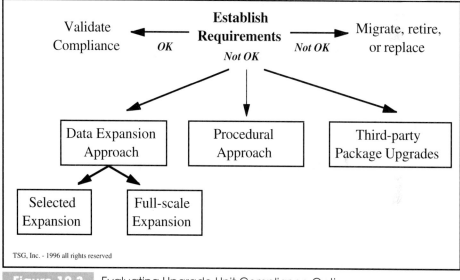

Figure 12.3　Evaluating Upgrade Unit Compliance Options

Systems being replaced, migrated, or phased out prior to 2000 and before their respective event horizons arrive are placed in a low-priority contingency status. Replacement or migration projects must be reviewed to assess risks. These risks stem from the late completion or the noncompliancy of systems produced by a replacement or migration project. Replacement centers on new development, while migration projects tend to contain a very high degree of component reuse. When a system is phased out, analysts must verify that the noncompliant system is eradicated from the software portfolio prior to its projected failure date. System contingency planning is addressed later in this chapter in section 12.8, *Year 2000 Implementation Strategy Finalization*.

12.6.2 Procedural Workaround versus Date Field Expansion

In-house, noncompliant upgrade units that are not scheduled for replacement, migration, or elimination must be slated for date field expansion or procedural upgrade. Approaches are selected based on end-user input, business criticality, and projected life. For example, a system with less than two years of life remaining may be a good candidate for a procedural workaround.

A procedural workaround enables a program to recognize cross-century data logic, even though the system continues to use a two-digit data format for a year. This approach has the benefit of making a system Year 2000 compliant for less cost through reduced implementation effort. According to analysts, a procedural approach requires roughly 20 percent less work than applying the date field expansion approach to that same system. This varies dramatically by system, however. The downside includes addition of more procedural logic, sort field problems, display complexities where full dates are required, permanent interface bridges, and regulatory interface limitations.

Candidates for a procedural workaround approach include systems with the following attributes.

- The system is being replaced within the next 3 years.

- The system is not date dependent and does not interface in any substantial way with other systems or data bases that are themselves highly date dependent.

- The system does not heavily rely on date dependent key fields for data access or updating.

- The event horizon is less than 6 months away, and system failure date is expected in the next 12 months.

- Management refuses to fund the date field expansion effort because the system does not strategically justify the expense.

- The system is being phased out over the next 3 years.

Date field expansion, on the other hand, represents a more complete and more permanent treatment of the Year 2000 problem. Once system upgrades are complete, key fields, sort fields, display fields, and calculations essentially continue to function without additional procedural intervention. This is not true with the procedural approach. The procedural approach is also more prone to having maintenance analysts misinterpret date workaround logic and erroneously introduce a program problem.

The procedural approach also has potential flaws that will be exposed if the solution was incomplete or if it was implemented incorrectly. For these reasons, many organizations have selected date field expansion.

Candidates for date field expansion include systems with the following attributes.

1. *Use of a fully expanded date field meets long-term business requirements based on the strategic value of the system.*

2. *The system is highly date dependent, making the complexity of a procedural solution untenable.*

3. *The system shares data with other systems that are undergoing a date field expansion.*

4. *A government regulatory agency has an 8-character date interface requirement.*

5. *Numerous report and screen displays use dates, and business end users have requested full representation on all end-user interfaces.*

6. *The system makes heavy use of date logic or processes high-volume monetary transactions that would make the use of procedural workaround logic risky.*

7. *Event horizons are far enough away and budget allocation has been set aside for the project.*

In reality, most organizations will apply a mix of the procedural approach and date field expansion across an enterprise. Occasionally, a system may require selected expansion of dates shared with another application even though that system is using a procedural approach. In order to plan for this eventuality, planning teams should obtain the processes, tools, and implementation expertise to accommodate both approaches. It is not recommended that application teams mix approaches within a given system because it has a tendency to complicate testing and can greatly confuse maintenance teams for years to come.

12.6.3 Application Package Software

Application package software, identified during the systems inventory process, requires special consideration and handling. Planners must segment application packages into well-defined upgrade units and determine an upgrade approach based on application area and package vendor input. This approach may include migrating to the latest vendor release or may include other options. The application package assessment process includes the following tasks.

1. *Contact the vendor to determine which release will be Year 2000 compliant, when this release will be available, and the approach selected to correct the problem.*

2. *Estimate the level of effort required to migrate from the current release to the compliant release.*

3. *Define the approach required to reimplement custom changes that may have been applied to the package or to software used to interface with the package.*

4. *Examine alternative options when a package upgrade is unavailable or economically not feasible.*

5. *Add the package to the list of in-house systems to be made Year 2000 compliant where in-house modifications make resynchronization with the vendor's compliant version of the package impossible.*

Packages and any interface components should be scheduled for Year 2000 compliance upgrades along with in-house systems. Embedded, obsolete technology in older vendor packages may require examination of alternate upgrade approaches. Regardless of the alternative selected, enterprise analysts must include application packages in enterprise planning and budgeting tasks. This includes adding all third-party systems to the repository tracking facility, tagging these systems and subsystems as vendor packages in the applicable attribute fields of the repository, and defining interface relationships with in-house systems, as needed. Finally, third-party coordinators should notify vendor contracting agents to correct deficiencies in the contract language.

12.6.4 System Software Strategies

System software and utilities, often ignored during an enterprise assessment, are by no means immune to the Year 2000 problem. Analysts should survey software systems support, data administration, operations, security personnel, and other areas. These survey results, coupled with a list of system software from the operations team, provide the assessment team with a reasonable starting point for determining system software Year 2000 upgrade requirements.

The system software inventory includes databases, teleprocessing monitors, compilers, library management systems, operating systems, interface routines, and utilities. Each of these systems must be examined and upgraded as required. Tasks associated with system software analysis include the following.

1. *Obtain a list of all system software and utilities for all mainframe, midrange, and workstation platforms.*

2. *Review each system package to determine if it will be retained through 1999; note that system software rarely has an event horizon that occurs before 1999.*

3. *Identify all inactive system software (not used at all within the shop), slating those systems for deactivation and eliminating them from the inventory list.*

4. *Determine if any obsolete packages or home-grown utilities can be deactivated and, if so, tag those systems for deactivation prior to 1999.*

5. *Identify duplicate software packages that can be consolidated (e.g., migrating from two library management systems to one) and schedule consolidation projects as needed.*

6. *For all remaining system packages and in-house utilities, contact vendors or in-house personnel to ascertain which release will be Year 2000 compliant and when that release becomes available.*

7. *Schedule release upgrades as upgrade unit projects and coordinate these efforts with application personnel where necessary.*

8. *Estimate the level of effort required to migrate from the current release to the compliant release and determine budgeting strategy with management team.*

9. *Update Year 2000 tracking facility to reflect system software updates—a repository setup option involves storing a utility type (e.g., database) as an entity and linking it to systems that use that utility to cross-reference system software utilization.*

Inventorying and updating system software on all platforms is a key requirement of the Year 2000 project. Ignoring these systems is common because the application managers that are responsible for driving a Year 2000 assessment may not be accustomed to dealing with operations management. Systems requiring particularly close attention include database software because of inherent date dependence, tape management systems for the same reason, and compilers because they may be directly involved with a Year 2000 upgrade. Compilers are often included in an application plan because a vendor, such as IBM, uses the Year 2000 as leverage for encouraging customers to update outdated software. Systems personnel must be closely aligned with these strategies.

12.6.5 End-user and non-IT System Strategy

IT analysts tend to ignore end-user and non-IT based systems during the assessment process. End-user-based systems are unique because they were commissioned or acquired by end-user departments without knowledge, input, or approval of IT. By definition, these systems are difficult to find and equally difficult to accommodate under a Year 2000 strategy. User-based systems are typically established because of some level of dissatisfaction with IT. These same end users tend to be reticent in sharing information about these systems. Non-IT based systems that are either used internally or produced for sale to third parties fall into a similar category. Researching end-user and non-IT systems poses a challenge to the assessment team but is a required task of the Year 2000 assessment.

Analysts should survey and take recommended action for end-user based systems as follows.

1. *Streamline survey forms to the minimal level of questions needed to ascertain data on end-user based applications.*

2. *Send these survey forms to applicable business area directors or vice presidents.*

3. *If there is a large number of end-user systems (end-user systems comprising more than 10–20 percent of the IT portfolio), assign a full-time end-user systems coordinator to a support role.*

4. *Depending on the IT charter for end-user systems, provide coaching and briefings to end-user areas on the Year 2000 problem and how users might correct package systems developed in-house or purchased.*

5. *Add significant end-user-based systems (but do not include small scale spreadsheets or similar PC-based systems) to the Year 2000 tracking facility and tag them as end-user systems for reporting purposes.*

6. *Continue tracking progress on these applications and report on end-user status in advisory board sessions as required.*

Non-IT systems include systems that are not under IT control and that are either used internally or sold to third parties. Internal candidates include ATM equipment, manufacturing control systems, entry systems, elevator systems, environmental control systems, or other equipment that contains a computer chip and related processing technology. These systems should be identified by the end-user-based systems analyst or facilities coordinator, working in conjunction with a vice president of administration. The main goal is to produce a vendor survey to determine if these systems will work when 2000 arrives and, if they will not function properly, how to proceed with a replacement initiative.

Non-IT systems that may be produced for resale by a company can include computerized dashboards, card entry systems, elevator systems, telephone chips, computers, or process control systems. This recital introduces the other side of the systems dilemma: companies that sell technology that contains Year 2000-related risks must be proactive in assessing potential impacts to their customers. If a company's primary purpose is to sell computer systems, executives should take immediate action to determine the level of legal exposure. The guidelines found in this book apply to systems developed for resale—although somewhat in reverse as far as risk factors are concerned. If these non-IT systems are just byproducts of the manufacturing process—computerized dashboards for example—then the level of analysis to be performed is fairly minimal.

12.6.6 Standalone Database Expansion Projects

When a large database is shared by numerous systems, all of which are deemed separate upgrade units, special projects may need to be commissioned to expand and reformat those databases. This approach, which applies only to a date field expansion strategy and is shown in Figure 12.4, requires a special project, executed by data administration, to reformat database structures to reflect expanded and redefined date formats. Multiple options can be pursued under this scenario; the following outlines the most common one in use today.

1. *Use the enterprise assessment inventory results to identify major databases and all systems and upgrade units accessing those databases.*

2. *If databases are either too large or are shared by too many systems, then schedule that database to be updated as a standalone entity to reduce the upgrade unit migration window.*

3. *Schedule each database in this category to be expanded as a funded upgrade project.*

4. *Include work tasks to expand all physical database date fields, segments, or record types and to create expanded and original versions of applicable database definitions.*

5. *Identify all impacted upgrade units, using cross-reference analysis results, to schedule API updates for each impacted program; these can be done by maintenance teams or special project teams.*

6. *Define the cost of all database projects in the final implementation budget as a project.*

7. *Schedule each upgrade unit API project as a related cost to that upgrade unit.*

8. *Include each upgrade unit again for complete expansion, based on other criteria, as for any other upgrade unit.*

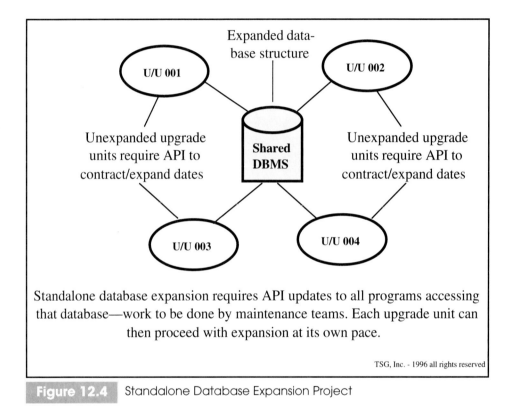

Expanded database structure

U/U 001

U/U 002

Unexpanded upgrade units require API to contract/expand dates

Shared DBMS

Unexpanded upgrade units require API to contract/expand dates

U/U 003

U/U 004

Standalone database expansion requires API updates to all programs accessing that database—work to be done by maintenance teams. Each upgrade unit can then proceed with expansion at its own pace.

Figure 12.4 Standalone Database Expansion Project

Another approach to database expansion is to add to the database layout new dates that essentially mirror the existing date, through the use of a duplicate date field with an expanded format. This alternate approach does not require any initial change to the existing system source code. Its disadvantage is that it requires analysts to add program logic so that throughout the migration process for the upgrade unit, two physical dates—essentially the same but with different formats—are kept synchronized within the same record. This approach works quite well if only one upgrade unit accesses a given database.

12.7 Existing IT Support Infrastructure Assessment

Chapters 5 and 6 discuss basic definitions and the importance of standards and Year 2000 specific infrastructure requirements. Topics include standards, configuration management, code freezing (change control), shared routines (reuse), migration technology, testing requirements, and migration environments. Assessing the readiness of the IT organization regarding these issues requires reviewing the IT support intrastructure and allows management to make more informed decisions when planning the Year 2000 implementation phase. These decisions may affect the ability of management to estimate how well project teams can deliver results in specified time frames. It may also lead to the commissioning of special projects to correct infrastructure weaknesses in parallel with Year 2000 implementation projects.

Dealing with infrastructure problems is a critical factor in delivering successful Year 2000 results. Risk levels and impacts should be evaluated for each area during the enterprise assessment. This analysis can be completed concurrently with upgrade unit planning and should be incorporated into the final Year 2000 strategy. Analysts should interview managers in charge of selected support functions in order to complete this assessment. In this way, infrastructure improvement projects can focus on selected functional areas or more broadly as required. Analysts should use their best judgment to determine if a topic is best assessed at an enterprise level or at an application area level. Infrastructure topics include management issues, standards, procedures, and test environments.

12.7.1 Management Infrastructure Readiness

If it is still an issue, analysts should confirm that executive sponsorship remains intact. This includes determining if the CIO and direct reports have the year 2000 on their monthly meeting agenda, if the working budget is still safe, if the Project Office director still retains access to the CIO, and if the Project Office deems that sponsorship is adequate. Analysts should also ascertain whether business unit sponsorship is adequate. This inquiry includes determining whether functional area leaders are apprised of the Year 2000 issue, whether working budgets have been discussed at their level, and whether they acknowledge the project as a critical agenda item for the next 2–3 years. If sponsorship is in jeopardy at any level, the advisory board or other executive governing body should be notified immediately.

Examine the level of the Year 2000 team's preparedness to determine if it is adequate to support the implementation phase. Determine if a

Project Office leader is in place and in charge and that assignments exist for coordinating software tools and tool vendors, methodology, communication, third-party support, status tracking and reporting, validation, change and configuration control, and technology transfer. Furthermore, ensure that representation is in place for quality assurance, the data center, operations, security, data administration, auditing, and the legal department. Determine that the project office budget and charter are in place through the end of the Year 2000 project. If these items are not in place, executives should be notified immediately to correct the problem.

Finally, analysts should ensure the adequacy of application area management support by verifying that managers and coordinators are assigned for each major area and that education of these individuals about the Year 2000 has begun or is planned in the near term. If sponsorship is not in place for any of these management issues, executives should be notified immediately. A lack of management infrastructure support going into the implementation phase could spell doom for the project.

12.7.2 System Support Standards and Guidelines

Standards and guidelines, covered in Chapter 5, strengthen the reliability of the project planning process. Analysts should verify that standards are in place as the organization enters the implementation phase of the Year 2000 project.

Year 2000 compliance standards should be available to ensure that the developers of new systems are making those systems Year 2000 compliant. These include:

- Standards requiring an 8-digit date in source code, on interfaces, and for data stores

- Guidelines defining when user views may diverge from an 8-digit date standard

- Guidelines defining when procedural workaround options are acceptable

- Contracted language for vendor package acquisition and upgrades.

- Communication guidelines for external entities (IRS, SEC, etc.)

- Standards exemption procedures for application teams

- Standards for acquiring hardware and system software

- A set of "date handling routines" and supporting documentation for all environments

In addition to the above standards, analysts should determine whether Year 2000 migration specifications are in place. This includes reviewing that:

- Specifications are ready to be communicated to outsourcing organizations

- Specifications are in place for internal migration teams

- Migration guidelines communicate clear responsibility for migration activities, interface development, testing, and change management

If these standards and guidelines do not exist, the Year 2000 Project Office should quickly establish these guidelines so that they will be ready for use by migration teams as the implementation phase is launched.

12.7.3 System Configuration and Categorization Procedures

Chapter 6 provided an extensive treatment of configuration management and change control issues. The analysis recommended at this point in the assessment process involves a basic review of issues that could cause significant problems during the implementation phase of the Year 2000 project. Topics include library standardization and integrity, distribution issues, and change control procedures. Depending on the structure of the organization analysts should apply this analysis at an enterprise, divisional, or application area level.

Analysts should review library standards to determine if the Year 2000 inventory process encountered well-defined source libraries at predefined locations. Analysts should also determine if the location of these systems was documented in the tracking facility during the analysis process. Additionally, analysts should indicate if configuration changes are formally updated through a central coordinator and available to all systems personnel. Finally, analysts should examine library integrity levels for naming convention quality, incidents of missing or duplicate components, and the existence of obsolete systems in production libraries. If any of these issues are identified, the advisory board should review options to resolve them.

Other issues complicate a Year 2000 implementation project: multiple source languages, support teams that not are trained in these languages, and no commitment from management to eliminate obsolete languages and compilers. A high degree of mixed or obsolete languages will drive up implementation costs and time frames. Another complicating factor is the degree of system and support distribution, across physical locations, found during the inventory process. If the majority of systems were identified during the initial inventory process, with distributed system locations now stored in the central tracking facility, there should be little problem implementing this project from a controls perspective. If this is not the case, the assessment team should reexamine its original analysis and correct this problem.

12.7.4 Change Control and Production Turnover

Change control and production turnover tend to be unique to a given application area and typically require multiple interviews to determine adequacy. Change control procedures are critical to the successful implementation of a large-scale Year 2000 project. This means that a well-defined change control process must be in place for the Year 2000 implementation effort, that production synchronization techniques must be documented for implementation teams, and that application staging procedures must be in place to manage multiple, work-in-progress libraries.

Analysts should determine if production turnover procedures are centrally defined and followed for applicable platforms and systems. They should also review whether the acceptance and actual turnover process is handled by a separate and centrally controlled group. If production turnover time frames are fairly long or if the process is neither tightly controlled nor well managed, analysts may want to recommend a separate project to adjust these procedures in anticipation of the Year 2000 implementation phase of the project.

12.7.5 Process and Procedure Review

Maintenance maturity, development reliability (e.g., the ability to meet target dates), project management maturity, quality assurance, and the use of a formal migration process all impact implementation projects. For example, if maintenance changes are not tracked, recorded, and grouped into well-defined work groups or no maintenance procedures exist, analysts may want to recommend that work for this particular area be taken off site or be performed by consulting teams. Similarly, if new development and replacement target dates are rarely attained or cost overruns are common, any replacement projects slated for that application may be suspect. This type of track record may require that management pay more attention to contingency plans for that area.

Strong project management ability is another factor driving the decision to perform work in-house versus using third parties to migrate systems. Analysts should determine if formal project management procedures are in place and required for all projects, if a formal process is applied to project management, and if project planning tools are used.

Quality assurance, a key task in Year 2000 migration projects, should already be a formally defined function performed by a team of people other than the personnel that produced the original work. Management should also consider getting the internal audit department involved if this has not already occurred. Analysts should examine the relationship between internal audit and quality assurance teams as part of this analysis.

12.7.6 Validation and Testing Infrastructure Analysis

Validation and testing readiness should be reviewed at the application area level because it tends to vary by team. The validation and testing process can be considered ready for the Year 2000 implementation project if the following are true.

- Testing process is documented and generally followed.

- Separate testing teams are established and used on a regular basis.

- Testing includes regularly tracking test logic coverage, and the level of coverage is at least 70 percent.

- Formal test files or databases that are not just copies of production have been set up for various functional areas.

- Validation for the Year 2000 implementation phase will be managed through a formal process.

- On-line testing includes some type of capture and playback facility.

- Validation assistance will be provided through a centrally defined process with technology transfer support.

If an application area is not meeting any of these criteria, the Project Office must recommend that procedures and tools be put in place to correct the deficiencies. These recommendations may result in several projects aimed at stabilizing the test environment, and the resulting test environments will be of value long after the Year 2000 project is over. The cost of each of these projects can be coupled with a Year 2000 upgrade unit plan or can be estimated as a separate project. Review Chapter 6 for more details on improving testing infrastructures.

12.8 Year 2000 Implementation Infrastructure

The last infrastructure category to be addressed is Year 2000 implementation technology and environments. The Year 2000 technology coordinator must research inventory, impact, migration, validation, repository, process/project management, communication, and presentation tools for the project and verify that all languages, platforms, and environments are considered. Various software tools enhance productivity and should be procured, tested, and deployed early in the implementation cycle. Research efforts can be streamlined by using a formal methodology to identify tools by category.

Work environments, repository support, implementation tools, and project management technology are described at length in Chapter 6. The detailed guidelines contained in Chapter 6 should be referred to during the process of setting up the implementation support infrastructure. The methodology discussion in Chapter 9 also provides valuable input to this process. Analysts should determine what is in place today and what work must be completed in order to establish a functioning work environment for Year 2000 projects. The categories described in the following pages, should be included in this analysis. Each category is prefaced by a discussion regarding management ideas about where the implementation work should be performed.

12.8.1 Implementation Tool Support

Implementation technology is typically required for most organizations. IT groups wanting to perform Year 2000 upgrades in-house must procure certain tools. If a consulting house is performing the upgrade work on site, these tools will still be required, although the consultants may provide them. Even companies that tend to shun automated solutions will want to use impact analysis tools to help identify date fields, and inventory and cross-reference tools to audit component changes. Products within these categories should be procured for major platforms. Based on the approach applied to the majority of the upgrade units, an automated or semiautomated field expansion or a date routine technology can also be added to this list.

Validation tools are required for Year 2000 implementation projects, because the bulk of the testing typically is performed on site. Tools for validation should minimally include dynamic analyzers, playback tools for on-line testing, automated comparison tools, and data manipulation tools that also support data conversion and interface development. Implementation and validation technology is discussed in greater depth in Chapters 13, *Year 2000 Implementation and Deployment*, and Chapter 14, *Validation Strategies*, respectively. At this stage of the planning cycle, analysts should verify performance of the following tasks.

1. *Identify prevailing upgrade unit scenarios based on the Year 2000 migration strategy.*

2. *Select tools that best support those implementation and validation approaches for primary hardware and software platforms.*

3. *Examine tool categories (Chapter 15), and tool vendor options (Appendix A).*

4. *Procure tools to support work that is definitely going to be performed in-house.*

5. *Add total projected tool costs to the enterprise budget and obtain approval of required tool acquisition.*

6. *Procure tools after checking with customer references and third-party consultants that may provide input to the planning process.*

7. *Deploy tools in selected pilot projects in actual conversion conditions to fine-tune the tools and the process.*

Refer to Chapter 13 and Chapter 14 for more information about implementation and validation tool categories. At this point, identifying, procuring, and implementing those tools is the main priority for the Project Office technology coordinator.

12.8.2 Repository Tracking Facility

Analysts should verify that the repository tracking facility set up during the enterprise assessment has been kept up-to-date for use in the implementation phase of the project. If this repository was not populated during the enterprise assessment, it is typically too late to attempt to activate that repository during implementation: the inventory process would have to be repeated or information in the inventory tools would have to be updated and then ported into the repository facility from scratch. If the repository is populated, however, the technology analyst should take the following steps.

1. *If a simple data model was used during the enterprise assessment project, determine requirements for moving to a formal repository for implementation.*

2. *Obtain budget approval for repository technology as required and finalize procurement process.*

3. *Establish and institutionalize an inventory refreshment capability using automated inventory tools, manual techniques, and multiple repositories to feed a central tracking facility.*

4. *Define any adjustments required to transition the repository from the enterprise assessment phase to the implementation project tracking phase.*

5. *Document these procedures and the level of effort required to keep the repository information current.*

6. *Add this information to the budget planning process for the enterprise budget.*

7. *Verify that the repository facility is used in any pilot projects.*

Review Chapter 13 for more in-depth information on the use of the repository as a tracking facility.

12.8.3 Implementation Work Environments

Work environments, described in Chapter 6, provide streamlined access to tools and methods during the course of a project. The prevailing platform, mainframe, for example, typically drives the type of work environment to be selected for a Year 2000 project. This may be augmented by a workstation-based environment if a significant amount of maintenance and development work is performed there. When tools permit, as much of the upgrade work as possible should be performed on the platform where that application is currently maintained. If additional hardware is required for upgrade unit migration projects, analysts should add the cost of that hardware to the enterprise budget. Excess hardware requirements are discussed below.

12.8.4 Excess Hardware Requirements

Because production environments must be replicated to support Year 2000 project implementation and testing, extra disk space and hardware capacity must be allocated for internally executed projects. The operations area must provide input on hardware, system software, and storage upgrade requirements for the Year 2000 project, based on what is used today. A rule of thumb is that organizations should plan on using up to 20 percent more hardware capacity and disk space during peak migration than what is currently used. Much of this capacity is driven by testing requirements—work that is likely to be performed in-house regardless of where the migration work is performed.

Options for satisfying excess hardware requirements include using disaster recovery sites for excess testing time, leasing more hardware, or using excess capacity, if available, within other divisions or areas of the company. Other alternatives may include off-loading conversion work to factory or outsourcing vendors to minimize in-house hardware utilization or off-loading some work to workstation platforms, thereby minimizing upgrade costs. As stated earlier, the most efficient migration platform is usually the environment where the systems are maintained, and this implies that workstation off-loading strategies may limit productivity in the short term. Planning for hardware requirements must occur prior to implementation, and analysts must attempt to gain an accurate picture of excess capacity requirements. Excess hardware expenditures are incorporated as a line item expense of the enterprise section of the Year 2000 budget that was defined in Chapter 10.

12.9 Year 2000 Implementation Strategy Finalization

The year 2000 implementation plan includes an infrastructure upgrade plan, a system software and hardware upgrade plan, an upgrade unit migration schedule, strategies to perform work in-house or to outsource certain portions of the project, a validation plan, and a summary budget for the implementation phase. The implementation phase and validation activities are discussed in depth in Chapters 13 and 14, respectively. The other deliverable, that is not technically part of the enterprise assessment but typically performed in parallel, is the pilot project plan and results. Pilot projects are discussed in the next section of this chapter.

12.9.1 Infrastructure Upgrade Plan

The infrastructure upgrade plan is a direct result of the infrastructure assessment and includes required upgrades to facilitate a successful implementation, system software and hardware upgrades, recommended work environments, and software tool requirements.

Potential infrastructure upgrades, based on the findings of the infrastructure assessment, may include the following tasks.

1. *Adjust the management and reporting infrastructures where weaknesses have been identified.*

2. *Upgrade, finalize, distribute, and train key personnel in standards and procedures as required by the infrastructure assessment analysis.*

3. *Implement standardized library configuration management and change control technology and procedures across selected application areas.*

4. *Incorporate the repository tracking facility into the configuration management facility.*

5. *Eliminate all duplicate or obsolete systems and system components found during the inventory process.*

6. *Introduce quality assurance, change control, production turnover procedures, and audit techniques into selected application areas where deficiencies were identified.*

7. *Stabilize maintenance procedures in application areas where existing policies present a change control or change management risk to the Year 2000 upgrade project.*

8. *Correct weaknesses in testing procedures that were discovered during the validation and testing infrastructure analysis—corrective action is outlined in Chapter 6 and in the validation strategy discussion later in this section.*

Based on the analysis of system software and hardware requirements, pursue the following action items where applicable.

1. *Based on the number of noncompliant system software upgrade requirements, summarize the systems to be upgraded and eliminated.*

2. *Summarize systems to be upgraded, required time frames, and associated costs so that these can be rolled into the upgrade unit timeline, discussed in the next section.*

3. *Determine if current hardware processing capacity is sufficient to handle a peak load increase of 20 percent envisioned during the Year 2000 implementation and testing projects.*

4. *Identify and recommend a hardware upgrade, backup hardware site or off-load plan, and associated costs, to address peak hardware processing requirements.*

5. *Determine if current storage capacity is sufficient to handle a peak load increase of 20 percent envisioned during the Year 2000 implementation and testing projects.*

6. *Identify excess storage capacity acquisition and budget costs as required.*

7. *If any hardware platforms (e.g., old PC hardware) were deemed noncompliant during prior assessment tasks, summarize the cost of those upgrades by application area and add these to the upgrade unit budget.*

Recommended work environment and tool requirements are summarized in these tasks:

1. *List all implementation tools, as discussed in section 12.8* Year 2000 Implementation Infrastructure.

2. *List all work environment upgrade requirements, including hardware, process management tools, or other items defined in Chapter 5 and required for project implementation.*

3. *Add these lists as line items of the Year 2000 enterprise budget.*

Incorporate each of the aforementioned items, as required, into the Year 2000 enterprise budget. Justification for many of these items hinges not just upon the success of the Year 2000 project, but also on the long-term benefits provided by these infrastructure improvements. Most of these upgrades will occur in the early stages of implementation, and the budget allocation plan should reflect this fact.

12.9.2 Upgrade Unit Migration Schedule

Inputs to the migration planning process include the business risk assessment, upgrade unit segmentation and migration strategy, system software and hardware plans, and other data that has been collected to this point. The final deliverable from this process is the list of upgrade units and associated systems to be made compliant, projected start dates, completion time frames staggered over a multiyear implementation window, and related costs for each upgrade unit.

Once analysts have identified all Year 2000 upgrade units and the approaches to be applied to each of those upgrade units, sequencing of each project may begin. Sequencing depends on event horizons, project duration, and resource availability. Figure 12.5 represents a multiyear implementation schedule for an enterprise Year 2000 initiative at a medium-sized company with about 14 million lines of code. Table 12.1 summarizes a Year 2000 implementation plan that can be used to report project status to senior executives and to the advisory board.

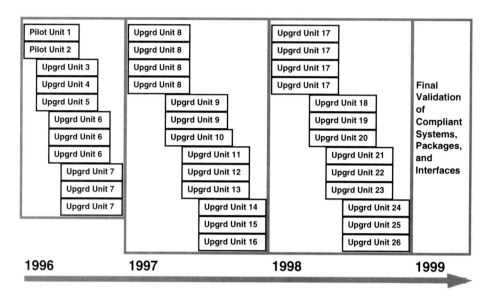

Figure 12.5 Year 2000 Upgrade Unit Prioritization Plan

Defining the plan in Table 12.1 requires that the following tasks be performed.

1. *Obtain a list of upgrade units and systems included within those upgrade units; keep a separate list for system software.*

Table 12.1 Upgrade Unit Implementation Plan Summary

Upgrade Unit	Systems	Planned Startup	Planned Duration	Budget Estimate	Approach	Strategy
001A	Payroll Pension	1/1/97	90 days	$1.8 million	Expansion	Outsource
002C	A/R A/P	2/15/97	100 days	$2.7 million	Package Upgrade	In-house w/ consultants
etc.	etc.	etc.	etc.	etc.	etc.	etc.

2. *Review event horizons, approach, and business criticality for each upgrade unit to create an initial project priority sequence within a defined multiyear time frame.*

3. *Based on the approach and related metrics unique to that upgrade unit, create a project estimate, using activity-based or alternative cost model.*

4. *Examine related system software, database upgrade, or upgrade unit interdependencies and adjust startup time frames as required.*

5. *Assign project start date, expected duration, and project end date for each upgrade unit.*

6. *Create a representation of this multiyear plan (e.g., Figure 12.5 and Table 12.1) as needed to communicate and summarize the Year 2000 implementation strategy.*

Detailed activity-based cost models and formulas can be found in commercially available methodologies and blueprints. A high-level estimating example, required to perform a complete (screens, reports, data, programs) date field expansion project, is shown below. These estimates represent an upgrade unit that contains 3 systems, 100 data files and database segments, 5 shared interfaces, 21 batch data interfaces, 240 source programs, 100 batch reports, 85 screens, and 90 job control members.

Upgrade unit plan development:	2 days
Detailed upgrade unit design:	80 days
Upgrade unit implementation plan:	2 days
System component expansion:	90 days
Data store expansion and interface creation:	80 days
Validation:	120 days
Total work effort:	374 days

Note that many of the tasks and related factors are not shown in this estimating example. Note also that the interface development and certain data expansion tasks may also be construed as validation activities. This means that validation, as a percentage of the total project, still encompasses one-third to one-half of total project effort. Calculation of projected costs can be adjusted depending on who is slated to perform the work. Activity-based cost models should be created for all procedural workaround options, application package upgrades, or other types of projects scheduled during the implementation phase. Individual upgrade unit project plans should be drafted in detail as supporting documentation for the overall plan.

12.9.3 In-house Upgrade versus Outsourcing Strategies

Work to be performed in house, either with or without consulting support, has certain levels of responsibility associated with it. The decision process that dictates whether an organization takes the project outside or performs the work in-house is based on numerous factors. An upgrade unit should be migrated in-house if the following situations are prevalent.

- In-house staff or third-party consultants are available to perform in-house conversion work.

- Migration environments, tools, and methodology are either in place or being put in place to support in-house migration work.

- The upgrade unit is either a third-party package or is of such a sensitive nature that it precludes the shipping of an upgrade unit off site.

- Management wants this work to be performed in-house because of control issues or other relevant factors.

If an upgrade unit is outsourced, which includes shipping code off site as well as providing off-site links to in-house systems, exact specifications must be communicated to the vendor for this type of project. Issues that would drive an upgrade unit project to be shipped offsite include the following factors.

- In-house staff is either unavailable or unable to perform upgrade.

- Migration environments and tools are not available to support in-house work.

- The upgrade unit is not a package and is not of a proprietary nature that restricts sending that upgrade unit off site.

- Management is more comfortable with shipping work off site to minimize impacts on in-house project work.

Chapter 17 outlines basic service obligations that relate to various third-party support approaches. In-house work, with or without third-party consulting help, is still considered in-house work and subject to the guidelines outlined above. Shipping upgrade units to a factory or having a third party link into an in-house system both imply that external personnel are performing work on in-house systems. Where work is to be given to a third party, management has the following obligations.

1. *Define upgrade unit boundaries and all components that belong to that upgrade unit.*

2. *Ship all of those components to the factory site as a well-defined upgrade unit.*

3. *Understand the interfaces to be created by the external service provider.*

4. *Set the approach to be applied and the extent of the approach (e.g., screens and reports left as is).*

5. *Assume responsibility for data conversion, change control, validation, and production implementation.*

6. *Manage the relationship very closely.*

Once management has defined the key issues related to all upgrade units across the enterprise, they should perform one final review to verify that the entire plan is cohesive and realistic. This should include identification of consultants and factory vendors—by name. Naming actual third-party consultants requires that the Project Office research third-party service providers in parallel with the planning for implementation. Any other unique, outstanding implementation requirements should be included at this time.

12.9.4 Contingency Planning

Management should develop contingency plans for all mission-critical systems, systems with near-term event horizons, and systems scheduled to be replaced. This means that, in the event that a project runs late (a common occurrence in IT environments) and causes an existing application to fail because of a date problem, management will have a fallback position. Typically, business management must be involved in contingency planning because of the nature of the solution, which may require an end user to work without a computer for a period of time. It could also mean that, as event horizons near, selling a business unit or some other type of radical solution may gain greater appeal.

12.10 Pilot Project Planning

Pilot projects are an important element in fine-tuning estimates and approaches. Results are fed back into cost models so that estimates reflect actual implementation experience. This process is important because each organization has unique policies, technologies, and politics. Pilots are the first project for a language or platform type or the first project with a given third-party service provider.

Pilot requirements, including major languages, platforms, databases, teleprocessing monitors, vendors, tools, and outsourcing options, should be documented in the final section of the assessment report. If pilot projects have not been executed at this point, plans to do so should be noted. Pilot projects should ideally be executed during the planning stage and prior to finalization of budgets and deployment plans. Chapters 13 and 14 discuss various implementation and testing issues that should be addressed during pilot project planning and execution.

If pilots are used as a test for outsourcing vendors, send different systems with different attributes to each of those vendors and make sure that application teams move compliant systems into production when testing is completed. Pilot tests should never be an academic exercise—time is too short—and converted systems must be returned to production in all circumstances.

12.11 Enterprise Assessment Finalization and Ongoing Coordination

One of the biggest challenges faced by companies that have had external consultants perform an enterprise assessment is that the deliverables from that assessment were incompatible with requirements of other consulting firms or in-house analysts. This resulted in in-house or third-party consultants having to essentially rework portions of the enterprise assessment to recast the deliverables in a format that could be understood by others. The responsibility for this lies with the management team and Project Office that chartered the assessment in the first place.

To avoid this problem, all RFP or contract documents should contain a well-defined set of deliverable requirements that clearly state the content and format of the enterprise assessment deliverables. These deliverables should include reports, repository formats, and project work plans resulting from the assessment. If this set is not specified in advance of the enterprise assessment, then each in-house or outsourcing consulting firm that works on this project will eventually end up reworking much of an analysis that should only be performed once.

Project scope, budgets, and timelines for upgrade unit migration, established during enterprise planning, typically require ongoing adjustment. Change is the only constant in an IT environment and must be accommodated. This means that the Project Office roles described earlier in this chapter must be maintained throughout the project where applicable. It also means that status tracking and related shifts in plans or budgetary issues should be expeditiously communicated to IT management and the advisory board. This practice may not be standard with other IT projects, but most of those projects do not have such an unforgiving deadline as the year 2000.

Chapter 13

Year 2000 Implementation and Deployment

This chapter discusses the Year 2000 implementation phase. It describes the execution of the implementation phase of a Year 2000 project, in which the organization performs detailed conversion analysis, conversion, testing, and implementation of each upgrade unit identified in the enterprise plan. Note that the activities described in this chapter are subject to enterprise guidelines discussed in Chapter 12. Readers who have not familiarized themselves with the enterprise assessment process may want to review Chapter 12 before continuing.

Deliverables from a Year 2000 implementation project and related activities, all discussed in this chapter, include the following.

- Deliverable: Summary of roles and skills for implementation phase
  Activity: Finalize roles and skills requirements.

- Deliverable: Summary of implementation technology and infrastructure
  Activity: Finalize implementation technology requirements.

- Deliverable: Infrastructure upgrade project
  Activity: Implement selected infrastructure upgrade options.

- Deliverable: Finalized analysis plan for upgrade unit
  Activity: Create upgrade unit detailed analysis plan.

- Deliverable: Detailed design analysis for upgrade unit
  Activity: Complete upgrade unit detailed design analysis.

- Deliverable: Finalized migration plan for upgrade unit
  Activity: Implement upgrade unit package upgrade.

- Deliverable: Date field expansion solution for upgrade unit
  Activity: Implement upgrade unit date field expansion.

- Deliverable: Procedural workaround solution for upgrade unit
  Activity: Implement upgrade unit procedural workaround.

- Deliverable: Package upgrade solution for upgrade unit
  Activity: Implement upgrade unit package upgrade.

- Deliverable: Activated/deactivated interfaces
  Activity: Implement data store and upgrade unit interface routines.

- Deliverable: Solution for data migration
  Activity: Perform data store migration.

- Deliverable: Strategy for change control and production turnover
  Activity: Perform change control and production turnover procedures.

Other activities, also described in this chapter, include the following tasks.

1. *Update central tracking facility.*

2. *Synchronize upgrade projects.*

3. *Execute contingency plans.*

4. *Finalize enterprisewide Year 2000 project.*

Figure 13.1 summarizes activities unique to a given upgrade unit conversion. The top half of the figure, titled "Upgrade Unit Conversion," illustrates the scope of this chapter; validation and testing are addressed in Chapter 14.

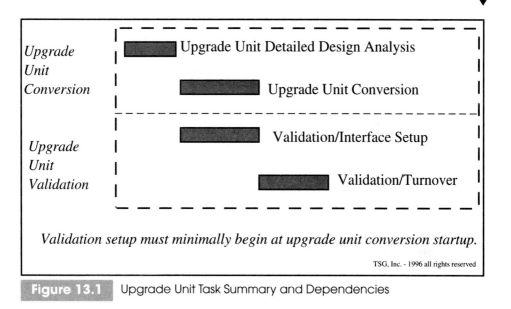

Figure 13.1 Upgrade Unit Task Summary and Dependencies

13.1 Implementation Roles and Skills Summary

Year 2000 implementation projects require a mix of roles and skills for in-house or, alternatively, externally performed projects. The basic roles described below are common to most date field expansion or procedural workaround projects. Special coordination is required and discussed for upgrade unit conversion work that may be performed off site or for projects where package software is involved. References to testing personnel are provided in Chapter 14, *Validation Strategies*.

- **Year 2000 migration specialist.**

  A Year 2000 migration specialist is skilled in a variety of detailed analysis and conversion techniques. These techniques include finding dates, fixing dates, inserting standard date handling or workaround routines, interface development, data migration, and library synchronization. Some of these skills are optional, depending on the type of project performed. This specialist must also be knowledgeable in the platform type and the languages to be converted.

  Depending on the size of the upgrade unit, there may be one or more migration specialists assigned to a given upgrade unit conversion project with various skills distributed among them. For example, one person may be skilled in system expansion, while a second individual focuses on data store expansion. Implementation techniques and tool knowledge transfer can be provided by the Year 2000 Project Office or third-party consultants and is highly recommended in most situations.

- **Upgrade unit migration project manager.**

  The upgrade unit Year 2000 conversion project is a self-contained project that requires planning, resource assignment, and status tracking. Each project requires a project manager to be responsible for these activities.

- **Year 2000 software tools and technology analyst.**

  When software tools are used in conjunction with a system, individuals with knowledge of those tools should provide project support. This knowledge should extend to all relevant tools listed in section 13.2 on implementation technology and section 13.3 on infrastructure support. For larger projects, skills can be distributed among multiple individuals. For example, one analyst might work with the impact and cross-reference analysis tools, while another analyst works with interactive or automated conversion tools. Year 2000 Project Office personnel can provide valuable software tool skills transfer as a means of offsetting the long learning curve typically associated with software tool deployment.

- **Application area analyst.**

  Application area analysts can participate in or advise a Year 2000 upgrade project. The minimum level of participation required by the application area analyst is that of an advisor, because application knowledge is needed to help identify upgrade units, provide input on date usage, install interfaces, and test and implement a system. In some cases, application management may want only the individuals responsible for a system to be working on it. In other cases, management may want to minimize application personnel involvement because of other commitments. Upgrade unit planning should determine the minimum and maximum level of involvement for application analysts at the beginning of the project.

- **External business partner coordinator.**

  When external application software vendors or interfaces to external business partners are a consideration, someone must be assigned responsibility for coordinating with these third parties. This person may be an application area analyst or may be someone assigned from the Year 2000 Project Office. Regardless of the individual assigned, it is important to formalize and coordinate this role at the beginning of the project.

- **Project Office participation.**

  The Year 2000 Project Office provides technology and process knowledge transfer to project participants as required. The Project Office also participates in status tracking. The Project Office also provides information regarding existing and newly defined data interfaces and related upgrade unit project status.

- **Special roles for off-site work or third-party packages.**

  When upgrade units are shipped off-site, or offshore resources are linked to in-house computer systems, a coordinator must be assigned to interface with the applicable service provider. The responsibilities of this coordinator include establishing offshore or off-site coordination and packaging standards, establishing specifications for the upgrade unit to be processed or shipped off site, and verifying that participants followed adequate procedures.

13.2 Implementation Technology Summary

Year 2000 implementation projects require certain basic software tools. The tools selected to migrate a given upgrade unit to Year 2000 compliance depend in part on tools used to perform the enterprise assessment, platform and language types, conversion approach selected for that upgrade unit, who is to perform the work, and where the work is to be performed. If, for example, a consulting firm performing the work uses a proprietary software tool to perform the conversion, selecting a conversion tool is a nonissue. If conversion work is to be shipped off site, in-house personnel need not concern themselves with the tools to be used.

Note that selected upgrade unit implementation technologies are recommended regardless of the migration options chosen to support change integration and quality assurance reviews. These tool categories are discussed in more depth in Chapter 15, and specific vendor tool references can be found in Appendix A. Technology validation and testing is discussed in Chapter 14.

- **Inventory and cross-reference tool**

  In the implementation phase, cross-reference tools ensure that all components are included in the upgrade process and that all related components are updated with the same formats. We highly recommend the use of this tool on implementation projects. Chapter 15 and Appendix A provide more insight into the options available to implementation teams.

- **Impact analyzer**

  Using an impact analyzer to identify date fields during an upgrade unit conversion effort provides significant value to the implementation team. Planning teams should note that an impact analyzer provides value regardless of the approach used to achieve Year 2000 compliance.

- **Tracking facility or repository**

  The tracking facility populated during the enterprise assessment should be integrated into the implementation phase. If available, analysts will want to extend repository use to support automated population by the cross reference tools. Use of this tool is discussed later in this chapter section 13.12, *Central Project Office Communication and Status Reporting*.

- **Calendar routines—standardization and workaround logic support**

  Vendor tool support for standardizing date manipulation logic may be required if standard date handling routines are not available to support cross-century date values. Tools that provide standard date logic typically also offer procedural workaround capabilities. These tools are required for workaround projects unless in-house technology exists.

- **Interactive date change facility**

  Finding and fixing date fields is a tedious activity that lends itself to automation. This date change facility allows analysts to interactively find and fix dates. If there are no plans to use a date field expansion tool, interactive change support is a definite benefit. Synchronization with the conversion methodology is critical for this tool.

- **Date field expansion tool**

  If automated date field expansion is a goal, analysts should investigate the platforms supported by these tools and match them to in-house environments. Use pilot projects to verify levels of automation and reliability.

- **Interface/bridge generator**

  The creation of APIs and bridges can be automated to some degree by certain tools. This includes some of the tools that provide automated date field expansion. Analysts should keep this in mind during tool research efforts.

- **Comparison/change integration facility**

  Auditing code changes is a basic requirement supported by comparison tools. This tool supports the quality assurance walk-through and change integration analysis—tasks so prevalent in an upgrade unit conversion that this tool is one of the most important tools found in a Year 2000 implementation project.

- **Data migration tool**

  Developing physical data migration routines to expand date formats is another tedious task that benefits from automation. Note that certain date field expansion tools also support data structure conversion. In-house tools, particularly for databases, also support this need.

13.3 Infrastructure Upgrade Projects

The Year 2000 Project Office may recommend certain infrastructure improvements that focus on standardization or stabilization of support environments. These projects may include consolidation of redundant production libraries or data stores, implementation of standardized date routines, or improvements in testing infrastructures, to name just a few. Most infrastructure projects recommended by the Project Office relate directly to streamlining Year 2000 implementation effort and time frames. The type of project to be avoided is one involving an architecture upgrade to critical applications that may thus risk missing an event horizon delivery window. In the implementation phase, three types of infrastructure projects must be coordinated closely with upgrade unit projects. These projects involve date routine standardization, test environment improvements, and system software upgrades.

13.3.1 *Common Date Routine Deployment*

Standardizing date routines requires commitment from system software and application support teams. System software teams must review in-house routines and, where applicable, replace those routines with an in-house standard or a third-party set of calendar routines. Another option is to update an existing common date routine to support multi-century calendar processing and to provide documentation for widespread use of this routine. When selecting a date routine, consider the following points.

- Date handling should be standardized to avoid hundreds, or even thousands, of hours of conversion work that may be required for existing routines.

- Date routines should support multiple conversions and validation for general and industry-specific date processing requirements, including:

  — Validation of input dates in Julian, Lillian, Edited, Gregorian, and other formats

  — Cross-century date specification, including holidays, work days, and fiscal dates

  — Date-to-date conversion from any format to any format

  — End-point calculations, day-of-week indexing, and century interpretation if a century indicator does not exist

  — Date calculations that support banking, insurance, securities, and other industry-specific formats

- Date routines can be acquired or can use existing in-house routines but should not involve development of new routines because of limited time.

- Acquired tools tend to come with procedural workaround options that may be useful for certain upgrade unit compliance projects.

- Routines should be portable across multiple platforms and environments.

- Use of non-standard date routines will result in migration chaos.

Date routine implementation requires performing the following tasks.

1. *Establish common routines and procedures at the outset of the project.*

2. *Provide all application teams with the new routines and associated documentation.*

3. *Have executives issue a directive for application areas to implement common routines prior to the actual upgrade unit compliance project, when possible.*

4. *Test these routines as for a standard maintenance upgrade.*

Implementing common date routines prior to initiating an upgrade unit compliance project is not a requirement but can dramatically reduce the time required to convert an upgrade unit. This is especially desirable when system maintenance volatility requires that implementation windows remain relatively short.

13.3.2 Testing Environment Improvements

Synchronization of upgrade unit implementation projects with the stabilization and improvement of the test environment used by a given upgrade unit can dramatically streamline the overall conversion effort. Each upgrade unit relies on a stable test environment to validate the results of a Year 2000 upgrade. This validation process can take a significant amount of time to complete when a given test environment has exceptionally poor test data, a lack of standards, no tool support, or poorly defined procedures. When these situations exist and the enterprise assessment recommended upgrading specific, application-area test environments, the Year 2000 implementation phase must synchronize the timing of upgrade unit conversions and test environment improvements.

The validation process, detailed in Chapter 14, discusses the types of activities to perform to prepare for and execute a Year 2000 validation effort. Many of these activities can be performed prior to actual startup of a Year 2000 conversion. For example, compiling and testing the original system to determine the percentage of logic that has actually been tested can be performed at any point leading up to the actual validation stage. If coverage is below 60 to 70 percent, it must be brought up to that level of test logic coverage in order to thoroughly test a Year 2000 upgrade. Because most production cycles cover only 5 to 10 percent of the logic in a system at best, most systems without a formal set of test data require some degree of improvement. All mission-critical, application-area test environments, depending on the recommendations made by the enterprise assessment, can be candidates for the following procedures.

1. *Compile, test, and check logic coverage levels for all programs.*

2. *Upgrade logic coverage levels to achieve a 60 to 70 percent degree of execution coverage.*

3. *Upgrade test procedures, establish standard test libraries, and standardize production acceptance testing where required.*

4. *Procure and deploy software tools to support dynamic coverage analysis, data store comparison, on-line test script capture and playback, and interactive testing analysis.*

One final point to note is that improvements to the testing infra-structure serve to streamline Year 2000 validation efforts and technology upgrade validation efforts because logical equivalence testing is the de facto validation strategy for both projects. For more information on Year 2000 validation and testing approaches, refer to Chapter 14. Given existing tight, project time constraints, dictated by extremely close event horizons, successful implementations will be best achieved through a proactive approach to upgrading existing test environments.

13.3.3 System Software Upgrades

System software upgrade plans are established during the enterprise assessment phase. Ideally, these system software upgrades minimize the amount of work required by application groups; however, this is not always the case. A compiler upgrade, for example, whether driven by the year 2000 or unrelated issues, requires that application source code be upgraded, recompiled and tested to verify that the system still works properly. If the validation process is well-defined and carefully followed, compiler upgrades can be coupled with a Year 2000 compliance project. Ideally, a compiler upgrade would precede a Year 2000 upgrade project to simplify the complexity of the project and reduce project time frames. In some cases, the Year 2000 project may be semidependent on a compiler upgrade where the current date is available only in a linefeed 6-digit format.

Other system upgrades should be integrated into the overall sched-ule and Year 2000 budget where required. For example, macro-level CICS, or older versions of various database products, will not function properly in a post-Year 2000 environment and must be upgraded sometime before the end of the century. These projects may involve extensive modifications or may be limited to minor application adjustments. In most situations, application technology upgrades should be scheduled around Year 2000 compliance projects because two, compacted delivery windows are better than one, longer window when the deadline cannot slip. Separate projects also decrease testing complexities and increase the percentage of successful projects.

13.4 Upgrade-Unit, Detailed-Design

The detailed design phase of an upgrade unit project is similar to the detailed design phase of a development project. This phase finalizes upgrade components and detailed relationships, external data store links, date field occurrences, record groupings, data definition language, screen maps, reports, date routines, approach, and project time lines. The project plan includes resource assignments and task estimates for conversion, interface development and deployment, data conversion, validation setup, testing, change control, and production turnover. The types of tasks performed vary according to the implementation approach used on a given upgrade unit. There are several differences between the detailed design activities performed for a date field expansion project and those performed for a procedural workaround project. Where applicable, these variations are highlighted in the following project task summaries.

13.4.1 Upgrade Unit, Detailed Design Plan

Once a given upgrade unit is ready for migration, analysts must answer several questions. Does the approach identified at the enterprise level still hold true? Is the originally specified in-house or outsourcing strategy still valid? What resource mix of consultants and in-house staff should be applied to internally performed project tasks? Have upgrade unit boundaries shifted because of related projects or other factors? Is the cost model and project plan still accurate? All of these questions are addressed in the upgrade unit planning phase and result in a final upgrade unit analysis plan and preliminary implementation plan.

Upgrade unit, detailed analysis tasks include upgrade unit boundary, component, and relationship finalization, detailed data definition impact analysis, end-user interface analysis, data store and external interface analysis, and the finalization of the upgrade unit migration plan. Most of these tasks involve detailed discovery of dates across the upgrade unit and finalization of how those dates are to be modified to achieve Year 2000 compliance. Project managers should note that the greatest variation in analytical techniques between a date field expansion and a procedural workaround project occurs during the detailed, data-definition impact analysis.

13.4.2 Inventory and Cross-Reference Analysis

The inventory and cross-reference task utilizes, where available, inventory technology to create a final list of physical components to be analyzed and made Year 2000 compliant. This list is based on actual component usage derived from analysis of executable control language and job scheduling facilities. In an IBM environment for example, these facilities include JCL, CICS control tables, and job scheduling tools unique to that environment. Figure 13.2 shows many of the interdependencies that can exist among components in a systems environment.

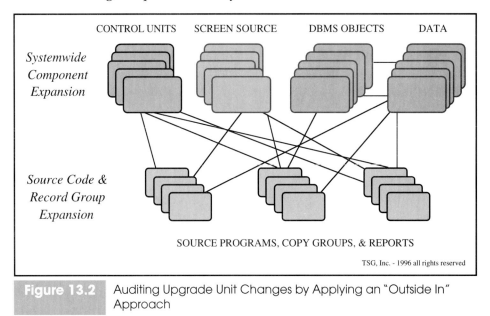

CONTROL UNITS   SCREEN SOURCE   DBMS OBJECTS   DATA

Systemwide Component Expansion

Source Code & Record Group Expansion

SOURCE PROGRAMS, COPY GROUPS, & REPORTS

Figure 13.2 Auditing Upgrade Unit Changes by Applying an "Outside In" Approach

Cross-reference analysis ensures that unused components are excluded from the upgrade project, that all relevant components are included in the upgrade project, and that data structure integrity is maintained across systems and throughout the upgrade process. Automated, or manual, component cross-reference analysis produces the following references or mappings.

- Control language, Job Step to Executable Program

- Executable Program, Data Definition Name to Physical File or Database

- Executable Program to Source Module Names

- Executable On-line Program to Screen Member Definition

- Copy/Include to Program(s) and Program to Copy(s)/Include(s)

- Calling Program to Subordinate Called Program(s)

- Called Program to Calling Program(s)

- File/Database Name to Executable Program(s)

- Executable Program to File/Database Names

- Screen to Source Program(s)

- Source Program to Screen(s)

This information is captured, stored, and presented in a variety of ways depending on the tool used to capture this data. Tools using an embedded repository may support both ad hoc and fixed format reporting while other tools may support only fixed format reporting of cross-reference data. Analysts should make every effort to incorporate inventory results in the Year 2000 central tracking facility. Ideally, data is captured during the inventory process, loaded into an intermediate repository via automated population facilities, and uploaded into the central, high level tracking facility maintained by the Year 2000 Project Office. In a worst case scenario, analysts may periodically update the central tracking facility with high-level physical information as it is tracked through an upgrade unit project.

Cross-reference analysis results, once reconciled for duplicate and missing components, is the basis for finalizing inputs to subsequent analysis and upgrade tasks. Project teams that do not complete deliverable requirements from this task will encounter audit, change control, and upgrade unit, boundary definition problems throughout the remainder of the upgrade unit implementation project. In addition to basic environmental information, many of the inventory tools are capable of producing data definition cross-reference results. This information is typically available "on request" from many of these tools and provides highly valuable input to the next task: date and data definition impact analysis.

13.4.3 Date and Data Definition Impact Analysis

Data definition analysis, within the context of a Year 2000 project, involves more than running an impact analysis tool to identify date fields within program source code. First, dates appear in screen definitions, database definitions, control language members, data stores, and other system components that an impact analyzer may or may not find. Second, impact analysis tools can omit entire record structures or other data constructs that will need to be updated along with program source code. Finally, rather than solely relying on the impact analyzer as a way of verifying date occurrences use inventory and cross-reference tools as a powerful means of helping to find hidden date fields and audit changes to a system.

13.4.4 Data Definition, Cross-Reference Analysis

The main difference between analysis performed for a date field expansion project versus a procedural workaround project is that identifying and cross-referencing every date definition is critical for date field expansion to ensure that all format changes are synchronized, and not critical for a procedural project. The cross-referencing of data definitions can therefore be omitted for a procedural workaround project.

Inventory and cross-reference tools, discussed in section 13.4.2, identify relationships among various data definition constructs. Data definition cross-reference analysis includes the ability to determine whether:

- Copied and included code is related to hardcoded, in-line record group definitions

- Group-level and locally defined data elements represent the same physical data

- Program source code identifies date occurrences in physical files and databases

- Screen definitions are linked to program record definitions

Figure 13.3 depicts the process of reviewing candidate record structures that have been linked to the same physical data structure. The list of all input/output (I/O) data structures, categorized into groupings that define the same physical data, is called a record grouping report. This report can be produced by a number of inventory and data definition cross-reference analysis tools or can be created from information extracted from those tools. For a record to be included in the same, logical, record grouping category it must minimally have the following characteristics.

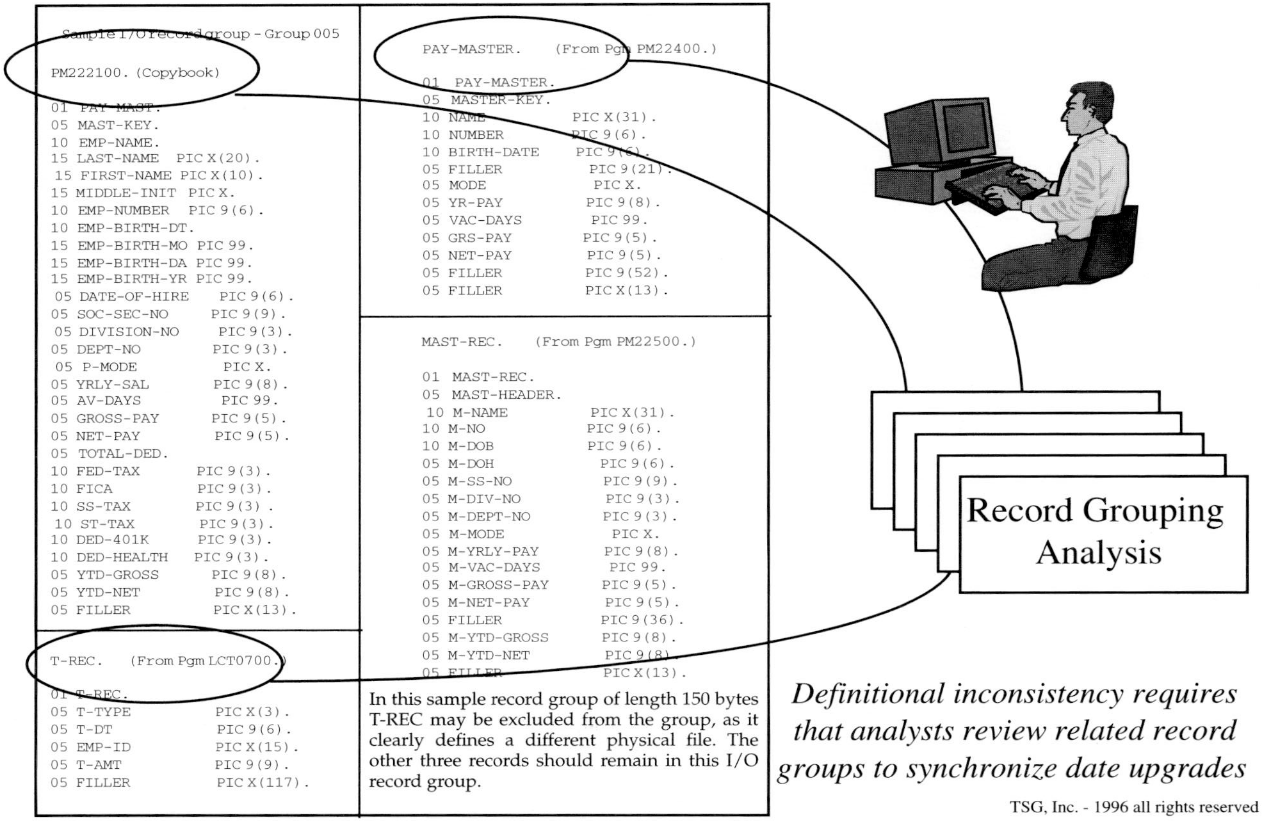

Record Grouping Analysis

Definitional inconsistency requires that analysts review related record groups to synchronize date upgrades

Sample I/O record group - Group 005

```
PM222100.  (Copybook)
01 PAY-MAST.
 05 MAST-KEY.
  10 EMP-NAME.
   15 LAST-NAME     PIC X(20).
   15 FIRST-NAME PIC X(10).
   15 MIDDLE-INIT PIC X.
  10 EMP-NUMBER   PIC 9(6).
  10 EMP-BIRTH-DT.
   15 EMP-BIRTH-MO PIC 99.
   15 EMP-BIRTH-DA PIC 99.
   15 EMP-BIRTH-YR PIC 99.
  05 DATE-OF-HIRE    PIC 9(6).
  05 SOC-SEC-NO      PIC 9(9).
  05 DIVISION-NO     PIC 9(3).
  05 DEPT-NO         PIC 9(3).
  05 P-MODE          PIC X.
  05 YRLY-SAL        PIC 9(8).
  05 AV-DAYS         PIC 99.
  05 GROSS-PAY       PIC 9(5).
  05 NET-PAY         PIC 9(5).
  05 TOTAL-DED.
   10 FED-TAX        PIC 9(3).
   10 FICA           PIC 9(3).
   10 SS-TAX         PIC 9(3).
   10 ST-TAX         PIC 9(3).
   10 DED-401K       PIC 9(3).
   10 DED-HEALTH     PIC 9(3).
  05 YTD-GROSS       PIC 9(8).
  05 YTD-NET         PIC 9(8).
  05 FILLER          PIC X(117).
```

```
T-REC.      (From Pgm LCT0700.)
01 T-REC.
 05 T-TYPE            PIC X(3).
 05 T-DT              PIC 9(6).
 05 EMP-ID            PIC X(15).
 05 T-AMT             PIC 9(9).
 05 FILLER            PIC X(117).
```

```
PAY-MASTER.      (From Pgm PM22400.)
01 PAY-MASTER.
 05 MASTER-KEY.
  10 NAME           PIC X(31).
  10 NUMBER         PIC 9(6).
  10 BIRTH-DATE     PIC 9(6).
  05 FILLER         PIC 9(21).
  05 MODE           PIC X.
  05 YR-PAY         PIC 9(8).
  05 VAC-DAYS       PIC 99.
  05 GRS-PAY        PIC 9(5).
  05 NET-PAY        PIC 9(5).
  05 FILLER         PIC 9(52).
  05 FILLER         PIC X(13).
```

```
MAST-REC.     (From Pgm PM22500.)
01 MAST-REC.
 05 MAST-HEADER.
  10 M-NAME         PIC X(31).
  10 M-NO           PIC 9(6).
  10 M-DOB          PIC 9(6).
  05 M-DOH          PIC 9(6).
  05 M-SS-NO        PIC 9(9).
  05 M-DIV-NO       PIC 9(3).
  05 M-DEPT-NO      PIC 9(3).
  05 M-MODE         PIC X.
  05 M-YRLY-PAY     PIC 9(8).
  05 M-VAC-DAYS     PIC 99.
  05 M-GROSS-PAY    PIC 9(5).
  05 M-NET-PAY      PIC 9(5).
  05 FILLER         PIC 9(36).
  05 M-YTD-GROSS    PIC 9(8).
  05 M-YTD-NET      PIC 9(8).
  05 FILLER         PIC X(13).
```

In this sample record group of length 150 bytes T-REC may be excluded from the group, as it clearly defines a different physical file. The other three records should remain in this I/O record group.

Figure 13.3 Data Definition Record/Component Grouping Analysis

331

- Record structure is part of an I/O routine that can be traced back to a physical file or database definition.

- Record structure is linked indirectly to a physical data store, via an implicit or explicit data transfer to a record structure identified as above.

- Record structure has the same length and a layout that does not conflict with other records defined to that group.

If, in the example in Figure 13.3, this record group also included another 150-byte record that had no subordinate data elements and contained only a generic filler area, it would be difficult for an impact analysis tool to identify this record as a field expansion candidate. Cross-reference analysis, however, identifies this record structure as a date field expansion candidate because it belongs to a record group that also contains one or more date fields.

To track down hidden or implicit upgrade requirements a analyst, or tool, must know which data structures are related, based on the data or user view components that they represent. Considering the potential problems and project delays that missing these constructs can cause, it makes sense to cross-reference these system components during the design stage of the project. As stated earlier, a procedural workaround project is not particularly dependent on this level of analysis because only explicit date field occurrences, as discussed in the next section, need to be identified.

13.4.5 Date Field Identification

Both the date field expansion and the procedural workaround project require identification of date fields. Impact analysis tools facilitate date identification by providing lists of date fields and in-context date usage across system components. These lists are used as direct input to the date change process, regardless of the solution applied to that upgrade unit.

Date field expansion projects are primarily concerned with identifying all nonprocedural date definitions but not in-context procedural occurrences, because the date field expansion process corrects most issues related to procedural date calculation and comparison logic without requiring any procedural changes. Date formats have a direct impact on conversion time frames and overall approach. For example, numerous occurrences of binary and packed date fields can increase conversion time. Similarly, date fields that are embedded in other fields, such as a customer number, can also increase conversion efforts. Detailed analysis of these formats, identified in the upgrade unit source code, is input to the date field expansion design process. In-context procedural date usage can be examined on a case-by-case basis to ensure that no further procedural adjustments are required.

Procedural workaround projects primarily focus on in-context date calculation and comparison logic and secondarily focus on date definitions themselves. In-context usage analysis is important in procedural workaround projects because subroutines to fix the date processing must be added wherever this logic occurs. Establishing procedural workaround subroutine parameters also requires analysis of date definition formats. In situations where key fields, sort fields, or birth dates exist, augment procedural workaround logic with other techniques to ensure that the system will function properly across multiple centuries. Date impact analysis tools, which provide both in-context procedural and date definition identification, are discussed in more depth in Chapter 15. The key point to keep in mind during this analysis is to let the type of project determine the type of analysis report and to not rely solely on impact analysis tools to guide the process of date identification.

13.4.6 End-user Interface Analysis

Procedural workaround projects may need to accommodate date modifications to screens or reports when users want to differentiate one century from another but the display headings provide no clue as to which field is the year and which is the month. In a date field expansion project, these same facts apply for systems in which internal dates are fully or partially expanded, whereas display dates remain in their original formats. When all dates, including screens and reports, are to be expanded, detailed analysis is required for all user interfaces. If end users or business analysts are struggling with the decision to expand or ignore screen and report date fields, analysts should ask them when the following date occurs: 01/09/02. If display headings provide no clue, expansion may be desirable.

If end-user interface changes are planned, analysts must review all screens and reports. This task requires that analysts collect samples of all user views. These can be generated by selected inventory tools or can be provided by application analysts. The quickest way to reduce the level of screen and report analysis and conversion work is to deactivate all screens and reports that are obsolete. Shutting off selected reports in production for a week or so is one way to find out if anyone uses them. If this is done, it should be tried during the analysis step so that reports can be deactivated prior to startup of upgrade unit conversion. The deactivation process should be assigned to application personnel and typically requires changing source to comment out unnecessary report or screen logic.

Each screen and report for which date field expansion is envisioned should be reviewed to determine if space is available for expanded date displays. If there is no room, analysts can choose to bypass screen or report field expansion on a case-by-case basis. Where no room exists and fully expanded dates are considered a necessity, application analysts will have to participate in a redesign of selected screens and reports. This may complicate the testing process by invalidating automated comparison tool capabilities (see Chapter 14 for more information on this issue).

One final point should be made regarding user-related interface media. Many organizations produce preprinted checks, forms, and other documents that contain hardcoded century fields. End users may need to help identify and schedule these forms for date-related changes. Reports and screens also may contain hardcoded century values. These fields should be adjusted during the process of expanding screen and report fields.

13.4.7 Data Store and Bridge/API Requirements

Finding all physical data stores during the detail design process for an upgrade unit is a primary goal. Even when procedural workaround techniques are selected for a system, each of these data stores must be used as input to the testing process. The level of analysis for a procedural workaround project can be slightly less comprehensive than that used for a date field expansion project.

Date field expansion requires all physical files to be identified during the inventory and cross-reference process performed during the early stages of the analysis project. Each of these files and databases must be linked with source component definitions containing date field definition. These components include database, screen, copy and include, control language, and program source code. The result of this analysis produces the exact number of physical files, database segments or tables, generation data sets, or other types of physical files to be converted during the data expansion task of the implementation phase.

Identification of data store utilization, coupled with preliminary analysis of interface requirements completed during the enterprise assessment, produces an API and bridge design strategy. All databases and on-line files shared with other upgrade units ultimately require development of an API within the code. If a standard API was not previously developed by another migration team or by data administration, analysts must include a task to do so in the migration plan. Batch files received from or sent to other upgrade units require development and implementation of conversion bridges. Central status coordinators must track API or bridge routines that already exist. Reuse and deactivation of API and bridge routines are covered in more depth later in this chapter.

13.4.8 Upgrade Unit Migration Plan Finalization

Once all of this information has been collected, analysts will finalize the original plan established during the enterprise assessment project. This may involve changing the entire approach or may just involve finalizing the tasks, resource requirements, and budget estimates. Implementation tasks for a date field expansion include the following items.

1. *Perform upgrade unit expansion.*

    a. Expand record groups and source code.

    b. Code for special date format handling.

    c. Expand report definitions.

    d. Expand screen definitions.

    e. Expand database and data file definitions.

    f. Adjust control language components.

    g. Perform quality assurance walk-through.

2. *Expand and migrate data stores.*

3. *Build and activate/deactivate API interfaces.*

4. *Build and activate/deactivate bridge interfaces.*

5. *Set up validation processes.*

6. *Perform validation tests.*

7. *Certify system Year 2000 compliant.*

8. *Perform system and acceptance testing.*

9. *Implement upgrade unit into production.*

Implementation tasks for a procedural workaround include the following items.

1. *Perform upgrade unit compliance change.*

    a. Create or adjust special date handling routines.

    b. Propagate date handling logic across source code.

    c. Adjust and expand special case situations.

    d. Perform quality assurance walk-through.

2. *Adjust control language components.*

3. *Bridge to external data store where required.*

4. *Set up validation processes.*

5. *Perform validation tests.*

6. *Certify system Year 2000 compliant.*

7. *Implement upgrade unit into production.*

The level of effort associated with these projects varies according to the tasks included in the activity-based cost model, skill levels, tools, and upgrade unit size. The estimating example provided in Section 12.9.2 works as a starting point and should be adjusted downward if tools are in place to automate the process and skilled personnel are available to perform the tasks. Analysts may alternatively adjust estimates upward if no tools are available or numerous nonstandard constructs are present in the code and data structures.

13.4.9 Augmentation of Year 2000 Implementation Plan

Certain issues may arise that require the standard work task list to be augmented in some way. One issue, missing components, requires the addition of a task to recover those components. Unless a program has absolutely no date logic associated with it, that program must be recovered for date field expansion and procedural workaround projects. Otherwise, that component will fail when it encounters 2000-related date data. Automated recovery tools are available on the market for this purpose. A second option involves rewriting the program for inclusion in the Year 2000 project.

Other issues include upgrading obsolete technology, performing a compiler upgrade, or other technologically prohibitive factors that prevent a system from being Year 2000 compliant. Some of these tasks, a compiler upgrade for example, can be integrated into the Year 2000 plan, whereas other tasks, for example, a CICS macro to command-level migration, probably should be handled as a standalone project. Regardless of the issue, the final project plan for an upgrade unit should reflect the reality of what is to be accomplished within the scope of that plan.

13.5 Library and Environmental Setup

For library setup requirements, assume (1) production code is always left intact (2) a copy of unmodified production code is used for audit and comparison, and (3) one working version of source code is minimally required in order to apply changes to that code. When a combination of automated tools and manual changes is being applied, a second working copy of the source is recommended to differentiate between automated updates and manually applied changes. The recommended naming conventions for each library setup during this process are as follows:

Original production copy:	original (or some abbreviation thereof)
Updated production copy:	modified (or some abbreviation thereof)
Updated copy with additional changes:	final (or some abbreviation thereof)

Initially, analysts must populate each of these libraries with copies of all source code components, including source programs, screen definitions, data definition language, copied or included routines, macros where applicable, and control language members. Qualifiers, differentiating the component type (e.g., source code versus JCL), should be added to each library name where applicable and should use in-house naming conventions.

Data is migrated separately for migration and validation testing. Analysts must copy and reformat production data stores for date field expansion, validation coverage enhancement, and certification teting. These library conventions generally hold true for date field expansion and procedural workaround projects, although data migration requirements are not an issue for procedural workaround projects. Analysts should make the appropriate adjustments when libraries need to be added or eliminated for a given project.

In addition to library management issues, other environmental setup requirements should be finalized prior to actually moving forward with upgrade unit modifications. These requirements include finalizing the tools to be used on the project, the methodology to be applied, and the work environment. If work is to be performed in the environment in which the system is currently maintained, library setup and tool enablement are the main components of this process. If a migration project is to be performed on a workstation or other platform, analysts must migrate all source components to that environment and set up all applicable libraries at that point. If the facilities are available, analysts should verify that all compilers, editors, and even test simulation technology are in place, along with any migration tools to be used on the project. A Project Office coordinator should check migration environments to verify that they have been set up properly.

13.6 Upgrade Unit Date Field Expansion

A date field expansion project may require that all dates, including screens and reports, be fully expanded to an 8-character, or comparable, format or may entail expansion on a more selective basis. Variations on a complete date field expansion project include expanding data stores and programs—but not user views—setting a century indicator, or forcing expanded values into current work areas by using binary formats. All expansion options have one thing in common: some or all dates are changed to an expanded format.

Regardless of the extent of the date expansion process, an "outside in" change and audit approach is recommended. This approach expands data stores, data definition language, screens, job control, and reports within an upgrade unit. These changes are driven through source modules via cross-reference facilities found in various tools. The outside-in approach improves the reliability and auditability of the end result and is particularly useful when automated date field expansion tools are unavailable. Automated expansion tools eliminate much of the manual date conversion work but do not affect the need to audit component changes.

Date field expansion projects include finalization of date conversion formats, screen and report expansion, data language expansion, source code expansion, control language upgrades and data migration. Updating each of these component types is discussed separately in individual sections; the process itself requires reciprocal analysis and change techniques across an upgrade unit. Other tasks, described in later sections of this chapter, include interface deployment, change control, and production turnover. Validation, an integral part of any Year 2000 project, is discussed in Chapter 14.

13.6.1 Existing Date Utilization: Considerations and Options

Date impact analysis, performed during the upgrade unit detailed design effort, identified the various types of date formats or hidden date issues embedded in a given upgrade unit. Analysts should assume that any of the date formats listed in Table 13.1, and numerous other variations on these formats, will be encountered during the course of the date field expansion process. Procedural date implementation can also require detailed review and specialized solutions to make the code Year 2000 compliant.

Basic conversion planning should include an analysis of the following items, which, if found, can be addressed as indicated.

- Compilers, database software, telecommunication systems, and other potential sources of conflicting base date values should use current date source.

Table 13.1 Date Format Conversion Options and Requirements

	Old Format		**New Format**
Basic Year Format:	*96*	*to*	*1996*
Gregorian Date:	*961225*	*to*	*19961225*
Julian Date:	*960359*	*to*	*19960359*
Display Date Format:	*12/25/96*	*to*	*12/25/1996*
Display Date Format:	*Dec. 25, 96*	*to*	*Dec. 25, 1996*
Selected COBOL Formats:			
01 ALPHA-DATE	PIC X(6)	to	PIC X(8)
01 NUM-DATE	PIC 9(6)	to	PIC 9(8)
01 PACKED-DATE	PIC 9(7)	to	PIC 9(9) COMP-3
01 DISPLAY-YEAR	PIC X(2)	to	PIC X(2)
Embedded COBOL Date Field:			
01 PART-NUMBER.			
05 PART-ID	PIC X(12)	to	PIC X(12).
05 PART-DATE-MADE	PIC 9(6)	to	PIC X(8).

- Binary, packed, and other existing date formats may allow for the addition of a 1-byte century indicator if a physical data structure cannot be expanded.

- Encoded dates may require that decoding tasks be included in the project plan for systems using those date formats.

- Existing dates may already have a century indicator stored in a high-order bit (typically, Assembler), in the half-byte not used in a packed field, or in other nonstandard areas.

- Dates embedded in nondate fields, such as part numbers, customer numbers, or other fields, may require expansion of those fields as well.

- Key field date and sort field date formats may be difficult to identify but must be expanded along with other date fields.

- Hardcoded literal fields that define date values are common in many programs and should be expanded, using the same guidelines that analysts are using to expand variable date fields.

Generally, date field expansion projects should avoid adding any procedural logic to compensate for an incomplete or partially thought-out solution. Nevertheless, situations do arise that may necessitate this type of fix. For example, a date filed expansion project may incorporate a single-byte century indicator (versus a 2-byte century field) if required or recommended as a solution to the date problem. This type of date filed expansion—single-character century indicator—requires procedural logic to display a complete date, to move 8-character date formats into data stores using that format, and to compare that date to other 8-character dates.

If expansion is the selected strategy and space or reformatting constraints do not restrict the size of a date field, analysts should expand the year field to a full 4-character field. If packed, binary, or other data formats are used to store date fields, the equivalent of a 2-character century field should be added to that numeric date field in order to represent an 8-character date value. Hardcoded literal definitions, regardless of the format used to define a given field, should be checked so that a "19" does not automatically enter system data values. Any hardcoded century values, such as a "19," must be modified so either the current date value or a user-entered date value is placed into the century field.

Analysts should try to avoid moving century fields to areas of a data store that do not directly precede the date being expanded. This "date splitting" approach requires procedural logic to move the century indicator into a full date definition to support comparison logic, key fields, and other situations that arise. It can also evolve into a maintenance burden for future generations of programmers. Other date field expansion solutions, regardless of how clever they are, should similarly avoid the addition of procedural logic, because these solutions tend to lengthen implementation time frames and increase future maintenance complexity.

The "clever solutions" to be avoided category includes strategies that attempt to save time by not expanding every date field in a system. Analysts can spend more time identifying dates that do not need to be expanded—because they are not used in calculations or comparisons—than they would spend by just expanding every date field. Furthermore, the risk of missing a date that happens to be related to an expanded date, and causing problems as a result, are high. The risk of introducing future maintenance problems by using this approach is also extremely high because a programmer may not know which dates have been expanded and which dates were left in their original format.

Finally, incorporating prior date-compliant solutions into the date field expansion project is something that may occur from time to time. Analysts may have partially expanded certain date fields to correct a previously encountered event horizon problem but left all other date fields in original formats. The bottom line regarding date field expansion projects is to expand all dates to an 8-character format where possible, avoid date encoding tricks, and avoid adding procedural logic unless absolutely required.

13.6.2 Expansion of Screens, Reports, and Other Presentation Media

End users, along with IT analysts, determine whether or not screens and reports are to be expanded. This requirement may be attributable to external regulations or internally defined date standards. Screen and report date field expansion is the recommended approach for systems that will be around for a long time or systems that manage critical information or financial data. Regardless of the motivation, the expansion of end-user screens and reports adds an additional level of effort to the project. This discussion applies to any end-user presentation media requiring date field expansion.

The following considerations apply to expansion of dates that are found on screens and reports.

- Do not expand obsolete screens or reports commonly found in old systems; validation testing process can accommodate deactivated screens and reports.

- If fully expanded dates do not fit but are still desirable, leave screen or report date fields unexpanded during this project and selectively redesign them later.

- Expansion of display format fields should, in most cases, not involve the addition of procedural logic once the year field is changed to a 4-character format.

- Screen field formats, defined outside the source code, must be expanded along with in-line source code record definitions.

- Identification of report layouts, embedded in source code, requires a review of record groups of a defined length (e.g., 132 bytes, 133 bytes) and confirmation that those groups represent actively used output reports.

- Reporting utilities could hide report definitions in a way that may involve redesign work.

Eliminating obsolete screens and reports during a Year 2000 project is a valid way to streamline costs and delivery times. Conversely, redesigning screens and reports during a Year 2000 upgrade is one way to lengthen delivery time frames. Analysts performing date field expansion for on-line screens should perform the following tasks.

1. *Identify all screen definition members and the source code record definitions that define those screen work areas to various source programs.*

2. *Use record grouping analysis to find all record definitions that are linked to initially defined source definitions via data transfer, subroutine, or conditional logic.*

3. *Use an impact analysis tool to find all screen record structures that contain dates (this information was produced during the detail design stage).*

4. *Expand all screen definitions, including all primary and secondary record structures containing date fields.*

5. *Verify that all source record definitions and copy/include members are now of the same length, using inventory and cross-reference tools (if available).*

6. *If tools are available to print screen mock-ups from a screen map definition, run those tools and review newly expanded screen layouts.*

Analysts performing date field expansion on report layouts should consider the following tasks.

1. *Scan record group reports produced during data definition cross-reference analysis.*

2. *Identify all 132-byte, 133-byte, and any other record groups that appear to be output reports.*

3. *Use record grouping analysis to find all other records that are linked to initially identified source definitions via data transfer, subroutine, or conditional logic.*

4. *Use an impact analysis tool to find all report record structures that contain dates (this was produced during detail design stage).*

5. *Expand all report definitions, including all primary and secondary record structures containing date fields.*

6. *Verify that all source record definitions and copy/include members are now of the same length, using inventory and cross-reference tools (if available).*

If screen and report definitions are to be excluded from the date field expansion process, these steps can be omitted.

13.6.3 Data Definition Language Upgrades

Physical data definitions that represent files and databases are defined in various ways, depending on a system's platform and environment. Data stores and related layouts can be externally defined macros that are linked to internal source code definitions or can be wholly defined within a source program. In an IBM IMS environment, for example, data is defined in DBD and PSB macro layouts that are redefined within the source code itself.

Regardless of where system components are defined, analysts must locate and expand all those that define physical data stores containing one or more date fields. Linking these components to each other and to the physical data stores they represent allows analysts to verify that all record and file formats are concurrently expanded along with the physical data stores they represent. Data definitions that define physical data files or databases should be expanded as follows.

1. *Use inventory and cross-reference analysis results to identify relationships between physical files and program definitions (via control language references) and between databases and applicable database definition language members.*

2. *Identify relationships between data definition language members and the source code definitions that define those work areas to various source programs.*

3. *Use record grouping analysis to find all record definitions that are linked to initially identified source definitions via data transfer, subroutine, or conditional logic.*

4. *Use an impact analysis tool to find all data definition-related record structures that contain dates (this was produced during detail design stage).*

5. *Expand all data definitions directly or indirectly related to physical data structures containing date fields. These definitions include data definition language members, in-line source definitions, and copy/include source code.*

6. *Ensure that any special setup work required for adjusting newly expanded key fields containing dates is completed as required.*

7. *Verify that all source record definitions and copy/include members are now of the same length, using inventory and cross-reference tools (if available).*

This process is designed specifically for auditing the changes that have been applied and not necessarily to enhance the speed at which the changes are made. If tools are available to expedite the upgrade, analysts should apply the tools as required while using the aforementioned guidelines to verify that all relevant changes were applied.

13.6.4 Source Code Expansion

If the previous guidelines were applied to all record groups that directly or indirectly define screen, report, and physical data definitions, the changes remaining at the source program level are limited to a handful of internally defined work areas and numerous locally defined date elements. In other words, date field expansion, when viewed at a system level rather than a program level, can be defined as a well-structured process. Again, partially or highly automated date change tools impact the approach selected but should not impact the approach an analyst would use to verify that all components have been expanded in a uniform and consistent fashion.

At this point, each program can be scanned with an impact analysis tool to find and expand, either manually or in some automated way, all date definitions. The following techniques should be applied.

1. *Identify all definitional occurrences (versus procedural occurrences) of dates, using the data definition and date identification results produced during earlier analysis steps.*

2. *Expand each occurrence of date fields and formats in the data definitional segments of each program.*

3. *Accommodate special date formats as needed.*

4. *If screen or report fields are being left unexpanded, verify that data transfer logic accommodates the truncation or the move of only the last two digits of the date to the screen and report.*

5. *Identify any procedural exceptions that would still leave the upgrade unit noncompliant.*

6. *Correct all procedural or other issues that may cause the system not to be compliant even though all date fields were expanded.*

If the aforementioned expansion techniques were applied to I/O record groups, copy/include members, screens, reports, and physical data definitions, certain inventory and cross-reference tools can be used to analyze field length mismatches. Field length mismatch tools highlight a field that is being moved either to or from, read into, written from, transferred via a subroutine, or compared to another field not of the same logical length. Running this tool against a program with expanded record groups and unexpanded, locally defined elements is a fast way to identify, and subsequently expand, all date definitions unique to a given program. The field mismatch tool also verifies that no fields were missed during an expansion project that applied an alternative process or that used automated tools to expand date fields. Refer to Appendix A for a list of inventory and cross reference analysis tools.

Once these changes have been applied, a first-level quality assurance review is required, in which analysts compile all updated source code to make sure that no errors or field problems were introduced. Once this task is completed, additional quality reviews by individuals other than those that performed the original code changes should proceed as outlined in Section 13.11 *Change Control, Quality Assurance, and Production Turnover.*

13.6.5 Data Migration

The inventory and cross-reference analysis, performed at the outset of the detailed design stage of the upgrade unit migration project, identified physical data stores through analysis of control language and related execution facilities. Reviewing, preferably through the use of automated tools, all versions of production runtime environments is the most thorough way of finding data stores that may require date field expansion. While not all data stores contain dates—and this varies by system and industry—the majority of data stores in a given system usually do contain some date fields. Identifying and expanding physical data stores require that analysts perform the following tasks.

1. *Use the cross-reference analysis to identify all physical databases and data files used by the system.*

2. *Eliminate databases and on-line files that require API interfaces, because they are shared with other upgrade units. See enterprise assessment and interface coordinator for support.*

3. *For all remaining data stores, review the cross-reference analysis showing links between program definitions and physical data stores to determine which data stores contain dates.*

4. *Use the old and the new record structures to create a conversion routine to input the old data store and output the newly formatted data store.*

5. *If this is a database requiring special utilities to perform this operation, obtain assistance from the data administration area.*

6. *Test the conversion routines and document their high-level function for implementation purposes.*

7. *Keep a list of all data stores requiring API or bridge interfaces (see enterprise assessment or interface coordinator) for later reference.*

13.6.6 Control Language Upgrades

Control language components execute program object or load modules, specify data stores and related parameters to be used within the scope of a given job step, and execute utility functions. Control language can initiate batch jobs, as is the case with IBM JCL, or can control on-line environments, as is the case with IBM CICS control tables. Each control language member should be reviewed in order to find and adjust date-related items that may explicitly or implicitly exist within those control language members. The following guidelines apply.

1. *For each data store that was reformatted due to a date change, determine where record lengths, blocking factors, or other physical attributes require modification.*

2. *Use cross-reference tools to verify that all control members and data stores are identified.*

3. *Expand record lengths, adjust block sizes, and correct any other length or format issues defined in control language members.*

4. *Verify that any sort utility parameters are expanded to reflect larger key fields.*

5. *Carefully track these changes, which are to be made in the modified library and not the original, so that they can be audited during the testing and the turnover process.*

If any other system components, other than the ones explicitly discussed in the date field expansion project summary, exist in the upgrade unit being converted, analysts should review and update those components accordingly.

13.7 Upgrade Unit Procedural Workaround

The procedural workaround approach requires the creation and implementation of a subroutine or in-line logic to set and test a fixed or rolling (adjustable) date window to determine if a 6-character date falls in a century beginning with a "19" or a "20." Issues related to the selection of this approach were discussed in the procedural workaround versus date field expansion section in Chapter 12. If this approach is selected for an upgrade unit and is to be applied in whole or in part to that upgrade unit, analysts should complete the applicable portions of the detailed design analysis with a focus on date identification. Once system components and dates have been identified by basic impact analysis tools and techniques, analysts should finalize options, customize and implement required date routines, and correct any special requirements that arise.

13.7.1 Existing Date Utilization: Considerations and Options

Analysts should review the results of the date identification process, in which each date in the system was highlighted by the impact analysis, in order to finalize the implementation approach to be used. Analysts should take the following action.

1. *Review all compiler, database, telecommunication, and other software as potential sources of base date values.*

2. *If necessary, determine how a current date in an 8-character date format is to be reformatted into a 6-character date format.*

3. *Obtain date identification analysis results from the detailed design analysis.*

4. *Tally all procedural comparison and calculation logic occurrences to finalize the number of instances of date routines that need to be added.*

5. *Review special handling requirements when the procedural workaround does not support a given function or date format. This review includes key fields, sort fields, birth dates, literals, or other exception cases.*

6. *Finalize an approach to deal with all exception cases.*

7. *Inventory all date formats used in calculations and comparisons to verify that date subroutine workaround logic will handle those formats.*

This analysis verifies that all issues are identified and accommodated before proceeding with the actual procedural workaround process.

13.7.2 Date Routine Development or Customization

Unless a procedural workaround is to be used in only very specific and limited situations, analysts will want to create reusable routines that can be accessed, as needed, by application programs. This can be done via copy/include commands or by applying special subroutines. The approach depends on the programming language and environment. Including or copying source code in-line can become a maintenance problem for a number of reasons. Thus, in most situations, a separate callable subroutine that receives and returns date-related parameters is the recommended approach.

Date routines are commercially available or they can be developed internally. The benefit of obtaining routines from a third party is that they are documented, tested, supported, and generalized to fit many circumstances and formats. Basic procedural workaround routines should do the following:

- Calculate an 8-character date from any 6-character date

- Allow a user to specify a window of time to be used in calculating an 8-character date

- Set return codes to indicate the success of the routine's work

- Optionally calculate the time frames between two different 6-character dates

- Offer other options as required by the user or provided by the vendor

Figure 13.4 depicts the logic that has been added to an existing program to replace a test to determine policy valuation. In this situation, the existing logic would have not handled a valid claim when the policy date expired in the next century. In the updated code shown in Figure 13.4, analysts modified the code to pass the 6-character policy expiration date, the current date, and a 40-year rolling date value to the subroutine. The routine then returns to the program an 8-character date (full date) that can be used to provide a valid test to determine if the policy is valid.

Move current-date to current-date-now.   (current-date is 1996/12/30)
Move 40 to future-years.   (set rolling window 40 years out)
Move policy-expiration-date to in-date.   (in-date = 01/12/31)

Call "CONVRTN" using in-date, full-date, current-date-now, future-years, date-flags.

If current-date is less than full-date   (1996/12/30 is less than 2001/12/31)
        perform process-claim-request
else
        perform reject-policy.

Subroutine allows a program to continue to use a 2-character year field for data, but still be able to accurately interpret events that span a century window.

Figure 13.4   Procedural Workaround—Date Routine Utilization

The actual subroutine logic, shown in Figure 13.5, demonstrates very basic functionality that is used to create an 8-character date from a 6-character date. Extended functions, such as calculation of time differences between two dates that span different centuries, and parameter initialization and manipulation, have been omitted from the example. Off-the-shelf procedural workaround routines provide a wealth of additional functionality that should be investigated before an organization attempts to create its own routines. Once the required date subroutines have been created or obtained, tested, and deployed, Year 2000 implementation teams can begin using them to create procedural workaround solutions for various upgrade units.

CONVRTN using in-date, full-date, current-date-now, future-years, date-flags.

Calculate midpoint-ccyy = future-years + current-date-now-ccyy.

If in-date-yy is less than midpoint-yy   (in-date-yy = "01" is less than
        move "20" to full-date-cc   midpoint-yy = "36")
else
        move "19" to full-date -cc.

Move in-date-yy to full-date-yy.
Move in-date-mm to full-date-mm.
Move in-date-dd to full-date-dd.

Return to calling routine.

Subroutine tests an input year value against a calculated rolling midpoint and creates an 8-character date based on the result.

Figure 13.5   Procedural Workaround—Date Subroutine Logic

13.7.3 Date Routine Implementation

Implementing procedural workaround routines, once they are generally available, is fairly straightforward. Analysts must obtain the list of dates and the "in context" usage analysis created during the detailed design stage of the upgrade unit project. This inventory, coupled with subsequent analysis to examine exception cases and format requirements, is a high-level guide to the implementation process. As with other Year 2000 implementation tasks, the process is partially dependent on the tools available to support code changes. Interactive date change tools can locate dates interactively so that analysts can simply plug in the routines at each point.

The process to insert procedural workaround routines is summarized as follows.

1. *Apply the date routine implementation process to one program at a time, unless interactive analysis tools suggest an alternative process.*

2. *Use the impact analysis report to find each instance of date field comparison and date calculation logic in the program.*

3. *Prior to each date comparison logic statement, insert (copy, paste, or in some way add) the date setup logic and subroutine call to the program.*

4. *Verify that date formats are either converted prior to being moved them to the subroutine date areas or that the subroutine can recognize that date format.*

5. *Insert any return code logic tests and transfer any date values back into the working date fields for the program, as needed.*

6. *Perform the date comparison, using the fully expanded date or dates.*

7. *For calculation logic, determine whether the subroutine performs the calculation or whether the application code is responsible for the calculation.*

8. *Pass the applicable date values to the subroutine and either let the subroutine perform the calculation or perform the calculation with the fully expanded date values.*

9. *Upon completion of program conversion, compile and link the modified program and subroutine (or routines, if required) and verify that everything links properly.*

Analysts should continue this process for all programs in the system, noting where exception cases exist. Exceptions include key fields, birth dates, sort fields, and other dates where an 8-character date is required to properly process a function in a system.

13.7.4 Special Date Handling Considerations

Exceptions are the rule in a procedural workaround process. This means that many types of dates can be encountered that will require analysts to expand values or add logic to accommodate shortcomings in a procedural workaround project. The most common example is birth dates. Many birth dates span multiple centuries and a 105-year-old may be mixed up with a 5-year-old under a procedural workaround solution. When dates span multiple centuries, analysts have two options. If the situation is extremely rare, the system can be left alone and end users warned of the shortcoming. For example, will a lot of people be driving cars at the age of 116? The second option involves expanding specific dates, as needed, to 8 characters. These dates must be transferred to special work areas prior to comparisons and calculations involving 6-character dates.

Sort fields containing date field values will sort records in the wrong sequence if left as is. Analysts, again, have more than one option to correct this problem. Year 2000 tool coordinators should contact the vendor that furnishes the sort routine to see if that vendor has created a way of handling the sorting of date fields. Certain vendors have committed to providing an upgrade that allows the application user to tell the sort which fields are date fields. The sort utility, in turn, applies an approach similar to the workaround strategy outlined earlier. This means that sort fields containing 6-character date values can be left in their existing format, as long as vendor instructions are followed to tell the sort utility that a given field is a date. If the sort utility does not have this option, the sort field will have to be expanded, using the same subroutine approach that was applied earlier. Standalone sorts and in-line program sorts should both be included in this process.

Key fields, central to identifying and retrieving records from databases and keyed file structures, typically contain date field values. When these date field values begin to roll over in the next century, there is an increasing level of risk that key fields for different records will end up being duplicated. If this is a risk, these key fields should be expanded to an 8-character date to avoid the problem. If expansion is contemplated and the data stores in question are shared with other upgrade units or application areas, analysts must contact all owners or users of those data stores to communicate the data format changes. Any other exception situations should be handled appropriately.

If an upgrade unit undergoing procedural workaround conversion finds that exceptions have forced modifications to screens, reports, data stores or other components, then analysts should follow the applicable guidelines in section 13.6 for guidance on relevant issues.

13.8 Upgrade Unit Package Upgrade Solution

Package upgrades may not be as simple as they first appear, and management should be prepared for the level of effort involved. The number of release levels, customized changes, and surrounding additions to a system all combine to complicate the upgrade project. New releases must be certified compliant, deployed, synchronized with in-house changes, and, where applicable, interfaced with in-house data stores and other systems.

13.8.1 Upgrade Review and Certification

Upon receipt of a package release that is Year 2000 compliant, analysts must go through a number of tasks to verify that the system meets in-house or advertised requirements. These tasks include the following items.

1. *Verify that the approach used by the vendor is the one that they claimed they used.*

2. *If source code is available, analysts can use an impact analyzer to check for fully expanded date fields or, alternatively, procedural workaround techniques.*

3. *If no source is available, check the data store and file layouts provided with the package.*

4. *Verify that all documentation is complete and reflects the type of date upgrade performed.*

5. *Generally determine the number of release components and changes that have been added to the system.*

6. *If in-house developed code was inserted into the package software, finalize estimates to retrofit these changes into the new release.*

7. *If additional programs were developed to surround or interface with a package, determine the approach and the level of effort required to make these programs compliant.*

8. *Follow applicable date field expansion or procedural workaround guidelines on all in-house developed programs included in an application package upgrade unit.*

9. *Finalize the implementation and validation plan as dictated by in-house standards.*

13.8.2 Customized Retrofit Requirements

If a vendor supplies the source code for an application package and a customer has applied changes to that source code, these changes must be added back into the new release before that version can be deployed. This is not always the case, of course. The vendor may have added enhancements that make in-house changes obsolete, and this should be considered during the upgrade. In a worst case scenario, in-house updates may be so extensive or the in-house release may be so out of date that the in-house version of the code no longer even resembles the new release of the package. If either of these possibilities is true, the application team should investigate applying a date field expansion or a procedural workaround solution to the in-house package and dropping maintenance on the product.

If in-house upgrades need to be reapplied to a new vendor release, analysts should obtain documentation specifying which in-house changes have been applied to the vendor-supplied source code. If this information is unavailable, analysts should obtain the original version that was, hopefully, frozen in a backup library and run a code comparison tool against that original system and the current production programs and related system components. This comparison should provide a summary of baseline changes applied to the system since the last release.

If the last release was relatively current, these changes can then be retrofitted into the new release of the vendor package. Change integration technology is available to assist with automating at least part of this retrofitting process. Changes should be applied only as required to restore the package to end-users' minimal level of requirements so users can take advantage of the new, Year 2000-compliant vendor package.

13.8.3 Package Interface Component Upgrades

If file formats were modified as part of the vendor Year 2000 upgrade, these new formats must be assimilated into the in-house environment. Similarly, if in-house developed programs surround a package environment, those programs must be brought into line with the vendor package software.

Interface requirements should be identified prior to the arrival of the new release of the package. The vendor should supply a high-level specification indicating the Year 2000 approach to be used and the impact that this approach is to have on files and databases employed by the package. Based on these high-level guidelines, the Project Office interface coordinator should specify API or bridge requirements for a package. These API and bridge interfaces can be developed by use of techniques described in section 3.10.

Any in-house developed code that is part of the upgrade unit but not part of the new vendor release must be made Year 2000 compliant, using the approach applied to the rest of the package software. If in-house developed code relies heavily on data structures that are copied or included, the changes may be relatively easy. If the vendor supplies tools or techniques to assist with the upgrade of in-house code, these should be used whenever possible. Otherwise, analysts should seek out the techniques described in Section 13.6, *Expansions Upgrade Unit Date Fields,* and Section 13.7, *Upgrade Unit Procedural Workaround.* Validation and testing should proceed, just as with in-house systems, using the guidelines described in Chapter 14. Planning teams and management should remember that the work on a package product just begins the moment it arrives from the vendor.

13.9 Off-site Upgrade Unit Migration Project

Performing Year 2000 upgrade projects off site, either at a conversion factory or through an offshore/off-site service provider, demands unique packaging and specification requirements. In addition to identifying the upgrade unit, conversion approach, time frame, and budget, analysts must synchronize off-site conversion activities with in-house upgrade unit tasks. Analysts must ensure that the following in-house tasks are executed properly.

1. *Identify upgrade unit components and conversion requirements during the enterprise assessment.*

2. *Define time frames for project startup, conversion duration, and return to production.*

3. *Contact vendor to determine their requirements and to set up ongoing communication with vendor project management.*

4. *Prior to shipping the system to the vendor, in-house analysts must do the following:*

   a. Specify conversion approach to be used on the upgrade unit.

   b. Finalize all deliverables required from all parties for each stage of migration project.

   c. Accurately identify all components to be included in the upgrade unit.

   d. Obtain and synchronize vendor packaging requirements with in-house capability.

   e. Define the data stores that require bridge interfaces or APIs to the vendor.

   f. Communicate special date formatting or conversion requests.

   g. Establish an in-house point of contact and a vendor site point of contact.

5. *While the upgrade unit is being processed off site, analysts must do the following:*

   a. Monitor vendor off-site progress to adjust for timing slippage.

   b. Set up and test data store migration routines, if applicable, based on approach.

   c. Set up and finalize the Year 2000 validation environment and plan.

   d. Monitor and prepare to synchronize upgrade unit with in-house maintenance work.

6. *Once the upgrade unit is converted and returned by the vendor, analysts must do the following:*

   a. Verify that all deliverables are intact and complete according to specification.

   b. Optionally, run an impact analyzer to review code change results.

   c. Synchronize maintenance changes for any components modified during conversion.

   d. Use comparison tools to integrate maintenance changes back into the code.

   e. Execute final data store conversion, if applicable, under this approach.

   f. Install and test all interface routines developed by the vendor, as needed.

   g. Compile and test Year 2000-compliant version of upgrade unit.

   h. Run comparison analysis on output results and certify system Year 2000 compliant.

   i. Finalize any system testing requirements and complete production turnover process.

Shipping an upgrade unit off site does not relieve the in-house team of all responsibility for the Year 2000 conversion project. On the contrary, analysts must be even more vigilant on projects where much of the work is beyond their control. Chapter 17 discusses the use of conversion factories and offshore facilities in more depth.

13.10 Interface Creation, Activation, and Deactivation

Interface implementation is an in-house activity that is required any time date fields change formats in shared data stores, regardless of where upgrade unit changes or the interface development is actually performed. The creation of a bridge or an API is only part of the challenge. System testing and implementation is a key component in verifying that all components work properly once upgrade units are activated within a production environment.

Recall this terminology: A batch bridge is a standalone conversion routine that compresses or expands data sent to or received by other batch upgrade units; an API is a subroutine or in-line logic that interactively expands and contracts data formats between systems and on-line files and shared databases. Both interface types can be present in the same upgrade unit and it is critical that the project office interface coordinator play an active role in the determination of where bridge interfaces and APIs are to be activated, as discussed in the following sections.

13.10.1 Batch Bridge Creation and Implementation

Batch bridges must be enabled and disabled throughout the migration cycle in order to avoid nullifying bridges. Nullification occurs when one upgrade unit compresses an expanded data file so that downstream systems can still read that data. Then, subsequent upgrade units may undergo expansion and insert an expansion bridge between that previously compressed data store. This worst case scenario is avoided by having a central coordinator monitor all interface activity.

Bridges are an outgrowth of phased Year 2000 migration projects. Let us examine a very simple example where an upgrade unit receives one batch data file as input and sends one batch data file as output. The upgrade unit undergoes a complete date field expansion, which includes these two data files. No other surrounding upgrade units have undergone conversion at this point. To allow other systems to continue processing normally—a given rule of the phased migration strategy—two bridges are created as follows.

1. *The input file, received from another system, has a job step inserted to read the old format and write a newly expanded format to be used by the converted upgrade unit.*

2. *This job step executes a modified copy of the conversion routine used to expand this file during the original conversion effort.*

3. *If the sending upgrade unit was already expanded, the existing contraction bridge would be deactivated and no new bridge would be created.*

4. *If no existing bridge is in place, the job step and expansion bridge are moved into the production job stream along with all other upgrade unit components.*

5. *The output file, produced by this upgrade unit, has a job step inserted to read the expanded format and re-create the old, unexpanded format for upgrade units requiring this data in the old format.*

6. *This job step executes a "reverse" version of the conversion routine used to expand the code originally.*

7. *If all receiving upgrade units were already expanded, the existing expansion bridge would be deactivated and no new contraction bridge would be required.*

8. *If no existing bridge is in place, the job step and contraction bridge are moved into the production job stream along with all other upgrade unit components.*

This is an simplified, but very real, example. Figure 13.6 demonstrates how several upgrade units, in varying states of date field expansion, cause batch bridge activation and deactivation throughout the life of a Year 2000 initiative. The interface coordinator from the central Project Office must closely monitor this process to ensure that extra work and confusion are avoided. Upgrade unit support teams should concur on the ultimate date and file formats in advance

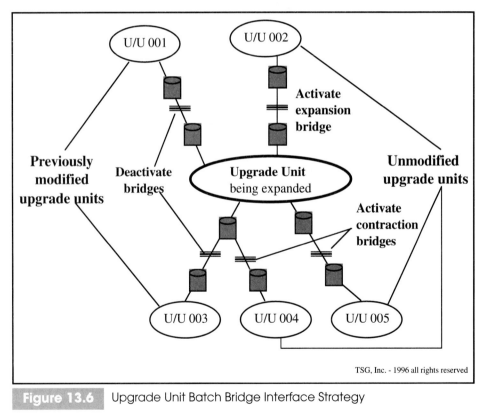

Figure 13.6 Upgrade Unit Batch Bridge Interface Strategy

13.10.2 Shared Data Store API Creation and Implementation

Databases or on-line files accessed by multiple upgrade units require an interactive API to facilitate phased implementation. The main difference between an API and a bridge is that an API is an interface program that adjusts data store formats while the program is actually running, whereas a bridge runs before or after a given application program. An API can also be shared and reused by many different programs and upgrade units throughout the life of a Year 2000 project. The use of an API facilitates independent expansion of data stores and allows for smaller, more manageable upgrade units. How these API interfaces are applied is up to the implementation teams responsible for a given upgrade unit.

A simple example illustrates the application of an API. Let us assume that one database is shared among multiple upgrade units. A database example was selected because a database API requires more setup and coordination than a shared, on-line file API. Setup and deployment of this type of API are accomplished by the following tasks.

1. *A planning team determines the need for an API, based on a decision to expand dates in a major database independently from each system accessing that database.*

2. *Data administration defines expanded formats for each hierarchical database segment containing a date and finalizes the conversion process for the database.*

3. *That same team creates an API for the database that allows upgrade units to access the database without going through a complete migration as follows:*

   a. Retain all existing processing logic and data definitions in the source programs accessing the database.

   b. Define new database segments in the form of expanded data definition language and the include members of the corresponding source record layout.

   c. Create a subroutine for each modified segment (a single subroutine may be employed if it can discern which segments are to be accessed).

— for a data retrieval function, the subroutine moves data from the retrieved, expanded segment layout into the original layout and returns this data to the application program

— for a data send function, the subroutine moves data from the original segment layout into the expanded segment format and updates the databases accordingly.

— Database return codes should be mimicked accordingly

4. *Once task #3 is completed, support personnel must make the following changes to the application programs accessing the expanded segment layouts.*

    a. Wherever an expanded database segment is accessed, replace the database call with a subroutine call that accesses the expanded segment format.

    b. Compile and link each impacted source program with the applicable subroutines and verify that the program works properly via a test execution against the new database.

5. *As each given upgrade unit is migrated, replace the original database commands as appropriate.*

Figure 13.7 depicts the phased expansion of various upgrade units that share a major database. An on-line data file API essentially uses a simplified version of this same process but does not require the same degree of conversion and setup effort. Note that other approaches can be used to accomplish this process. Certain software tools, for example, automatically generate and include API logic into the source code. Other approaches may expand the data last and use APIs in a process that is basically a reversal of the process described above. The important point to remember in implementing an API and a bridge interface strategy is to control the interfaces that are being planned and deployed through a central coordination facility so that redundant work can be avoided.

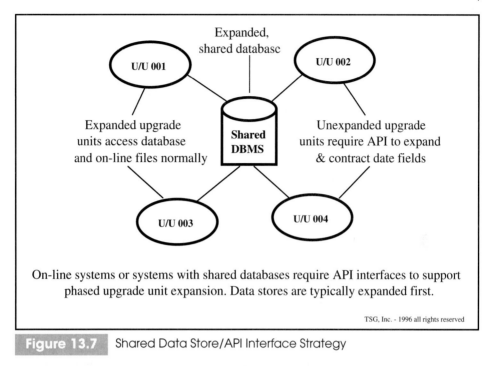

On-line systems or systems with shared databases require API interfaces to support phased upgrade unit expansion. Data stores are typically expanded first.

Figure 13.7 Shared Data Store/API Interface Strategy

13.11 Change Control, Quality Assurance, and Production Turnover

The change control and quality assurance processes are highly intertwined in a Year 2000 implementation project. As is the case with the detailed design and conversion stages of a migration project, each upgrade unit has its own unique change control and quality assurance requirements. Production turnover is similarly unique to each upgrade unit and must be coordinated with other production turnover efforts at the enterprise level to ensure that all projects remain synchronized. Each of these important components of the Year 2000 implementation phase is discussed in the next sections.

13.11.1 Change Control Techniques

Systems personnel tend to view change control as a barrier to Year 2000 migration. Copies of source code, as defined in Section 13.5, *Library and Environmental Setup,* can be periodically refreshed with production changes to manage volatile environments. Of course, any production changes while upgrade units are actually being converted and tested should be avoided. However, it is a common fact that, in most IT environments, change cannot be avoided or even delayed in many cases. One basic rule should be followed whenever possible: baseline versions of an upgrade unit must be protected from functional upgrades, or validation time frames could increase exponentially.

The change control process is predicated on the use of the library versions set up at the beginning of the upgrade unit conversion process. When a production change has been made, the source code and all related components should be submitted to the Year 2000 conversion team. The team then runs a code comparison utility against the controlled production version and the newly submitted modified versions. Analysts should use the audit report produced by the code comparison tool to carefully retrofit all maintenance changes into the modified versions of the source code. The original production versions should always be updated by replacing all modified components in their entirety. This discipline will provide analysts with a reliable baseline during the quality assurance walk-through and validation cycle.

The Year 2000 team should verify that the maintenance team is tightly controlling all source changes during the upgrade cycle. Change control can be reduced to a relatively minor issue in a Year 2000 migration project when it is managed systematically. Such management should appease users that are anxious for system fixes or other critical requirements during the upgrade unit conversion process.

13.11.2 Quality Assurance Process

Quality assurance should be established as a formal function in a Year 2000 project. This means that the following guidelines should be reviewed and applied by the Year 2000 project office or some other managing body.

1. *Formalize the quality assurance (QA) process.*

2. *Identify a responsible party to perform QA for the project. This person can be someone from the Year 2000 Project Office or the application team can be a consultant.*

3. *Establish a set of deliverables from each project that are to be provided to the QA reviewer, including:*

   a. compiled versions of all final source code and related components version

   b. access to the version libraries used during the migration process

c. copies of any interface or API routines developed for the project

   d. audit trail results for execution process for the test data conversion (or whatever outputs are produced by the data conversion tools)

   e. final results demonstrating that "clean" compiles have been obtained for the final source code versions

   f. audit trail report showing all changes between the original production baseline components and the final versions

   g. audit trail report listing differences between automatically converted and manually modified versions of an upgrade unit (where manual changes were used to compensate for weaknesses in the conversion tool)

4. *Review (QA individual) all components and changes, looking for irregularities and missing deliverables.*

5. *Report inconsistencies to the project manager so that they can be rectified prior to validation testing.*

This process can be phased over the life of the project by having conversion analysts provide components and deliverables to the QA reviewer when certain portions of the upgrade unit are completed. Sign-off forms provide a formal mechanism for tracking the results of a QA walk-through. Many project managers may think that this activity is extraneous and unnecessary. A project of this nature, however, must have a formal vehicle for ensuring that work was completed to specification. The erroneous belief that the validation process is that checkpoint will dramatically increase the costs of the project.

13.11.3 Certification Acceptance

Year 2000 certification is a direct result of the validation process discussed in Chapter 14. Analysts must determine that a system will properly interpret time-dependent events when century boundaries are being crossed. Regardless of the quality of the work performed during the actual conversion itself, the validation process is the final certification qualifier. Who performs this certification process and what the final sign-off process entails is up to the Project Office and the project manager for that upgrade unit. The Year 2000 Project Office should establish guidelines for conversion teams to follow. Support for this process can be derived from internal audit teams, outside consultants, the Project Office, or other senior analysts. The bottom-line requirement is that a formal review and sign-off are key to successful implementation efforts. The guidelines in Chapter 14 provide detailed insights into this process.

13.11.4 Production Turnover

The operations team tends to dictate when and how upgrade units are to be promoted into production. The advisory board should have established, at a high level, what degree of risk the production support team is willing to take when it comes to the turnover process. How many critical systems can go into production at one time? What documentation is required for the process? How often will turnover occur and what are the lead times? All of these issues should be addressed during project mobilization and documented for the implementation teams.

13.12 Central Project Office Communication and Status Reporting

Throughout this chapter, we have referred to the role of the central Project Office in project coordination, status reporting, migration support, setting up formal QA and turnover procedures, and other aspects. All of these roles are important, but the one that should be reiterated one more time is the need to track and coordinate any activity that crosses an upgrade unit boundary. This includes the activation and deactivation of interface routines, method and tool utilization, managing cross-functional, external business partner relationships, large database migration projects, budget adjustment, and transfer of upgrade unit conversion skills. The Project Office cannot disappear during migration but must play an even more visible role than during the enterprise assessment phase of the project. The truly successful implementation project team manager will keep this in mind.

13.13 Contingency Options and Project Finalization

As Year 2000 implementation and the year 2000 near, one thing will become increasingly clear: all upgrade units will be Year 2000 compliant or they will not. For those systems that are about to pass their event horizon (past the point of making a managed transition to compliance), contingency plan implementation must be invoked. This means that, in the event of a total failure, users may need to invoke manual techniques to replace automated functions. When minor system glitches arise, users will have to be trained in workaround techniques to keep the business functioning.

As failures due to non-compliance loom, software triage, discussed in Chapter 4, will begin; this is when business and IT personnel will discover the real importance, or unimportance, of various systems. Every organization and every business area will have contingency issues. Proper contingency planning will keep executives from making rash moves that could be avoided or will allow them to make those moves with the most information at hand.

Many companies believe that Year 2000 projects will come to some orderly conclusion near the end of the century. We contend that the actual end of the project will be difficult to truly determine. First of all, much of the conversion work will likely be implemented in an abbreviated manner that leaves screens, reports, and other components untouched. The full impact of this may cause end users to demand that these components be expanded once the initial version of this upgrade unit moves into production. The shortcut approach is likely to be commonly applied, given the time frames that IT is facing with this project.

In addition, project-introduced errors and unconverted systems will continue to haunt IT and end users well past the turn of the century. Transitions can be streamlined by having a transition team in place and on call for the last 3 months of 1999 and first 3 months of 2000. A Project Office SWAT team will likely need to remain in place to "clean up" problems for one to two years, or more, beyond the onset of the year 2000. Organizations should not be shocked by this. Rather, executives should budget some amount of money to provide a controlled and orderly shutdown to the project.

Validation
Strategies

Year 2000 validation is the last chance for an organization to keep date-related problems out of production. Validation determines that no errors were introduced during the conversion process. This determination is critical because a latent error could cause large monetary losses, legal concerns, or a loss of goodwill to the organization. Year 2000 compliance certification testing, using post-Year 2000 date values, is covered in Section 14.6. The importance of validation to the success of the overall project motivates this chapter's in-depth treatment of the issue.

This chapter discusses the resources, technologies and techniques required to ensure that migrated applications will function as they encounter events beyond the year 2000. This chapter also provides an overview of the validation process, including two different implementation options, and descriptions of key components within the overall process. Note that validation approaches vary according to industry, system, regulatory requirements, in-house standards, time constraints, and a host of other factors. Note, too, that this chapter is not a replacement for any of the more extensive discussions on testing available through numerous other books and sources.

Finally, as with any Year 2000 task, validation should be performed with the assistance of skilled experts whenever possible. All of these issues should be considered when establishing enterprisewide and upgrade unit-specific validation strategies. The topics reviewed in this chapter will, we hope, enrich this process.

Deliverables and related activities from a Year 2000 validation project, all discussed in this chapter, include the following.

- Deliverable: Validation role and skill requirements
  Activity: Finalize role and skill requirements.

- Deliverable: Validation technology requirements
  Activity: Finalize validation requirements.

- Deliverable: Year 2000 validation strategy
  Activity: Select and establish an overall validation strategy.
  Activity: Finalize validation environment, location, and resources.

- Deliverable: Test results and execution coverage analysis for original upgrade unit
  Activity: Perform initial tests on the original version of upgrade unit.

- Deliverable: Upgraded test data to support enhanced execution coverage
  Activity: Enhance test data as required to improve execution coverage.
  Deliverable: Comparison results between original and converted upgrade unit outputs
  Activity: Perform validation test on converted version of upgrade unit.
  Activity: Perform comparison analysis between original and converted versions of upgrade unit.

- Deliverable: Test results for converted Year 2000 upgrade unit
  Activity: Review and correct any validation discrepancies.

- Deliverable: Test data to support post-Year 2000 certification testing
  Activity: Populate input test data stores with post-year 2000 date values.

- Deliverable: Certified Year 2000-compliant upgrade unit
  Activity: Perform Year 2000 certification testing.

- Deliverable: System test results and production sign-off
  Activity: Finalize change control and code synchronization issues.
  Activity: Complete upgrade unit integration testing.

- Deliverable: Post-implementation audit facility
  Activity: Establish post-implementation audit facility.

14.1 Validation Roles and Skill Requirements

Validation, as with all other phases of a Year 2000 project, requires certain skill sets to ensure that the project is a success. These skills include a project manager, a validation process specialist, a tool and technology expert, validation analysts, application area experts, and a certification specialist. Each of these skills is required for a successful validation project, but a single individual can assume multiple roles.

- **Validation project manager.**

  — The validation project manager is typically the same manager who is managing the Year 2000 implementation project for that upgrade unit.

  — On a very large upgrade unit, this could be a separate manager assigned to manage validation tasks.

  — Skills include the ability to manage the validation workplan developed during the enterprise assessment and to ensure that the testing and certification process is completed properly, on time, and within budget.

- **Year 2000 validation specialist.**

  — A validation specialist is typically a Project Office representative who has knowledge and experience with Year 2000 validation projects.

  — Skills include the ability to define the overall validation process, help fine-tune test scripts, review comparison results, certify systems to be Year 2000 compliant, and train validation team members as needed.

  — This individual should also have general testing knowledge and skills.

- **Validation tools and technology expert.**

  — The validation technology expert is typically a Project Office representative who has experience using testing tools within the applicable systems environment.

  — For example, if this is a mainframe environment, this individual has experience with tools that support mainframe testing.

  — The technology background for this person should include comparison technology, coverage analyzers, virtual date utilities, data migration tools, and, optionally, on-line testing tools.

- **Validation analyst.**

  — Validation analysts are the individuals that actually perform the validation testing and certification work.

  — These individuals should have solid testing experience and a willingness to follow the guidelines set forth by the validation specialist and the tools and technology expert.

- **Application area expert.**

  — Application area experts identify the test data to be used for validation, assist with any security issues, and provide general input regarding the overall test environment.

  — Application area experts, more often than not, can also be the same analysts that actually perform Year 2000 validation.

- **Year 2000 certification specialist.**

  — This individual is responsible for certifying an upgrade unit to be Year 2000 compliant.

  — Skills include the ability to review output results and determine that the system is correctly processing date values that cross the century window.

  — This person may be the validation specialist, the project manager, or even someone from internal audit.

  — To avoid a conflict of interest, however, this person should not be the same individual who performed validation work on the system.

14.2 Validation Technology Requirements

Testing tools provide a tremendous degree of leverage in stream-lining the validation process. This means that certain basic, repetitive functions can be handled by tools, while analysts focus their time on more critical tasks. This is particularly true with comparison facility and test coverage analyzers. These tools, along with on-line playback and capture tools, virtual date utilities, and data migration tools, help streamline validation efforts. Validation tool categories are discussed in more depth in Chapter 15; specific vendor tool references are listed in Appendix A.

14.2.1 Comparison Utility

A comparison utility provides the minimum level of tool support required for validation projects. Key features include an ability to bypass certain fields where old and new formats differ and, optionally, to deter-mine that two data values, while different, are correct based on offset cal-culations.

14.2.2 On-line Capture and Playback Tool

On-line capture and playback tools create consistent, reusable input data for on-line systems and provide significant value to on-line system validation projects.

14.2.3 Test Coverage Analyzer

Dynamic analyzers highlight the percentage of a program that has been executed; static analyzers help analysts modify test data so that a greater degree of logic is invoked. These tools play a key role in valida-tion setup and execution. Only qualified analysts should apply these tools during an implementation project as they have a long learning curve.

14.2.4 Virtual Date Utility

Testing a system to see if it works after the turn of the century requires that programs believe the year to be 2000 or beyond. Virtual date utilities offer this capability in varying degrees and are required unless testing is performed in a standalone environment or on a workstation.

14.2.5 Data Migration and Data Upgrade Tools

Data migration tools can be useful for adding or updating date values that reflect future events—a key requirement for Year 2000 certification testing. Analysts should thoroughly research these tools to support validation efforts.

14.3 Validation Planning and Preparation

Before the validation process begins, multiple levels of planning and preparation must occur. The enterprise assessment reviewed testing infrastructures and, where applicable, recommended certain improvements or upgrades. Validation preparation typically includes mobilizing a validation team, establishing a Year 2000 testing process, and deploying testing tools. Centralized or distributed validation teams work with application areas throughout the Year 2000 implementation project to improve Year 2000 test environments, perform validation tasks, and certify systems Year 2000 compliant.

The enterprise assessment may also have identified the need to stabilize the testing environments of selected application areas. The Project Office should focus its attention on areas found to have exceptionally poor test environments and on mission-critical systems. The activities needed to stabilize system testing environments include the following:

1. *Introduce common testing procedures and testing tools to the application team.*

2. *Find and document all test data and execution control facilities.*

3. *Analyze the level of execution coverage and increase it if necessary.*

4. *Reduce test data volume by eliminating redundant test cases.*

5. *Set up on-line data capture and playback facilities.*

6. *Establish and document unit and system testing scripts, as required.*

Test scripts include documentation, test data, compile and link guidelines, and procedures for performing unit and system testing. System testing, also called integration testing, determines that a system works properly when integrated with related applications and the surrounding environment. This is particularly important when one considers the number of interfaces, data format changes, and other modifications involved in a Year 2000 project.

A wide variety of testing improvements can be implemented before work begins on a given upgrade unit. Documenting and upgrading test scripts, for example, are valid goals for any application area, regardless of the motivating factors. Once conversion work begins on an upgrade unit, however, all validation tasks applied to that upgrade unit must be narrowly focused toward achieving Year 2000 compliance. Validation goals should be limited to upgrading test data as needed to maximize execution coverage and the Year 2000 certification process itself.

The timing of these events is critical. If an upgrade unit migration project is scheduled to begin immediately after completion of the enterprise assessment, for example, extensive upgrades to the testing environment could not be accommodated. In these cases, work should be focused on stabilizing the validation environment. The remainder of this section discusses logistical planning, high-level validation strategies, and a summary of tasks to be performed in parallel with upgrade unit implementation.

14.3.1 Validation Logistical Planning

Logistical planning for validation is determined by platform, hardware, and resource restrictions. Where testing is performed, for example, depends on who is performing the work and on which platform the system runs. Who performs the testing is dictated by application management requirements and the availability of resources. There are options, however, that can and should be explored.

Validation is best managed as an in-house activity, close to the upgrade unit's support personnel and native operating environment. This means that proposals from consultants that advocate off-site testing should be viewed with some skepticism. Relocating hundreds of files and databases, and re-creating exact operating environments can lengthen upgrade unit delivery schedules beyond required event horizons. If processing windows and storage facilities are at peak capacity, however, the upgrade unit may need to be tested on a system other than the machine on which it normally resides. Planning teams, in these cases, should explore the following options.

- Interview disaster recovery service bureaus (ideally, sites that are already used by your organization) as potential backup testing sites.

- Where available, examine the option of running unit tests on workstation environments that simulate native database, compiler, and telecommunication facilities.

- Review the use of scaled-down versions of the mainframe that run operating system, database, telecommunications, and other software required to test the system.

- Examine offshore options, based on existing relationships with offshore service providers.

One factor to consider when reviewing off-site testing options is that final system acceptance testing should be performed in an upgrade unit's native environment. Doing otherwise is highly unreliable. When considering off-site testing, consult tool specialists to determine if the testing tools used in the native environment can be transferred to other platforms or if comparable tool support is available in a simulated testing environment. One last consideration regarding testing sites is that validation must be closely integrated with change management. If an upgrade unit is subject to volatile maintenance activity, off-site testing may not be the best approach.

The decision as to who performs the testing tends to reside with the owners of a given application. Usually, the persons responsible for maintaining and enhancing a system will want to perform the testing. These individual efforts can be supplemented by outside consulting staff and project office personnel for specific tasks. In some cases, management may select outside consulting staff to perform the testing, with application analysts providing input as needed. Determining who is to staff validation tasks should be finalized when the upgrade unit project starts up.

14.3.2 General Validation Strategy

At a high level, most validation projects have many tasks in common. The basic process includes the following steps.

1. *Test the original version of the upgrade unit to establish a baseline set of output data against which to validate the converted version of the upgrade unit.*

2. *Adjust test data to increase execution coverage and confidence in the final results.*

3. *Execute the converted upgrade unit by inputting the same data used to test the original version of the upgrade unit.*

4. *Compare all output results to verify that original and converted upgrade units are functionally equivalent; correct any discrepancies.*

5. *Test the upgrade unit by using post-year 2000 data and certify it Year 2000 compliant.*

6. *Move the upgrade unit back into production.*

The concept underlying the validation process is fairly simple and rooted in a history of numerous systems redevelopment projects with goals very similar to those of a Year 2000 project. The process ensures that no functional differences or errors were introduced during the Year 2000 conversion process. It also prevents analysts from broadening the scope of the conversion process beyond that for the year 2000. This is a concept that management should embrace if they plan to complete the Year 2000 project on time and within a specified budget.

Organizations will undoubtedly pursue numerous variations of this basic strategy. For example, certification testing, using Year 2000-specific data, can be integrated with the validation process. This is called "single pass" validation and certification. Conversely, validation testing can be segregated from the Year 2000 certification testing process. This is called "dual pass" validation and certification. These two strategies, along with specific details describing each of the individual tasks within the validation process, are discussed in the remaining portions of this chapter.

14.3.3 Dual-Pass Validation Strategy

Figure 14.1 depicts the "dual pass" Year 2000 validation and certification process. This suggested default process applies a "divide and conquer" approach to the problem and assumes that verifying functional equivalence during a first pass validation test and then certifying Year 2000 compliance in a second execution test is a more straightforward process than attempting to meet both objectives at once. This conclusion stems from the fact that comparing output results from the original upgrade unit to output results from the converted upgraded unit is a highly automated process. If a difference occurs, it can be readily traced to the source of the error. Once this process is completed, the code can be moved back into production and made available to maintenance personnel as required.

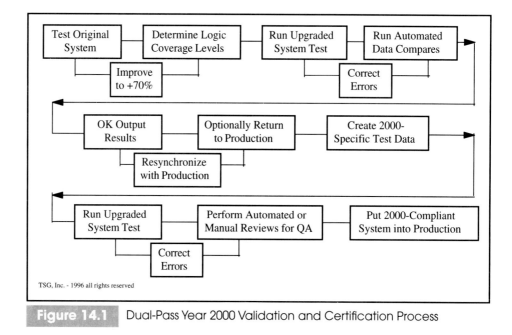

Figure 14.1   Dual-Pass Year 2000 Validation and Certification Process

While application support personnel perform maintenance upgrades for end users, validation analysts can continue populating input data stores with post-Year 2000 date values at a measured pace. Once post-Year 2000 date values are propagated across test input data stores, certification testing can begin. A number of circumstances make dual-pass Year 2000 validation and certification desirable.

- Upgrade units are constantly under maintenance making out-of-production windows extremely tight.

- The project involves a fairly comprehensive date field expansion that includes end-user screens and reports, databases, and other components.

- Test data stores are extremely complicated, numerous, or extensive, and updating these data stores is a difficult task.

- The system is extremely date dependent with many occurrences of date field values and date-sensitive logic.

- Other nonfunctional changes (e.g., a compiler upgrade) were concurrently applied to this upgrade unit.

Dual-pass Year 2000 validation and certification testing has a downside. Testing a system twice always takes more time and resources. Dual-pass validation is a more conservative approach, however, and should be considered for upgrade units that meet some or all of the above criteria.

14.3.4 Single-Pass Validation Strategy

Figure 14.2 depicts the "single pass" Year 2000 validation and certification process. The single-pass approach has advantages over the dual-pass approach. The main benefit of the single-pass approach is that, in an ideal situation, one test cycle is executed to certify an upgrade unit as Year 2000 compliant. This means that the comparison process between the output data generated by the original upgrade unit and that generated by the converted upgrade unit must use date value offsets, because the original system cannot process data that contains date values in the next century.

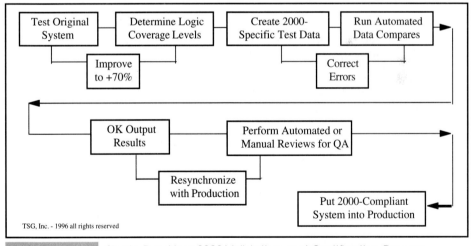

Figure 14.2 Single-Pass Year 2000 Validation and Certification Process

Single-pass validation significantly complicates problem tracking when a discrepancy in the validation process arises. Analysts may not know if the discrepancy was a weakness in the date offset calculations or was an error in the actual conversion process. The decision to apply the single-pass validation strategy is desirable when the following factors are true.

- The upgrade unit is not highly date dependent.

- Application support requirements are minimal and maintenance volatility is low.

- A procedural workaround approach was used to make the upgrade unit Year 2000 compliant.

- No other changes were concurrently applied to this upgrade unit.

- Data store utilization within this upgrade unit is not unduly complex.

- Very few API or bridge interfaces were introduced during the conversion.

- The upgrade unit is small (under 100 programs) and can be validated in a relatively short period of time.

- Acceptance testing cycles are long because of political or organizational issues.

- The upgrade unit event horizon is too close for analysts to apply a dual-pass strategy.

Ultimately, the decision between a dual-pass and a single-pass validation strategy is based on common sense. If analysts believe that the validation process for a given upgrade unit is relatively straightforward and maintenance volatility is low, a single-pass strategy can be used. Later sections of this chapter address validation tasks from both perspectives; consider these factors as input to the validation planning process.

14.3.5 Parallel Validation Setup Tasks

A number of validation setup tasks should be undertaken simultaneously with upgrade unit implementation efforts so that testing environments will be ready when conversion work is completed. The timeline and dependencies for these events is shown in Figure 14.3. Once data definition and impact analysis are finished and analysts have determined which programs are ultimately affected by date conversion, all original programs can be compiled and run through a preliminary test cycle. Data stores can be upgraded to adjust execution coverage at that point.

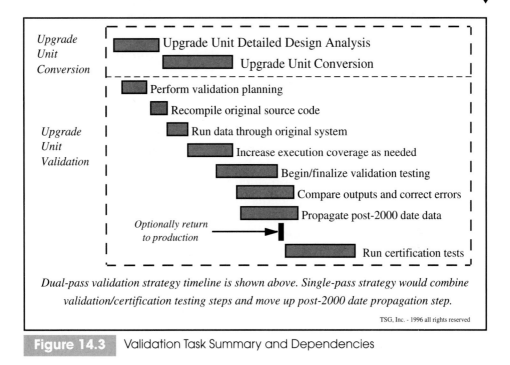

Dual-pass validation strategy timeline is shown above. Single-pass strategy would combine validation/certification testing steps and move up post-2000 date propagation step.

Figure 14.3   Validation Task Summary and Dependencies

As conversion work is completed on selected upgrade unit components, those components can be validated, using the newly upgraded data stores. The timing of the post-Year 2000 date propagation task varies according to the strategy selected. Figure 14.3 depicts dependencies for the dual-pass strategy. Personnel assigned to upgrade unit analysis and conversion tasks cannot be the same individuals assigned to the validation setup process. Upgrade unit project managers must synchronize implementation and validation tasks carefully so as not to create a resource utilization conflict and not to prolong project timelines unnecessarily.

14.4 Establishing a Validation Baseline

Establishing a validation baseline involves identifying all source components to be validated, compiling and executing all original programs targeted for conversion, determining execution coverage levels, and upgrading data stores to improve execution coverage as needed. This process is typically performed during the later stages of upgrade unit detailed design and the early stages of upgrade unit conversion. This preliminary validation testing stage becomes the baseline for the remaining validation tasks and should be performed with enough lead time to ensure that validation of the converted upgrade unit can begin as soon as various system components are released from the quality assurance review process.

14.4.1 Compilation of Original Upgrade Unit Components

Identifying and compiling all source code and related components is the first formal activity within the validation process. As a rule, the entire upgrade unit must undergo validation testing at the system level before being released to production. At the unit level, however, the goal is to test only those components that are impacted by the Year 2000 conversion effort. Impacted components are identified during the early stages of the detailed design process for the upgrade unit. The analysis team should release a list of these components to the validation team as soon as this analysis is complete.

All source programs that are directly or indirectly impacted by date field expansion or by procedural workaround conversion must be included in the initial unit test of the original system. It is easier to segregate components for testing purposes in a procedural workaround project because the impact of change is relatively isolated. In a date field expansion project, however, the effects of a change are much more far-reaching. Analysts must, therefore, ensure that any components that are even remotely impacted by the conversion process undergo a validation test. Because almost all data stores and system components accessing that data are impacted by a date field expansion, this type of project requires a greater degree of testing than a procedural workaround project.

The following activities should be performed by analysts to ensure that all of the proper programs are selected and prepared for the original upgrade unit test cycle.

- Identify all components assigned to the upgrade unit being validated; the inventory list can be used for these purposes.

- Identify all programs and related components impacted by the date upgrade project.

- Gather all compile, linkage, and other types of assembly job control members.

- Finalize compiler levels and related parameters as needed to compile source code components of an original upgrade unit.

- Optionally, introduce a dynamic analyzer tool or dynamic analysis compile options into the process at this point.

- Compile and link all source programs and other components as required.

- Verify that all programs have been successfully compiled and linked.

It is important to introduce the dynamic analysis technology into the compile-and-linkage process so that the test run of the original system produces execution coverage analysis results.

14.4.2 Validation Setup and Execution Coverage Analysis

Testing the original version of an upgrade unit meets several key validation objectives. It produces output data that can be compared to output produced by the converted version of the upgrade unit as a way of ensuring that no functional errors were inadvertently introduced during conversion. The results of this test also provide analysts with execution coverage analysis results and assist with determining whether data stores need to be modified to expand coverage analysis. Finally, this process ensures that all compile, link, and execution steps are documented prior to performing those same steps on the converted upgrade unit. The following steps allow analysts to complete the validation setup and run the original upgrade unit through an initial test cycle.

1. *Obtain all standard test scripts, guidelines, and input test data stores typically used to perform standard testing on the system or systems contained within this upgrade unit.*

2. *Identify all source programs directly impacted by the procedural workaround or date field expansion project; add these to the test plan.*

3. *Add any other programs that share a load module or a data store with these programs (inventory and cross-reference lists support this analysis) into the test plan.*

4. *Identify and verify that all execution job streams and on-line invocation facilities are available for the upgrade unit test.*

5. *Verify that all input data stores and upgrade unit execution components reside in the test environment selected for this validation cycle.*

6. *For on-line systems, obtain or establish fixed screen inputs, using on-line playback and capture tools.*

7. *Identify all output data stores to be used in the validation comparison process as follows:*

   - Obtain the entire inventory of output data stores for the upgrade unit.

   - Exclude output data stores that have no connection to any impacted components.

   - For on-line programs, exclude output screens that have no date values and that are not related to programs impacted by the date change.

8. *Establish output data capture requirements as follows:*

   - Verify that all relevant output files are assigned permanent addresses and names.

   - Freeze copies of input data stores to be used as input to the converted upgrade unit test cycle; this is critical for data stores updated during the original test cycle.

   - Assign report and other printed output data sets to permanent file names.

   - For on-line systems, verify that screen inputs and outputs are saved, using capture and playback facilities.

9. *Identify programs that require a high degree of execution coverage as follows:*

   - Include mission-critical programs as determined by application analysts.

   - Include programs that perform update functions to strategic files or databases.

   - Exclude reporting routines, utilities, or other less critical programs as identified by application analysts.

10. *For batch system components, obtain production runtime procedures to help guide the execution process.*

11. *Execute on-line programs and batch job streams in the sequence dictated by production runtime procedures and by application area analysts.*

12. *Review and record the level of execution coverage for each program identified in prior steps.*

13. *Capture and save all output results.*

As the initial test cycles for original upgrade unit programs are completed, analysts must verify that all outputs and audit trail reports from dynamic analysis are captured and catalogued for further analysis. The next section discusses the process of expanding the level of program execution coverage.

14.4.3 Assessing and Upgrading Execution Coverage

Dynamic analyzers produce audit trail reports that indicate what percentage of the total program was executed during a given test cycle. These tools also highlight the individual lines of the code that were executed during that same test run. This information should be reviewed for all programs identified during preliminary validation setup tasks. If the percentage of logic that was executed for a given program is low (a typical test falls in the 5 to 10 percent range), test data must be modified to increase coverage while minimizing the volumes of data and the number of test cases.

An acceptable level of coverage is anything over 70 percent. Although this may be unattainable, it is an excellent goal for validation analysts. There are two schools of thought on how to increase the confidence in and reliability of a given set of test data.

The first school of thought involves increasing execution coverage generally so that more logic, regardless of whether it is date related or not, is executed in a given test cycle. The reasoning behind this is that (1) singling out date related logic may be unduly time consuming; (2) if enough logic paths are invoked, much of the date-related logic is executed anyway, and (3) nondate logic should be tested because errors may be introduced and not caught if these logic paths are omitted.

The second school of thought states that analysts should focus on increasing logic path coverage based solely on date-related, conditional test cases. This concept is based on the premise that focusing solely on date logic saves time and produces more comprehensive test results. While this approach may be ideal, the reasons listed above for pursuing a more general approach to increasing execution coverage should be considered carefully. Regardless of the approach selected, knowledgeable analysts should apply test coverage analysis tools to programs in which test data did not provide a high degree of execution coverage. The process to expand execution coverage is summarized below.

1. *Obtain all audit reports, test data, and source code listings for programs having an inadequate percentage of execution coverage.*

2. *Use dynamic analysis results to determine where major routines were left unexecuted.*

3. *Trace high-level decision points from the beginning of the program to identify test cases that could be established to invoke these high-level routines.*

4. *Use the static analysis graph and any dynamic tools to examine how additional, lower-level routines, particularly those that contain date-sensitive logic, can be invoked.*

5. *Continue this process, noting where test data values can be added to invoke logic paths that were previously not executed.*

6. *Run some sample tests to drive up the level of execution coverage until management is satisfied that test data is comprehensive enough to support the validation process.*

7. *Capture all output results from the last or most comprehensive program execution so that these outputs can be used to validate converted upgrade unit output data.*

As the preceding sections make clear, the process of streamlining execution coverage should be performed with assistance from skilled testing and validation experts.

14.5 Year 2000 Validation: Functional Equivalence Testing

Year 2000 validation is based on the concept of proving "functional equivalence." This requires a comparison of output produced by the converted version of an upgrade unit with output produced by the original version of that upgrade unit. The basis for this concept is the fact that no functional changes were applied to the original or the converted upgrade unit libraries and that identical input data, when processed through the different versions, will yield identical output results excluding any time stamp differences. Run-date differentials can be adjusted by using virtual date utilities to set the current date to the same date for all tests.

In the case of a date field expansion project, functional equivalence testing must accommodate expanded input and output data store formats. In this situation, analysts must synchronize equivalence testing with the completion of related data store expansion efforts. Inputs to functional equivalence testing include all inputs and system components used to test the original upgrade unit, converted upgrade unit components, and, for date field expansion projects, expanded versions of input data stores. Figure 14.4 depicts this process and highlights the fact that expanded data formats were used as input to an upgrade unit that has undergone a date field expansion. Procedural workaround projects can alternatively utilize copies of input data stores that were used to test the original version of the upgrade unit.

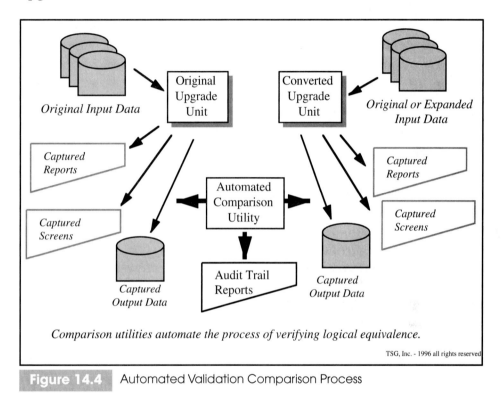

Comparison utilities automate the process of verifying logical equivalence.

Figure 14.4   Automated Validation Comparison Process

14.5.1 Upgrade Unit Validation Test

The procedure used to validate an upgrade unit that has undergone a Year 2000 conversion is similar to the process for setting up and executing the original upgrade unit test. The guidelines for identifying and compiling upgrade unit components, identifying data stores, finalizing the test environment, and executing the test itself remain fairly consistent. These guidelines, unique to preparing a validation environment to test the converted version of an upgrade unit, are:

1. *Job control facilities, used to compile and link original upgrade unit source code, should be duplicated and then modified to ensure that all converted load modules are placed in separate load libraries.*

2. *If this is a procedural workaround project (no data format changes), ensure that original input data sets are used as input to all on-line and batch execution facilities.*

3. *If this is a date field expansion project, ensure that the expanded data stores are used as input to all on-line and batch execution facilities.*

4. *The converted upgrade unit must specify output data set names different from those names specified by the original upgrade unit. This name difference avoids the overlaying of original output data sets that are required for validation comparison.*

5. *If a virtual date utility is available, verify that the date on each job is the same as that used on the original upgrade unit test execution.*

Once these items are finalized, analysts can proceed with testing the recently converted upgrade unit to determine if the new, upgraded system still functions properly.

14.5.2 Automated Comparison Analysis and Resolution

Automated comparison utilities help analysts determine if the results from one system, in this case, the original upgrade unit *without* Year 2000 changes, and a second system, in this case, the converted upgrade unit *with* Year 2000 changes, produce functionally equivalent results. This process, highlighted in Figure 14.4, is the most efficient way that analysts can determine that no errors were introduced during the process. Automated comparison techniques and technology can be applied in two different ways.

The first approach assumes that the same input data values were used, with the possible exception of a new century field in certain data stores, in determining logical equivalence. This approach, commonly used in dual-pass validation strategies, suggests that analysts employ the following steps.

1. *Identify all output data stores, captured reports, and simulated output screen data produced by the original upgrade unit test.*

2. *Identify all output data stores, captured reports, and simulated output screen data produced by the converted upgrade unit test.*

3. *Obtain the automated comparison tool and set parameters to ignore inconsistent values or new fields—with a specific focus on time stamp values and new century fields.*

4. *Run the comparison tools against all corresponding outputs produced by the original and the converted upgrade units.*

5. *Review the audit trail reports to determine any discrepancies.*

6. *Sign off on all valid results and correct errors found in the audit trail report.*

7. *Where discrepancies occur, work with conversion analysts to correct the error.*

8. *Rerun any tests to produce a valid audit trail report.*

9. *Turn over all results from the test to the quality assurance coordinator for the project.*

If a compiler-level upgrade or similar technological change that has no functional impact on the code was introduced during the conversion process, the results should be logically equivalent if all changes were applied correctly. In these cases, analysts should take care to keep multiple versions of all programs intact: one with compiler upgrades only and a second with compiler upgrades and the date changes (this protocol can be reversed). The first version can be retested to determine if the error was in the compiler upgrade. If not, analysts should look toward the date upgrades as the source of the problem.

A second approach to equivalence testing used in the single-pass validation strategy, uses date values set to points beyond the year 2000 to test the converted system. This comparison calculates logical date offsets in order to reconcile date values produced by the converted upgrade unit with date values produced by the original upgrade unit. If the validation team is pursuing a single-pass validation strategy, they are responsible for integrating the equivalence testing and certification testing processes. Integrated validation testing is explored in more depth in Section 14.6.3 *Certification and Equivalence Testing Integration Strategy.*

14.6 Year 2000 Compliance Certification Testing

The next and final stage of the validation process requires certification testing with post-Year 2000 date values. Certification testing is required both for procedural workaround projects and for date field expansion projects. Year 2000 certification testing is a more complex process than determining functional equivalence. This section discusses a passive versus proactive approach to certification testing, the population of data stores with future date values, the upgrade unit certification process, combining certification testing with validation equivalence testing, and certification sign-off.

Final compliance certification requires that converted upgrade units be tested with post-Year 2000 date values. The system cannot be certified Year 2000 compliant unless data that reflects events that have occurred after the year 2000 has been processed through that system. There are two basic ways to meet this requirement; they are based on the type of system and time constraints. The first approach, which is a more passive strategy, depends on the natural data flow found in highly isolated upgrade units. The second approach, which is much more proactive, manipulates existing date values to assemble a future date certification environment. The applicability of and related techniques involved in these two approaches are summarized in the following sections.

14.6.1 Passive Year 2000 Certification Testing

The passive Year 2000 certification approach uses the same data input facilities that the system uses in a production environment. Future date values are created by the system's standard front-end input facility. The execution of subsequent job steps causes these date values to eventually be filtered throughout all system data stores. This approach is applicable in the following types of situations.

- Year 2000 certification is performed apart from the functional equivalence validation process.

- The functionally equivalent upgrade unit has been returned to production.

- The event horizon is still far enough away that analysts can take a somewhat measured approach in certifying the system as Year 2000 compliant.

- Date offset analysis tools are unavailable to validation analysts.

- The application area prefers to generate data in the same way that it would be generated in a production environment.

- The system is not highly dependent on data that is generated from other systems beyond the control of the testing team.

If this approach is selected, analysts should establish a test environment to implement it as follows.

1. *Use the virtual date utility to establish a test environment with all active programs accessing a current date that is set to some point after the year 2000.*

2. *Have analysts or users begin entering different types of transactions, using various future dates. This may require customizing data entered through other means such as externally derived data files.*

3. *Continue this process with system date settings that include leap year dates, year-end dates, and other industry-specific future dates.*

4. *Include date values that project forward several years in time.*

5. *Execute the entire system through various iterations so that these future dates become propagated throughout all test data stores.*

6. *Have end-user analysts review the results to ensure that the system is functioning normally.*

14.6.2 Proactive Year 2000 Certification Testing

The proactive approach to certification testing involves the manipulation of existing test data to propagate post-Year 2000 date values into those data stores. This is a more complex, yet more efficient, approach to certification testing and, when selected, should be applied to upgrade units that meet the following criteria.

- The upgrade unit depends on input data that is either received from or shared with other upgrade units that are beyond the scope and control of the validation team.

- The upgrade unit must be validated for logical equivalence and certified Year 2000 compliant concurrently.

- Tools are available to calculate and insert offset date values.

- Event horizons are relatively close and the upgrade unit must be certified Year 2000 compliant quickly.

- The validation team is highly skilled with this approach and can implement it in a relatively short time.

- The application team prefers this approach because of resource constraints or other factors.

We believe that the proactive approach is the one that organizations will most often select because most upgrade units depend on data from sources that are beyond their control and because of event horizon constraints. Year 2000 certification testing is, in general, more difficult to perform than functional equivalence testing because original upgrade units cannot accurately interpret post-Year 2000 date values. Certain vendors have created data manipulation tools to address this issue. Depending on the product, these tools allow for the manipulation of date values and provide a means to compare and reconcile past and future date values during the output data store comparison process.

If the proactive certification testing approach has been selected, it is best applied immediately after completion of functional equivalence testing so that the original version of the upgrade unit and all other validation facilities remain valid and intact. The original, upgrade unit, output results are the baseline against which analysts should ideally be certifying the upgrade unit as Year 2000 compliant. Organizations undertaking the proactive Year 2000 certification testing should consider the following steps.

1. *Obtain all input data stores that contain date field references.*

2. *Obtain output data stores generated by the original upgrade unit during functional equivalence testing.*

3. *If available, obtain any data manipulation tools that can assist in upgrading these date values.*

4. *If available, obtain an intelligent comparison tool to compare date and data values produced by the original upgrade unit and those produced by the converted upgrade unit.*

5. *Develop an offset value to ensure that the date/day coordination is handled properly (e.g., adding 28 years to 1996 dates ensures that 2024 dates fall on the same day).*

6. *Verify that all date offset formulae are synchronized with unique industry requirements (e.g., cannot have a bank posting date on a Sunday).*

7. *Verify that date dependencies are properly established (e.g., a birth date does not occur after an employee start date).*

8. *Use data manipulation tools to upgrade all input data store date values to settings beyond 2000, based on predetermined offset values (e.g., increase all dates by 28 years).*

9. *Use the virtual date utility to reset system dates for all on-line and batch job facilities to a date that falls beyond the latest date in the data stores used for the test.*

10. *Execute various batch and on-line programs as determined in the earlier validation plan.*

11. *Run comparison tests on converted upgrade units using the same guidelines applied during functional equivalence testing.*

12. *If needed, run additional tests to verify that year end, quarter end, month end, leap days, and other factors are tested.*

13. *Run an intelligent comparison tool to check that all date values in the original output data stores are consistently offset by the date values in output data stores produced by the converted upgrade unit.*

14. *Ensure that the comparison process for data stores with expanded date field formats, ignores the century field and limits analysis to existing 2-character year fields.*

15. *Correct any errors or deficiencies found in the converted system during the testing process.*

16. *Where required, integrate production changes into the certified system and retest as needed.*

This process should be refined with skilled validation analysts and tool experts, as needed. The dual-pass validation strategy typically requires that analysts perform some degree of synchronization with maintenance changes applied before certification testing was complete. Section 14.7, *Change Control and Code Synchronization*, discusses how to synchronize the changes.

In some cases, an original upgrade unit may become so out of synch with the converted version of that upgrade unit that analysts can no longer generate a baseline set of data against which to validate the compliant system. If this is the case, the process used to certify Year 2000 compliance reverts to more traditional testing techniques, which involve analysts and end users reviewing and certifying that system outputs appear accurate. This is a worst case scenario, but is a very real possibility that hopefully can be avoided by prompt certification testing or by integrating certification testing with functional equivalence testing as in the following discussion.

14.6.3 Certification and Equivalence Testing Integration Strategy

Integrating the certification testing process with functional equivalence testing is driven by time constraints. Analysts should review considerations for performing single-pass validation, as opposed to dual-pass validation, prior to undertaking a single-pass approach. If single-pass validation is to be pursued, analysts should consider the following additional requirements.

1. *Obtain an intelligent comparison tool that can accommodate new fields, bypass different field values, and calculate equivalence based on value offset calculations.*

2. *Use the test results from the original upgrade unit output as the basis for comparing the test results of the converted upgrade unit output.*

3. *Modify input data store date values as described in Section 14.6.2,* Proactive Year 2000 Certification Testing.

4. *Set up comparison tool parameters to accommodate the following conditions:*

   - Bypassing or ignoring time stamps

   - For expanded dates, ignoring century fields and values

   - Calculating equivalence based on the offset guidelines as indicated in Section 14.6.2.

5. *Resolve discrepancies that occur in the output comparison results:*

   - Check the offset values to determine that setup errors or other discrepancies are not the problem.

   - Verify that the conversion itself was not in error.

6. *Work around a discrepancy that cannot be resolved:*

   - Rerun the converted upgrade unit test with data that contains no date value offsets.

   - Apply standard equivalence comparison techniques to resulting output data.

   - Trace the error, correct it, and rerun the test, using data containing offset date values.

As stated earlier, the single-pass validation approach makes it more difficult to prove that an upgrade unit is both functionally equivalent and certified Year 2000 compliant. As with any of these validation processes, skilled analysts and solid technology can go a long way to ensuring that systems entering production are indeed Year 2000 compliant.

14.6.4 Year 2000 Certification Sign-off

Compliance sign-off is a formal process by which a quality assurance analyst reviews all material resulting from the validation process and, given that all material is in order, certifies that an upgrade unit is Year 2000 compliant. The review process should include the following steps.

1. *Validation team reviews validation strategy for that upgrade unit with quality assurance analyst.*

2. *Quality assurance analyst is provided with:*

   - Access to all source code, execution guidelines, data generation reports, and other material for both the original and converted upgrade units

   - Access to all input and output data stores or related outputs such as screen captures

   - Audit trail results produced by the automated comparison tool

   - Coverage analysis reports for all major programs as determined in validation plan

   - A summary of all changes that had to be reconciled between the production version and the final version of the upgrade unit

3. *The quality assurance analyst must determine that:*

   - All input and output results are either identical or have had differences reconciled appropriately

   - No errors were introduced by the Year 2000 conversion process

   - All interfaces have been synchronized with the Project Office coordinator and data administration representatives

4. *Upon determining that results for the validation tests are correct, the quality assurance analyst certifies the upgrade unit Year 2000 compliant.*

Year 2000 certification personnel are key to a successful project and could involve internal audit, project office personnel, internal experts, or external consultants.

14.7 Change Control and Code Synchronization

If unsynchronized functional changes are applied to the upgrade unit libraries established during the implementation project, the functional equivalence process will no longer work. However, end users may want maintenance changes applied to systems during the conversion period. Handling change control requirements arising during the conversion process is discussed in Chapter 13. If any maintenance changes were made between the functional equivalence test and the certification test, the same techniques apply.

All source code and related components should be submitted to the Year 2000 validation team (conversion team might be disbanded by this point). The validation team should run a code comparison utility to highlight differences between the original version and the maintained version of the upgrade unit and then work with application analysts to apply all highlighted differences to the certified version of system. Application personnel should take responsibility for these changes and any special testing required to determine that these modifications are accurate.

14.8 System and Integration Testing

System testing is a standard requirement within most IT organizations, with application areas typically under some obligation to follow certain procedures and guidelines imposed by operations and production management. This section is not meant to replace those guidelines, but rather aims to augment standard system testing procedures with Year 2000-related testing requirements. These requirements include validating bridge and API interfaces and determining that an upgrade unit functions properly within the context of an integrated systems environment. Figure 14.5 highlights these issues within a multiple upgrade unit architecture.

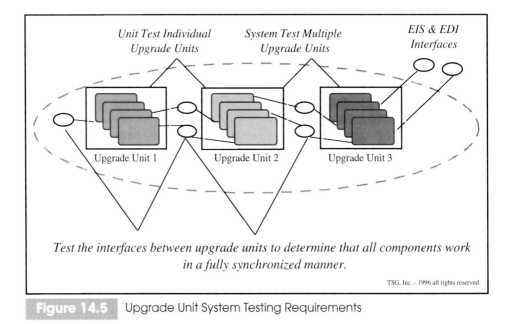

Unit Test Individual Upgrade Units

System Test Multiple Upgrade Units

EIS & EDI Interfaces

Upgrade Unit 1   Upgrade Unit 2   Upgrade Unit 3

Test the interfaces between upgrade units to determine that all components work in a fully synchronized manner.

Figure 14.5   Upgrade Unit System Testing Requirements

14.8.1 API and Bridge Interface Testing

Any upgrade unit that contains APIs to shared data stores or batch bridges to input/output files requires specialized integration testing. Upon completing functional equivalence or certification testing, and before releasing the converted upgrade unit to production, analysts should consider interface-related issues and test appropriately, as follows.

1. *Execute all bridge programs that produce input data stores to the converted upgrade unit; test the programs that receive those input data stores.*

2. *Execute all bridge programs that produce output data stores used by other upgrade units; have appropriate applications personnel test all programs accessing that data.*

3. *Verify that all programs that use API subroutines have had those subroutines exercised within the scope of the functional equivalence and certification tests.*

4. *Retest all programs that use API subroutines as follows:*

   • Test programs to access test databases or on-line files that contain a broader range of record types and data values.

   • Verify that any data stores required for system or integration testing have been included in this test cycle.

   • Work with applications analysts responsible for systems that access shared data stores to test programs that rely on this data.

5. *Provide all test results to the quality assurance analyst responsible for signing off on the results of this upgrade unit test.*

14.8.2 Year 2000 Integration Testing Requirements

If the interface testing process has been completed to the satisfaction of quality assurance analysts, relevant application analysts, data administration, and operations personnel, the validation and application support teams should complete all other system testing requirements. This means that, in addition to conforming to the procedures typically required during a system testing effort, validation analysts must ensure that when the upgrade unit enters production, no other system problems will occur. Analysts should consider integration issues and test appropriately, as follows.

1. *Verify that test versions of all software releases, including compilers, teleprocessing monitors, and databases, are synchronized with those used in production.*

2. *Verify that all data interfaces among systems contained in the upgrade unit work harmoniously when operating in a shared environment (required for multisystem upgrade units).*

3. *In addition to interface testing, verify that all data shared with systems external to the upgrade unit function harmoniously when operating in a shared environment.*

4. *Verify that any external data interfaces to an electronic data interchange, graphical user front-end system, or similar environment function according to specification.*

5. *Verify that all production and operations procedures to execute interfaces or other special case routines are in place prior to production turnover.*

6. *Finalize all other system testing requirements as required by internal system testing procedures.*

Once all system testing has been completed for a given upgrade unit, formal unit and system testing procedures (test scripts) should be institutionalized to support future testing and turnover. This should include procedures for deactivating bridge and API routines from the production environment as appropriate.

14.9 Post-Implementation Audit Facility

One component of the implementation process that may not appear on many deliverable lists is the need to verify that systems that have been made Year 2000 compliant remain Year 2000 compliant. This verification can be accomplished in a number of ways. One approach is to apply date impact analysis tools to highlight all date definitions for systems with expanded dates. Analysts can then review these definitions to verify that dates of an incompatible format have not entered the system. Where systems have been converted by the procedural workaround approach, impact analyzers can scan procedural date usage to determine if workaround logic remains intact. Another approach involves using source code comparison tools to verify that all date-related changes applied to an upgraded version of a system entering production are Year 2000 compliant.

All of these approaches depend on the sharp eye of a quality assurance analyst and the use of tools that may or may not be available to the application team. The one approach that is most likely to be employed by organizations—because it can be institutionalized in the testing process—

is adding one additional test cycle to the system testing process. Setting up this Year 2000 audit test cycle involves the following tasks.

1. *Obtain all input test data containing post-Year 2000 date values that was used as input to upgrade unit certification testing.*

2. *Retain and update any special instructions related to execution of this test data.*

3. *Establish a minimum periodic time frame (e.g., quarterly) when this test data can be run through the system during a regularly scheduled production turn-over cycle.*

4. *Remember to reset the system date, using the virtual date utility, for each post-implementation audit test cycle.*

5. *If a system is not updated that often, periodically (as determined by application management) retest it, using post-Year 2000 date values.*

6. *Using the techniques employed during certification testing or through normal end-user reviews, verify that the system is still functioning properly.*

7. *Document this procedure for each system upon completion of the validation effort.*

Establishing a post-implementation audit facility to ensure that systems remain Year 2000 compliant is the one way to verify that all of the work completed during implementation and validation is not wasted. This process should remain intact throughout the end of the century. Once the century window passes, this process can be phased out.

Chapter 15

Year 2000 Tool and Technology Selection

$\mathbf{N}$ext to people, software tools are the most important ingredient of a successful century-date compliance project. It is impossible to carry out the project without a strong array of tools for project management, analysis, component changes, version control, and testing. Tools provide a series of crucial benefits.

- **Tools reduce the time, effort and cost to complete the project.**

  There is simply too much work to perform a typical century-date compliance project within the allotted time without tools. People resources are too expensive and their availability will become too constrained to allow manually intensive approaches. Tools can perform in seconds or minutes tasks that would require hours or days of programmer effort.

- **Tools increase the coverage of identifying date issues.**

  Widespread usage of dates causes a huge number of date-related variables in program code. The number of interactions between those variables quickly becomes mind-boggling. Dates can be passed through layers of redefined and renamed variables, thereby obscuring century-compliance issues. Identifying and classifying all of the date fields affected by century-compliance issues is incredibly tedious and difficult to accomplish manually. Manual methods are highly likely to miss the less obvious interactions. In contrast, the proper tools are able to trace virtually every variable, guaranteeing a much greater level of date coverage.

- **Tools reduce the likelihood of errors.**

  Unlike humans, tools cannot be distracted, become fatigued, or make careless errors. An unpublished study by one of the authors found that programmers performing redevelopment work produced an average of 3 errors per 100 changes. Given the volume of changes in a typical century-compliance effort, this rate can translate into thousands of errors. Tools perform their operations in an absolutely consistent manner, avoiding a range of human errors. Even when a tool causes an error (through defects in its own programming), these errors occur consistently, making them easier to find and correct.

- **Tools reduce tedium.**

  At the planning and strategy end of the effort, century-compliance projects offer challenging assignments for their staff. In contrast, the implementation level involves endless repetition of the same operations program by program, file by file, and application by application. This effort quickly becomes tedious and mind-numbing to the programmers charged with implementation. The tedium increases error rates, discourages volunteers for century-compliance efforts, and causes project burnout and turnover. Tools automate many of the most tedious activities, allowing programmers to concentrate on the more interesting activities where they provide the greatest value.

- **Tools offer long-term value.**

  Aside from a few Year 2000-specific tools, century-compliance projects use tools that can be applied to standard application support activities. Any investments in tools and training will translate into greater future productivity. Normally, the greatest challenge for implementing a new tool is encouraging programmers to adopt that tool. Century-compliance projects force programmers to quickly adopt and become proficient with the tool. This experience ensures that the tools become successfully integrated into the company culture for use in future application support efforts.

Perhaps the greatest endorsement for the value and applicability of tools is their adoption by offshore outsourcing vendors. These vendors have resource costs that are significantly below the costs for most IT organizations. Despite their low costs, these vendors aggressively employ software tools for the reasons listed above and to increase their competitiveness with mainstream consulting organizations.

IT organizations may already own many of the tools that they need for their century-date compliance project. The tools and support environments used for standard maintenance apply to century-date compliance projects. However, these existing environments often lack the robustness needed for projects of the scale of century-date compliance efforts. Gaps exist in tool coverage and integration, usage skills, version control processes, and test data availability. While IT organizations can make effective use of existing tools, many of these tools are poorly deployed. Further, these tools may not be century-date compliant themselves.

Before selecting any tool strategy, IT organizations must inventory their existing tools to identify issues and gaps. Ensure that tools are available to cover all of the categories described in this chapter. Audition the existing tools against the tool selection criteria recommended in Section 15.2, *Tool Selection Criteria.* This project is large and costly enough to justify the replacement of an existing tool if one of higher productivity is identified. Sometimes an existing tool will duplicate the function of a tool within a vendor's multifunction tool set. Weigh the benefits of keeping an existing tool for the sake of familiarity and cost reduction against the benefits of integration offered by purchasing a full tool suite. Find new tools to fill all gaps in tool coverage.

Chapter 6 provides an overview of tool strategies. These include performing the conversions off site, using Year 2000-specific tools, and obtaining maintenance tools. It also describes combining tools into workbench environments to support major categories of project activities. This chapter describes how to select the right tools to support these strategies. It provides a technical background, covers basic tool selection criteria, and lists all of the major categories and types of tools that can be applied to a century-date compliance project.

The information in this chapter is useful even for those IT organizations seeking to fully outsource their migration effort. One of the best ways to judge a potential outsourcing vendor is to examine the tools they use to support their practice. The quality and completeness of their tool set is a clear indicator of their level of experience and sophistication in performing century-compliance projects. Vendors that do not rely on automation to reduce their costs and ensure the quality of their work products or those that use inferior tools should be avoided.

15.1 Technical Background

Some technical background is useful for distinguishing between the capabilities of the tools on the market. Vendor claims notwithstanding, tools can only be as powerful as their technical underpinnings. Understanding these differences enables tool evaluators to make informed decisions about the strengths and weaknesses of a particular technology. The following discussion concentrates on the capabilities required for the analysis and code conversion activities. These features are unique to century-date compliance projects. Other tool categories, such as testing and configuration management, are more generally applicable outside of century-date compliance projects and are adequately described in other books available on the market.

15.1.1 False Positives and False Negatives

Both analysis and code conversion require the same basic set of capabilities to perform their tasks. They must be able to "understand" program source code in order to identify data descriptions and operations that involve dates. Their level of sophistication at this activity determines the accuracy of their results. This accuracy can be described in terms of false positives and false negatives. A false positive occurs when a tool identifies a date field as potentially at risk when it is not at risk. A false negative is the converse: it occurs when the tool fails to identify an at-risk date field. The perfect tool would find no false positives or false negatives. Unfortunately, 100 percent accuracy is not technically feasible within the limits of current technology. False negatives are the most problematic situation. If an at-risk field is not identified and corrected, the program will not be compliant and will fail or produce incorrect results. Testing is the activity of last resort for finding false negatives before reaching production.

False positives produce different issues in analysis and conversion activities. During analysis, it is better to find too many false positives than to allow false negatives. As a result, analysis tools tend to err on the side of overreporting possible impacts. Unsophisticated tools grossly overreport false positives, leading to excessive effort on the part of programmers to eliminate false positives before proceeding with conversion activities. During conversion, false positives are a bigger problem. Automatically converting fields falsely identified as a problem will introduce other potential errors into the program. Unlike analysis, the preference during conversion is to err on the side of converting only the fields that are unquestionably at risk. All other questionable fields must be identified and segregated for human analysis. The less sophisticated the technology, the greater the number of fields that fall into the questionable category. This forces programmers to perform tedious and error-prone correction activities on the fields falsely identified as negatives.

In order to find the fields within a program that contain year information and are potentially at risk, a tool has to perform an analysis of all program variables. These variables are analyzed by name, definition, and use. If the name of a field refers to "date," "year," "YY," or other such clue, it becomes a potential suspect. Unfortunately, programmers use a great variety of reasonable and unreasonable names for their variables. Variables can also be passed through generic identifiers, such as "FILLER" in COBOL, that prevent identification solely through name. Definitions associate a given variable name with its characteristics. If a year variable is defined as two digits, it has a range from 0 through 99 and is at risk. As with names, definitions vary widely. Many other nondate variables can use the same definition formats as dates. Thus, definition alone is not sufficient to identify a date, although its size is an important characteristic for determining risk. Use is the final characteristic for determining risk. If a date variable is used simply to print a year on a report, the program is not at risk for failure or producing incorrect data (although in some cases, the result may still be undesirable). Year variables used for calculations, comparisons, sorts, and as index keys are all at risk for producing incorrect or undesirable results.

Using the three variable analysis criteria—name, definition, and use—allows variables to be identified as at-risk candidates for century-date migration. The perfect candidate is clearly identified as a year through its name (named), has a definition that is too short to support century dates (short), and is used in an at-risk operation (at risk). While these are the perfect candidates, they are not the only candidates. A date variable may not be identifiably named, but it can still be short and at risk. Conversely, a variable named YEAR-TO-DATE-TOTALS can be named, short, and used in an at-risk operation but has nothing to do with dates. The short, at-risk category can contain many false positives, because many variables can have short definitions and be used in at-risk operations. Correctly finding all true candidates requires knowledge about all ways that a date can enter a program and a thorough analysis of everything that can happen to those dates within the program.

15.1.2 Analysis Techniques

Performing an extremely thorough analysis to identify at-risk variables requires a series of increasingly sophisticated techniques, starting with scanning and processing through parsing, control flow analysis, and data de-aliasing, to data flow analysis. The number of tools using each technique drops off quickly as the level of sophistication increases. For example, a majority of the analysis and conversion tools on the market do not progress beyond string searching in their analysis. Going beyond that level requires training in compiler development and a much greater investment of time and development dollars. This increased investment is usually reflected in the cost of the tool.

The benefit of progressing up the levels of technique sophistication is increased accuracy, that is, fewer false positives and false negatives. This decreases the human effort required for analysis and conversion and reduces the likelihood of human error. For this reason, it is advantageous to obtain the most sophisticated tool available for any given language. Given the level of knowledge and investment required, the most sophisticated tools will be found only for the most common languages such as COBOL. Purchasers of tools for uncommon languages will have to make do with a lower level of sophistication. Even less sophisticated tools are faster and more accurate than performing the same tasks by hand.

It is difficult to determine the true sophistication of a tool from marketing literature and sales claims. Marketing hype often misuses terminology, but vendor claims are easily verified or disproved with an understanding of each level of analysis. If a tool with a lower level of sophistication is selected, be aware of its limitations. Knowing these limitations permits an organization to create techniques to overcome them during conversion.

15.1.3 Tool Sophistication Levels

This section describes the advantages and disadvantages of the analysis techniques at increasing levels of sophistication.

15.1.3.1 Scanning

Scanners are tools that perform string searches of source code looking for specific text patterns. Scanners start with "seeds," which are lists of patterns that may refer to candidate fields. For example, a scanner may search for text fields containing "YEAR," "YY," "YR," "DATE," and it may search for variable definition patterns such as "99" or "9(6)." Most scanners allow their users to add to their seed tables to include or exclude particular patterns. This enables users to customize the scanner to meet the situation within their environment. Scanners are very easy to write, hence they are commonly used for "quick hit" analysis tools. Vendors that rapidly add new languages to their tool portfolio are most likely using scanning technology. Since scanners perform a very simplistic analysis, they are very forgiving of errors in language syntax. Thus, scanners can operate on a wider range of language versions or even on non-compileable pieces of code.

The simplicity of scanners is also their downfall. Scanners have many limitations. These include:

- **Limited to text patterns.**
  Scanners can find variables only by name or by using a common date definition pattern.

- **High numbers of false negatives.**
  Dates passed through poorly named variables will not be found. Thus, date fields with names such as TEMP-VAL or FILLER will go undiscovered.

- **High numbers of false positives.**
  Scanners cannot differentiate between the "YEAR" in an active source code statement and the same text in a comment. Similarly, since they have no understanding of variable usage, they will find false pattern matches such as variables containing the term "GOOD-YEAR."

- **Names that are not unique.**
  Scanners cannot determine if two variables using the same name are truly the same. Conversely, they are also unable to identify the same variable redefined or renamed to another name.

- **Inability to understand usage.**
  Scanners cannot determine if a variable is at risk because of its use in a given operation. They simply list the source code lines where the code is found and leave the determination to their user.

15.1.3.2 Parsing

The next layer of sophistication is parsing. Parsing uses compiler techniques to understand the syntax of the language. Figure 15.1 shows the parse tree created for the following section of COBOL code:

```
MOVE DATE1 TO YY.
IF YY > 95
        MOVE DATE TO XX
ELSE
        COMPUTE AGE = XX - DATE-OF-BIRTH.
```

Breaking each statement into its component parts following the syntax of the language allows the parser to determine the use of each element. Thus, the parser can determine which language elements are variables and which variables are used in at-risk situations. In this example, the parser determines that "YY," "XX," "DATE1," "AGE," and "DATE-OF-BIRTH" are variables. Additionally, the IF and COMPUTE statements put "YY," "XX," "AGE," and "DATE-OF-BIRTH" at risk. Interpreting language usage prevents the parser from making scanner-type mistakes, such as finding "YEAR" within a comment or within a procedure name.

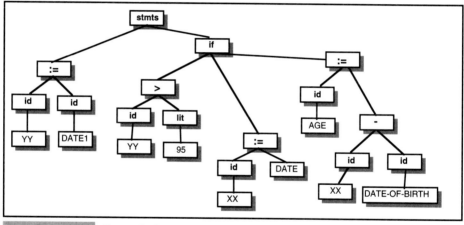

Figure 15.1 Example Parse Tree

Parsers represent a significant improvement over scanners. Their additional intelligence greatly reduces the number of false positives. However, parsing techniques still have limitations. These include:

- **Inability to determine if a statement is actually used.**
  A parser cannot determine if the control flow of the program reaches a given statement; it does not recognize branching around the code with a GO TO statement or if the statement is nonoperable (dead) code.

- **High levels of false negatives.**
  Parsing does not follow data flow. Thus, a parser alone will miss the connection between dates that are passed through multiple variables or reset through a "Redefines."

- **Correct language syntax required.**
  Because parsers follow the specific syntax of a given language, they are sensitive to the specific version of the language used and to the correctness of a program's source code. This causes parsers to reject code that would be accepted by a scanner.

The advantages of a parser over a scanner outweigh its disadvantages. However, parsers are considerably more difficult and time consuming to write. As a result, despite vendor claims, fewer tools truly use parsing techniques. To test whether a tool is using scanning or parsing techniques, create a small test program containing a name such as "YEAR-1" used in a variable, comment, and paragraph name. If the tool finds all three occurrences, it uses a scanner. If it creates an error message because "YEAR-1" is used as both a variable and paragraph name, it uses a parser.

15.1.3.3 Control Flow Analysis

The next step of sophistication is combining control flow analysis with a parser. Control flow analysis follows the implications of each control statement within the source code. In COBOL, these control statements include GO TOs, PERFORMs and ALTERs. By mapping the flow of the entire program, control flow analysis enables the connection to be made between the definition of a variable and its actual use. For instance, variables appearing in unreachable, or "dead," code are safely ignored. This increases the accuracy of the analysis and further reduces the number of false positives. The main limitation of control flow analysis is that it does not follow the flow of the data between variables. Thus, it will still miss data that is passed between multiple variables.

Control flow analysis is used by a number of more sophisticated tools, such as system-level analyzers, program analyzers, and restructuring tools. To be effective, control flow analysis must be combined with a parser to ensure that the resulting control flow map is accurate. To test whether a given tool is analyzing control flow, create a test program that contains intentional "dead code" by commenting a PERFORM of a section of code. If the tool still finds variables within the dead code, it is not analyzing control flow.

15.1.3.4 Data De-aliasing

Data de-aliasing is a set of techniques that reduces false negatives by reconciling data naming and usage issues. Computer languages provide a variety of methods for addressing a particular piece of storage. This technique enables data to be set or accessed through a number of different aliases, that is, different variable names that refer to the same piece of storage. Tools that do not use data de-aliasing miss situations such as the one shown in Figure 15.2. In this example, data de-aliasing is required to identify that START-WS is the same as DATE-WS and contains YEAR-WS. Without this knowledge, the IF statement is not identified as containing an at-risk variable.

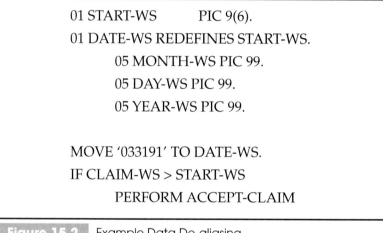

```
01 START-WS        PIC 9(6).
01 DATE-WS REDEFINES START-WS.
      05 MONTH-WS PIC 99.
      05 DAY-WS PIC 99.
      05 YEAR-WS PIC 99.


MOVE '033191' TO DATE-WS.
IF CLAIM-WS > START-WS
      PERFORM ACCEPT-CLAIM
```

Figure 15.2 Example Data De-aliasing

Data de-aliasing is used to resolve a number of different situations involving ambiguity (two variables with the same name) and aliasing (multiple names for the same variable). Specific examples include:

- **File remapping.**
  Different overlays are used to extract the same information from a record within a file.

- **Group moves.**
  Date data within a larger data structure is moved into another variable.

- **Anonymous reference.**
  Date data can be passed anonymously, such as within FILLER in COBOL.

- **Renames.**
  Multiple names are applied to the same piece of data.

- **Redefines.**
  The same section of storage is renamed and possibly reformatted for another use.

The use of data de-aliasing significantly reduces the number of false negatives by ensuring that all methods of referencing a given variable are identified and incorporated into the analysis for at-risk operations. Data de-aliasing does not resolve situations where date data is passed through multiple variables.

Data de-aliasing is an integral part of compilers and is found within the most sophisticated program and system-level analysis tools. To test whether a given tool is using data de-aliasing techniques, create a test program that uses the construct shown in Figure 15.2. If the tool recognizes that START-WS is a date variable, it employs de-aliasing.

15.1.3.5 Data Flow Analysis

Data flow analysis follows the flow of data across multiple variables. Figure 15.3 illustrates two situations that can be resolved only through data flow.

```
01  START-WS      PIC 9(6).
01  DATE-WS REDEFINES START-WS.
      05  MONTH-WS  PIC 99.
      05  DAY-WS  PIC 99.
      05  YEAR-WS  PIC 99.
01  XJS-15        PIC 9(6).
01  RX7-WS        PIC 9(6).

MOVE '033191' TO DATE-WS.
MOVE START-WS TO XJS-15.
MOVE XJS-15 TO RX7-WS.
IF RX7-WS > DATE-WS
      COMPUTE XJS-15 = XJS-15 + 3
ELSE
      COMPUTE RX7 = RX7 + 1.
```

Figure 15.3 Example Data Flow Analysis

Data de-aliasing resolves that DATE-WS and START-WS refer to the same data. Data flow analysis is used to show that XJS-15 and RX7-WS contain the same data. Without this analysis, these two variables would be missed, becoming false negatives. Combining control flow analysis with data flow analysis allows the resolution of the second situation. Given the data flow, RX7-WS will always be equal to DATE-WS. Thus, the IF statement can never be true and the COMPUTE of XJS-15 will never occur.

It is easy to see how a complete data flow analysis would virtually ensure that false positives and false negatives are eliminated. As long as all dates entering a program can be identified, a combination of the techniques described above would ensure that all at-risk situations are identified. Unfortunately, full data flow analysis is an extremely difficult and computationally expensive problem to solve. The number of possible data flows rises exponentially as a program increases in size and complexity. Resolving even an average program by using a brute force method of data flow analysis exceeds the capacity of the largest computers currently available. As a result, only limited data flow capabilities appear in tools currently on the market. Interactive program and system level analyzers allow their users to follow data flow out to a preset number of layers on a variable by variable basis. Limiting the analysis to a single variable reduces the size of the analysis to manageable levels. It is the responsibility of the programmer using these tools to trace all relevant variables.

Another approach involves data flow pruning to eliminate extraneous data flows during the analysis. This approach increases the level of automation by tracing all identified date variables in a single session. At the time of this writing, only one tool uses this highly advanced technique.

15.1.4 Analysis Process

Given the current state of technology, analysis and conversion remain a two-step process. Proper conversion tools must have full analysis capabilities to ensure the correctness of their conversion, but they still need to be fed the results of the analysis before they attempt an automatic conversion. The analysis must be seeded with names and patterns for potential dates. Even the most sophisticated tools must start with this information. After the tool identifies all affected variables and operations, a programmer must review the list to eliminate false positives and research the possibility of false negatives. This is the effort that is reduced through greater tool sophistication. Once a verified list of affected variables and operations has been created, the conversion tool uses this list to perform the selected conversions.

15.2 Tool Selection Criteria

Selecting tools for a century-date compliance project can be a daunting activity. The level of noise and conflicting claims in the market is incredible. The already large number of vendors and products is growing daily. Virtually every major software company is seeking methods to enter the market, and many entrepreneurs are cloistered in garages building new tools. At the time of this writing, the Year 2000 tool market is attracting tremendous interest in the investment community, leading to even more new companies and products. This type of overheated market draws profiteers along with reputable vendors. Not all products are equal and not all claims are true. Many vendors overpromise and underdeliver.

The challenge for an IT organization is to separate the "wheat from the chaff" to obtain the right set of tools. This section describes the criteria that an IT organization can use to differentiate between hype and reality. It describes truisms about tool purchases to help IT organizations avoid common mistakes. A discussion of key technology provides the background needed to differentiate vendor capabilities. This discussion is followed by tool selection criteria. The section concludes with a discussion about how to best work with software vendors.

15.2.1 Tool Truisms

The following set of truisms apply to all categories of software tools used for century-date compliance efforts. Although some of these principles appear obvious, it is amazing how few tool evaluation committees actually apply them. Following these principles will help the IT organization avoid costly and time-consuming mistakes.

- **Tools will get better.**

  In the Year 2000 market, software tools are like personal computers—the next version is always better than the last. The competition among vendors and the potential for large profits for new and improved tools is steadily increasing the quality and capabilities of the tools on the market. Vendors are extending and tuning existing tools to better fit century-date compliance projects, and new tools are arriving to plug gaps in capabilities.

- **Don't wait for future tools.**

  As with buying a PC, one can always defer a purchase until a better version arrives. Since improvement is constant, there will always be a better version in the future. Given the tight project time frames, deferring tool purchases for century-date migrations is foolhardy at best. Purchase the tools that are currently on the market to begin receiving their value immediately. While new tools will be better, they will not improve to the level that justifies the time lost by waiting.

- **Upgrade as needed.**

  Do not worry about replacing tools as better tools appear. Start with available tools and upgrade every time a significant advance appears. The project is so large that tool expenditures pay back very quickly. If the difference in productivity afforded by a new tool exceeds its purchase price and implementation cost, it is immediately beneficial to perform the upgrade.

- **If a tool seems too good to be true, it is.**

  Vendor claims for many tools severely stretch the bounds of credibility. There are no "silver bullets" in this market. No tool can completely automate the migration process. Use the technical background and selection criteria in this chapter to weed out hype from reality. For example, tools based on scanning technology cannot guarantee completeness. Beware of vendor claims that cannot be verified. It is easy for a vendor to claim the use of advanced techniques; however, the real proof can be found in the product's results.

- **You get what you pay for.**

  Budget-constrained IT organizations can be easily tempted by tool vendors offering low-cost solutions. The market adjustments forced by a capitalist economy guarantee that true price inequities are quickly corrected. For example, if one vendor's $10,000 product is really the same as another vendor's $100,000 product, the second vendor would not be able to maintain their price. Further, unless the first vendor's motivations are strictly altruistic, they are unlikely to sell their product for less than its worth. The difference in product cost is often due to product quality and reliability, vendor experience, and level of available support. Given the overall size of a Year 2000 effort, the difference in cost between products is less significant than their level of productivity. Purchase products based on capabilities rather than price.

- **Avoid "analysis paralysis."**

  Act quickly to eliminate the less credible vendors from the tool selection process. Once this is done, avoid overanalyzing the tool evaluation and purchase. Many tool evaluation groups spend more time and money selecting the perfect tool than the cost of buying all of the top candidates. Most tools are competently built and will provide much-needed productivity gains. Slight differences between competing tools are less important than a quick and successful tool implementation. "Time box" the selection process to make a quick decision.

- **Don't shortcut the implementation.**

   A tool is productive only if it is used. The best tool sitting on a shelf provides less value than a mediocre tool that is actually used. Be sure that tool purchases include enough support and training to allow the tool to be successful.

15.2.2 Selection Criteria

Selecting the proper set of tools will greatly facilitate the speed and accuracy of a century-date migration project. While there are many good tools on the market, not all tools are equal. The size of the Year 2000 tool market has attracted a great variety of tool vendors. These vendors vary dramatically in terms of skill and experience, and the tools they offer vary in sophistication. The market has also attracted many companies with products that have, at best, a tenuous connection to the century-date issue. We receive product literature almost daily from new vendors entering the market. This explosive growth of vendors offers many benefits, but it also presents IT organizations with significant challenges.

Competition among the vendors is rapidly improving the quality and functional coverage of tool solutions while keeping prices somewhat in check. This competition, however, is also forcing vendors to resort to ever-increasing levels of hype to differentiate their offerings from those of other vendors. Another hazard is found in vendors using market desperation to float weak product offerings. These vendors flourish by preying upon IT organizations eager to believe their questionable claims for low cost and high levels of automation. IT organizations must somehow sift through this hype to select the vendors and tools that best match their migration requirements.

The selection criteria described below offer a general checklist to apply against the tool offerings on the market. These criteria apply to all tool categories. Obviously, more specific criteria are required to contrast the capabilities of tools within the same category. However, starting with the list below will help to eliminate questionable choices before progressing to the next level of analysis. For the next level of tool selection analysis, use the descriptions in Section 15.3, *Tool Categories* to develop more detailed criteria.

- **Reputation and experience of vendors.**

  As just described, the Year 2000 market is attracting many vendors who seek to profiteer from the situation. One method to avoid these profiteering vendors is to examine the vendor's reputation and experience. Do not simply trust the references that the vendor provides. Attend tradeshows and ask the other attendees about their experiences. Ask the major consulting firms about the tools that they use. Because these firms rely heavily on tools for the success of their projects, and hence their profitability, they carefully select their tool sets. If the company is publicly traded, request copies of their financial statements through their annual report and 10K filing. Request a financial analysis report from Dun and Bradstreet. Strong financial performance is indicative of excellent management and is likely to be reflected in the quality of the tools. Further, successful companies will be around to support their products after the turn of the century.

- **Tool sophistication.**

  Try to obtain the most technically sophisticated tools available for each language and product category. As described in Section 15.1, *Technical Background,* the greater the level of sophistication, the greater the accuracy of the results and the less effort required for the migration. Compromises in tool sophistication will be required for less common languages and environments. Verify vendor claims about the technologies used by their tools through test programs. Remember that it is much easier to claim a capability than it is to actually build that capability.

- **Integration of tool sets.**

  At the time of this writing, several vendors are approaching "one stop shopping" in the breadth of their Year 2000 offerings. While there can be a trade-off between buying best-in-class tools for each category or buying an integrated tool set from a single vendor, often the level of integration can be the deciding factor. Strong integration provides a common interface between tools, which decreases learning effort. The results of each tool should support, or even feed, other tools in the set. This eliminates the need to repeat the same operation, using two different tools. This capability is especially important as a project progresses through increasingly detailed levels of analysis to feed the final conversion.

- **Tool accuracy.**

  The accuracy of each tool is extremely important. This accuracy is more important than the level of coverage provided by the tool. For example, it is far better to have a conversion tool that handles 50 percent of the conversion activity with 100 percent accuracy than it is to have a tool that handles 100 percent of the activity with 85 percent percent accuracy. Failures in tool accuracy are extremely difficult to find and correct. Use of a low-accuracy tool requires a far greater level of testing to ensure correct results.

- **Tool strategy.**

  Pick the tools that best fit the organization's long-term tool strategies. If the strategy is to gain long-term value, avoid Year 2000-specific tools in favor of those tools that can be used for future maintenance. If future maintenance support is not a requirement, Year 2000-specific tools can be applied. If the strategy is to perform the conversion through an outsourcer or off-site facility, examine their tools with the same rigor that would be used for internally purchased tools. Remember that the accuracy of their efforts will be based on the quality of their tool selection. Tool strategies are discussed in Chapter 6.

- **Flexibility.**

  Most IT organizations will use several different conversion strategies to handle their applications across the enterprise. Be sure that the tools obtained can support each of these strategies. Even if the default strategy for an organization is the procedural approach, there will be situations that require data expansion. Purchasing a set of tools that locks the organization into a single strategy will require other strategies to be implemented manually or necessitate the purchase of a separate set of tools.

- **Tool support.**

  Tools don't run themselves. Programmers must be trained and supported in the use of these tools. This is especially important for the activities, such as system-level analysis, that programmers have never really performed in the past. While it is simple to read and understand tool features from a manual, applying those features to real-life situations is far more difficult. The best tool vendors offer a mix of methodology, training, and consulting support to ensure that their tools are assimilated quickly, applied effectively, and remain useful. Lack of support will overcome any technical advantages offered by a given tool. Over the life of the project, the level of support offered by a tool vendor is more important than small differences in tool features when selecting a tool. Be sure to examine all forms of support offered by the vendor. Call the support line to evaluate the quality of technical support. Do not trust vendors who claim that their product is so simple that it does not need support.

15.2.3 Working with Tool Vendors

Tool selection in many IT organizations is a complex activity performed by a separate technical support organization. This organization decides which categories of tools to evaluate, finds potential vendors, performs trials, selects tools, and recommends their implementation. Given the level of effort needed to support this activity, only a limited number of tools are evaluated and selected each year. This process, although valid in normal situations, is too cumbersome and time consuming for century-compliance projects. These projects require flexibility and fast decisions to enable tools to be deployed and upgraded as needed to keep the project on track. Ultimately, the Year 2000 Project Office must have the responsibility for tool selection.

The best method to fast-track tool selection is to do some tool research before contacting vendors. This saves considerable time and is fairer to the vendors. Understanding the organization's tool strategy and environment and applying the criteria listed in this chapter will greatly reduce the number of tools that need detailed evaluation. Contact only those vendors whose tools fit the criteria. When those vendors respond, attempt to eliminate as many tools as possible before agreeing to a trial. If possible, select only one tool for the trial. If this tool fails, then move to the next tool. If the tool evaluators performed their research correctly, few, if any, evaluations will have to proceed to a second tool. Although vendors are disappointed to lose a sale, they appreciate not having to spend money supporting an evaluation that they have little chance of winning.

Unfortunately, many IT organizations are excessively swayed by the personality and opinions of the vendor's sales people, causing them to buy lesser technology or to avoid buying the right technology. Although it is important to evaluate all aspects of a vendor's organization, do not attach excessive importance to the sales person. Great tools can have poor sales people and poor tools can have great sales people. Although a strong relationship with the sales person facilitates the sales process and can assist in obtaining future resources, it is far more important to judge the organization by the quality of its tools and support. Judge the tool and support on their own merits, and view a good sales person as an added bonus. In contrast, if the consulting staff or technical support organization is poor, do not select the vendor. Poor technical support is symptomatic of greater problems within the vendor organization.

When conducting the actual tool trial, use as much vendor assistance as possible to guarantee its success. Rather than viewing the evaluation as a chance to find fault with the tools, use the reverse approach: look for methods to make the tool successful. No tool achieves perfection. The goal of the evaluation is to quickly determine if the tool meets the project's requirements and, if it does, to immediately roll into purchase and implementation.

15.3 Tool Categories

This section describes the wide variety of tools that can be used within a Year 2000 project. These tools are divided into six major functional categories. This classification is introduced in Chapter 6, and it categorizes individual types of tools by their primary use within a century-date compliance project. The use of an individual tool is by no means limited to this arbitrary classification; some tools will be used throughout all phases of the project. The purpose of this classification is to provide a quick method for members of the Year 2000 Project Office to find the right type of tool for a specific project task. These six categories are:

- Management tools

- Repository technology

- Analysis tools

- Migration tools

- Redevelopment tools

- Testing/verification tools

The tool types within these categories are likely to increase as tool vendors develop new offerings for the Year 2000 market. Specific vendor tool offerings may not fit neatly into any single category. Through packaging, some vendors offer workbench solutions that cut across multiple categories. To evaluate these offerings, consider their features against the tool capabilities described in each category.

This section intentionally avoids mentioning tool and vendor names. Those seeking a list of vendors and tools can find this information in Appendix A. The Year 2000 tool market is so highly volatile that any information included in this chapter would quickly become obsolete. Numerous products from multiple vendors are available for most of the tool categories described below. Space limitations preclude a detailed discussion of the merits of each vendor's offerings. Directly contacting the vendors that support a desired solution capability is the best method for receiving up-to-date information on the tools and their functionality. Additional information about vendors and tools can be obtained from research organizations such as the Gartner Group and through tool reference guides offered by Datapro and other vendors.

Tools are available in every category for the most common languages and platforms. This support quickly drops off as the language or platform become less common. Vendors are continually adding to their lists of supported languages; however, those IT organizations with concentrations of rare languages may have to develop their own tools.

Do not assume that an IT organization is required to have a tool from each tool category or tool type to complete its migration effort. Although a complete set of tools would facilitate a full-scale effort, major categories such as repositories and redevelopment tools are highly recommended, but not essential, for the project. Compare the capabilities listed below against the current set of tools within the IT organizations. Many programmers use only a fraction of the capabilities of a given software tool. Those unused and forgotten capabilities may be perfect for the migration effort. Although in most cases it is cheaper and more expedient to buy tools from a software vendor, certain special-purpose tools can be developed internally. Such development is often necessary to handle uncommon environments or shop-specific modifications to a common technology.

15.3.1 Management Tools

Management tools are essential for century-date compliance projects regardless of the overall implementation strategy selected for the project. Even if the bulk of the project effort is outsourced, project management tools are still needed to coordinate outsourcing efforts with internal efforts. These projects are far too large and complex to manage with ad hoc methods. In fact, the sheer number of tasks and sub-projects within the compliance effort will stretch the capabilities of many project management tools. Project management support is needed at two levels: first, for managing individual sub-projects and second, for monitoring the execution of those sub-projects at the enterprise level.

The tools in this category have to perform several critical functions. They must support the following: estimation of new tasks for sizing and budgeting purposes; the scheduling, assignment, and tracking of all project tasks; the monitoring of the migration status of project components; and the communication of project information across the organization.

- **Project management tools.**

    This category includes the traditional tools used by project managers to schedule and track project tasks, time, and resources. These tools generate time lines, show project dependencies, and calculate completion dates and resource conflicts. Each sub-project uses a project management tool to create its own project plan and to track its progress against the plan. The individual project plan information must be "rolled up" to the enterprise-level master plan that is monitored by the Year 2000 Project Office.

    To be useful within a century-date migration project, a project management tool must be able to handle both levels of project management. While many of the simpler tools support individual plans, a more robust tool is needed to handle high-volume information sharing between the master plan and the sub-project plans. The project management tool must also support "what if" analysis to assess the impact of a given strategy on the overall project schedule. This enables project managers to weigh the project ramifications of each migration or triage strategy before making a final selection.

- **Estimation tools.**

    A variety of project estimation tools are available on the market. Some tools create high-level estimates based upon parameters fed by the project manager; others perform a full analysis of the source code that composes an application to issue their estimates. Performing a full analysis of the source code produces the most accurate estimate but requires the greatest level of effort. Parameter-driven estimators can produce ballpark estimates with very little effort; however, the value of the estimate hinges on the accuracy of the parameter information.

- **Project tracking facility.**

    This is a repository of project management information. It contains a high-level inventory of all applications, packages, system software, and other project components. This inventory is supplemented with vendor contact information, interfaces between internal and external applications, project sizing estimates, migration statuses, and other information useful to the Year 2000 Project Office. At the start of the project, this information aids in project sizing and selection of analysis and implementation strategies. As the project proceeds, it serves as the master checklist of application-level components that require migration. Although some consulting firms have their own version of this repository, most IT organizations will have to create their own, using a relational database. The basic repository can be implemented on a workstation database with relatively little effort. If the organization is currently using a full repository this database can be created within that repository, or the workstation version can be tied to the master repository for information exchange.

- **Methodologies and blueprints.**

  Methodologies are commonly used to support new development projects, and they are equally useful for century-date migration projects. A Year 2000 project methodology offers a step-by-step guide for implementing the phases and tasks of the compliance effort. A methodology combines manual and automated steps, describing the appropriate stages for using tools. The Help facilities provided with software tools tend to be feature based and tool specific, whereas the methodologies are task based and tools-independent. Methodologies also describe task deliverables, resource requirements, and effort estimation information. Consulting companies are heavy methodology users; many have their own methodologies, and others use commercially available tools. Use of a methodology eliminates the need for trial-and-error learning and facilitates consistency and the use of the most effective practices. Although an IT organization can create its own Year 2000 methodology, it is faster and more cost effective to obtain a commercial version.

- **Process managers.**

  Process managers provide a method for automating access to project methodologies, software tools, and repository information. Process managers provide an infrastructure for incorporating these components into a project workbench. By automating the project methodology, process managers guide their users through their migration tasks while simultaneously gathering project management information, tracking deliverables, and triggering the appropriate tools at the proper time. Because of their all-encompassing nature, the initial setup of a process manager can be effort intensive and can draw resistance from programmers used to ad hoc methods of programming. However, once implemented, these tools provide tremendous benefits. They eliminate many tedious project management tasks, enforce standards and methodology use, and automate the execution of standard programming tasks.

- **Communications technology.**

    Effective communications technology is essential for coordinating activities across a century-date compliance project. This capability is particularly important where organizations are highly distributed and direct access to support personnel is limited. The high level of interdependency among projects requires fast communication of project status information to avoid implementation gridlock. Communication tools typically include some type of an electronic mail facility and data gathering capability that facilitates information capture via remote access. Workgroup communication software that allows the posting and sharing of project information across internal networks or even intranets or the Internet further enhances project communication. Spreadsheets also offer a convenient format for recording survey data captured during the assessment. While desirable, spreadsheets are not essential to this task if the information to be gathered is alternatively loaded into an electronic mail facility or similar tool set. One final option is to provide direct access to the facility that is actually going to store the information. The repository discussion that follows contains more information on this concept.

- **Presentation technology.**

    A plan, summary reports, presentations, and other deliverables normally result from most sizable projects, and Year 2000 projects are no exception. Presentation tools should be designated in advance for the assessment team to use. This includes word processing, presentation, spreadsheet, and database tools that support both narrative and graphic deliverable results.

15.3.2 Repository Technology

Use of an enterprise-level repository is highly recommended for any Year 2000 project undertaken by any large, complex, or highly distributed IT organization. This repository provides the ability to represent relationships among systems and system components, via a logically defined meta-model, to support Year 2000 planning projects. A recommended meta-model that supports this analysis process is included in Appendix C. Implementing this meta-data in a repository or database during an enterprise assessment provides an easily referenced summary view of the enterprise. It also forms the basis for subsequent tracking and coordination tasks required during the implementation phase. Unlike the project tracking facility previously described, an enterprise-level repository contains significantly more detail about the physical components that compose each application.

Basic requirements for a Year 2000 repository include the ability to reflect system components as objects within the repository model and the ability to populate, in some way, that model from a legacy environment. A secondary, and optional, requirement involves accepting an automated load format based on tools that parse and analyze legacy environments. In the absence of a true repository, a relational database can be designed and loaded with this information. However, a repository product can support more data, more relationships, and more users than can a simple database storage facility.

If a Year 2000 repository is employed, the information from the project tracking facility should be integrated into the repository during the implementation phase of the project. Analysts may also want to extend the use of the repository to include automated population by the cross-reference tools used on the project.

15.3.3 Analysis Tools

Analysis tools are a foundation technology for century-date compliance projects. Correctly and completely locating all affected source code is virtually impossible without high-quality analysis tools. At the highest level of the project, analysis tools are used to build a complete inventory of the entire portfolio of applications and their components. Once the inventory is known, impact analysis tools are used to assess the level of date use and sharing across multiple programs and multiple applications. This information determines the extent of the conversion effort and identifies which programs and files require conversion. Program-level analysis tools examine individual programs to identify the specific data items and lines of source code that need to be modified. Information from these tools is valuable for selecting optimal conversion strategies, planning test scenarios, and auditing project activities.

Analysis tools vary widely in terms of the technology they use to perform their searches. As described in Section 15.1, *Technical Background,* the greater the level of sophistication, the more complete and accurate the results of the analysis. Although ultimately the Year 2000 Project Office should invest in the most sophisticated analyzers available for their environment, the role of an analyzer varies by project phase. Enterprise planning requires that a tool have high-speed and high-volume analysis capability and run on the platform on which the bulk of the systems reside. Implementation activities require significantly more sophisticated cross-reference and impact analysis capabilities to ensure the completeness of their analysis. Because implementation activities are performed on an upgrade unit level, they have dramatically reduced volume constraints, which enables the use of tools that capture and analyze greater levels of detail. For these reasons, the inventory and cross-reference technology used for implementation may not be the same as that used during the enterprise assessment. For example, most workstation tools that fall into this category have sophisticated cross-reference analysis and reporting features but do not support enterprise-level volume requirements. Thus, an IT organization may rely on mainframe tools for enterprise planning but switch to a mixture of mainframe and PC tools for implementation.

- **Inventory and cross-reference tools.**

  These tools help to automate much of the process of collecting a large-scale systems inventory. Without automation, the task of gathering inventory data across numerous libraries is quite time consuming. Key requirements include the ability to parse and cross-reference system components (control language, source, load, etc.) across multiple applications. A second basic requirement is the ability to report this information in a variety of lists and summary cross-reference formats. This information is gathered from the production hardware and software environment to ascertain which systems, and which components within those systems, are either in or not in production. This information is also used to determine how to divide the enterprise portfolio into effective upgrade units.

  Several vendors provide tools that are specifically designed to perform the inventory and cross-reference functions for large volumes of code. These tools tend to use scanning technology, which, while limiting the completeness of their analysis, enables fast operation and increases their ability to support multiple languages. Another solution is to use the same system-level analysis tools described in the following text for impact analysis. These tools require greater effort to load but provide far more analysis capabilities.

  At least one vendor offers an inventory tool for system software. This tool finds all currently operating versions of system software, utilities, and programming tools and provides version information for the software it locates. This is invaluable for identifying situations where old, back-level versions of software are still in operation.

- **Impact analyzer.**

  System-level impact analyzers provide the most significant and recent advance in tools for application maintenance. These tools enable their users to follow data and control flow across one or more applications. This capability automates many critical analysis tasks, such as true impact analysis, which until recently could only be performed manually. Thorough impact analysis at the upgrade unit level is a critical requirement for success in century-date compliance projects. These tools must be able to track date occurrences through actual use at the program and system level. This tracking includes following a given date variable through files and variable redefinitions, as well as identifying all other variables that set or are set by the original variable. Figure 15.4 illustrates some of the data flow transformations that an impact analyzer must follow to connect a date within dataset A with the same date in dataset D.

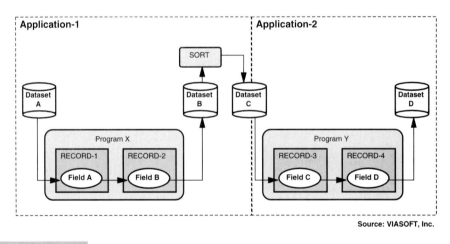

Source: VIASOFT, Inc.

Figure 15.4   Impact Analysis Complexity

Performing these functions requires highly sophisticated parsing, control flow, and data flow technology. Scanning tools that rely on name searches are not recommended for this task. Tool analysts should be sure to verify that the tool that they select truly contains the sophisticated technology required for impact analysis. An impact analysis tool provides value regardless of the approach being used to achieve compliance.

During implementation, analysts must ensure that all components are included in the upgrade process and must also ensure that all related components are updated with the same formats. For example, multiple record definitions, representing a common data storage layout, must be updated at the same time and in the same way. The cross-reference features inherent in an impact analyzer provide this capability.

- **Static analyzers.**

  Static analysis tools are batch-oriented tools that provide reports and cross-references for individual programs. Unlike interactive analyzers, where the analysis paths are chosen by the tool's user, static analyzers produce a complete "snapshot" of program control flow and data use. These tools are available in either mainframe or PC environments and are used primarily to create printed reports for program-level impact analysis. Although their printed reports can be voluminous, these tools are a useful adjunct to an interactive analyzer. Some versions can even incorporate their documentation into program source code as comments for future reference.

- **Interactive analyzers.**

  Interactive analyzers enable their users to dynamically follow the control flow and variable use within an individual program. These tools typically offer both text and graphical views of their information. They support the analysis and migration phases of a century-compliance project by providing program-level impact analysis and source code change capabilities. They enable programmers to verify the results of application-level impact analysis and to assess the impact of their intended change on a program's control flow. Because of their graphics requirements, these tools operate in workstation environments.

- **Data analyzers.**

  Data analyzers supplement the knowledge gained from source code analysis by searching for dates within file and database data. Most analysis tools find date variables by searching through program source code. These searches are complete only if *all* potential input dates can be identified. Data analyzers recognize the data patterns for a variety of date formats to identify date fields that would otherwise be missed. They find date fields that cannot be recognized through their variable names or that are hidden within a larger data structure. Once these fields are identified in the data, their displacement within the data record can be used to tie the date to a variable name within a source code record description. This variable name can then be used for impact analysis.

- **Environmental analyzers.**

  Century-date compliance projects require more information about applications and their operating environments than can be gathered through inventory tools and impact analyzers. There are numerous types of special-purpose environmental analyzers that handle special-purpose functions, such as determining the compiler version and options used to create a particular load module or documenting Job Control Language (JCL) streams in mainframe environments. IT organizations often own these types of tools within their operations areas.

15.3.4 Migration Tools

Migration tools are used in the Implementation and Deployment phase of the Year 2000 project. Migration activities tend to be the most routine and tedious and therefore have the highest potential for gaining efficiency from automation. While some tools are specialized for century-date migrations, most migration tasks use the same software tools to perform standard maintenance and enhancement tasks. As a result, a wide range of tools is available to assist migration efforts. Further, most tools acquired for the migration effort have value for future support activities.

Tools in this category handle application source code migration, data conversion, change integration, and data bridging activities. The application source code tools required for migration activities range from standard programming tools such as compilers and editors to automated change facilities for automatically converting large volumes of source code. While standard tools such as compilers and editors are an absolute requirement for century-date migration efforts, they are already present in most IT organizations and are not discussed below.

When considering the purchase of migration tools, the Year 2000 Project Office should consider the sophistication of the tool's technology and the degree of automation provided. The highly repetitive nature of migration tasks lends them to automated approaches; however, low accuracy will wipe out the benefit of automation by increasing testing and correction effort. The greater the sophistication of the tool's underlying technology, the higher the accuracy of its results. Because most Year 2000 efforts require a mixture of implementation strategies, the tools acquired must support the changes required for both data expansion and process-based conversion approaches.

- **Calendar routines—standardization and workaround logic support.**

  Several vendors offer libraries of standardized date logic routines that handle a large variety of calendar functions, such as distance between two dates, verification of day of the week, and holiday calculation. These libraries are very useful for IT organizations that are not already employing standard date routines. Many of the commercially available tools that provide standard date handling logic also incorporate procedural workaround capabilities. At least one vendor offers a tool to assist the implementation of the calendar routines by automatically generating the necessary subroutine calls in the application programs.

- **Automated change facility.**

  Whether an organization selects a date field expansion or procedural workaround approach, finding and fixing date fields is a tedious and repetitive activity that lends itself to a degree of automation. While no tool provides foolproof automated solutions, many tools can take much of the burden off the analyst to change every single occurrence of a date field from one format to another. There are two basic approaches to this automation process. The first provides an interactive date change facility that operates under the control of the analyst charged with the migration. This tool is essentially an extended feature of many of the impact analyzers in the market and allows analysts to interactively find and fix date fields. The second approach is more batch oriented. These tools perform a detailed analysis of the code to be converted and generate a list of conversion parameters or instructions. The analyst verifies and modifies these instructions for use as input to the conversion portion of the tool. The actual conversion is then executed in one step. These tools often support several types of conversion strategies and allow their users to change strategies by simply changing parameters.

- **Interface and bridge generator.**

  Technology to bridge the differences in files shared between compliant and noncompliant applications is an absolute requirement for any migration effort that employs a date expansion strategy. These requirements are described in greater detail in Chapter 5. Generating required APIs and bridge interfaces can be automated through four different strategies: custom interface creation, bridge generators, data migration tools, or automated conversion tools. Writing custom interfaces is not overly difficult; however, the effort required to create the hundreds or thousands of interfaces that may be deployed during the course of a Year 2000 implementation project is daunting. Bridge generators create either subroutines that are linked into the compliant software or separate bridging utilities that handle file differences between compliant and noncompliant applications. Some of the data migration tools that provide automated date field expansion can provide API and bridge generation as well. Finally, highly automated source code conversion tools can provide "virtual" bridging capabilities if they support both process-based and field expansion migration strategies. In this case, the application is initially converted by using a process-based approach to avoid impact on file structures. Once all applications sharing a given file are converted, the application is reprocessed through the conversion tool to employ the field expansion approach.

- **Configuration manager.**

  The control and management of all versions of all source code components is an essential requirement of a century-date compliance project. Many IT organizations will be conducting regular maintenance and enhancement activities in conjunction with their migration projects, thereby increasing the importance of ensuring that the correct versions of each component are combined into an application release. Failure to implement version control through configuration management enables noncompliant components to be inadvertently mixed with compliant components, undermining the entire compliance effort. Most IT organizations use library management software to control the configuration of their mainframe software. This software is the repository for all application source code, and programmers are required to check out and check in the components that they change. Most configuration managers track, and can report on, the differences between different versions. These reports are useful for verifying that all indicated changes were performed and are essential for auditing. PC and multiplatform configuration managers are available for non-mainframe platforms. If an IT organization is not currently using a configuration manager, it is highly recommended that such a tool be purchased and installed during the early stages of the century-compliance effort.

- **Comparison/change integration facility.**

  Reviewing manual or automated code changes by comparing previous and current versions of a system is a basic requirement supported by intelligent comparison technology. These tools support quality assurance walk-through and data storage comparison tasks required during validation testing. These basic tasks are so prevalent in an upgrade unit compliance effort that comparison utilities rank along with impact analyzers as the most important technology for a Year 2000 implementation project.

There are many comparison utilities on the market, and those utilities vary widely in intelligence. The simplest utilities compare two versions of a given file and produce a report listing line-by-line differences. This can produce voluminous results for small differences. More advanced versions can interpret differences in sequence to identify added or deleted lines, and they can ignore expected differences in line numbers or even date fields. These tools are available for source code and standard data files. The source code versions generally have some understanding of language syntax to permit more intelligent analysis. Most configuration management tools perform version comparisons for the source code contained within their libraries.

This same comparison technology is useful for determining if code changes were applied to baseline production versions and, if so, how those changes can be reincorporated back into expanded versions of that same system. Change integration technology, a more sophisticated extension of the comparison category, is useful when analysts find themselves repeatedly integrating maintenance changes into compliant versions of those same systems. This tool is particularly important if a majority of work is performed off site, where change integration opportunities are limited by vendor system-freeze requirements.

- **Data migration tool.**

When a date field expansion strategy has been selected, the application's files and databases must be expanded into the new format. This expansion may require interpreting existing dates to introduce the right century data into the expanded fields. Developing data migration routines to handle these expansion tasks is another straightforward, yet tedious, task that benefits from automated tools. Certain date field expansion tools can convert data structures in addition to expanding data definitions within source components. If these features are available in tools selected for automated conversion, analysts should use these facilities where applicable.

Analysts may optionally research data manipulation technology as a means of generating data conversion routines. Note that the overlap between interface generation tools and data conversion tools is more than coincidental, and this fact has not been lost on many vendors: many vendors that provide interface generation also offer data migration technology, and vice versa.

15.3.5 Redevelopment Tools

Software redevelopment is a form of perfective maintenance used to improve the technical quality of an existing application, redistribute its functionality, or update its language, database architecture, or platform. Redevelopment is used to extend the life of an existing application, reduce its cost of maintenance, or correct problems in operations or support. Specific redevelopment activities include language conversion, logic structuring, data name rationalization, module splitting, and reverse engineering.

Although redevelopment tools and activities are not always required for a century-date compliance project, they offer a means to add long-term value to the migration. Redeveloping the most highly maintained programs within an application provides a very high return on the investment in those programs and will facilitate century-date migration and testing activities. Applications that use obsolete technologies will need to be migrated to a technology that supports century dates.

- **Metrics analyzers.**

  Metrics analyzers measure the technical quality of a piece of software. They use industry-standard metrics to assess a program's maintainability through its size, complexity, structure, and other measures. This information is used for quality assurance, standards enforcement, and to select programs for other redevelopment activities. The information gathered by a metrics analyzer is useful in the estimation and quality assurance activities of a century-date compliance project. It identifies highly complex programs that will require greater effort to test and verify.

- **Data name rationalizer.**

  Confusing and inappropriate data names are one of the biggest complicating factors in a century-date compliance project. Data name rationalizers are tools that permit researching, understanding, and renaming data names across an application. Redundant variable definitions can be eliminated, and unnecessary aliases can be removed to significantly reduce future maintenance costs and facilitate the use of reverse engineering techniques. Although this can be an expensive and time-consuming activity, the payback is high. Century-date compliance projects offer an opportunity to at least rationalize all date-associated variables.

- **Structuring tools.**

    Program structuring tools reduce the complexity and increase the modularity of older legacy programs. These tools effectively rewrite old code, changing their convoluted logic into new programs that fully follow the rules of structured programming. The resulting programs are far simpler to understand, change, and maintain. Although the structuring tools on the market are fully automatic, better results will be obtained by performing a few manual improvements along with the structuring process. Within a century-compliance project, these tools can be used to simplify the most convoluted programs before performing any century migration activities. Some structuring tools have the ability to isolate input/output and CALL statements into standalone paragraphs. This simplifies the process of adding internal bridging routines. Structuring is a highly recommended prelude to code slicing and reverse engineering.

- **Code slicers.**

    Code slicing tools are used to break a large, complex program into multiple, smaller programs or to extract code to create reusable subroutines. This simplification reduces the size and complexity of application code and reduces long-term maintenance costs. The tools function by extracting sections of procedural logic and associated data definitions and then creating a new program based upon that code. Within century-date migration projects, these capabilities can be used to create reusable date subroutines and to remove redundant date processing logic from programs.

- **Language migration tools.**

    Numerous language migration tools are available for migrating source code from an older version of a language to a more recent version of the same language or from one language to another. Language migration between versions is required in century-date migration projects when the older version of the language is not century-date compliant. For example, the date functions used in older versions of COBOL do not support century-dates, whereas the latest versions of

COBOL contain functions to aid century compliance. IT organizations may want to consider migration to another language if the original language is not commonly used within the organization. Many organizations have isolated pockets of languages that are obsolete or were "orphaned" by changes in technical direction. Converting applications written in these languages to a more common language before century-date migration, provides access to a greater set of tools and expertise for the migration and reduces future maintenance costs.

- **Reverse engineering tools.**

  Reverse engineering tools analyze existing applications to identify and extract their functionality for migration into a repository or a model-based support environment. Once the application's underlying logic has been migrated into the new environment, it can be extended and regenerated into a new application or quickly ported to new platforms. Other types of reverse engineering tools identify the business rules that exist within the program source code. Although this technology has significantly improved over the past few years, it is still far from a totally automated process. It is useful for situations in a century-date migration project where it is desirable to migrate an application to a new platform or environment as a method of gaining extra value from the migration effort.

15.3.6 Testing Tools

Century compliance for a given software system cannot be guaranteed unless that system has been thoroughly tested with century dates. While testing is an obvious requirement for applications that have undergone migration, it is also required to certify supposedly compliant applications. As a result of these requirements, validation is the most costly and difficult phase of a century-date compliance effort, accounting for as much as 50 percent of the overall project cost. Testing tools provide a tremendous degree of leverage in reducing the effort required for the validation process. They allow certain basic, repetitive functions to be handled by tools, allowing analysts to focus their time on more critical tasks. Tools handle activities that would be difficult or impossible to complete manually. This is particularly true for the functions provided by comparison facilities and dynamic coverage analyzers. These tools, along with on-line playback and capture tools, virtual date utilities, and data migration tools, help streamline the validation process. Finally, tools such as test coverage analyzers enable an IT organization to manage the level of risk they are willing to assume. These tools allow the organization to decide how much testing is enough. Unfortunately, despite the opportunity for automation, there are relatively few strong testing tools compared to the number of tools in the other categories.

Testing requirements fall into three categories: the ability to create test data, the ability to execute system-level tests, and the ability to verify the results of those tests. The first category requires tools to identify testing requirements, generate test data, and monitor the coverage of that data. The second category requires tools to simulate various operational environments, including setting system dates into the next century. The final category requires data comparison programs to enable programmers to verify that tests completed successfully when they are run over large volumes of data.

- **Test data generators.**

    Creating test data is a tedious and time-consuming process. No tool can automatically create a complete set of test data for an application. Test data generators automate parts of the effort by generating test cases based upon parameters provided by an analyst. These tools are useful for adding or updating date values that reflect future events. Records may be added, for example, that establish an employee start date in 1999 and a termination date in 2003. Another approach is to strip test records from production files during the data migration process. Data migration tools reformat and regenerate files and databases that have been impacted by a date field expansion project. These same capabilities can be used to strip and update data for test scripts.

- **On-line capture and playback.**

    Test data generation is much more complex for on-line and client/server applications. On-line capture and playback tools provide the ability to create reusable test scripts for on-line systems. These test scripts are precisely controlled sets of input data that guarantee predictable results when used as input to a given test cycle. These tools operate by capturing the data input to an on-line system and placing that data into the test script. The playback portion of the tool provides the ability to direct the identical on-line screen inputs into a system test cycle over and over again. This capability offers the high level of test input consistency and repeatability required for a Year 2000 validation test.

- **Test coverage analyzers.**

  In order to perform comprehensive testing, analysts must determine what percentage of a given program has been tested. Dynamic (executes while the program is running) coverage analyzers report on the percentage of program logic that has been executed during a given test cycle by tracing execution paths based on a fixed set of test data. These tools tell the analyst how much code was executed during a given test run and whether the test cases should be expanded to improve this coverage. If the percentage is low, analysts will want to adjust the test data to improve the reliability of the end result.

  Static test coverage analyzers examine program source code paths, tracing all possible control flow paths. These tools are used by testing teams to expand the coverage of their tests by helping them identify the specific areas of logic that need to be covered by test data. When execution coverage by dynamic analyzers is deemed to be too low, static analyzers provide graphical analysis that helps analysts enhance test data so that a greater percentage of logic is invoked. Static analyzers provide significant value during the testing of infrastructure improvement and validation setup projects. The long learning curve and the overriding dependency on process required by these tools suggest that only qualified analysts should attempt to use these tools during a Year 2000 implementation project.

  The most sophisticated level of test coverage analyzer parses programs and analyzes the data itself to suggest where redundant records or database segments can be stripped away and where new records can be added to increase execution coverage. As with the static analyzers, the learning curve for this product restricts its use to skilled validation teams—particularly if these tools are to be used under the constrained time frames commonly found in a Year 2000 migration effort.

- **Virtual date utility.**

  Testing a system to see if it works after the turn of the century requires that programs expect the year to be 2000 or beyond. Virtual date utilities intercept and reset the current date and other similar registers used by the application, so that mainframe system dates do not have to be reset. Depending on the tool, virtual date utilities allow analysts to reset the system date to a valid date setting in batch and on-line environments. This enables the organization to conduct its compliance testing without impact on other production applications sharing the same computer system. An alternative to using this type of tool is to test a program on a standalone testing mainframe or in a PC-based environment.

- **Environment simulators.**

  Full-scale tests of on-line environments can be very time consuming to set up and execute. Although live testing is ultimately required for these applications, many preliminary tests can be conducted at the unit testing level through an environment simulator executing on a workstation. These tools simulate common mainframe database and teleprocessing monitor environments, enabling an analyst to quickly set up and execute multiple tests. Problems uncovered in these tests can be analyzed and corrected on the workstation and quickly reexecuted.

- **Execution simulators and debuggers.**

  Thorough unit testing reduces the time and cost of system-level testing. Execution simulators and debuggers are two types of tools that support unit testing activities. Execution simulators step through a program's source code, following its control flow. These tools do not actually execute the program, so they do not require data. The tool's user is queried at each decision point to supply the necessary information to continue execution. These tools allow quick verification of program changes. Debuggers use test data to monitor the actual execution of a program. These tools enable an analyst to set breakpoints, examine the data contained in variables, and step through a program's execution in various sequences. These tools are used to verify the actual results of each date calculation and decision. Both categories of tools can be found in mainframe and PC versions.

- **Comparison facility.**

  A basic comparison facility is the minimum level of software tool support required for a Year 2000 validation project. Fortunately, basic versions of these tools come with many operating systems. This tool allows an analyst to compare the results from two output data stores to determine that the results produced by the original system and the Year 2000-compliant system are identical. This can be the same tool previously described under migration tools. If a language-sensitive comparison utility is used for source code version comparisons, a generalized comparison utility is required for file compares. Key features include the ability to skip over certain data fields where old and new formats may differ and, optionally, the ability to determine where two data values are different, yet still correct, based on an offset calculation. This second feature is available only in highly specialized versions of these products, typically created for Year 2000 projects.

References

[1] The technical background section is adapted from a presentation written by Dr. Eric Bush for Eleventh Hour Software, LLP, 1996.

Chapter 16

Small Information Technology Organizations

Small companies and IT organizations may not have the budget or the resources to create a comprehensive Year 2000 delivery capability. This chapter provides these organizations with various alternatives for keeping information systems functioning in the face of the Year 2000 crisis. Small IT organizations are a microcosm of larger organizations and have many of the same requirements, but these requirements must be fulfilled in unique and creative ways. Discussions in this chapter are aimed at small companies with an IT staff of 1 to 10 people, minicomputer operations, individual or franchise operations using small network systems, and "mom and pop" organizations with no full-time IT staff. This last category includes the independent entrepreneur with little or no knowledge of information systems technology.

16.1 Defining the Small Organization or Business Unit

Many different types of IT organizations can be considered small. For example, certain companies that one would not necessarily consider small, may maintain an IT staff of 5 to 10 people. Other small shops, and there are thousands of these types of organizations, may have just one person working on information technology requirements for that company. In the most extreme cases, a sole proprietorship or partnership may have no one in charge of IT but still use some type of computer system. Individual personal computer users should consider themselves in this last category for purposes of understanding and preparing for the impending millennium problem.

16.1.1 Determining Size: Portfolio Size and Resource Limitations

There are a number of ways to determine if your company has a small IT organization. The first, and most obvious for purposes of Year 2000 planning, is based on the resources available to address IT-related issues. If a company has 2 to 20 people performing IT-related work, including systems and operations personnel, this is considered small. In these cases, there may be only a handful of individuals responsible for maintaining application systems. The remaining individuals likely have network, communication, operations, or management roles. A medium-sized shop, on the other hand, may have 20 to 40 people in IT.

A medium-sized shop might be able to establish a small Year 2000 Project Office, but small shops may not be able to mobilize a Year 2000 team without causing major disruptions in ongoing support functions. Medium-sized shops may find that the suggestions made in earlier chapters of this book can be applied in more conservative measures, but small IT shops are typically not as fortunate. If you have the personnel constraints mentioned here, the suggestions and guidelines in this chapter will provide insights into dealing with the Year 2000 issue. Medium-sized IT organizations can also benefit from many of the concepts presented in this chapter.

16.1.2 Constraining Factors: Low Budget Ceilings

Budget is another driving factor in the Year 2000 challenge. Typically, organizations with small budgets have small IT staffs. Companies recently may have slashed IT budgets for a number of reasons and are simultaneously reducing IT staff. A medium-sized IT shop may suddenly find that it is now a small IT shop with the same level of support responsibility.

Budgetary constraints dictate, to a great degree, how an organization responds to the Year 2000 problem. If we examine a large company with an IT budget of anywhere from $10 million to $100 million, there is typically some degree of discretionary dollars that can be allocated to the Year 2000 solution over a 2 to 3 year period. That is not to say that all large shops are doing a stellar job in dealing with budget allocation. It is, in fact, the main reason so many large companies are slow to address the issue.

However, once management at these large shops turns its attention to the Year 2000 matter, the money can be made available through the cancellation or delay of a data warehouse project, a package deployment effort or some other strategic initiative that can temporarily take a lower priority in the budgeting process. This is not the case for most shops with small IT budgets. An organization may have 2–3 million lines of code, with an estimated Year 2000 solution costing $3 to $4 million. The total IT budget for this organization may be only $5 million per year, including operations, management salaries, essential new hardware, and other, non-discretionary factors. Management has a real dilemma on its hands.

Finally, some shops may be small because of historic reasons that are no longer valid. For example, companies with rapidly growing revenues may still employ a highly understaffed IT function because this is the way it has always been. Recent growth, however, may be driving management to expand IT capabilities at the same time the Year 2000 problem is discovered. If this is the case, it may be an advantage to the company to expand IT operations while simultaneously addressing the Year 2000 issue. Growth strategies typically include major revamping of systems that served the company during initial startup but no longer support rapid expansion in revenue, customers, or other areas. The strategy, in this case, may be to deploy new applications to avoid the Year 2000 problem altogether. If a company falls into this category, management should examine the strategies discussed in this chapter and integrate these ideas in their expansion plans.

16.1.3 Small Divisions in a Large Corporate Infrastructure

A large company may have small divisions that, for whatever reason, have been left out of the corporate IT solution. This will become increasingly true as management focuses on salvaging mainstream IT functions as the end of the century nears. In other words, big corporations may let marginal or remote divisional operations sink or swim on their own as they struggle with keeping mission-critical systems running. These "orphaned" IT shops should look to the strategies embodied in this chapter for guidance but should also attempt to gain an advantage by reviewing progress made at their sister divisions. This may include attending Year 2000 advisory board and project office meetings at the other divisions, obtaining sample plans for these other divisions, meeting with in-house experts, and leveraging the use of the technology used on sister company systems. These divisions or subsidiaries must not be forgotten in the Year 2000 crisis.

16.1.4 Organizations With No In-house Information Technology Staff

The largest category of organizations that must deal with the Year 2000 problem is the small entrepreneur who has no full-time IT support staff. Examples include the local dentist, independent pharmacies, the doctor's office, retail operations, independent car service centers, lawyers, real estate companies, architects, churches, and any other types of small business service or product provider. These businesses typically buy or lease a system, along with support as required, from specialty software providers. Many of these systems are rarely enhanced or upgraded. In fact, many of these small businesses find it difficult to get software providers to upgrade even basic functions within these systems.

This problem is not unique to the small business community. Some public agencies may not have any appreciable in-house information technology support and could be in similar situations. For example, small-town or small county governments may own or lease systems to run basic service functions. These systems are typically customized to facilitate functions unique to small public agencies. The vendors of these systems are selected on a low-bid basis and may not have the resources to support an upgrade of these systems. Local governments may be in an even greater bind because of severe procurement restrictions. Finally, individual home users of personal computer technology, while not at severe risk, certainly are not immune to the Year 2000 issue.

Having no in-house staff makes the task of dealing with the Year 2000 problem even more problematic because no one at a given organization has the skills to identify the problem, let alone solve it.

16.2 Problem Determination: How Do You Know You Have a Problem?

Determining that there is a Year 2000 problem when little information has been dispatched to the general public about the issue is a real challenge. Whereas larger IT organizations can afford to send people to conferences, subscribe to professional publications, test new technology, and assign individuals to research high-priority issues, small shops do not have this luxury. With limited resources and budgets, many small shops find that they must fend for themselves in many areas. Unfortunately, IT professionals in these small, and often isolated, organizations find themselves reinventing the wheel when it comes to approaches and tools required to solve numerous IT challenges. The year 2000 clearly falls in this category as stories begin to emerge of small shops inventing their own scanning tools and processes for addressing this issue.

16.2.1 Hearing About the Year 2000 on the News

Because many smaller IT organizations may not have heard about the Year 2000 problem until very recently and because they may not be privy to leading edge strategies emerging in the industry as a whole, many professionals rush to solutions that have already been discounted in mainstream markets. Indeed, the last two years have seen numerous cases of companies pursuing solutions that were tried and discounted long ago. The pressure to do so arises when the director of IT, usually the top-ranking information technology position at many smaller shops, hears about the Year 2000 on a news show and demands quick identification and resolution of the problem.

16.2.2 Taking Stock of the Issue

If an organization primarily uses in-house developed applications, senior application analysts must be consulted to determine if there is a Year 2000 problem. If there is any doubt as to the reliability of information provided by these individuals—and many times in-house experts are reluctant to admit that the systems they created may have a flaw—management may need to look into the issue themselves. If this is not possible, an outside expert can be called in for a few days to review the problem. As stated earlier, widespread use of 4-character date does not guarantee Year 2000 compliance. Upon determining that there are potential Year 2000 risks, management should charter a full-scale effort to pursue a solution.

Many smaller shops make extensive use of application package software. In these cases, management should immediately contact package vendors to determine the type of Year 2000 compliance that they will provide and when this level of compliance will be available. If there is any risk of these vendors not providing compliant versions of these systems within the event horizons required, management should quickly investigate alternative options. The research guidelines outlined in prior chapters can be used to research both systems developed in-house and vendor packages.

16.2.3 Spreading the News

If analysts encounter the Year 2000 problem and find that management is unwilling to listen to their concerns, they should review and apply relevant guidelines outlined earlier in this book for building awareness.

As with larger companies and government agencies, analysts may need to educate management on the topic of the year 2000. The special concern in smaller shops is that these analysts may not be able to find allies to support their cause. As in larger companies, seeking advice and support from internal and external audit or general press clippings should help these analysts spread the word about the Year 2000 problem.

16.3 Solutions and Strategies for Small IT Shops

Seeking a solution in a small IT organization with limited staffing and budget resources has different types of challenges than performing this same task within larger, more resource-rich environments. These differences exist in the Year 2000 management infrastructure, technology considerations, assessment effort, and strategy development.

16.3.1 The Skeleton Year 2000 Management Infrastructure

Building a Year 2000 management infrastructure in small IT environments involves a much less formal process than in larger IT environments, because there is a much shorter chain of command and fewer full-time professionals that can be dedicated to this effort. Figure 16.1 depicts a skeleton support infrastructure for a small IT organization.

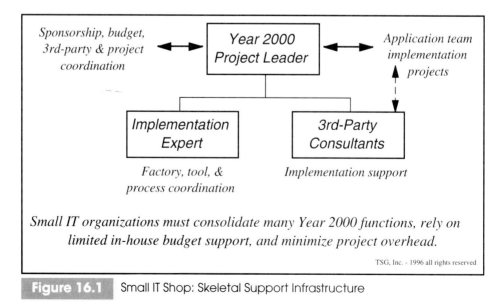

Figure 16.1   Small IT Shop: Skeletal Support Infrastructure

This infrastructure shown in Figure 16.1 suggests the following positions and responsibilities.

- **Project leader.**

  This individual, who could be the Project Office director or a manager, works with sponsors, application teams and third parties to facilitate the project. This person is responsible for managing communication, the budget, the plan, vendors and consultants, in-house project team personnel, and project deadlines.

- **Implementation expert.**

  Depending on the approach selected, this individual coordinates in-house tools and technology or, in the case of in-house systems being sent off site, factory specification and day-to-day coordination.

- **Third-party consultants.**

  These should be contracted through and coordinated with the Year 2000 project leader.

This infrastructure will, of course, vary, depending on the size and composition of the shop. The key fact to consider is that the formalities, size, and reporting structure found within a larger IT organization are not necessarily applicable to a small environment. The IT director should assign these responsibilities to a trusted manager and give this person wide latitude in addressing the Year 2000 issue.

16.3.2 Technology Support Considerations

The software tools and technologies required to plan and implement a Year 2000 project differ from those recommended for large organizations. Tools are recommended only when a portfolio contains a significant number of applications developed in-house and where management envisions that much of the work is to be done on site. Package-based shops, for example, should avoid the acquisition of implementation tools when possible. If in-house applications dominate the portfolio, certain planning and implementation tools are available to reduce tool budget requirements.

For planning, analysts should focus on workstation-based tools to inventory portfolios with fewer than 3–4 million lines of code. Workstation-based inventory and cross-reference tools are normally based on repositories that cannot store or report on medium-to-large software portfolios. Another planning tool constraint is that many smaller shops may be running IBM DOS VSE, IBM AS/400,™ DEC VAX, Wang, or other environments where Year 2000 tools are hard to find. If tools can be found to process systems running on these platforms, budget constraints may preclude the acquisition of these tools. Low-cost (e.g., workstation, home-grown) tools should be reviewed, procured, and deployed to support planning projects at small IT shops where in-house systems dominate.

If implementation work is to be performed by in-house application teams, workstation-based tools should be used to support the process of identifying and changing dates within upgrade unit components. The process of converting data stores and generating interfaces is typically more suited to technology that runs on a given upgrade unit's native platform. Validation, a process that is almost always performed in-house, requires some minimum level of tool support in almost all cases. For small shops, justification of validation tools may be difficult, even though these tools have long-term value for application teams. If this is the case, analysts at least should procure source code and data comparison tools, because this is the minimum level of technology required for the validation phase of the project.

A final consideration regarding tool procurement depends on how consultants are used for various Year 2000 tasks. Some consultants bring commercially available tools to a Year 2000 project. Others consultants use proprietary tools that they developed or that they leased from a third party. If consultants that contracted to perform in-house assessment or migration work bring their own tools to the project, the cost of these tools should be embedded in the cost of that phase of the project. This approach can be absorbed into the budgeting cycle more readily than separate line items for software tools that may not be used again. Key points to remember regarding tool utilization for small IT shops is to minimize costs by looking at workstation solutions, look to consultants where possible for required technology, and, when tools are needed for the project, identify uses for those tools beyond the Year 2000 project.

16.3.3 Rapid Planning and Assessment

Figure 16.2 depicts a rapid assessment strategy for small IT organizations. Owing to resource, budget, and staffing limitations, the following quick inventory and planning guidelines should be applied, as an alternative, in small IT environments.

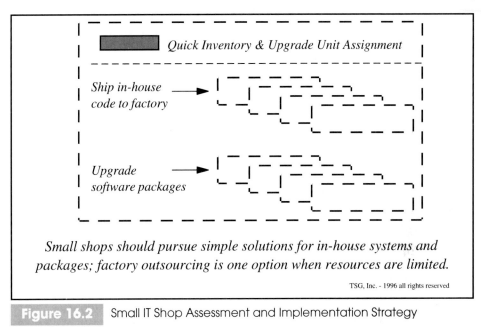

Quick Inventory & Upgrade Unit Assignment

Ship in-house code to factory

Upgrade software packages

Small shops should pursue simple solutions for in-house systems and packages; factory outsourcing is one option when resources are limited.

Figure 16.2 Small IT Shop Assessment and Implementation Strategy

1. *Inventory all systems, based on quick surveys of all application, system software, and user-based system owners.*

2. *Bypass the use of formal forms and collect this information, using a word processor or a spreadsheet where possible.*

3. *Identify major databases and master files through application area experts.*

4. *For segmentation purposes, treat each major system as an upgrade unit.*

5. *If a system is too big to be processed in a timely manner, based on general estimating guidelines found in prior chapters, subdivide it by subsystem as needed.*

6. *Finalize all system and upgrade unit groups and discuss implementation approaches with application personnel.*

7. *Develop a general estimate for each system and upgrade unit and move forward with pilot activities as required.*

Differences between the rapid planning approach of small shops and the full-scale planning approach typically used in a large-scale IT environment are matters of depth and degree. Small shops should reduce or eliminate the level of formality that is found in a larger project. Common sense should drive the shortcuts exercised during a Year 2000 planning project at the small IT organization.

16.3.4 Strategies for Resource-Limited Shops

Once basic assessment and planning work is completed, management should create an implementation strategy. The approaches selected are based, to a great degree, on the same factors that a large IT shop would consider. However, the differences are driven by the fact that justification for a Project Office support function, certain tools, in-house expertise, and other requirements is more difficult because of smaller budgets. The Year 2000 planning team should use the following guidelines.

1. *If systems have been deemed redundant, expendable, or obsolete, establish a plan to phase out or consolidate these systems.*

2. *If packages make up a portion of the portfolio, meet with applicable vendors, determine Year 2000 upgrade status, and establish upgrade plans as needed.*

3. *If tools and in-house expertise are not available, consider shipping in-house systems to a factory or having consultants perform in-house conversion work.*

4. *Review factory strategies (see Figure 16.2) as a first-priority consideration for any in-house systems that require Year 2000 migration if the following are relevant:*

    a. Multiple or nonstandard hardware platforms or application languages make in-house conversion unnecessarily expensive.

    b. In-house skills or resources are not available.

    c. Consultants to perform in-house work are unavailable.

    d. No tool expertise or tools are available for the environment being used.

5. *If other sources of assistance are not readily available, consider working with the hardware manufacturer to determine a Year 2000 strategy.*

6. *Consider moving to application packages for selected areas, where available.*

7. *In some limited cases, pursue selective redesign or migration of an existing system, if already planned and if it can meet the required event horizon.*

Smaller organizations may find difficulty in getting help with the Year 2000 issue. Hardware vendors, industry trade groups, external auditors, or other third parties can be good sources of help in these situations.

16.4 Implementation Options for Small Companies

When it comes to implementing a Year 2000 solution at a small IT organization, the supply-and-demand factor for scarce resources comes into play. Many of the mainstream solution providers are not working with smaller companies because larger projects yield larger profits. For this reason and those stated earlier in this chapter, small IT organizations may need to be more creative in their efforts to find and procure outside resources to assist with the Year 2000 migration project. Strategies for dealing with various organizations are outlined below.

16.4.1 Package Upgrade Options

Small IT organizations that utilize application packages should pursue strategies similar to those of larger organizations that use application packages. Management should contact the applicable package vendors, determine if or when each package is to be made Year 2000 compliant, determine the compliance approach that the vendor is using, and establish upgrade plans accordingly. Organizations that use packages almost exclusively while relying on third-party vendors for a solution, should have less to worry about than those shops that use in-house developed software. Of course, this is only true if the vendors in question have upgraded, or plan to upgrade, their systems to be Year 2000 compliant within the appropriate event horizons.

Some issues that are unique to a small IT organization include an overriding dependence on a small number of application package vendors. This dependence puts the information processing capability of a company at risk if that vendor decides not to upgrade the package. Timing is also an issue for small companies that may not be given appropriate lead times between the time a compliant version of the package becomes available and when it is projected to fail in production. A company that is highly dependent on a single vendor package may find, for example, that the upgrade and deployment process, including customization of in-house developed programs, may take longer than the event horizon demands. In these cases, a company may have to work with user groups or other organizations to have the vendor reassess the priority of the upgrade effort.

A worst case situation involves vendors that have chosen not to upgrade their package or that will not have the package upgrade ready in time. In these cases, management may be forced to shop around for a new application package to replace the obsolete package. One alternative, if package source code is available to the IT team, is to upgrade the package to be Year 2000 compliant as an in-house project. This option requires that no contract restrictions prevent in-house upgrading from occurring, that the source code is available, and that management is willing to assume ownership of this system.

Finally, analysts must review all system software to determine if it is Year 2000 compliant and, if not, which release will be Year 2000 compliant. The strategies here are similar again to the large IT shop and include determining system availability, scheduling the upgrade, synchronizing system software and application software upgrades, and adjusting the budget and workplans to accommodate these requirements.

16.4.2 In-house Application Strategies

Eliminating redundant, obsolete, or little-used systems from a Year 2000 plan is always a recommended first step, particularly when obsolete technology is prevalent. Once this cleanup process is completed, applications can be shipped off site or processed by internal staff working with outside consultants. When in-house application systems dominate a portfolio, small shops must determine if an internal solution can be managed under the current infrastructure. If, for example, management has no way of freeing up staff or processing resources to make those systems compliant, shipping systems to a Year 2000 conversion factory is likely the best option. If the management team alternatively believes that in-house personnel are best equipped to perform the Year 2000 conversion, in-house migration projects should be deployed. While the best approach depends on many factors, in small organizations the best approach is typically that which least impacts in-house activities.

Factories, described in more detail in Chapter 17, are basically off-site processing centers where systems can be upgraded to Year 2000 compliance. The benefit to a small shop is that an implementation team and environment need not be mobilized if work is shipped off site. This mobilization process is particularly difficult and costly in diverse technical environments. If this option is selected, packaging systems into upgrade units to be shipped off site can be assigned to a central coordinator who works with application experts as needed. Once a system is returned to in-house personnel, application personnel can validate and deploy those systems on a schedule of their own choosing.

In-house strategies for small IT organizations should focus on minimizing many of the formalities required in larger, system migration projects. This means that if migration work is to be performed by applications personnel, these teams should have access to basic, high-level conversion guidelines and workstation tools. A central specialist should review project progress, generate interfaces as required, provide tools support, and assist with testing and deployment. The goal again is to minimize overhead, but consulting experts can be selectively assigned to special support tasks where needed.

A second approach to in-house migration efforts is to have a consulting team take over the conversion project and use the application team to provide input to the project as needed. This approach is best suited to situations where the infrastructure supports conversion teams and tools, excess computing power is available, management wants to minimize application personnel involvement, and the budget provides for external consultants. When this approach is selected, in-house personnel act in support roles as required by the external consulting team.

16.4.3 Streamlining Validation Options

Validation testing is almost always an in-house activity that depends heavily upon the skills of application experts. To reduce costs and related efforts, application experts should test all non-mission-critical systems with near-term event horizons, using current in-house testing guidelines. All mission-critical systems and systems with more relaxed event horizons should use standard validation techniques and comparison utilities to verify logical equivalence between production and converted applications. Certification testing should be expedited for all mission-critical systems. Management may want to defer certification testing for all non-mission-critical systems, based on resource and budget availability. Where time and budget permits, management should consider upgrading test scripts for mission-critical systems with a life expectancy of more than 3–4 years.

16.4.4 The Scrap-and-Replace Option

One thing that small shops or shops with extremely limited budgets may find is that system software, or hardware, for that matter, is so old that upgrading it may require an inordinate amount of resources and budget. This resource drain may be well beyond what management is willing to pay to upgrade highly dated technology—particularly if management is of the mind that the current environment has outlived its usefulness.

If this is the case, smaller organizations may want to scrap the entire hardware and software platform in favor of an entirely new set of systems. This is an option for very small shops that do not have overly sophisticated processing requirements. Management should determine if their organization is a candidate for this type of solution by reviewing the following considerations that dictate a total replacement strategy.

- The hardware and software is obsolete and no longer supported by the vendor.

- Most of the systems support basic accounting, payroll, inventory, or other off-the-shelf functions.

- The company is not overly information system-dependent (e.g., not an insurance company, financial institution, or the like).

- The systems can be readily replaced by commercially available solutions.

- A major hardware vendor has divisions that specialize in installing totally new hardware, system software, and ready-to-run applications.

- No tools are available and no vendors will help with making in-house systems Year 2000 compliant.

- The total cost of a full replacement is close to the cost of a Year 2000 upgrade.

When these situations arise, management may want to consider the year 2000 as a blessing in disguise. Management should use extreme caution in pursuing this approach, because tight time frames dictate that only very small IT environments could sustain such a major shift in technology.

16.4.5 Seeking Third-Party Support

One important consideration for small IT shops is to determine where management can go for assistance with the Year 2000 problem. The types of assistance that a small IT organization may require includes planning, outsourcing (factory) interfacing, conversion project management, implementation assistance, tool or task review and guidance, and third-party coordination or validation support. Planning the small-shop, Year 2000 upgrade requires special sensitivities to small budgets, limited staff size, and the skills of long-standing, in-house application and systems support experts. The following types of professional firms and associations should be considered as resources to help with planning and implementing a Year 2000 project.

3. *On a Saturday—or another day when regular business is not being transacted— restart the system from scratch and reset the system date to December 29, 1999.*

4. *Enter several transactions as they would be entered during the regular course of business.*

5. *Shut the system down and restart it, using a system date of (Monday) January 3, 2000.*

6. *Enter several more transactions as they would be entered during the regular course of business.*

7. *Run reports that summarize inventory status, payroll status, accounting status, or other summaries that force the system to look across the 1999 and 2000 dates including:*

   a. Receivable aging across the 1999/2000 year gap

   b. Employee start and termination dates across the 1999/2000 gap

   c. Inventory aging across the 1999/2000 gap

   d. Other examples that cross the century gap

8. *Restart the system one more time and verify that the system date is still set to January 3, 2000.*

9. *Prepare for trouble if any of the following occur:*

   a. System does not work at all when the system date is reset to 2000.

   b. System date resets itself to a date that is prior to 2000 or even to the current date.

   c. The application shows inaccurate information on screens and printed reports.

   d. The system will not accept information at all.

   e. Other abnormalities occur during the test.

10. *When finished, replace all system data with data from the prior day's backup.*

If the system date resets itself to a date prior to 2000 on the second restart, the system BIOS (basic input output system) is likely in need of correction. If the system does not start at all after the second or the third restart attempt, the BIOS and the hardware may be at fault. If the system restarts and the system date remains accurate on each restart but the information on various screens and reports is incorrect (e.g., receivables aging = 98 years), the application code is likely in need of repair. Everything working correctly does not mean that there are no problems, but it does indicate that the system can be easily corrected by the vendor. A true test of this problem requires running several iterations of the system cycle across multiple periods and close inspection of the results by system experts. The vendor will likely be the one to perform this operation to ensure that everything works properly.

16.5.2 Where to Get Help and What to Do About the Problem

The best case scenario is for an existing vendor to communicate a system's exact Year 2000 status to the customer or client. If a system upgrade is required, the vendor should communicate the time frames and the costs related to obtaining this upgrade. The small business provider will have to incorporate this upgrade into future budgets and capital expenditure planning. Maintaining an open and honest relationship with these vendors is the best way to weather the Year 2000 storm.

If the current service provider is either not providing any input or support regarding the Year 2000 dilemma or is just generally in bad standing with the company licensing the system, outside help is probably needed. Figure 16.3 identifies sources of assistance for the small organization that uses in-house systems but does not have in-house information technology expertise.

These sources of assistance, in general order of preference, include other readily accessible system vendors, professional organizations that have member companies with similar information requirements, small business audit services, and outside consulting experts. The general order of preference is based on how much information a company may have about other systems in the market.

An upgrade to a new system requires installing the system, converting or reentering data from the existing system to be used by the new system, user training, and implementation. As a rule, the vendor providing the system will support the bulk of these requirements. When researching the new system, verify that the system is Year 2000 compliant and that the contract clearly states that the system will support data that spans the century mark. If management is unsure of the vendor's level of Year 2000 support, users can try some of the self-diagnostic techniques discussed earlier to verify that everything works properly.

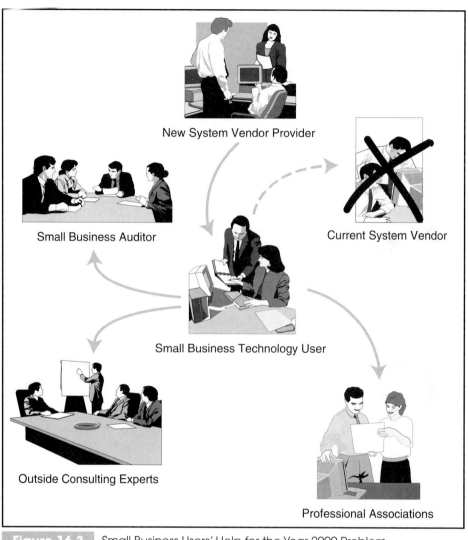

New System Vendor Provider

Small Business Auditor

Current System Vendor

Small Business Technology User

Outside Consulting Experts

Professional Associations

Figure 16.3 Small Business Users' Help for the Year 2000 Problem

16.5.3 Service Bureau Customers

Some small businesses run their system on a service bureau; that is, the system itself is not on the company site and users are linked to a shared system that is installed at the service bureau provider's site. All of the same factors hold true for determining if there is a Year 2000 problem and seeking third-party help to address it. The main difference is that any one user does not control system date settings and cannot fully determine if a system is Year 2000 compliant. In other words, service bureau users are more reliant on truthful vendors than are companies with the system installed at their site.

16.6 Options for Individual Personal Computer Users

Some small companies, such as the small service provider, and individuals running standalone PC systems are not totally immune to the year 2000. These small organizations and individuals may not have any business-specific applications (e.g., accounts payable, payroll), but they may have developed systems using spreadsheets or other facilities that were purchased at the local computer store along with the PC that these systems rely on. The diagnostic tests suggested earlier for small organizations with no in-house technology support also apply to the individual PC user. Because mainstream suppliers of PC-based business software are moving toward Year 2000 compliance and because most users eventually upgrade to newer releases over time, the applications themselves are likely to be immune to the Year 2000 problem.

Systems developed under these applications, however, could be at risk. Spreadsheets and similar financial software should be checked to determine if 2-character date fields are used for business or personal functions. The BIOS problems will probably correct themselves as well, given that users upgrade hardware during the next three years. The self-diagnostic tests suggested earlier can determine if there are BIOS problems with a PC. If so, a quick check with the manufacturer can hopefully provide a resolution as more and more customers become aware of the Year 2000 problem.

16.7 Stay Aware, Be Calm, and Act Judiciously

Barring any laws being passed to force all software vendors to label systems as Year 2000 compliant (these are under discussion by lawmakers in various countries), most small-system users, as well as large-system users, must determine their level of exposure to the Year 2000 problem. The key thing to remember is that small IT organizations or individual PC users have a much smaller problem than that of large-scale IT organizations. The corollary to this point is that smaller organizations have less access to Year 2000 information, tools, large consulting firms, resources, and budget money to address the problem. This being the case, small information technology users should judiciously investigate compliance requirements and the options to be pursued.

Staying aware of how to respond to these issues may be a matter of searching the Internet, sending a representative to conferences, attending local Year 2000 user group sessions, and working with other sources of information. There is no need to panic at this point. Most small companies, with 1–5 million lines of code, should remember that it could be worse. Many multinational corporations and government agencies have 50–100 million lines of code or more. The challenge is here and it clearly will not go away by itself. The sooner small companies proceed with analysis and correction steps, the better their standing when the millennium arrives.

Selection of Year 2000 Service Providers

Chapter 17

Despite the best efforts of many of the top tool developers around the world, century-date compliance projects remain heavily dependent on people resources. Many tasks simply cannot be automated. Even tasks that can be automated require the intervention of trained individuals to interpret findings and verify results. The people involved in a century-date compliance project must have a wide range of abilities, from highly skilled project managers through junior programmers. The number of resources required to complete the project by the turn of the century grows with each delay in project initiation. Further, few IT organizations will be able to defer other pending business requirements. These assignments will tie up resources that would otherwise be assigned to century compliance. As a result, most IT organizations will turn to consultants for many project activities.

Almost every consulting company offering IT services of any form has entered the Year 2000 market. This presents the IT consumers with an unparalleled selection of service offerings to fulfill almost any type of requirement, from supplemental staffing to complete project outsourcing. Among them, consulting firms have access to the widest imaginable range of skills. Many firms have considerable experience at managing large, complex projects, while other firms have strong redevelopment and conversion expertise. Given the number of consulting companies and consultants on the market and range of choices available, it appears that IT organizations are well covered for their century-compliance projects.

Unfortunately, despite their apparent abundance, there are not enough consultants to go around. Even the largest consulting firms can service only a fraction of their client base. The demand for the top consultants is enormous, and many firms will be entirely booked well before the turn of the century. As demand exceeds supply, prices will inevitably rise. Latecomers will pay top dollar for lesser resources. The IT organizations that leap into the market early will get the best resources for the lowest rates. Thus, the best tactic for the Year 2000 Project Offices is to quickly determine their consulting strategy and resource requirements. Armed with this knowledge, they can select and contract the appropriate consulting firms early in the project to guarantee access to these resources when they need them.

This chapter discusses the options for obtaining consulting resources and strategies for selecting and applying those resources. The first section describes the reasons for using consulting services and the benefits that can be expected from those services. The next section covers the range of consulting strategies, both in terms of available types of consulting services and methods for best applying those services. Each type of consulting resource is described along with its benefits and drawbacks. The next two sections discuss vendor selection criteria and the process of writing a Request for Proposal (RFP).

The section on criteria for vendor selection begins by describing the types of consulting vendors in the market along with their normal methods of operation. This is followed by a list of criteria for evaluating these vendors. The large size and fast growth of the Year 2000 market has attracted many marginal consulting vendors, and these criteria will help IT organizations separate hype from reality.

Many IT organizations use RFPs as a method for their vendor selection process. A well-conceived and well-written RFP provides valuable information and can eliminate vendors that do not fit the organization's selection criteria. In contrast, a poorly written RFP will drive away the best vendors, delay the selection process, and even increase the overall cost of the project. Because Year 2000 consulting services are a seller's market for the top consulting firms, many of these firms will not even respond to RFPs that contain unrealistic requirements. The final section of the chapter describes how to create an RFP that accomplishes the selection goals of the Year 2000 Project Office.

17.1 Why Consultants?

The first question an IT organization may ask is, why use consultants at all? These organizations may have large armies of programmers that can theoretically handle their century-compliance projects. Whether an internal staffing approach is even possible depends on the constraints imposed by the project and the ongoing operations of the IT organization. The first constraint is the sheer volume of the effort. Most companies have built their portfolio of applications over thirty or more years. The project teams currently maintaining those applications are staffed to change only a small portion of each application per year. The fixed deadline imposed by the turn of the century requires those resources to be expended over a relatively short period of time. IT organizations that could have completed their compliance project themselves if they had started 5 years ago do not have enough resources to complete the same volume of project work over the next 3 years.

Expertise is another limiting factor. IT organizations have begun to shift their mix of technical skills to newer environments while still supporting their legacy applications that use older technology. Although they may have the number of programmers to complete the migration effort, many of these programmers may not have the necessary language and platform skills. In-house skills may no longer be available for some of the orphaned technologies that still operate in production.

Although Year 2000 projects will cause discretionary initiatives to be deferred, essential business requirements cannot be delayed. The highest payback, most mission-critical new development projects will continue, and strategic initiatives will still be funded. Critical maintenance efforts will similarly continue. These projects will compete for the same internal resources needed for century-date compliance efforts. Given the choice of staffing either new development projects or century-compliance projects with existing staff, most organizations will opt for new development, farming out to consultants the work deemed to be less desirable.

The wide range of consulting services available on the market enables IT organizations to apply consultants in whatever manner best suits their needs. Some of the most common uses for consulting services include:

- **Augmenting in-house staff.**

  This is the typical supplemental staffing approach in which external consultants fill internal resource gaps. Consulting staff can be mixed with existing staff to extend a team or substituted for existing staff, allowing those team members to be reassigned to other projects.

- **Off-loading activities.**

  Activities that do not offer long-term value to the IT organization can be off-loaded to consultants on a project basis. These activities include projects that are not strategic, are deemed undesirable by internal staff, or require skills not available within the IT organization.

- **Adding expertise.**

  Perhaps the best use of consulting services is to add expertise to the project. Consulting companies accumulate expertise from years of delivering large numbers of projects in many different environments. Obtaining this expertise enables IT organizations to decrease their learning curves, gain knowledge in specific technology categories, obtain assistance in project planning and data interpretation, and acquire "best in class" practices for project implementation.

- **Providing direction.**

  The top-tier consulting firms have considerable expertise in managing large scale projects. This level of experience is often lacking in many IT organizations. This expertise is backed by experience in planning and executing analysis and conversion efforts.

  The use of consultants brings many valuable benefits to IT organizations. These benefits should be familiar to those IT organizations that regularly use consulting services in their normal operations.

- **Offer an external perspective.**

  The external perspective offered by consultants helps IT organizations to avoid mistakes and to jump-start their project efforts. Consultants bring the experience of having seen best and worst practices in many IT organizations.

- **Reduce risk and save costs.**

  IT organizations can significantly reduce their risks and save costs by using consulting expertise at strategic points in the project. The experience of the consultants avoids the organization's need to learn by trial and error. Although consultants may seem costly at first, they are often more productive than internal staff, resulting in cost savings over the life of the project.

- **Reduce project time frames.**

  Adding more resources to the Year 2000 project team is often the only method for reducing the project's elapsed time to fit within the century deadline.

- **Retain internal staff.**

  Subcontracting the most rote tasks to consulting firms helps staff retention by avoiding burnout. Internal staff can be applied to projects that offer career growth opportunities.

- **Control headcount.**

  Year 2000 projects require large, but temporary, increases in headcount. Using consultants to gain this headcount avoids the costs and management attention needed to find, hire, and train staff that will be released after project completion.

17.2 Consulting Strategies

There are almost as many consulting strategies as there are consultants. IT organizations have choices in the form of consulting they purchase, the way they apply that consulting, and the type of vendor from whom they purchase the service. These choices are not black-and-white; rather, they are a sliding scale of options that can be set to match almost any situation. Figure 17.1 illustrates this point.

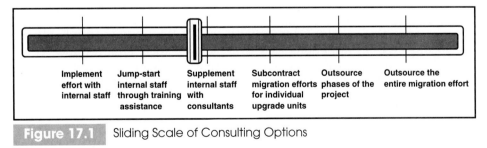

| Implement effort with internal staff | Jump-start internal staff through training assistance | Supplement internal staff with consultants | Subcontract migration efforts for individual upgrade units | Outsource phases of the project | Outsource the entire migration effort |

Figure 17.1   Sliding Scale of Consulting Options

At one extreme is the "do it yourself" approach, using only internal resources; at the other extreme is full outsourcing, using only consultants. There are numerous choices between these extremes. These approaches can be applied on an enterprise basis, or they can be applied by individual projects. Small IT organizations can pick one vendor and one standard approach. Large, distributed IT organizations will require several approaches and potentially many vendors.

The following section describes the different forms of consulting available for Year 2000 projects. No form is perfect for all situations. Each option has its own advantages and disadvantages. The major criteria for selecting the most appropriate form of consulting are the level of expertise required, the number of resources needed, and the level of project management responsibility desired.

Following the forms of consulting is a discussion of approaches for deploying consulting resources. These approaches help an IT organization to determine the most productive methods for applying consultants in their organization.

17.2.1 Types of Consulting Projects

There are five major categories of consulting projects. The first form, internal staffing, doesn't use consultants but is included for comparison. Each of the forms is discussed as a broad category. Needless to say, each form can have numerous variations.

- **Internal staffing.**

    This is the approach used by IT organizations that intend to implement their century-date compliance project themselves. Although some targeted consulting resources can be applied to jump-start the project, all other resources are provided internally. To be successful, the IT organization must have the expertise to plan and manage its project, the skills needed for implementation, and enough resources to complete the project on time. IT organizations should verify their ability to meet these criteria before attempting to apply this approach. IT organizations that overestimate their abilities and require additional resources mid-project may be unable to find those resources on the market. Given its requirements, this approach makes the most sense for IT organizations with limited century-date exposure.

    Advantages

    — Little additional cost; uses staff that is already on the payroll.

    — Internal staff has business-specific knowledge about operations and application design.

— Internal staff has (theoretically) greater loyalty to the company.

— Internal staff is motivated to do the best possible job—they will inherit the results.

Disadvantages

— Draws internal staff away from other projects.

— Requires strong internal project management expertise.

— Requires sufficient staffing levels.

— Requires expertise in performing century-compliance projects as well as all technologies within the enterprise.

— High-stress, low-challenge century-compliance tasks may increase staff turnover.

- **Supplemental staffing.**

  Supplemental staffing is the standard form of consulting used by most IT projects. The project manager determines the number of individuals required and the types of skills desired, then contacts a consulting firm to provide those resources on a time-and-materials basis. These consultants are typically placed on a project alongside internal resources. Although any level of technical skill and management experience can be obtained from this approach, it is more commonly used to gain implementation resources. For instance, few IT organizations will be able to obtain a Year 2000 project manager in this manner. These skills are too rare and too valuable for a consulting firm to provide as supplemental staffing.

  Century-date compliance projects will use supplemental staffing approaches primarily to gain extra resources or to gain specific technical skills. These consultants will be used as temporary labor on resource-intensive activities such as detailed analysis, code and data migration, and testing. In fact, many project consulting firms and tool vendors will use the supplemental staffing approach to augment their staff on project assignments.

  Effectively employing supplemental staffing requires strong internal project management. These consultants arrive with only their skills and must be provided with direction, tools, and methodology. Supplemental staffing is a low-cost alternative for IT organizations that know how to implement a century-date compliance project but lack sufficient implementation resources.

Advantages

— Internal staff manages the project and provides company-specific knowledge.

— Undesirable work tasks can be off-loaded to consultants.

— Supplemental staffing has the lowest cost per resource.

— Gains necessary resources and technical expertise.

— Frees internal staff for other projects.

Disadvantages

— Consultants have little stake in the project; they will not support the applications after migration.

— The IT organization must supply the project methodology and tools.

— Supplemental staff consultants are only as effective as their direction.

— Although supplemental staffing is currently a commodity business, costs will rise and quality resources will become scarce as the year 2000 approaches.

— IT organizations will compete with other IT organizations, vendors, and consulting firms for the best resources.

- **Training and Jump-starting.**

  This approach uses highly experienced consultants to assist IT organizations in setting up Year 2000 projects. These consultants can provide a variety of services ranging from initial project plans to methodology implementation and tool training. Although this approach is usually used to support internal staff, it can also be used to provide project expertise for supplemental staff. These types of services are typically provided by Year 2000 solution vendors, training organizations, and independent consultants. Solution vendors focus on the successful implementation of their tools, and they may provide their own methodology to guide the project. These organizations do not have enough consultants to provide more than training and high-level project planning and management assistance. Training organizations focus on transferring technical and project management skills as well as basic implementation techniques. Independent consultants offer services such as strategic planning,

Year 2000 Project Office setup, tool and vendor selection, training, and ongoing project reviews. The services provided by these consultants are highly dependent on their individual skills.

Advantages

— Helps IT organizations avoid project pitfalls.

— Reduces project costs and risks.

— Can be used with most implementation strategies.

Disadvantages

— These organizations provide only knowledge; implementation results are dependent on the quality of project management and staffing.

— Must be selected carefully to get quality results.

• **Project.**

In this form of consulting, the IT organization turns over a complete project to a consulting vendor. The consulting firm provides the resources and project management to complete the project. The firm often provides its own tools and methodology. Projects range widely in scope and size. The consulting firm may take responsibility for a phase of the overall effort, such as enterprise planning, the migration of an upgrade unit, or the implementation of a testing architecture. These projects can be provided on a fixed price or time-and-materials basis. They can be implemented on site, off site via a conversion factory, or by using offshore resources.

IT organizations will heavily use project consulting to implement their century-compliance efforts. A typical approach will be to divide an enterprise-level Year 2000 project into a series of manageable subprojects to be contracted to project consulting firms. Although the IT organization must monitor project completion, they are freed from the project's daily management and implementation details. Project consulting can be mixed with other forms of consulting to handle special requirements. For example, an IT organization may prefer to handle its own verification activities but contract out the code migration effort. IT organizations can save the expense of tool acquisition and training for peripheral technologies by subcontracting those projects to consultants.

Advantages

— Off-loads full responsibility for all aspects of a project's implementation.

— Uses the consulting firm's expertise, methodology, and tools.

— Avoids the need for internal staff to develop specialized skills that are not useful in the future.

— Project management is provided by the consulting firm.

— Can utilize resources in cheaper locations.

Disadvantages

— In some cases, it is more expensive than other approaches.

— Internal staff doesn't gain experience or expertise from the project (although skills transfer can sometimes be contracted as part of the project.)

— The IT organization is highly dependent on the consulting firm's execution of the project.

— The consultants have limited access to company-specific knowledge.

- **Outsourcing.**

Outsourcing is a larger-scale version of the project form of consulting. In this case, the consulting firm takes responsibility for most of the Year 2000 effort for a large business area or even an entire enterprise. The consulting firm may provide all of the resources for the project, or it may serve as the general contractor, providing project management capabilities and using conversion factories, supplemental staff, and offshore resources to handle various project tasks. In all cases, the consulting firm has total responsibility for successful project completion.

Outsourcing does not eliminate the IT organization's responsibility for the overall Year 2000 effort, nor does it cover all activities. Important tasks, such as negotiating interface and support issues with company customers, cannot be handled through outsourcing. Further, unless the IT organization outsources future application support to the same vendor, they will inherit the results of the project. For these reasons, an IT organization will still need to maintain a Year 2000 Project Office and supply some technical and managerial resources to the project.

The outsourcing approach makes the most sense for IT organizations that can more profitably devote their resources and management attention to other projects. Although outsourcing frees internal resources for other uses, it requires significant funding to cover its costs. One typical scenario is to outsource long-term support for legacy applications. The consulting firm assumes responsibility for all support activities, including century-date compliance. In this scenario, the consulting firm remains responsible for the application after the year 2000.

Advantages

— The consulting firm handles the entire migration effort.

— Internal resources are freed for other tasks.

— Consulting firms devote their best resources to their largest projects.

— If the project is coupled to support outsourcing, the consulting firm has long-term incentive to control the quality of the project.

— Offshore and onsite project work can be combined to establish round-the-clock, 24-hour conversion activity.

Disadvantages

— The IT organization is entirely dependent on the performance of the outsourcer.

— Outsourcing requires careful vendor selection and complex contract negotiations.

— This is the costliest approach in terms of extra budget dollars, as all resources are provided by the outsourcer.

17.2.2 Deployment Strategies

Consulting services can be deployed in a number of different manners. These options are not mutually exclusive but can be applied in any manner that fits the requirements of the IT organization. The deployment strategies listed below primarily apply to project consulting. They offer different means of partitioning projects among consulting firms and internal staff or even other consulting firms. Figure 17.2 illustrates how a century-date compliance project can be partitioned through deployment options.

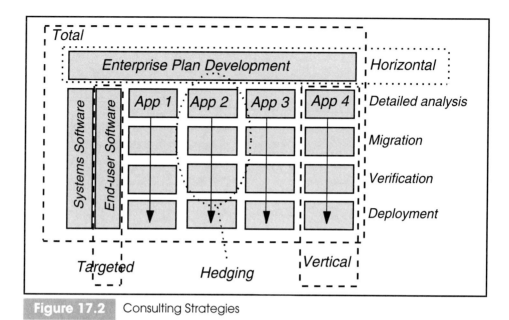

Figure 17.2 Consulting Strategies

IT organizations may want to consider the use of more than one consulting vendor as a method of reducing project risk. This approach decreases the organization's dependence on the performance of any single vendor and provides backup in case of problems. This solution is not without trade-offs. Consulting firms may have difficulty cooperating with each other on projects, and they may not devote their best resources to projects where they have only a limited stake.

- **Total.**

  This deployment strategy turns over full responsibility to the consulting vendor for an enterprise or business area migration project. It is the same as the outsourcing form of consulting just described.

- **Horizontal.**

  The horizontal strategy partitions projects by implementation phases. In this strategy, enterprise assessment is one consulting project, detailed assessment and migration is another, and so forth. This approach allows the IT organization to contract each assignment to a consulting firm specializing in that type of project. Strategic IT consulting firms are best equipped to handle enterprise assessments. Migrations can be handled by offshore vendors or through conversion factories to reduce costs. Testing can be performed by internal resources or a consulting firm that specializes in testing. This approach optimizes the performance of each project phase, but it may be difficult to manage and lead to fingerpointing if problems arise between layers.

- **Vertical.**

  The vertical strategy partitions projects by business area, technology, or upgrade unit. In this case, the selected vendor or internal team is responsible for all activities, from assessment through testing for their project. This approach is well suited for decentralized IT organizations or for situations where applications vary widely by strategic value and volatility. Older, highly stable applications can be sent for off-site conversion, while highly volatile and strategic applications are converted by internal staff. This strategy is easy to manage and results in the greatest level of independence between projects.

- **Targeted.**

  This strategy chooses isolated projects to contract to consultants. The IT organization uses internal staff or supplemental staffing to handle the bulk of the migration effort but turns over any projects that fall outside of their standard implementation approach. These projects may be selected by their technology, platforms, skill requirements, or even physical location. This method is useful for avoiding the need to invest in skills and tools for handling isolated situations. Internal staff is devoted to migration tasks with future value.

- **Hedging.**

  The hedging strategy applies to IT organizations that want to reduce their overall corporate risk while implementing a full century-date compliance effort. In this strategy, the Year 2000 Project Office immediately identifies the few most mission-critical applications for the corporation. Minimum effort should be devoted to this effort. These applications do not need scheduling or assessment to determine when they should be migrated—the company will suffer severe damage if they fail. The detailed assessment and conversion of these applications is immediately contracted as project work to a consulting vendor. In the meantime, the Year 2000 Project Office continues with the enterprise assessment and other standard project phases for the remaining applications. Migrating the most critical applications removes some of the pressure from the bulk of the project and lowers the overall risk to the corporation. The experience gained from their migration can be applied to the remaining applications.

17.3 Selecting Consulting Vendors

Given the importance of consulting support to century-date compliance projects, IT organizations should select their vendors carefully. The fixed deadline for century-date compliance provides little leeway for mistakes in vendor selection. IT organizations forced to switch vendors midstream are in double jeopardy—they are already late in the project and finding a replacement vendor will be difficult because the best vendors will already be booked. For this reason, IT firms should consider contingency strategies for their vendors.

There are several ways to mitigate this risk. The first is the use of multiple vendors, as discussed above under deployment strategies. Another method is to limit vendor selection to top-tier consulting firms. These firms depend on long-term relationships with their customers for future business and are large enough to guarantee access to project resources. Given their experience, they are less likely to overcommit resources. A third approach is to engage the IT organization's preferred vendor(s). Almost every IT organization that frequently uses consultants has one or more local consulting firms that consider it a strategic account. These firms, regardless of size and background, are far more likely to invest whatever effort is necessary to make the project successful. This third strategy is recommended for smaller IT organizations. Most of the larger consulting firms have less interest in providing support to smaller, peripheral customers than those that they consider strategic accounts. However, even the smallest IT organizations have smaller regional consulting firms that consider them a strategic account.

When selecting a consulting vendor, remember that for Year 2000 consulting companies, while still competitive, it is a seller's market. Consulting firms can support only a fraction of their existing customer base and are likely to limit their engagements to those customers that they feel will be successful and that will lead to business in the future. The top vendors can easily avoid those IT organizations that request onerous contract terms, are too price sensitive, or have a history of being difficult. Although the term "partnership" is overused in describing relationships between consulting firms and their clients, it has meaning for century-date compliance efforts. When faced with the inevitable staffing and support pressures that will arise in the last two years of this century, IT organizations having strong relationship with their consulting vendors will get the best support. The extra resources that they need will likely come at the expense of IT organizations that used a bargain-hunting approach to their staffing needs.

17.3.1 Types of Vendors

Virtually every consulting firm with any legacy software experience has entered the Year 2000 market. Even firms without a direct connection to Year 2000, such as client/server development firms, position themselves as a potential solution, recommending themselves as an alternative to migration. The style, cost, and level of service provided by a consulting firm varies widely by its type. Understanding the types of firms on the market enables IT organizations to select the range of services that best meet their requirements.

- **Tier 1—The "big six" and equivalents.**

    This category consists of the largest multinational consulting firms and outsourcers. These organizations are present in all major markets, offer a full range of services, and have access to enormous numbers of consultants. They are methodology oriented and have strong, large-scale project management experience. Given their size, geographic distribution and long-term stability, these firms are well suited to handle large, widely distributed century-compliance projects. These firms tend to be quite expensive compared to their peers, but they are a good choice for IT organizations seeking to outsource major portions of their projects.

- **Tier 2—National project-oriented firms.**

    These are large IT-oriented consulting firms with thousands of consultants and a wide distribution of offices. This category of consulting firm has been the most aggressive in pursuing Year 2000 business. These firms tend to have the greatest level of experience in supporting legacy applications. They are project-focused and have project management capabilities. Firms at this level have Year 2000 methodologies and either their own tools or partnerships with major tool vendors. Because their pricing structure is significantly less than the tier-1 firms, these vendors are a strong choice for larger project consulting and outsourcing for most IT organizations.

- **Tier 3—National supplemental staffing firms.**

  This category comprises consulting firms that specialize in supplemental staffing services on a multiregional or national basis. These firms are generally not project oriented; however, they can, if needed, assemble a project team. Some of these vendors have begun specific Year 2000 practices but most supply resources to their clients' existing projects or supplement the resources on projects won by tier-1 and tier-2 firms. These firms may have relationships with tool vendors or conversion factories. Firms at this level are not suited for managing large century-date projects, but they are cost-effective for project work and supplemental staffing.

- **Tier 4—Regional and local contract programming firms.**

  These firms specialize in placing contract programmers. They rarely have access to strong project management experience and are mostly too small to have methodologies or relationships with major tool vendors. While some of the firms attempt to bid project work, they rarely have the experience to handle major projects. Their primary advantage is the ability to supply lower-cost resources to supplemental staffing projects managed by their clients.

- **Year 2000 firms.**

  Several consulting firms specialize exclusively in Year 2000 support. These firms tend to concentrate their services in the enterprise planning and assessment phases of the project, but they may branch out as their clients progress to implementation and testing. Although these firms gain considerable Year 2000-specific experience, they do not have the resources and national presence to handle very large projects. As a result, these firms are most useful in a horizontal, consulting deployment strategy.

- **Independent consultants.**

  A large number of independent consultants are entering the Year 2000 market. The best of these consultants can save IT organizations significant time and money in starting their Year 2000 projects. IT organizations are best served by engaging independent consultants directly rather than through a larger consulting firm. This practice enables the consultants to be truly independent in their recommendations. Use independent consultants for strategic planning, vendor selection, and ongoing project quality reviews.

- **Offshore outsourcers.**

  Numerous offshore consulting firms have entered the market. Indian outsourcing firms have received the most press, but offshore resources are available from Eastern Europe, the Philippines, and even the Canadian Maritimes. The largest offshore outsourcing firms have offices in the U.S. and staff their projects with a mixture of on-site and offshore resources. This geographic diversity enables these firms to take advantage of time zone differences to run three-shift migration operations. Smaller outsourcers have relationships with tier-1 and tier-2 consulting firms to provide low-cost staff during resource-intensive phases of the project. While IT organizations view the primary advantage of these firms as low-cost staffing, offshore vendors often have access to excellent technical staff and have considerable experience in delivering projects. Given their cost structure and skills, offshore vendors are an excellent option for project work that can be easily packaged and for rarer technologies that are not supported by programming tools.

- **Conversion factories.**

  Conversion factories fall between consulting companies and software vendors. These vendors operate an off-site conversion facility that uses their own set of tools for detailed analysis, conversion, and unit testing of application code. Their customers package and ship their applications by upgrade unit for conversion at this facility. Most of these vendors began in the conversion business by offering other types of conversion, such as those between hardware platforms, operating systems, or databases, and have adapted this technology for century-date compliance projects. By mixing tools and consultants in an off-site facility, these vendors avoid the need to create the documentation and robust product interfaces needed to sell their tools directly. Some conversion vendors pursue business directly; however, most work together with other consulting firms offering their services within a larger contract. The consulting firm assumes responsibility for selecting and packaging the code for conversion and the testing and production integration of the results.

- **Software vendors.**

  Many of the software vendors in the Year 2000 market maintain their own consulting organizations. These organizations enable the vendors to offer full solutions rather than solely products. These consulting organizations usually specialize in planning, training, and tool deployment. These services are provided directly to the vendor's clients or are supplied to the vendor's consulting partners. Some software vendors take their services a step further by accepting project work. In these cases, the vendor provides project managers and subcontracts the staffing of the project to a tier-2 or tier-3 consulting firm. Software vendor consultants tend to be expensive; however, their skills are honed to Year 2000 projects, usually making them a good value.

- **Computer resource providers.**

    Many IT organizations do not have enough computer resources to adequately handle their Year 2000 efforts. These organizations must either purchase additional hardware or purchase time from a computer service bureau. These service bureaus offer a number of services that go beyond simply supplying additional computer resources. They provide rigorous testing environments that can be set up to emulate the Year 2000 crossover. These environments enable their clients to fully test an application with all of its associated system software across the century transition. Most service bureaus require that the IT client bring all system software and tools needed to run these tests. These firms also supply consulting assistance for their clients in analysis, migration, and testing activities.

17.3.2 Selection Criteria

Given the large variety of consulting firms and available service options, it is impossible to develop one set of evaluation criteria that will fit all situations. For instance, an IT organization seeking supplemental staff is taking an entirely different risk than an organization seeking to outsource an enterprise-level migration effort. Both organizations will use a different set of criteria to select their vendors. The first organization is less concerned about the reputation and skills of the vendor but highly concerned about the skills of the individual being hired. Conversely, the organization considering outsourcing will care very much about the consulting firm and very little about the individuals that will staff the project.

Cost considerations are a factor for most IT organizations. Costs are directly related to the level of service received and the level of risk assumed by each party. If an IT organization requests a fixed price bid from a large consulting firm for the entire project after providing only minimal data about the application portfolio, they will pay the highest possible price for their services. Conversely, organizations willing to break the overall project into smaller pieces and subcontract those pieces to the most effective consulting sources will pay the lowest price for their project. Price should not be the primary consideration when selecting a vendor. Inexperienced vendors will underprice a project and then fail in its execution. Further, high quality skills and services cost money; skimping on cost will usually result in lower quality support.

The following selection criteria are meant primarily for IT organizations evaluating consulting firms for project work or outsourcing. Many of these criteria are based on common sense and can be applied to any type of consulting situation. Any consulting firm can claim to handle century-date compliance projects, but their ability to deliver those projects is based on their reputation, project management capabilities, and expertise.

- **Reliability and reputation.**

    The best method for judging a consulting firm is by its track record. Given the importance and risk of a century-date compliance project, it is essential to select a vendor with the experience and track record for delivering complex projects on time and within budget. While there are no infallible criteria for evaluating the potential success of a given project, the following criteria provide a good indication of the vendor's track record.

    — *Length of time in market:* Evaluate both the length of time the vendor has been providing IT consulting services and the length of time the vendor has been in the Year 2000 market. The best vendors have a long history in the IT market, as shown by steady growth and consistent profitability. This is indicative of successful results. Similarly, the timing of the vendor's entry into the Year 2000 market indicates an understanding of customer needs as well as their experience level.

    — *Number of century-compliance projects underway:* Successful vendors are winning many century-compliance projects. Those vendors are gaining valuable expertise in project delivery. Clear indicators of quality service are a high percentage of follow-on projects and quick progression between project phases in ongoing projects.

    — *Customer base and references:* The types of companies in a vendor's customer base are a strong indicator of their ability to handle projects for IT organizations of a given size and industry sector. IT organizations should select consulting firms with experience in companies similar to theirs. Checking references is a must. Do not restrict reference checks to customer names provided by the vendor. Network at tradeshows and in professional organizations to find other customers of the vendor. Forewarned is forearmed.

— *Post-2000 strategy:* What will the vendor do once the century-compliance project is complete? Look for vendors with a long-term business strategy. This ensures that the vendor will support the results of the migration work after the turn of the century. Vendors looking for outsourcing projects and future development work have added incentive to perform a quality job during migration.

- **Project management capabilities.**

  Year 2000 projects are predominately an exercise in project management. Do not select any vendor that does not have a demonstrable track record in project management. Interview potential project managers carefully. Be skeptical of any vendors that must recruit project managers for their projects. The market for Year 2000 project managers is already very tight at the time of this writing. Few vendors will be successful at recruiting quality managers in such a tight time frame.

- **Expertise and resources.**

  Year 2000 projects require a great deal of expertise and a large number of resources to execute. Be sure that any selected consulting firm has sufficient quantities of both to support its level of consulting. Although a firm's marketing literature may be impressive, its actual practices are more telling. Strong staff-training programs, availability of a formal Year 2000 methodology, and solid relationships with tool vendors demonstrate the firm's experience and commitment to the Year 2000 market. Consulting firms without these characteristics should not be considered for project assignments.

  — *Consultant base:* Ensure that the consulting firm has a strong base of trained consultants that are locally available to staff and manage the project. Be sure that the firm's skill base matches organizational needs. Beware of overcommitment. Firms will sometimes sell more projects in an area than they are able to support. Request staffing guarantees in the project contract.

— *Tool usage:*   An excellent method for determining the skills and sophistication of a consulting firm is by evaluating their tool vendor relationships. The top consulting firms will have relationships with the top tool vendors. Other consulting firms have developed their own tools. Internally developed tools are fine as long as the vendor is willing to adopt better tools if they become available. Consulting firms that do not have specific tool vendor relationships often claim that they will use "the best tools for a given project." This is a weak excuse for inexperience and lack of investment in the market. Firms with strong vendor relationships or proprietary tools have experience using those tools and have heavily invested in staff training.

— *Methodology:*   The availability of a strong Year 2000 methodology is the best indicator of a consulting firm's commitment to the market and ability to execute. The use of a methodology enables the firm to replicate its best practices in all of its projects and guarantees consistent results.

While the preceding criteria can be applied to any large consulting firm, independent consultants need their own criteria. Unfortunately, anyone can become an independent consultant, leading to great variation in expertise and quality. The top independent consultants meet or exceed the expertise available in major consulting firms, whereas the lowest-level consultants may be castoffs from those firms. Select independent consulting firms using a modified form, described below, of the above criteria.

- **Length of time on the market.**

  Very few independent consultants survive in the market beyond two years. Exceeding this time span is an indicator of the consultant's success, which in turn is related to project delivery capabilities.

- **Reputation.**

  Given the variance in independent consultants, it is especially important to check references and evaluate experience. Top consultants will have impeccable references. The consultant's publications and speaking engagements are also indications of reputation and expertise. Top consultants are widely published and are frequently requested for industry conferences.

- **Market knowledge.**

  Select consultants for strategic planning projects, based upon their overall knowledge of the market. Consultants must keep abreast of market developments, such as new tools and techniques, in order to offer value to the project.

- **Customer base.**

  The number and quality of the consultants' customers are another important indicator of their capabilities. Beware of consultants whose entire experience encompasses only one or two clients.

- **Industry relationships.**

  The best independent consultants have relationships with many tool vendors and consulting firms but are not tied to any specific firm. The consultant should disclose any potential conflicts of interest before the start of the engagement. The consultant's relationships are extremely valuable to the client as a source of potential solutions. Using these relationships, consultants can assemble solutions unavailable through other means.

17.4 Writing an RFP

Although Requests for Proposals (RFPs) are not required to contract with consulting service providers, they are frequently used by IT organizations in both the public and private sectors. The goal of an RFP is to facilitate vendor selection. Project requirements and constraints are documented within the RFP and sent to all interested vendors. Vendors that meet the requirements within the RFP respond with a proposal. In theory, since the proposals all meet requirements, the IT organization can easily select the best proposal by comparing their respective merits. Used properly, a well-conceived and well-written RFP provides valuable information and can eliminate vendors that do not fit the organization's selection criteria. Unfortunately, many RFPs are poorly written and overly ambitious in content. These RFPs often bring responses that are the exact opposite of the intended result. Unrealistic RFPs drive away vendors who realize that they cannot profitably deliver the project. Because Year 2000 consulting services are a seller's market for the top consulting firms, many of these firms will not even respond to RFPs that contain unrealistic requirements. The firms that do respond either do not understand the requirements or are so desperate for business that they are willing to accept onerous terms. Neither situation is likely to end in a successful project. If RFPs are going to be used at all, they must be realistic and clearly written.

17.4.1 When to Use an RFP

RFPs are not required for all projects. If the project requirements are clearly defined and the list of potential vendors is small, the IT organization can forego creating an RFP, meet with vendors directly, and evaluate the resulting proposals. Because century-compliance projects contain many similarities from organization to organization, vendors do not need all of the information typically contained in an RFP to create their proposals. Most vendors can obtain the necessary information through interviews and other data collection methods. Avoiding the RFP process can save valuable time.

When the IT organization needs assistance in refining its requirements, RFPs are useful as a method of consolidating project requirements into a single document. This document can be shared and reviewed within the organization to ensure that it truly reflects project needs. Used in this, manner the RFP is valuable as a means of coming to a common understanding about the project with the vendor.

An RFP should never be created to gather basic information about a project topic. The individuals creating the RFP must be well versed in century-date compliance projects before they begin writing. Failure to do so will result in an overly broad RFP and will communicate the organization's lack of understanding to potential vendors. Attending training sessions and scheduling initial vendor presentations before writing an RFP will help the writers focus their requirements to match the capabilities available on the market.

17.4.2 Guidelines for Writing RFPs

A complete discussion on how to write an effective RFP merits its own book. However, the following guidelines will measurably improve any RFP. RFPs are the most valuable when they are well researched and are limited to reasonable requests. The consulting contract process is ultimately a matter of shifting work and risk for cost. The greater the work and risk for the consulting firm, the higher the cost of the project. The goal of the RFP writer is to reflect the correct balance between the RFP's requests and the likely cost of the project.

- **Thoroughly understand project requirements before including them in an RFP.**

  This rule follows the cliché "be careful about what you ask for, because you might just get it." RFP writers often include marginal requirements that greatly increase the cost and difficulty of the resulting project. Be sure that all requirements are absolutely necessary and be willing to accept alternatives if a vendor suggests a more optimal solution.

- **Be forthright about project information.**

  Consulting firms need information to refine their proposal to effectively meet client needs. The less information they receive, the more generalized their proposal and the more contingency effort has to be included in the proposal, leading to a higher price. Inadequate information forces a vendor to create an estimate large enough to cover any project contingency.

- **Keep requirements realistic.**

  It is easy to create requirements that no vendor can meet. Often, unrealistic requirements reflect a lack of knowledge on the part of the writer. They provide little purpose other than to waste time and eliminate knowledgeable vendors. Rather than aiming for perfection, select requirements that can actually be delivered.

- **Avoid draconian terms.**

  Another common flaw in RFP writing is requiring vendors to agree to unreasonable performance terms, both in the delivery of the proposal and the delivery of the project. Some IT organizations actually boast about the vendor cost of responding to their RFPs. Since this is a seller's market for consulting services, no vendor will respond to draconian terms. For example, do not require the vendor to respond with a 100-page proposal within one week, or to warranty their project results at a level greater than that achievable with internal resources.

- **Avoid overspecifying the details of project delivery.**

  The RFP should restrict itself to project requirements and leave the details of meeting those requirements to the vendor. For example, requiring a vendor to use a conversion factory as the method for handling code migration may preclude that vendor from offering an even more cost-effective method.

- ## Be careful about tying pricing to requirements.

  Pricing is an important characteristic of any RFP. It makes no sense to receive proposals that greatly exceed the IT organization's budget. However, pricing is directly related to project requirements. A common mistake in RFP writing is to place pricing restrictions that preclude vendors from meeting the RFP's requirements. If budget is a consideration, it is better to state a budget restriction and allow the vendors to propose the level of effort possible within those bounds. Conversely, if the requirements are absolute, let the vendors determine the pricing.

- ## Avoid excessive vendor influence.

  Vendors are always happy to assist the RFP writing process in any way they can. Be wary of vendor suggestions for requirements that may eliminate other vendors or that skew the RFP too closely to their offerings. If an RFP is written to favor a particular vendor, why not simply skip the process and hire the vendor directly?

- ## Be flexible when reviewing RFP responses.

  Despite everyone's best efforts, vendors may not be able to completely meet RFP requirements. If most of the responding vendors cannot meet a specific requirement, it is probably unreasonable. A vendor may respond with a solution that doesn't meet RFP requirements but offers a solution that is superior to those requirements. In each of these situations, the IT organization is best served by being flexible in its selection process. The RFP should be a tool for obtaining the best possible solution rather than a barrier against innovation.

- ## Seek assistance.

  When in doubt, seek assistance in creating the RFP. This assistance is easy available from independent consultants or consulting firms specializing in RFP creation. Using a subject matter expert ensures that the RFP is reasonable and that the IT organization is adequately protected against omissions.

Part 4

Strategic Implications of the Year 2000

Most IT organizations view the Year 2000 problem as a necessary evil that will cost tens of millions of dollars, tie up endless resources, and net absolutely nothing. This fatalistic view is shared by most people as the century draws to an end. A growing number of individuals, however, have discovered that there are hidden benefits in applying a comprehensive solution to the Year 2000 problem. These people are viewed with skepticism by IT counterparts. What good, after all, can come of a project with such narrowly defined goals? The answer is that significant value can be gained, based on a willingness to fully understand the nature of the Year 2000 challenge and its myriad of solutions.

Uncovering hidden opportunity in a Year 2000 project requires that management examine the issue in a broader light. Although it is one of many initiatives presented to senior management, the Year 2000 has several unique aspects. A Year 2000 project demands complete accounting of IT and non-IT systems during the inventory phase. It requires broad scrutiny of 2- to 3-year plans to determine migration, replacement, and phase-out strategies. Additionally, long-standing infrastructure issues must be addressed in order to achieve success. Finally, the year 2000 is likely the first legacy-related project requiring a multiyear budget in excess of $20–$30 million.

This type of high-cost, low-payback problem tends to draw little time or interest from senior executives. The most common response is to assign a manager or task force to determine the cost of a solution and then pay a third-party service supplier to make the problem go away. A monthly or quarterly status meeting becomes the sole link between senior executives and the Year 2000 project. This raises several questions.

- Why does management ignore the relationship between this high-cost initiative and other strategic planning efforts when one directly impacts the other?

- How can configuration management, quality assurance, internal audit, and other areas ignore data collected by the Year 2000 team that directly benefits these areas?

- Can management afford not to institutionalize the benefits accrued from the most expensive initiative likely to be implemented in this, or the next, century?

How senior management addresses these issues impacts the ability of the organization to compete successfully well into the next century. The successful IT organization must leverage critical software assets and scarce resources by synchronizing strategic planning and infrastructure stabilization activity with the Year 2000 project. To ignore this requirement is more than just an opportunity lost—it could impact the long-term viability of the organization itself.

Chapter 18

Gaining Value from a Year 2000 Effort

The dawning of the year 2000 and its impact on computer systems have raised industry consciousness about production applications. IT organizations throughout the world are suddenly realizing the importance of their "bread and butter" application systems and the impact on their corporate operations if these systems fail to faithfully execute. Unfortunately, rather than inspiring IT to invest in the future of its legacy applications, this new awareness is tainted by the misplaced belief that most IT organizations will spend millions of dollars modifying these applications to handle Year 2000 dates and get nothing in return. This viewpoint stems from the conviction that the role of IT is building new systems and that anything that diverges from that role is valueless.

A constant request from IT managers is to find a way to gain value from a century-date compliance project. These managers are often disappointed in their hopes to use their Year 2000 initiative as justification for replacing their legacy applications. Unless the project can deliver new business functionality, they reason, it does not offer any benefits to their corporation.

While project time constraints preclude gaining benefits from wholesale application replacement, Year 2000 compliance initiatives are far from a low-value project. Aside from offering corporations the ultimate benefit—allowing them to remain in business—Year 2000 initiatives enable IT organizations to apply many of their century-date compliance investments to the long-term betterment of their production application portfolios and support infrastructure. They can apply the knowledge gained to their new development activities to build higher-quality applications and prevent the occurrence of future Year 2000-type problems.

Enlightened IT organizations take a broad view of their role within their corporation. They see themselves as an integral component of the businesses that they support. They are willing to invest their efforts wherever they will maximize the return to the business. For these organizations, Year 2000 conversions, while painful and costly, offer an opportunity to correct mistakes from the past while positioning for the future. Viewed from this perspective, Year 2000 initiatives can be leveraged to provide considerable organizational value with little, if any, additional investment of resources or capital.

This chapter explores some of the key ways that IT organizations can leverage their experience from Year 2000 initiatives to gain future value. It explores four principal areas for gaining value.

The first area views the Year 2000 solution as building a foundation for implementing formal application management techniques to more effectively manage the application portfolio in the future. Application Management changes the role of the IT organization from a reactive maintainer of production applications to a proactive manager dedicated to optimizing the value of those applications to the corporation.

The second area examines the improvement of the quality of the application portfolio. By slightly redirecting their century-date compliance efforts, IT organizations can eliminate useless applications, technologies, and programs from their portfolios as well as take measures to enhance quality to reduce future maintenance and enhancement efforts.

The third area takes advantage of century-date compliance investments to improve the application support environment. The knowledge, tools, techniques, and test environments built and acquired for a Year 2000 initiative are fully applicable to future support activities.

The fourth, and perhaps most important, area explores the lessons that can be learned from the Year 2000 crisis and how those lessons can be used to gain a better understanding of the development and support processes. The difficulties encountered during this project justify standards, reusability, and other improvements in development processes and support environments. This will ensure that IT staffers will not encounter the same difficulties in future projects. Reflecting on the aftermath of a century-date compliance effort offers hope for avoiding similar crises after the year 2000.

18.1 Foundation for Application Management

Application Management is an objective, business-oriented approach for proactively managing a portfolio of business applications in order to maximize their ability to support corporate business strategies. Although applications are not "physical" assets, from a management perspective they share many of the same characteristics of capital assets such as plants and equipment. They have a life expectancy, they must be maintained or they break down, they can become obsolete through advances in technologies, and their effectiveness is often determined by the skills of their operators and maintainers. Given these characteristics, it is surprising that most corporations use far less formal methods for managing their production software than they do for managing their production equipment.

The Year 2000 crisis developed to a large degree from supporting applications on an ad hoc basis rather than employing the formal asset management practices used elsewhere in the corporation. The high visibility of the Year 2000 issue in corporate boardrooms is causing senior executives to question the methods their IT organizations are using to manage their application assets. The growth of application outsourcing attests to their unhappiness with current approaches. Fortunately, IT organizations can use the knowledge they gained during their century-date migration efforts as a foundation to implement more formal approaches for managing their applications.

The Application Management approach rises above traditional distinctions between new development, enhancement, and maintenance activities. Although the greatest proportion of any IT budget is spent on existing applications, Application Management is not a discipline for application maintenance, but rather a method for determining the right mixture of IT investment in all phases of the application life cycle. It is based upon the following three principles.

- **Business applications are valuable corporate assets.**

  Business software represents a major investment of corporate financial and intellectual capital. This investment has grown significantly in value over the last 25 to 30 years. These applications are the foundation of many corporate operations and often provide the unique capabilities that form a corporation's competitive advantages. As demonstrated by the Year 2000 crisis, few corporations could recover from the loss of their application software.

- **These assets can be measured and managed as an investment portfolio.**

  Application performance measurements can be derived and used to determine the application's effectiveness at supporting its business function(s). Much of this information is gathered during the enterprise assessment portion of a Year 2000 project. In an Application Management approach, these measurements are used to contrast the applications in a corporate portfolio by investment needs and value to the corporation to provide an objective approach for directing IT strategies and investments.

- **Investments in business applications can be optimized to provide the greatest overall return for the corporation.**

  All applications are not equal. Some applications support mission-critical functions, whereas others are less strategic. Small investments in certain applications may provide large rewards for the corporation, whereas investments in other applications may never be returned. An understanding of corporate goals and application performance to attain those goals enables managers to target available resources to the applications and support strategies that provide the greatest overall benefit to the corporation.

  The foundation of Application Management is obtaining a full corporate inventory. Capturing this information and its associated measurements is necessary to perform investment analyses of business applications. These analyses are used to create a formal Application Management plan.

  Century-date compliance projects greatly facilitate efforts to implement Application Management by providing a full and accurate inventory of the corporate portfolio of applications. Every Year 2000 project captures this inventory during the enterprise assessment phase to scope the size of the century-compliance effort. This inventory is the basis for a corporate repository and is valuable for planning, scoping the size of future initiatives, and supporting maintenance impact analysis.

Century-date compliance projects also capture information about the functional quality, technical quality, strategic value, and life cycle stage of each application. This information is used during the project to select migration strategies, determine migration priority, and to develop triage strategies. Although not as detailed as would be required for an ideal Application Management plan, the information captured for a century-date compliance project is more than sufficient to develop an initial plan. Because the century-date compliance effort touches virtually every application across a corporate enterprise, it provides an excellent opportunity to proactively examine application strengths, weaknesses, and opportunities for improvement. It identifies applications that should be replaced, as well as applications that are good candidates for migration to newer technologies. This information is the basis for the Application Management plan. Figure 18.1 illustrates the use of a Portfolio Quadrant chart to rank the applications by their characteristics. This chart positions applications by technical and functional quality, illustrates their strategic value to the organization as well as their relative size. Figure 18.2 shows how that information can be used to develop high-level application investment strategies.

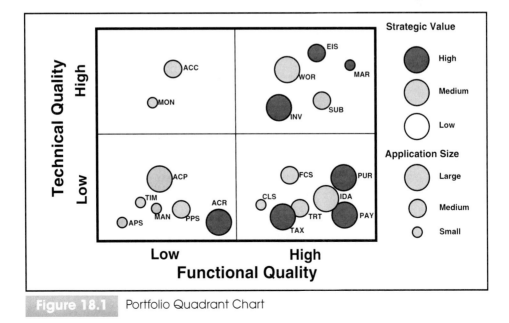

Figure 18.1   Portfolio Quadrant Chart

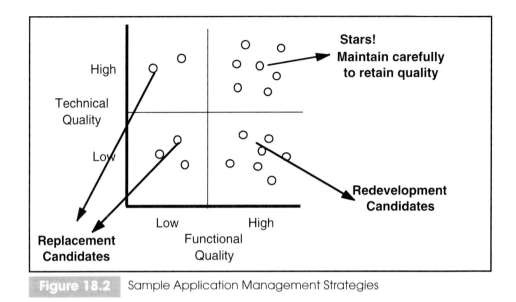

Figure 18.2   Sample Application Management Strategies

Once created, the Application Management plan provides IT managers with the data needed to make informed decisions about their application portfolios. This approach offers managers a number of valuable benefits over less formal approaches for selecting application strategies. These benefits include:

- **Targeting investments to provide the greatest return.**

  Contrasting applications by their strategic value and investment requirements enables managers to direct their resources to the applications and improvements that provide the highest level of value to the business.

- **Selecting the most appropriate optimization strategy for a given application.**

  The technical and functional quality ratings of an application identify the type of improvements that are necessary for an application. The strategic value determines the importance of making those improvements, and the cost and life cycle stage determine the appropriate strategy. Numerous strategies are available, ranging from developing a new system, purchasing a software package, renovating and extending an existing application, to simply sustaining an application "as is."

- **Providing measures for reevaluating performance.**

  The measurements from the initial Application Management plan serve as a baseline for future analysis. Data from subsequent analyses is compared to quantify the effect of improvements and to document changes in IT performance.

- **Providing data for cost justification.**

  Establishing the cost of application support and quantifying the business value of an application provide methods for justifying improvement costs or replacement efforts. The cost of making enhancements to an existing application can be compared to the cost of application replacement to offer a cost-based approach for determining application obsolescence.

- **Identifying and replicating "best practices".**

  Comparing the performance of similar applications enables the identification and replication of internal best practices.

- **Identifying and correcting problems before they become serious.**

  Similar to other assets, business applications require attention to ensure that they continue to operate in an effective manner. Contrasting data from subsequent Application Management plans allows managers to identify and correct slips in technical quality, functional quality, or support efficiency before the problems become critical.

18.2 Enhanced Application Portfolio

IT organizations can use their century-date compliance project to "clean up" and enhance the quality of their application portfolios. Software quality tends to degrade over the years from the effects of repeated maintenance, and application libraries accumulate many unused versions of application code. Because the century-date compliance effort necessitates identifying and certifying all active software, it presents an opportunity to eliminate unused software and to apply redevelopment techniques to improve the quality of the programs that remain. The time and resource constraints of most century-date compliance projects will prevent many IT organizations from implementing improvements that are not directly related to compliance efforts. Even limited improvements can have a significant effect on reducing future support costs. Further, it should not stop those organizations from noting candidates for future improvement projects.

The list below encompasses application portfolio improvements that can arise from a century-date compliance project. Some of these improvements are side effects from migration efforts; others require the use of additional resources. IT organizations should consider applying additional resources to gain these benefits if those resources are available, the incremental cost is very low for benefits gained, and the extra effort does not detract from other century-date compliance efforts.

- **Eliminate old technologies.**

  As described in Chapter 4, applications using old, odd, or difficult-to-support technologies increase the cost and difficulty of century-date compliance efforts. If these applications cannot be eliminated outright, they can be replaced or migrated as part of the Year 2000 effort. Migrating the applications to common technologies reduces the cost of Year 2000 migrations by enabling the use of commonly available tools, reduces future maintenance effort, and eliminates the cost of supporting orphan technical environments.

- **Eliminate old applications.**

  Year 2000 initiatives provide the impetus to remove marginal applications from corporate portfolios. Many old applications continue to operate even when most of their functionality has been replaced by new applications or has become obsolete. Inertia and user preferences enable these marginal applications to survive. The cost of modifying an old application to handle century dates may well exceed its business value, providing little incentive to migrate that application. If an application's functions can be provided through other, more cost-effective means, that application should be removed. This avoids century-date compliance migration costs as well as eliminating future maintenance costs.

- **Eliminate useless programs.**

  The complete application inventory developed as part of the enterprise assessment identifies all active application modules. Each of these modules must minimally be certified for compliance, and many will be modified to handle century dates. The remaining, untouched modules in the application libraries are no longer active and can be archived and removed. This reduces application library maintenance effort and prevents programmers from accidentally using the wrong version of a program in the future.

- **Re-create missing source code.**

  Almost every IT organization discovers during enterprise assessment that one or more of their production programs is missing its source code. If these modules cannot be discarded, the source code must be re-created in order to allow the module to be brought to century-compliance. Once recovered, this source code is available for future maintenance uses. Appendix A lists a vendor of source code recovery services.

- **Standardize data naming conventions.**

  Improper, redundant, and confusing data names increase the difficulty of finding and correcting program date fields. The Year 2000 project team migrating a given application can use the project as an opportunity to at least rationalize the date data names to facilitate future maintenance. The impact analysis tools used during the migration effort support finding all affected date fields, provide counts of those fields, and may even support the mass changes needed for rationalization.

- **Implement date subroutines and eliminate redundant code.**

  Unpublished data captured by a Year 2000 software vendor from 30 enterprise assessment projects discovered that 72 percent of all application programs contain date processing logic. As Year 2000 migration teams quickly discover, much of this logic is redundant. Replacing existing date logic with date subroutines eliminates redundancy, decreases the size of application modules, and reduces future maintenance effort.

- **Redevelop highly maintained programs.**

  Although redevelopment activities are not always required for a century-date compliance project, they offer a means to add long-term value to the migration. Redeveloping the most highly maintained programs within an application provides a very high return on investment and will facilitate century-date migration and testing activities. It extends the life of the application by stabilizing the most heavily maintained programs and decreasing the effort needed to incorporate future changes.

18.3 An Environment for Future Support

Many century-date compliance projects begin with heavy investment in infrastructure improvements, such as the purchase of tools, training and methodologies, and the development of adequate test libraries. Unlike the specialized tools and techniques used for other one-time projects, many of these tools, methodologies, and test environments from a Year 2000 initiative offer long-term value for future application maintenance. These future benefits are "free," as their costs have been included in the budget of the century-date compliance effort. Forward-thinking IT managers can use the Year 2000 crisis as a means for significantly enhancing their IT infrastructure. This will enable their organizations to devote fewer resources to future support and enhancement activities.

Some of the key infrastructure improvements gained by IT organizations include:

- **Enhanced project management skills.**

  As the largest and most complex project management challenge in the current history of IT organizations, century-date compliance projects will hone the skills of all of its project managers. These project managers will gain hands-on experience in delivering projects on time while under tight constraints. This experience will teach the project managers how to focus on only the most important tasks and teach them many new management techniques. These skills will be extremely valuable to the IT organization in all of its future projects.

- **Enhanced application support skills.**

  IT organizations that use internal staff to implement at least part of their century-date compliance effort will gain considerable experience in the use of the most advanced analysis, coding, and testing tools and techniques on the market. Because staff members will be forced to use the tools immediately and continuously throughout the project, the IT organization avoids the assimilation issues associated with typical tool roll-out efforts. By assimilating advanced programming methods such as those used for impact analysis, the IT staff will greatly increase their productivity and lower their future error rates.

- **Improved application support processes.**

  As discussed in Chapter 8, most IT organizations are using ad hoc processes to support their applications. Century-date compliance efforts force those processes to be documented and upgraded to increase efficiency and enable consistent results among projects. The time pressures of the compliance effort will cause many organizations to acquire and implement a methodology to provide their migration processes. Many of these new techniques and processes can be applied to future maintenance and enhancement activities. Processes such as those used for enterprise assessments are reusable in a different context to support Application Management planning activities. Documenting and assimilating these new processes will increase the effectiveness of the IT organization. Further, they will reduce the training curve for new IT employees.

- **Tools for application support.**

  The influx of investment capital to Year 2000 tool vendors is causing a rare burst in maintenance tool development. Software vendors have significantly enhanced the quality, packaging, and number of their tool offerings to take advantage of the Year 2000 market. This presents a significant opportunity for IT organizations to enhance and extend their collection of software tools to encompass the latest advances in maintenance technology. Most of the tools used for Year 2000 migrations are the same tools that IT organizations should use for their daily maintenance. These include application-wide and program-level analysis tools, intelligent editors, and testing tools. IT organizations can justify including tool purchases in their Year 2000 budget and recoup their investment in Year 2000 tool purchase and training by simply continuing to use the tools for ongoing application support.

- **High-quality test environments.**

  Enhancing and extending existing test environments within the context of a century-date compliance project is another method of gaining significant future support benefits. Few IT organizations have adequate test environments to support their Year 2000 effort. They will have to invest in the necessary test plans and test libraries to ensure that their applications will operate correctly after the conversion. This new test environment is entirely applicable to routine maintenance and support. By reusing these environments, IT organizations reap the benefits of thorough testing: fewer errors, reduced support costs, and higher-quality deliverables.

- **Large-scale change methodology.**

  Year 2000 projects are a massive proving ground for many techniques and practices that have never been applied before on a large scale. Unlike typical maintenance and development projects, these efforts involve careful coordination of multiple projects, large-scale version control, high-volume changes, and massive testing. If properly captured and retained, the methodology and approaches used to complete the century-date compliance effort can be adapted for future large-scale conversions or migrations. Example uses include European Currency Conversion, customer number expansion, changes in data interface standards (for example, Electronic Data Interchange [EDI]), and software package implementation.

18.4 Lessons for the Future

History has shown that unless we learn from the past, we are doomed to repeat our mistakes. Perhaps the greatest value IT organizations can take from a Year 2000 project is the knowledge gained from reflecting on the aftermath of the project. There are numerous lessons to be learned from our legacy applications and the challenges imposed by the century-date compliance effort. IT organizations were blindsided by an issue that was overlooked because it was so obvious. Procrastination changed a problem that could have been handled over time through routine maintenance into a global IT crisis. Correcting the problem exposed many weaknesses in the IT infrastructure. IT organizations discovered that they lack the tools, expertise, and support infrastructure necessary to effectively address the problem. Many organizations find themselves in the embarrassing position of being unable to even identify and locate the applications they manage! Misconceptions about the role, importance, and life expectancy of legacy applications explode when IT management faces a massive aging portfolio of applications whose failure threatens corporate survival.

Painful as these lessons are, they become a valuable investment in the future if IT organizations learn from them. This hard-won knowledge will repay itself many times over for those IT organizations that have the foresight to apply it to their new development projects as well as their application management efforts. IT organizations must ask themselves the following key questions:

- How did the organization end up in this predicament? Were there warning signs that were ignored? Was the problem underestimated, and if so, why? Could better access to industry information have identified the problem sooner? What type of procedures could facilitate faster identification of future issues?

- What changes in the environment would have facilitated the correction effort? What gaps in the environment were identified by the century-compliance effort? Were these gaps corrected during the project or do they still exist to impede future projects? What weaknesses appeared during the management of the project? Were communications and coordination efforts as successful as they should have been?

- How can similar issues be avoided in the future? How will the organization minimize the impact of a future century-date type of problem? What changes or improvements will facilitate early awareness and faster resolution of similar issues?

- Are there any latent century-date problems in the application portfolio? This is the most difficult question to answer. Application managers must carefully review the assumptions built into their applications. Boundaries and limitations that seemed unreachable when the applications were built may now be within the realm of possibility. Identifying these issues early offers IT organizations many more options for correction.

The purpose of these questions is not to assign blame but to serve as a means of developing solutions to prevent similar situations in the future. Information Technology is a relatively young discipline compared to major disciplines such as manufacturing, insurance, and banking. It is not surprising that IT organizations need additional evolution to reach maturity. Manufacturing organizations have experience in planning for the maintenance and obsolescence of manufacturing machinery, but the IT discipline is just beginning to learn about the issues inherent in 30-year-old applications. Fortunately, century-compliance projects provide plenty of data to aid the maturation of IT processes. Further, the high cost of century-compliance projects provides a solid yardstick for developing cost/benefit analyses for needed improvements.

Although some of the most valuable lessons are organization-specific, there are a number of lessons that apply to all IT organizations. The list below is by no means inclusive, but it provides a good starting point for discussion. It is our hope that IT organizations have the foresight to apply these lessons rather than return to "business as usual" at the conclusion of the century-compliance effort.

- **Production application maintenance is underrated in most IT organizations.**

  Many IT organizations appear to view their production applications as a liability rather than as an important corporate asset. As the Year 2000 issue shows, corporations cannot operate without their production applications. As those IT organizations forced to defer new development activities while they correct century-date issues discovered, production application support is more important than new development for the survival of the corporation. This realization should encourage IT organizations to invest greater financial and intellectual capital into methods for enhancing the effectiveness of their application support.

- **Applications last longer than planned.**

  Old applications rarely die. Many IT organizations discovered that they are routinely running applications written in the late '60s. Applications that were supposed to be replaced by new technology are still around, working in conjunction with their "replacement" system. Why? They still provide business value. There is no reason to suspect that this trend will not continue for many of the applications developed today. Thus, IT organizations must design new applications for the possibility that they will be in operation 15 or 20 years from now. This requires reversing the trend of optimizing application design to facilitate new development at the expense of future maintainability.

- **Shortcuts lead to high costs in the future.**

  Saving years in two-digit rather than four-digit date formats seemed like an acceptable trade-off at the time. How many similar shortcuts are being built into new applications developed today? Many IT organizations have a culture that favors short-term benefits over long-term consequences. Even though century-date compliance projects were caused by shortcuts, these organizations seek to correct the problem with shortcuts. These shortcuts will cost many times their savings in the future. Short-term efficiencies should not be implemented without fully weighing long-term consequences. It is always cheaper to perform the job right in the first place.

- **Reusability is a necessity, not a luxury.**

  Software reusability is widely discussed and rarely applied. The Year 2000 challenge would not be an issue if all software was designed to share the same handful of reusable date routines. Inordinate amounts of time are spent in century-date compliance projects correcting the same code in hundreds, if not thousands, of locations in each application. Organizations seeking to justify a software reusability initiative need only to point to the cost of Year 2000 compliance.

- **Standards exist for a reason.**

One has only to count the number of different date formats or examine the variations in date naming within a typical IT organization to realize the benefits of defining and enforcing standards. Astonishingly, many IT organizations have backed away from formal standards for their new development activities. The high cost of the Year 2000 effort should inspire IT organizations to invest heavily in standards for all future development activities.

- **Odd technologies are rarely an advantage in retrospect.**

Organizations that have deviated from commonly accepted technologies and languages are paying for their follies now. Excellent tools and assistance are available for COBOL, whereas most 4GL users are left out in the cold. This principle should be remembered before selecting that new "leading-edge" client/server development environment. Unfortunately, the development tool and technique marketplace is more fragmented than ever, increasing the risk of selecting a technology that may later leave the IT organization stranded. Given the long life of most applications, IT organizations must consider if a given technology and its vendor will still be viable in twenty years. This viability will have more organizational value than slight improvements in technical performance. This should be considered when adopting client/server, screen painter, interconnectivity tools, and other emerging technologies.

- **The sooner a problem is corrected, the less it costs.**

Year 2000 compliance could have been achieved through routine maintenance if IT organizations had begun early enough. As the century draws to a close, organizations that procrastinated scramble for resources, paying top dollar for armies of consultants to accomplish the conversion at the last minute. Proactive, long-term application planning enables organizations to detect and identify solutions for other major applications issues before they become crises.

- **Application replacement lead times are very long.**

  Many IT organizations believed that they could avoid the Year 2000 crisis by replacing their legacy applications with software packages or by developing replacement applications. These organizations quickly discovered that long project lead times prevented them from replacing more than a small handful of applications. The processes used to fund, design, develop, and deploy a new application are typically measured in years despite supposed breakthroughs in development technology. These lead times must be a consideration in any application planning activity. These lead times are another justification for early detection of application issues. IT organizations would have been able to replace many more applications if they had begun the century-date compliance effort several years earlier.

Chapter 19

Architecture Transition Strategies —Looking Beyond the Year 2000

The Year 2000 problem is irrefutable testimony to the fact that IT continues to face enormous challenges from aging legacy system architectures. Legacy architectures are responsible for locking IT organizations into a field size limitation 25 years past the point of when it should have been an issue. These same architectures are responsible for the fact that Year 2000 solutions will cost up to half a trillion dollars worldwide. This chapter discusses how IT can "turn the tables" on the Year 2000 problem by making the Year 2000 project a catalyst for strategic change.

Strategic change is required to transition legacy systems into the information technology architectures needed to support strategic business requirements in the next century. Management must face this issue now, because the Year 2000 is symptomatic of an even more serious problem: significant structural weaknesses in IT architectures and infrastructures. Management should exploit the potential of the Year 2000 project to form the basis of a long-term architecture transition strategy.

19.1 The Case for Transforming Legacy Architectures

Many IT executives believe that aging architectures will eventually be replaced with new, strategic systems. These same executives have believed this for more than 15 years. Initially it was fourth-generation languages (4GL) that would lead the way. Then it was the CASE (computer-aided software engineering) revolution. Most recently, IT believed that client/server systems would replace legacy environments by the mid 1990s. But the same systems continue to run in production year after year. Occasionally, a new system is developed to surround existing systems, but legacy systems are deactivated in only a small percentage of cases. According to the Gartner Group, more than 85 percent of the systems in production in 1995 will be around in the year 2000.

19.1.1 Legacy Architecture Challenges

To highlight IT architectural weaknesses, one need only look at what the industry has learned from attempts to address the Year 2000 problem. IT environments contain obsolete, duplicate, and missing components and lack basic documentation and configuration control. These issues stall enterprise assessment efforts and delay Year 2000 project deployment. Data definition redundancy, typically 60 to 80 percent at the source code level, slows date identification and conversion, while making the process complex and error prone. To envision the depth of this problem, imagine how easily and reliably analysts could find and fix dates if every single date field had "date" in its name. These issues, coupled with poor testing environments, can drive Year 2000 costs up by almost 80 percent. As bad as this sounds, these issues can be dealt with by applying straightforward techniques, such as data name rationalization, discussed later in this chapter.

The most significant challenge that IT faces in current systems environments stems from the underlying architectures upon which these systems are based. For example:

- Redundant data stores are common within legacy data architectures.

- Data is replicated across multiple data stores, making date expansion projects prone to mistakes.

- Aging, obsolete data structures make date field expansion risky or impossible. These data architectures force IT into a procedural solution in many situations where this approach may be undesirable.

- Legacy data architectures tend to store and represent data in ways that make this data inaccessible to end users for planning, query, and other purposes.

Underlying system architectures mirror the inconsistencies and redundancies found in legacy data architectures. Redundant, overlapping, and inaccessible legacy systems do not typically reflect or adequately support current and future business requirements. Figure 19.1 depicts a view of how existing systems map functionally to strategic business requirements. Functions tend to be either split or replicated across multiple physical systems, while no single system performs all of the functions required by a given user. Years of patchwork changes and maintenance workaround approaches have left a huge gap between how systems are currently implemented and how they should be defined to support long-term business needs.

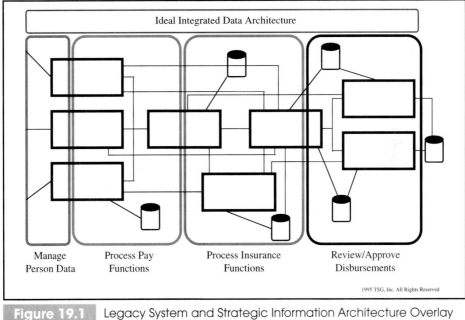

Ideal Integrated Data Architecture

| Manage Person Data | Process Pay Functions | Process Insurance Functions | Review/Approve Disbursements |

Figure 19.1 Legacy System and Strategic Information Architecture Overlay Mapping

19.1.2 Failure of Replacement Approaches

Some IT executives have given up trying to realign application architectures with business requirements; others continue exploring scrap-and-replace options that have not worked in the past and continue to show little promise. The Standish Group study, quoted in Chapter 4, found that only 9 percent of IT projects were implemented on time, within budget, and with all specified functionality—because IT organizations continue to attempt to integrate replacement systems into highly complex legacy architectures without considering how these architectures are impacted.

Little, if any, formal analysis of legacy applications is applied to replacement planning and analysis efforts. If a new system actually does make it into production, it usually ends up running in parallel with one or more mainframe systems that already perform many of the same functions. Manual reconciliation of replicated functions and redundant data adds yet another task to an increasingly complex end-user environment. The end-user situation, in this scenario, degrades, and executive management then renews discussions to outsource the IT environment to a systems integrator.

An alternative option being explored by management is to build a data warehouse to collect and consolidate legacy data into user-friendly formats. The data warehouse, coupled with enterprise data interconnectivity projects, is fast becoming the de facto strategy to provide end users with mission-critical data in ways that leverage the business to the best extent possible. Data interconnectivity strives to create an environment where disparate legacy data is brought together to facilitate ad hoc user queries. While these options are good interim strategies, building warehouses and interconnecting legacy systems and data stores is similar to building a house on quicksand. Eventually, the aging legacy infrastructure will collapse.

To change this situation, management must focus on transition requirements, using different approaches and strategies than those used during the past two decades. Transitioning existing systems into strategic architectures requires in-depth understanding of legacy environments and a practical plan to achieve improved target architectures. This will become even more important as business process reengineering teams pressure IT management to transform inflexible systems into dramatically improved, user-friendly, information technical environments that meet radically streamlined business requirements. While many IT people would agree with these assertions, few view the year 2000 initiative as an opportunity to establish the foundation for achieving strategic business and IT goals.

19.1.3 A Year 2000 Project Return on Investment

Many IT professionals believe that the Year 2000 project is a zero-gain proposition, providing little return on investment other than keeping systems functioning, but this is not the case.

- **Management must insist on gaining value from the Year 2000 effort.**

  It is likely that no IT initiative other than a Year 2000 project will ever be able to consolidate a comprehensive view of the IT enterprise. This effort is the largest, multiyear, must-do project that IT has ever faced—a one-of-a-kind IT initiative based on unusually open access to enterprisewide meta-data and the funding needed to keep this meta-data updated and current.

- **Management should institutionalize access to information.**

  Meta-data includes data about mainframes, distributed architectures, user-based systems, systems software, and non-IT, process-driven technologies. This information is critical to short-term and strategic planning efforts, and IT professionals must leverage it, both near and long term.

- **Management can use Year 2000 facilities in strategic transition planning and implementation projects**

  This cross-functional meta-data loaded into the central tracking facility during the enterprise assessment, and maintained throughout the Year 2000 implementation phase, is the core knowledge base that can be used by countless strategic transition projects. The Year 2000 tracking facility defines a subset of meta-data found in the legacy transition meta-model (LTM).

The remaining sections of this chapter discuss the relevancy and composition of the LTM, the types of IT initiatives that benefit from the use of this information model, redevelopment strategies to support these initiatives, and the role of IT within the context of this new paradigm.

19.2 Legacy Transition Meta-model: Baseline for Architecture Transition Planning

Legacy systems, ignored in strategic planning projects, contain embedded business knowledge that should be leveraged by the vast majority of IT projects. The enterprise version of the LTM, found in the Year 2000 tracking facility (see Figure 12.2 on page 288), only hints at the kind of information that can be tracked across an IT organization. The LTM is used within a Year 2000 project to track systems, cross-functional data store utilization, bridges and APIs, upgrade unit delineation, and physical scope metrics. The LTM's value outside the scope of a Year 2000

project extends to numerous systems management activities that include the following:

- Documenting all systems and shared data among those systems as input to planning and maintenance efforts

- Tracking change requests across diverse and complex environments

- Providing critical input to configuration management activities

- Tracking cross-enterprise data usage for impact planning and data architecture redesign projects

- Documenting the accumulated knowledge of existing business rules

- Managing transition activity (component activation/deactivation) throughout the life of a replacement or migration project

- Tracking shared or redundant data utilization to help analysts with ongoing reconciliation efforts

- Establishing a roadmap for any large-scale IT transformation project requiring knowledge of installed data, systems, and functions

19.2.1 Using the LTM

A Year 2000 project is a once-in-a-century opportunity to establish the baseline infrastructure required to catalogue physical and logical legacy knowledge. LTM meta-data is extensible to support numerous strategic initiatives and can be built by using any commercial repository, although some organizations use relational database technology to implement the LTM. The LTM stores information about current systems, cross-reference relationships, and commonalties across environments, maps this information between existing systems and target models, and manages system implementations across disparate environments. The LTM facilitates coordination of difficult projects through its meta-model, as shown in Figure 19.2.

Note that this illustration is a subset of LTM object types and relationships and is only meant to provide an overview of the LTM. Appendix C summarizes the LTM more completely.

The LTM is basically an entity relationship model with many-to-many relationships of current and target system components. Each instance of an entity (or object) can be represented in a repository. Current object types include job, step, proc, source module, copy member, screen, report, on-line table, record, file, and other system components. The LTM also defines attributes and relationships for each object. Relationship examples include step executes load module, and load module comprises source module or record defines file. Once established, the LTM has value as a documentation tool and provides strategic migration and redesign support. Physical object attributes vary, based on implementation factors, but typically include name, description, scan date, metrics, and applicable technical features such as language type.

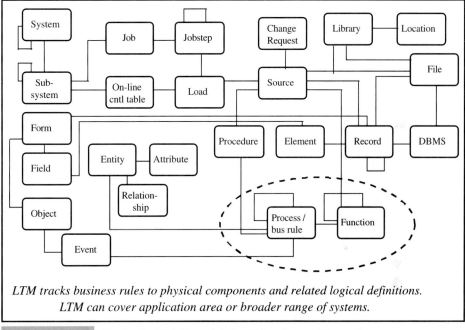

LTM tracks business rules to physical components and related logical definitions.
LTM can cover application area or broader range of systems.

Figure 19.2　Strategic LTM Capabilities Using Formal Repository

A second category of LTM objects includes logical components that map to various development paradigms. This category includes entities, functions, processes, screens, reports, and other models that may add value to the analysis process. The LTM also can represent objects, events, and business rules to support client/server migration to an event-driven design model. Figure 19.2 shows a typical set of logical objects within the LTM.

Objects are set up to represent both current and target components within the LTM. An example of this is the business rule object that uses a current/target indicator switch to tell an analyst if this repository object represents an existing rule or one that is planned for a new system. An existing rule, implemented in a physical system, can then be mapped to a target rule, defined in a logical design model. Reusing and deactivating legacy system business rules becomes a more manageable process with this type of tracking facility in place.

Because development paradigms vary to a great degree, organizations can use the LTM baseline to create a subset of these objects or to extend the model to reflect in-house methods and design paradigms. One important category of objects to be considered involves intangible components found within IT environments. An example is the end-user change request. Tracking and relating change requests to existing systems and systems in development transition verifies that specifications are synchronized with maintenance upgrades. Other examples include documentation, physical forms, or other "external" objects such as a director or management position. The LTM can be expanded or adjusted to reflect specific project requirements.

19.2.2 Building, Populating and Updating the LTM

While building and populating the LTM is step 1 in the process, keeping it updated with current meta-data about the enterprise environment is equally important. The basic LTM configuration requires a meta-model like the one pictured in Figure 19.2, a repository in which the meta-model can be defined, an underlying relational database (depending on the repository tool), and a population facility. Data administrators can use the meta-model in Figure 19.2 or Appendix C, customizing and entering it into a repository facility. Populating this repository with physical data requires parsing technology either developed in-house or purchased from a third-party tool vender. Some repositories come with the required parsers; others do not. Organizations should consider the following features in a repository population facility.

- Do parsers have the breadth of coverage to scan various components in a given environment?

- Do parsers run on the host or workstation?

- Do the loaders recognize and update only modified components to avoid a complete reload when refreshing is required?

- Does the repository population tool vendor have a contractual agreement with the repository vendor to provide a robust link to the repository?

Because the level of detail and breadth of coverage required from a given implementation of the LTM varies, data administrators may want to establish tiered repository structures. Such structures typically entail an enterprise-view LTM, which stores high-level meta-data and relationships similar to the original Year 2000 tracking facility, and multiple application area LTM repositories, which can store more detailed information, as depicted in Figure 19.2. The general approach required to build and maintain this meta-data requires each major application area to capture detailed information about its systems and load it into a localized LTM. Central coordinators can then extract selected information as needed and populate the enterprise LTM to support cross-functional planning or other types of transition projects. Data administrators can provide assistance in creating this tiered LTM infrastructure and the process required to populate it.

19.3 Leveraging a Year 2000 Project

Information captured during a Year 2000 project creates a foundation for strategic architecture transition initiatives. The enterprise assessment captures enterprise- and system-specific information that should be stored in the tracking facility, preferably using the tiered LTM infrastructure. The Year 2000 implementation of the LTM is the baseline for the more generalized and broadly applicable meta-model. The Year 2000 portfolio segmentation and upgrade unit prioritization phase of the project examines plans for every system in the enterprise. This systems migration and replacement information can then be entered into the LTM to extend the physical view of the IT environment to include short- and long-term systems planning data. This information should be added as planning comments in the LTM system object. Projects that are running late or that negatively impact Year 2000 implementation efforts quickly gain visibility at the enterprise level via LTM-generated reports. The mere fact that projects are being tracked, with status reports raised to an executive level of awareness, is likely to change the way decisions are made within the IT management ranks.

As the implementation phase of a Year 2000 project begins, analysts must ensure that information in the LTM remains current so that new systems, converted systems, and retired systems are reflected in the overall status tracking facility. Analysts can then track cross-functional data store usage, along with the interfaces developed over the course of the project. The ideal Year 2000 tracking facility reflects detailed information in lower-tier LTM repositories that can then be summarized at the enterprise level through the Year 2000 Project Office. Planners, designers, and managers can then extract and modify various incarnations of this data for short- and long-term planning.

19.3.1 LTM Meta-model Expansion

The main link between a Year 2000 project and strategic transition planning is the LTM repository facility instituted for the project. This tracking facility, representing an existing enterprise at a high level and individual applications in more detailed models, provides the core of the transition planning model. Physical and logical meta-data contained in this baseline model can be readily extended to depict a broader view of systems functionality. The extent to which this model is enhanced and applied is driven by ongoing systems planning requirements. The addition of new object types, including events, business rules, logical data types, business processes, or other information, is based on transition requirements.

Strategic initiatives using the LTM facility include data warehouses, data and system interconnectivity projects, package selection and implementation, system migration efforts, and architecture redesign projects. Many of these categories are driven by business-process reengineering initiatives that demand new and improved ways to access and process key information. The Year 2000 assessment itself is likely to include recommendations to proceed with system consolidation or elimination as a way to reduce expenditures and control system triage.

Once a repository is loaded and a process is established to keep it refreshed as new systems are deployed and data structures evolve, many areas of the organization can take advantage of this information, which includes basic configuration control, security, minor maintenance planning efforts, or other larger-scale activities to facilitate management of complex IT environments. Ongoing utilization of this facility requires that a permanent repository manager and LTM application coordinator be assigned to this task long term. The process of documenting and utilizing the LTM must be transitioned out of the hands of the Year 2000 Project Office and into a more permanent group as a Year 2000 project comes to a close.

19.4 Transition Mapping Approaches and Techniques

Defining a target architecture establishes a framework for systems development, redesign and migration efforts. Under most frameworks, a systems architecture includes conceptual definitions for business functions, data, and technical requirements.

- **Business architecture.**

  Defines how functions are to be distributed across the enterprise. Significant reorganization of current functional views is typically a given under a redesign scenario.

- **Data architecture.**

  Normally represented as an enterprise model that can then be defined in greater detail within a given business area. Organizations frequently err by attempting to depict the enterprise model at a level of detail that is too low. The enterprise model should synchronize data utilization across the enterprise, not define it to a minute level of detail.

- **Technical architecture.**

  Defines the hardware, software, telecommunication capabilities, and technical implementation of the business and data architecture models.

Once a target architecture has been drafted, mapping this architecture to the existing environment is the next step in a legacy transition strategy. The basis for this is that some systems only need to exist for an interim time, whereas others may be retained for an extended period. Mapping requirements against an existing architecture helps assess which systems are in which category. This process begins to shed light on a long term legacy system deactivation plan.

A second reason for current-to-target architecture mapping is that old and new system architectures rarely correspond on a one-to-one basis (see Figure 19.1). Portions of certain systems will be downsized, redesigned, integrated, reused, or eliminated. Mapping current functions to the target architecture ensures that legacy functions are consolidated, deactivated, and reused as required during the transition process. In other words, if you don't know where you are, a map won't help.

The LTM provides the basis to manage this mapping process on an enterprise and application area scale. Data warehouse, enterprise data interconnectivity, package assimilation, and systems transition projects all have a use for this data at some point. How these types of projects use this data is discussed below.

19.5 Data Warehouse Projects

Redundant data stores force many organizations to look toward short-term solutions to consolidate disparate data from cross-functional environments into a coherent data model that end users can access. This concept, called the data warehouse, is depicted in Figure 19.3. Data warehouse requires multisystem data capture and consolidation to create a relational view of legacy data. Repository support involves legacy data cross-reference tracking to highlight relationships among disparate data types. Once legacy structures are loaded into the repository, mapping between current data structures and target models facilitates model development and legacy data consolidation into a central query database. Changes in legacy data structures signal update requirements to the query database when the LTM is periodically refreshed from the legacy environment.

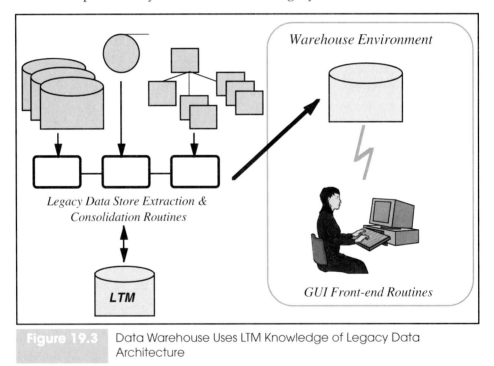

Warehouse Environment

Legacy Data Store Extraction &
Consolidation Routines

LTM

GUI Front-end Routines

Figure 19.3   Data Warehouse Uses LTM Knowledge of Legacy Data Architecture

Figure 19.4 represents cross-functional data mapping that focuses on tracking where redundant data resides, where it is used, and how it is presented to users. If an application changes data formats or other attributes related to the source of a data warehouse extraction process, analysts can immediately adjust the warehouse model, extraction process, or user interface.

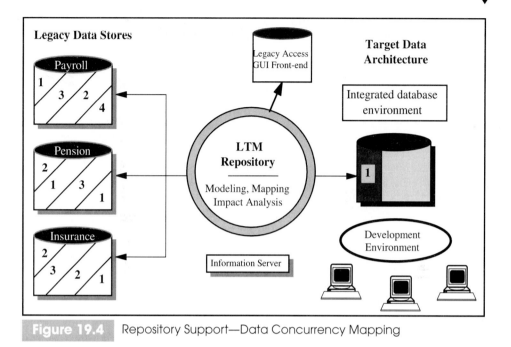

Figure 19.4 Repository Support—Data Concurrency Mapping

19.6 Enterprise Data Interconnectivity

Enterprise data interconnectivity uses middleware to connect front-end legacy systems and data stores to user-friendly, graphical workstation environments. This type of project has immediate value to end users and also serves as a stepping stone to client/server redesign. Building graphical user interfaces (GUI) involves identifying and isolating front-end edit routines, porting them to client environments, replacing character based front-ends with GUI interfaces, and building client-to-host data store links using middleware technology. This concept is depicted in Figure 19.5.

The LTM repository assists with documenting and tracking legacy data, functions, and interfaces developed as part of initiating an enterprise data interconnectivity project. This assistance includes tracking redundant data for consolidation and editing within the client environment, identifying host functions that may be replicated or superseded by new user interfaces, and serving as an audit trail to document increasingly complex, interconnected data environments. Data concurrency mapping, shown in Figure 19.4, ensures that as legacy data changes, the interfaces, middleware links, other data stores, and applications dependent upon that data can be updated to keep the overall environment synchronized. The LTM repository becomes a central facility for controlling and managing these emerging environments. This facility extends the concept of configuration management to the complex world of data interconnectivity.

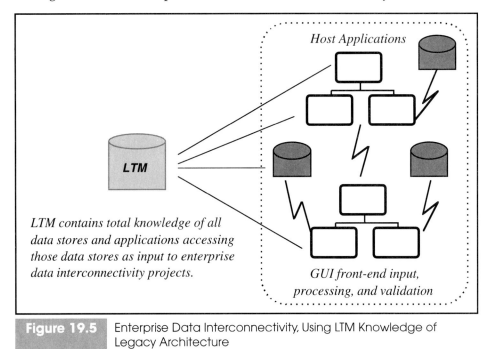

Host Applications

LTM

LTM contains total knowledge of all data stores and applications accessing those data stores as input to enterprise data interconnectivity projects.

GUI front-end input, processing, and validation

Figure 19.5 Enterprise Data Interconnectivity, Using LTM Knowledge of Legacy Architecture

19.7 Package Selection and Assimilation

A comprehensive assessment is required to determine that a package satisfies functional and technical needs, to establish a deployment strategy, and to clearly articulate cost benefit. Functional analysis involves multidimensional mapping of package functions to legacy functions and strategic requirements. Target requirements, derived from business process redesign and strategic planning, should be depicted by using formal functional decomposition to facilitate mapping between strategic requirements, the package(s) being reviewed, and in-house systems. Target planning models typically include entity relationship diagrams, function hierarchies, function/entity type matrices, or object models.

Models representing package functionality should come from the vendors themselves. A lack of formal specifications for a package can signal, in and of itself, a weakness in the process used to create that package. Fortunately, vendor-supplied models are becoming more common as new packages evolve. When these are not available, analysts may want to document what a package does inside the LTM.

Models representing legacy systems, on the other hand, are typically unavailable. Formal models can, however, be extracted from current systems through various reverse requirements tracing techniques. LTM meta-data is the central tracking facility for extracting this information. Application analysts can add comments reflecting business knowledge to LTM function or process objects and relate these objects to program occurrences in the LTM. As functional knowledge in the LTM is more fully expanded, analysts can generate reports showing the flow of business rules in an existing system, based on the execution sequence of the programs defining those functions. Analysts can then compare legacy functions to functional models in the package being selected or implemented.

The result of the assessment process (see Figure 19.6) provides a basis for verifying the integrity of strategic models, determining package components to be omitted, identifying legacy components to be deactivated, and finalizing a migration strategy. Once implementation activities in each of these categories are clarified, deployment costs can be clearly defined for one or more package alternatives. This process surfaces "hidden" costs well before implementation begins. Requirements mapping can be represented in the form of a matrix or in reports generated from the repository. They must show exactly where packages support given functions and where they do not. Packages that do meet functional requirements must similarly conform to technological standards.

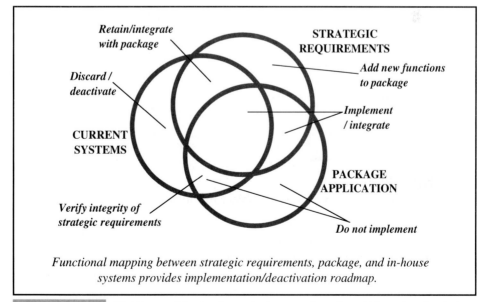

Functional mapping between strategic requirements, package, and in-house systems provides implementation/deactivation roadmap.

Figure 19.6   LTM Support for Package-to-Legacy Functional Mapping Analysis

19.8 Code-Based System Migration Projects

Code-based migration, conceptually depicted in Figure 19.7, requires that analysts review and perform data name rationalization, data structure redesign, program remodularization, and application component rehosting. The goal of this approach is to reuse source code components as a basis for the newly migrated system. Migration target environments typically, but not always, involve some type of client/server target. When systems contain a high degree of redundant or cryptic data definitions, analysts should perform data name rationalization on that system. This process reduces redundant names and record definitions to a succinct subset of well-defined names; it requires the inventory and cross-reference tools that were used during the Year 2000 project. Source code remodularization involves slicing and reconciling I/O routines and redundant functions across a physical system. This process supports the separation of data and presentation layers from business logic, as well as creating reusable routines. These routines become the source-based building blocks for the new system.

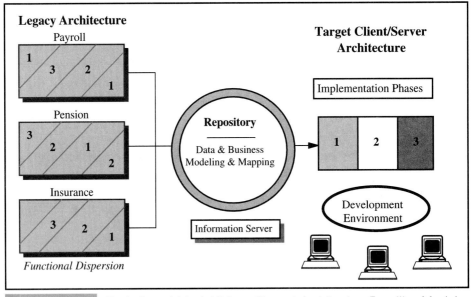

Figure 19.7 Code-Based, Model-Driven, Phased, Architecture Transition Model

Segregated I/O allows for GUI access to be linked via subroutines and simplifies replacement of legacy data access logic with SQL and the design changes that typically accompany a data redesign process. Analysts can then implement reusable functional routines in the new systems environment. LTM repository support includes mapping existing data and functions to target models, tracking functions, adjusting relationships during transition, and managing target-to-legacy data store concurrency during transition. Relationships between documented business rule and source program objects within the LTM are updated as legacy systems are remodularized. This process, shown in Figure 19.6, is particularly important when only selected functions of a legacy system are being migrated to the target environment.

19.9 Model-Driven Architecture Transition Projects

Model-driven architecture transition relies most extensively on repository support for target architecture migration. Model-driven transition does not reuse source code components, as in the previously discussed scenario, but relies on the abstraction of rules from the legacy environment and the repopulating of those rules into a target architecture. Support for this process relies on relationships within the LTM that facilitate a technique called reverse requirements tracing. In the model-driven scenario, reverse requirements tracing takes on a much more formal role that traces user views (screens and reports) back to system components responsible for producing those views. Screen and report headings are used as a "straw man" approach to performing current system functional decomposition. Functions are added to the LTM, linked to legacy source program objects, decomposed further by means of event derivation analysis, and then linked to program procedures.

Analysts can then capture and import business rules from legacy systems, using event and business rule models as the target. Examples of object and event modeling can be found in many object-oriented methodologies where a business rule is triggered by one or more initiated events. Based on prior functional mapping, analysts scan legacy modules, using interactive analyzers to find condition/action logic that can be mapped to the event or business rule paradigm for reuse in the target system. The LTM is both the guidemap to tracing this information and the interactive audit trail for verifying that each step of analysis is documented.

Duplicate rules occur when a current rule maps to another current rule. If a current rule maps to a target rule (defined during top-down analysis), current rules are used to accelerate specification of the target. Rule reconciliation proactively resolves situations where different systems apply the same rule differently. The LTM is updated to reflect one or more legacy locations where rules are to be deactivated by remodularization. The LTM provides a critical audit trail for analysts during this discovery process.

The LTM's return on investment, when applied to code-based and model-driven transition strategies, is based on streamlining specification time, reducing user retraining (rules are consistently applied), and avoiding post-implementation rework due to misinterpreting business rules that should not change. A second advantage is that portions of the new architecture can be migrated into production before activation of remaining target system functions. Figure 19.7 depicts how functional reconciliation can be implemented in a target architecture while legacy rules are selectively deactivated in current systems. The model-driven approach should be customized on a case-by-case basis but is impractical in the absence of an LTM repository to manage the process.

19.10 Adjusting the Focus of a Year 2000 Project

The Year 2000 Project Office, advisory board, and other participants need only make minor adjustments in focus during a Year 2000 project to take strategic advantage of the deliverables from this project. The advisory board must recommend that the LTM and other deliverables from the assessment and implementation phases of the project be released to quality teams, configuration management functions, and other areas that can leverage this information. The Project Office must drive the implementation of this information-sharing concept. Analysts from application planning areas should import and abstract selected meta-data from the LTM tiered repositories to assess cross-functional data warehouse, data interconnectivity, package system migration, and other redesign strategies. The critical requirement, however, is that management mandate that collateral benefits be derived from Year 2000 projects.

Another thing that organizations can do to leverage the Year 2000 project is to examine which pieces of the Year 2000 organizational and technological infrastructure can be expanded, enhanced, extended, or in some way generalized to support non-Year 2000 projects. This examination, of course, must be accomplished with no impact on Year 2000 delivery schedules. Organizational value can be derived by mirroring quality assurance, configuration tracking, testing, and other functions that were set up for the Year 2000 but have general value in a non-Year 2000 environment.

Similarly, Year 2000 technology can also be applied to other projects. One way to do this is to share technology access with application and other analysts that can use these tools for research or system upgrades on other projects. Many of the Year 2000 tools were, after all, derived from systems redevelopment technology that has value for many other types of legacy migration or transition projects. Inventory and cross-reference tools, date identification tools, and testing tools all have broader value in this context. Tool and repository coordinators should begin to institutionalize these capabilities as the Year 2000 project begins to draw to a close.

19.11 Beyond the Year 2000

Refocusing management attention on the value and the role of legacy architectures is critical to long-term IT success. This *is* the radical shift that many pundits and authors have been alluding to for the past several years, but that has somehow been masked by the emergence of new concepts such as CASE, object orientation, the Internet, and other new technologies. Refocusing IT emphasis requires redefining the role of IT and changing how executives budget for and appropriate resources to the IT function. These concepts will take time to institutionalize and will require a brave leader internally to champion these concepts.

19.11.1 Redefining the Strategic Role of IT

The reality of the situation is that IT does very little designing and building of new systems. IT fixes, evolves, and sometimes adds new pieces to existing application assets. One good analogy is that of a real estate portfolio manager. This individual keeps track of a vast amount of assets over long periods of time. Care and upkeep are the main goal of this person's job. When a new building is needed, or when a major retrofit of an existing structure is required, the portfolio manager hires the architects, engineers, and construction contractors that are required to fulfill these specialty roles. IT should act in a similar way. However, most IT personnel continue to liken themselves to their predecessors who spent much of their time building new systems. Executives should accept this new role of the asset manager and evolve IT strategies around it. If IT does not do this, it will be difficult for them to continue to function efficiently and service the businesses that require strategic information in rapid fashion.

19.11.2 Changing Old Habits

Management must communicate to senior executives deficiencies found within IT infrastructures. A strong individual must drive this communication. A second thing that IT must do is to stop investing in "quick fix" solutions that end up as canceled projects. The Standish Group study provides the background justification to support this decision. Management should also begin recognizing strategic value in the installed base of legacy systems. These systems are not going away, and IT should embrace the embedded business value they provide and build transition strategically around them.

Finally, executives must invest in IT strategies based on common sense and not on hopeless optimism. There is no way, for example, that entire legacy architectures can be moved into an object-oriented environment in this century or any time soon after the year 2000. Facing weaknesses discovered during the Year 2000 planning and implementation project is the best way to begin correcting them. Based on the difficulty that the industry has had coming to grips with the year 2000, IT does not have to look very far to find these weaknesses.

Vendor Lists

The vendor list in this appendix is offered as a service to the readers of this book. It lists examples of vendors offering the tools and services described within the book. It by no means represents all of the Year 2000 vendors on the market. Inclusion of a vendor on this list does not imply endorsement by the authors, nor does exclusion imply any negative opinions of the authors. Although the authors are thoroughly familiar with many of the tools on the market, they have not personally evaluated each offering.

This vendor list is meant as a starting point for research. We highly recommend that readers perform their own market survey when selecting tools or services. The Year 2000 tool market is so volatile that any vendor or tool list such as this quickly becomes obsolete. Since starting this book, we have seen dozens of companies enter the market and at least two vendors get acquired by other companies. Further, changes in vendor technology, management, or strategy can dramatically affect the viability of that vendor's solutions against its competition.

The list is divided into four subsections: consulting firms, software tool vendors, conversion services, and information about the authors' firms.

A.1 Consulting Firms

The following list represents only a small percentage of the consulting firms offering Year 2000 services. Vendor's tool usage is noted when a consulting firm employs its own proprietary tool set or has a strategic partnership with a tool vendor.

- **Andersen Consulting LLP**

  Address: Contact local Andersen office

  Telephone: NA

  Andersen offers a full range of strategic, project, and outsourcing services for century-date compliance efforts.

- **CAP GEMINI AMERICA**

  Address: 1114 Avenue of the Americas / 29th floor
  New York, NY 10036

  Telephone: (212) 944 6464 x 232

  Through its TransMillennium™ services, CAP GEMINI offers end-to-end project and outsourcing services for century-date compliance projects. CAP GEMINI supports its services with its own ISO 9001-certified methodology and a full set of proprietary analysis, migration, and testing tools.

- **CIBER**

  Address: 800 West Cummings Park, Suite 2000
  Woburn, MA 01801

  Telephone: (617) 932-6406

  CIBER offers project consulting services for all phases of Year 2000 initiatives. CIBER delivers its services through a combination of on-site consulting and an off-site automated conversion facility. The conversion facility uses Peritus technology.

- **Computer Horizons Corporation**

  Address: 49 Old Bloomfield Avenue
  Mountain Lakes, NJ 07046-1495

  Telephone: 1-800-321-2421

  Computer Horizons offers project and outsourcing capabilities for all phases of a Year 2000 initiative. Computer Horizons uses its own proprietary tool kit and methodology to support its consulting services.

- **Computer Sciences Corporation (CSC)**

  Address: University Office Park
  29 Sawyer Road
  Waltham, MA 02154-3423

  Telephone: (617) 894-0418

  CSC offers project and outsourcing services that cover enterprise assessments, migration, testing/validation, and acceptance deployment. CSC bases its practice on its own Year 2000 methodology and the use of Peritus technology.

- **Dun & Bradstreet Satayam Software (DBSS)**

  Address: 9 Technology Drive
  Westborough, MA 01581

  Telephone: (508) 871-5202

  DBSS is a division of Dun & Bradstreet with its headquarters in Madras, India, and offices in the U.S. DBSS offers impact analysis, migration planning, and Year 2000 upgrade implementation services, using its own set of tools and U.S. and offshore resources.

- **EDS**

  Address: EDS
  Technology Architecture
  H3-4C-16
  5400 Legacy Drive
  Plano, Texas 75024

  Telephone: (214) 605-4109

  EDS offers Year 2000 services for large projects and outsourcing engagements. Given its size and resources, EDS has the capability of implementing global, enterprisewide projects.

- **Information Management Resources (IMR)**

  Address: 26750 U.S. Highway 19 North, Suite 500
  Clearwater, FL 34621

  Telephone: (813) 797-7080

  IMR is a U.S.-based company with dedicated offshore facilities. IMR has the capabilities to handle large millennium update projects through automation and offshore resources. They use their own proprietary methodology and reengineering tool set.

- **HCL James Martin**

  Address: HCL James Martin, Inc.
  3050 Chain Bridge Road, Suite 400
  Fairfax, VA 22030-2834

  Telephone: 888-GET-TSRM

  HCL James Martin, Inc., provides quality systems redevelopment and Year 2000 solutions. The company is dedicated to providing solutions to help clients leverage their investments in existing business-critical systems while preparing them to meet information technology demands of today and tomorrow. They also provide the TSRM methodology as an off-the-shelf, commercially available product for Year 2000 and other redevelopment projects.

- **IBM/ISSC**

  Address: 1743 Great Falls Street
  McLean, Virginia 22101

  Telephone: (703) 734-2305

  IBM/ISSC offers an extensive set of strategic, project, and outsourcing services targeted at century-date compliance efforts in Fortune 500 companies.

- **Keane, Inc.**

  Address: Ten City Square
  Boston, MA 02109

  Telephone: 1-800-239-0296

  Keane is a large national services firm offering project and outsourcing Year 2000 services that include enterprise assessments, planning, application migration, and testing. Keane uses its own methodology and is partnered with VIASOFT, Inc.

- **KPMG Peat Marwick**

  Address: 99 High Street
                   Boston, MA 02110

  Telephone: (617) 988-1060

  KPMG offers a full range of century-date compliance service offerings ranging from application migration to application replacement.

- **Mastech Corporation**

  Address: 1004 McKee Road
                   Pittsburgh, PA 15071

  Telephone: 1-800-311-1970

  Mastech is a large software services firm serving businesses globally. It maintains three offshore development facilities in India. Mastech offers a full range of Year 2000 offerings that can be performed on site, off site or offshore.

- **PKS Information Services**

  Address: 11707 Miracle Hills Drive
                   Omaha, NE 68154

  Telephone: (402) 496-8500

  PKS offers both computer resources and consulting services. PKS professional services handle evaluation, planning, migration projects, and establishing customer-specific migration environments within PKS's processing environment. PKS is partnered with VIA-SOFT, Inc.

A.2 Tool Vendors

The following vendors sell software tools that are useful for century-date compliance projects. Some of these vendors offer solution packages that include consulting and training services in addition to software.

- **Applied Business Technology Corporation (ABT)**

  Address: 361 Broadway
                   New York, NY 10013

  Telephone: (212) 219-8945

  ABT offers project management and methodology management tools.

- **Computer Associates International, Inc.**

  Address: One Computer Associates Plaza
                   Islandia, NY 11788-7000

  Telephone: (516) 342-5224

  Computer Associates (CA) offers a combination of products and services through its CA Discovery 2000™ offerings. CA handles MVS, VSE, and PC platforms and includes tools for configuration management, COBOL to COBOL/370 migration, change integration, dynamic coverage analyzer, impact analysis, migration environments, and testing.

- **Compuware Corporation**

  Address: 31440 Northwestern Highway
                   Farmington Hills, MI 48334-2564

  Telephone: 1-800-535-8707

  Compuware offers a combination of products and services to handle all phases of a century-compliance project. Its tools operate on mainframe and PC platforms. Compuware has tools for data migration, execution simulation/debugging, metrics analysis, structuring, testing, and virtual date setting.

- **David R. Black & Associates**

  Address: P.O. Box 9013
                   Akron, OH 44305

  Telephone: (216) 688-2741

  David R. Black & Associates offers tools for date field expansion and data migration.

- **Gladstone Computer Services**

  Address: 28203 Shelter Cove Drive

                   Saugus, CA 91350

  Telephone: 1-800-709-7800

  Gladstone offers software tools for data analysis, data migrations, file comparisons, and test data generation.

- **INTERSOLV**

  Address: 3200 Tower Oaks Boulevard
                    Rockville, MD 20852

  Telephone: 1-800-777-8858

  INTERSOLV offers PC-based tools for configuration management and impact analysis at the program and system levels.

- **INTO 2000 Limited**

  Address: NSE, Inc.
                    1100 Abernathy Road, Suite 625
                    Atlanta, GA 30328

  Telephone: (770) 551-8163

  INTO 2000 offers tools and a methodology for RPG applications on the AS/400 platform. Its tools handle inventory and cross reference, impact analysis, and automated coding changes.

- **Isogon Corporation**

  Address: 330 Seventh Avenue
                    New York, NY 10001

  Telephone: (212) 967-2424

  Isogon offers an inventory tool that locates, identifies, and monitors usage of all mainframe software. It also offers a virtual date utility.

- **Mainware, Inc.**

  Address: 7176 Pioneer Creek Road
                    Maple Plain, MN 55369

  Telephone: (612) 932-9154

  Mainware, Inc. offers a virtual date utility.

- **McCabe & Associates**

  Address: Twin Knolls Professional Park
                    5501 Twin Knolls Road, Suite 111
                    Columbia, MD 21045

  Telephone: 1-800-638-6316

  McCabe & Associates offers products for code slicing, metrics analysis, and test coverage analysis.

- **Micro Focus**

  Address: 2465 East Bayshore Road
  Palo Alto, CA 94303

  Telephone: 1-800-872-6265

  Micro Focus offers a series of PC-based solutions for mainframe and PC applications. Its product set covers inventory and cross-reference, impact analysis, interactive analysis, date field expansion, environment simulation, and testing

- **Platinum Technology, Inc.**

  Address: 1815 South Meyers Road
  Oakbrook Terrace, IL 60181-5241

  Telephone: (708) 620-5000

  Platinum Technology offers a wide range of products, including those formerly sold by ADPAC. Its capabilities include configuration management, inventory and cross-reference, impact analysis, interactive date analysis, repository technology, and testing.

- **Prince Software, Inc.**

  Address: 1000C Lake Street
  Ramsey, NJ 07446

  Telephone: 1-800-934-2022

  Prince Software offers a series of tools and migration services. Its tools cover cross-referencing, COBOL version migrations, data migration, impact analysis, automated change, interface/bridge generation, and virtual date testing.

- **Princeton SOFTECH**

  Address: 1060 State Road
  Princeton, NJ 08540-1423

  Telephone: 1-800 457-7060

  Princeton SOFTECH's Version Merger™ is a tool for change integration in application source code. This facility is useful for reconciling different versions of package software and merging compliant source code with other maintenance changes made during the migration process.

- **SEEC**

  Address: 5001 Baum Blvd.
  Pittsburgh, PA 15213

  Telephone: (412) 682-4958

  SEEC offers PC-based tools that handle inventory and cross-reference, impact analysis, and interactive analysis.

- **Serena**

  Address: 500 Airport
  Burlingame, CA 94010

  Telephone: 1-800-699-6850

  Serena offers a file compare utility source code and data files.

- **Software Emancipation Technology, Inc.**

  Address: Kiln Brook V
  20 Maguire Road
  Lexington MA 02173-0843

  Telephone: (617) 863-8900

  Software Emancipation offers tools for code slicing, inventory and cross-referencing, and impact analysis for C and C++ applications.

- **Sterling Software–Application Engineering Division**

  Address: 5900 Canoga Avenue
  Woodland Hills CA 91367

  Telephone: (818) 716-1616

  Sterling Software offers a combination of software and training courses. Its software tools cover audit support, data migration, impact analysis, interactive analysis, static analysis, metrics analysis, structuring, and testing.

- **TransCentury Data Systems**

  Address: See Platinum Technology, Inc.

  Telephone: 1-800-837-7989

  TransCentury Data Systems offers calendar date subroutines and a date logic generator. TransCentury was recently acquired by Plantinum Technology, Inc.

- **VIASOFT, Inc.**

  Address: 3033 N. 44th Street
  Phoenix, AZ 85018

  Telephone: (602) 952-0050

  VIASOFT offers a full range of century-compliance solutions that can include products, training and consulting services. VIASOFT's tool set covers estimation, inventory and cross-reference, impact analysis, static analysis, interactive analysis, metrics analysis, code slicing, testing, and virtual date setting.

- **Vector**

  Address: 9318 North 95th Way, Suite 201
  Scottsdale, AZ 85258

  Telephone: (602) 966-2770

  Vector offers software for analyzing and identifying date utilization in Unisys Mapper source code and related data stores.

A.3 Conversion Vendors

The vendors listed below fall between tool vendors and consulting firms by offering a specialized mixture of tools and consulting. These vendors specialize in a variety of conversion services, and many have adapted existing conversion software and techniques to handle Year 2000 projects.

- **Avatar Solutions, Inc.**

  Address: 8300 Boone Blvd., Suite 315
  Vienna, VA 22182-2626

  Telephone: (703) 821-3200

  Avatar uses its proprietary technologies to handle impact assessment, plan development, and code migration. Avatar uses a combination of on-site consultants and its remediation facilities to process its client's code. In addition to COBOL and PL/I, Avatar handles 4GL languages such as Mark IV and Natural™.

- **Ernst & Young RE Products bv**

  Address: Varrolan 1000
  P.O. Box 3101
  3502 GC Utrecht
  The Netherlands

  Telephone: +011 31 30 258-8345

  Ernst & Young RE Products offers an automated conversion service for migrating PL/I to COBOL. This service is particularly useful for IT organizations with a small number of PL/I programs in a primarily COBOL environment.

- **Formal Systems, Inc.**

  Address: 16 Zokol Crescent
  Kanata, Ontario, Canada K2K 2K5

  Telephone: (613) 591-1896

  Formal Systems handles Year 2000 analysis and migrations for the Natural language. Formal also offers support for migration between versions of Natural.

- **IBS Conversion Services**

  Address: 2625 Butterfield Road
  Oak Brook, IL 60521

  Telephone: 1-800-5555-IBS

  IBS provides a variety of language, platform, database, and Year 2000 migration services. IBS utilizes its proprietary tools to perform the project on or off site. IBS has scanners to Easytrieve™ and Focus™ in addition to more common languages. IBS also offers training courses in implementing Year 2000 projects.

- **Peritus Software Services, Inc.**

  Address: 304 Concord Road
  Billerica, MA 01821-3485

  Telephone: (508) 670-1173

  Peritus has created a process and a set of software tools for analyzing, migrating, verifying, and generating test data for Year 2000 projects. Although Peritus offers its services directly, it primarily offers its facilities through other consulting vendors.

- **The Source Recovery Company, Inc.**

  Address: 992 East Freeway Drive, Suite A
  Conyers, GA 30207

  Telephone: (770) 760-7316

  The Source Recovery Company offers services for re-creating missing source code from load modules. Their services recover COBOL, assembly language, and BMS maps.

A.4 The Authors' Firms

The following listings are provided for those readers interested in contacting the authors or learning about the services provided by their firms.

- **Clarity Consulting—Ian S. Hayes**

  Address: 40 South Street, Suite 104
  Marblehead, MA 01945-3274

  Telephone: (617) 639-1012

  Email: 70661.1063@compuserve.com

  Clarity Consulting specializes in improving the effectiveness of Information Technology (IT) organizations. Founded in 1993, Clarity Consulting works with IT organizations, product vendors, and other consulting organizations to develop comprehensive solutions to complex IT issues such as the Year 2000 crisis. Clarity Consulting's Year 2000 offerings include strategic planning, enterprise assessments guidance, solution development, and ongoing quality assurance/migration issue resolution.

- **Tactical Strategy Group, Inc. —William M. Ulrich**

  Address: 2901 Park Avenue, Suite C3
  Soquel, CA 95073

  Telephone: (408) 464-5344

  Email: tsginc@cruzio.com

  Founded in 1990, TSG has helped hundreds of organizations develop strategies required to transform legacy systems into strategic information architectures. Clients include Fortune 500 companies, the federal government, hardware and software vendors, and major service providers. Year 2000 services include strategy development, Project Office setup, project audit reviews, and executive advisory services. TSG is also a founding sponsor of the Year 2000 Conference & Expo.

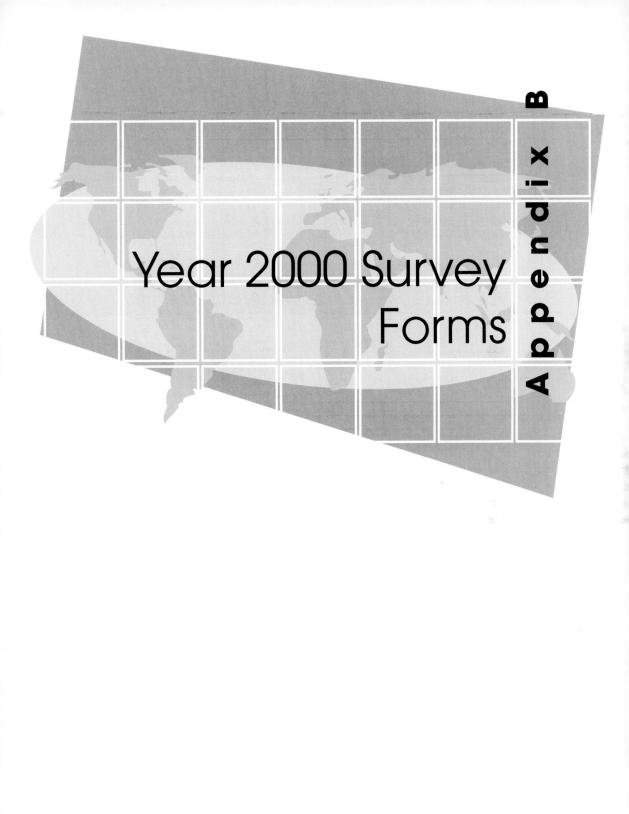

Year 2000 Survey Forms

B.1 TSRM Year 2000 Enterprise Survey Form 047

Enterprise Planning Survey

Company Name: _____

Date: _____

Contact Name: _____

Phone: _____

Contact Address: _____

Fax: _____

_____

_____

Title: _____

1. What stage of the Year 2000 effort are you currently engaged in?

   (Check all applicable items)

   _____ Early research
   _____ Preliminary planning
   _____ Enterprise assessment
   _____ Enterprise RFP effort
   _____ Implementation RFP effort
   _____ Pilot projects
   _____ Implementation

2. Is there high-level (CIO) sponsorship in place?

   _____ Yes
   _____ No

3. Is there a management-level person assigned to the project?

   _____ Yes
   _____ No

4. Is there a Year 2000 management team in place?

   _____ Yes
   _____ No

5. The budget development process is currently at what stage?

   _____ Working preplanning budget
   _____ Estimated enterprise budget
   _____ Actual enterprise budget

6. What is the projected estimate of your enterprise Year 2000 budget?

   $_____

7. In which of the following stages do you plan to use consulting services?

   (Check all applicable items)

   _____ Preliminary planning
   _____ Enterprise assessment
   _____ Project coordination
   _____ Pilot projects
   _____ Implementation

TSRM Year 2000 Enterprise Survey Form 047—Source: HCL James Martin

8. Is outsourcing an option for implementation?   ____ Yes
     ____ No

9. What is the estimated size of your application portfolio in terms of number of systems?
     ____ Less than 100
     ____ 100–250
     ____ 250–500
     ____ 500–1000
     ____ Over 1000
     ____ No idea

10. What is the estimated size of your application portfolio in terms of number of source programs?
     ____ Less than 5,000
     ____ 5,000–10,000
     ____ 10,000–20,000
     ____ 20,000–40,000
     ____ 40,000–60,000
     ____ 60,000–80,000
     ____ Over 80,000

11. What is the estimated size of your application portfolio in terms of number of lines of source code?
     ____ Less than 5 million
     ____ 5–10 million
     ____ 10–20 million
     ____ 20–30 million
     ____ 30–40 million
     ____ 40–60 million
     ____ 60–80 million
     ____ 80–100 million
     ____ Over 100 million

12. How many physical application support locations exist?
     ____ 1–2
     ____ 3–5
     ____ 6–10
     ____ 11–15
     ____ 16–20
     ____ Over 20

13. Applications support is spread across

     (Check all applicable items)
     ____ Multiple cities
     ____ Multiple states
     ____ Multiple countries

14. What date file and database management systems are used in your organization?

     (Indicate rough percentage of each type)
     ____% VSAM
     ____% Sequential files
     ____% Generation Data Groups
     ____% IMS DB
     ____% DB2
     ____% IDMS
     ____% Other: _____

15. What primary operating systems are used in your organization?

(Indicate rough percentage of each type)

_____% MVS/ESA
_____% AS/400
_____% DOS VSE
_____% UNIX
_____% OS/2
_____% MS Windows (et al)
_____% UNISYS 1100
_____% UNISYS A Series
_____% Other: _____

16. What primary hardware systems are used in your organization?

(Indicate rough percentage of each type)

_____% IBM Mainframe
_____% AS 400
_____% IBM PC/Compatible
_____% UNISYS Mainframe
_____% Other: _____

17. What primary teleprocessing systems are used in your organization?

(Indicate rough percentage of each type)

_____% CICS
_____% IMS DC
_____% IDMS DC
_____% Batch processing
_____% Visual Basic
_____% Middleware: _____

18. Has your organization experienced any Year 2000 problems to date? (e.g., Abends, corrupt data, inaccurate reports...)

_____ Yes
_____ No
_____ Don't know

19. Are configuration management tools used in your organization?

(Indicate rough percentage of each type)

_____% Mainframe tool utilization
_____% Client/server tool utilization
_____% Cross-platform utilization

20. Has your organization ever managed a cross-enterprise project similar to the Year 2000?

_____ Yes
_____ No

21. Is the Year 2000 project an immediate priority for your organization?

_____ Yes
_____ No

B.2 TSRM Year 2000 System Survey Form 045

System Survey

Application Area/Division Name: _____

Date: _____

Contact Name: _____

Phone: _____

Location: _____
_____
_____

Fax: _____

Supervisor: _____
_____

Title: _____

---

1. What is the name and acronym of the system?

Name: _____

Acronym: _____

2. What is the type of system?

_____ In-house business application
_____ System software
_____ 3rd-party business application
_____ User system
_____ Process control system
_____ Mixed (package & in-house)
_____ Other: _____

3. What are the acronyms of subsystems within this system? (List only if applicable)

System type is different from question #2

Acronym: _____
Acronym: _____
Acronym: _____
Acronym: _____
Acronym: _____
Acronym: _____
Acronym: _____
Acronym: _____
Acronym: _____

4. If system/subsystem is vendor package:
–Is system on maintenance?
–Is package Year 2000 compliant?
–If no, is vendor planning a Year 2000 upgrade?
–Do you modify package source code?

Yes No
___ ___
___ ___
___ ___
___ ___

Number of releases behind current release
_____

Current production release # _____

5. What primary function does the application serve? (e.g., master file reconciliation, tape management utility, receipts tracking...)

Primary Function:
_____
_____
_____

TSRM Year 2000 Enterprise Survey Form 045—Source: HCL James Martin

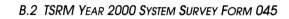

6. Do you expect the application to be replaced or in some way eliminated?

    If yes, when: _____

    _____ Phased out
    _____ Migrated to new architecture
    _____ Replaced/rewritten
    _____ Replaced with package
    _____ Updated with new package version

7. Does system import or export files to external entities such as other government or private institutions?

    _____ Yes
    _____ No
    _____ Don't know

    If yes, list file names and point of contact (attach additional documentation if more space is needed)

    _____
    _____
    _____

8. Is diagrammatic documentation available for system? (e.g., execution flows, operational flows, job flows...)

    _____ Yes
    _____ No
    _____ Don't know

    If yes, what type of documentation is available?

    _____
    _____
    _____

9. What is the estimated number of programs in the application?

    Estimated number of source programs:
    _____

10. Is system source code available?

    _____ Yes
    _____ No
    _____ Partially

11. What is estimated number of lines of source code in system? (Use program source code line counts with expanded copybooks and macros)

    Estimated lines of program source code:
    _____

12. What is estimated number of files and database segments, records, and/or tables in the application?

    Estimated files, segments, records, tables:
    _____

13. What is estimated number of batch reports in the application?

    Estimated number of batch reports:
    _____

14. What is the estimated number of on-line screens in the application?

    Estimated number of on-line screens:
    _____

15. What are the primary programming languages used in the system?

(Check all applicable boxes)

_____ COBOL
_____ Assembler (ALC)
_____ C or C++
_____ PL/I
_____ Visual Basic
_____ 4th GL: _____
_____ Mapper:
_____ Other: _____

16. What data file/database management systems are used by the system?

(List with corresponding percentage)

_____% VSAM
_____% Sequential files
_____% Generation Data Groups
_____% IMS DB
_____% DB2
_____% IDMS
_____% DMS 1100
_____% Other: _____

17. What operating systems does the system run on?

(List with corresponding percentage)

_____% MVS/ESA
_____% AS/400
_____% IBM VM
_____% DOS VSE
_____% UNIX
_____% OS/2
_____% MS Windows (et al.)
_____% UNISYS 1100
_____% UNISYS A Series
_____% Other: _____

18. What hardware does the system run on?

(List with corresponding percentage)

_____% IBM Mainframe
_____% AS/400
_____% IBM PC/Compatible
_____% UNISYS Mainframe
_____% Other: _____

19. What is the primary teleprocessing system used?

(List with corresponding percentage)

_____% CICS
_____% IMS DC
_____% IDMS DC
_____% Batch processing
_____% Visual Basic
_____% Middleware: _____
_____% Other: _____

20. Number of control language members?

_____

(see below for control language types)

21. What type of control language is used?

    (List with corresponding percentages)

    _____% IBM JCL
    _____% Unisys ECL
    _____% Unisys WFL
    _____% DEC DCL
    _____% Shell Scripts
    _____% AS400 CL
    _____% DOS VSE JCL
    _____% Other: _____

22. Are configuration management tools used
    on the system?

    (List with corresponding percentages)

    _____% Mainframe tool use
    _____% Client/server tool use
    _____% Cross-platform use

23. Does system share data stores with other
    systems?

    _____ Yes
    _____ No

    If yes, how many shared batch files? _____
    Please list files below (or continue on back of form)
    _____
    _____
    _____

    If yes, how many shared on-line files? _____
    Please list files below (or continue on back of form)
    _____
    _____
    _____

    If yes, how many shared databases? _____
    Please list files below (or continue on back of form)
    _____
    _____
    _____

24. Are 2-digit year representations (e.g., '95' for
    1995) used in the system?

    _____ Yes
    _____ No

25. Does your application contain forward date
    calculations?

    _____ Yes
    _____ No

    If yes, how far forward (2 months, 6 months,
    etc.)?
    _____

26. Are standard date routines implemented
    across the application?

    If yes, please list them by name:
    _____
    _____

    _____ Uses systemwide standard
    _____ Uses organization standard
    _____ Partial use of standard routines
    _____ No standard routines used

27. What are top 3 most commonly used date formats?

    (e.g., Gregorian, formatted, packed)

_____

_____

_____

28. Rate the system's dependence on date processing:

    Heavy _____

    Medium _____

    Light _____

    None _____   (None means system has no dates at all)

29. Has the system experienced Year 2000 production problems to date? (e.g., aborts, corrupt data, inaccurate reports...)

    _____ Yes

    _____ No

Legacy Transition Meta-model (LTM)

The Legacy Transition Meta-model or LTM is an entity relationship model representing current and target system components that can be depicted in a repository. LTM defines attributes and relationships for each entity or object in the repository model. Physical object types include job, step, proc, source module, copy member, screen, report, record, and other implementation-specific components. Logical object types include entity, function, event, process/business rule, and various other models and diagrams. External objects include change request, location, and other user types added as required. Relationship examples include step executes load module, process/business rule maps to procedure, and record maps to entity.

The LTM model allows organizations to customize the baseline by adding or eliminating object types as needed. Physical object attributes vary according to implementation factors, whereas logical object types vary depending on development paradigms. It is unlikely, for example, that a given project would use all of the Information Engineering and object/event representations within the LTM. Customization can also occur if an enterprise view is used to store high-level meta-data collected during an enterprise assessment. This enterprise model can then feed business area-related information into project-specific models.

Experience with Year 2000 and redevelopment projects has shown that large-scale transition from legacy to strategic architectures requires:

- Managing vast amounts of meta-data collected across multiple project phases

- Establishing an audit trail to track and verify step-related activities

- Tracking legacy-to-target relationships as they evolve

- Tracking redundant data and processes by having LTM objects map to themselves

- Flagging items for deactivation or reuse in target or legacy systems

- Establishing a comprehensive vehicle for integrating disparate tasks across a wide range of tools, techniques, or platforms

The LTM was developed in cooperation with certain vendors, repository and redevelopment experts, and user organizations to support redevelopment tasks defined in the HCL James Martin, Inc. TSRM (The Systems Redevelopment Methodology). The LTM maps to underlying models used in inventory and cross-reference analysis tools. This mapping simplifies population and other interface requirements between these tools and repositories. The LTM is best implemented under an open repository where organizations can add or remove object types, relationships, and attributes as required by the environment or project.

LTM objects (also called entities) are defined below. The LTM does turn difficult or impossible management assignments into projects that will succeed, using a defined audit trail for tracking activity and results. One requirement for implementing LTM in a repository is to populate and refresh the model. Some repository vendors offer these facilities. Others link to commercial tools. Organizations should consider certain features in a repository population facility:

- Do parsers scan all required physical components in a given environment?

- Do parsers run on the host or workstation?

- Do the loaders recognize and update only modified components to avoid a complete reload when updating is required?

- Does the population vendor have an agreement with the repository vendor to provide a "robust" link?

Because each project will have to adjust the LTM for project-specific requirements, there is a degree of leeway in how the LTM is used. Analysts should note this as they plan a given project. For example, a technical assessment, applied either as a first phase of a large assessment effort or as a standalone analysis project, would utilize only physical objects within the LTM. Additional object types could be added in subsequent project phases. Similarly, if target architecture mapping is not required, target entity and function relationships would not be created. Furthermore, modeling paradigms that do not apply to a given environment should be eliminated completely. For example, analysts would exclude event and object from the LTM if an Information Engineering paradigm was being used. The bottom line is that analysts should use good judgment in applying the LTM to various redevelopment efforts.

Once the LTM is initially populated, an infrastructure must be created to maintain its relevancy. This infrastructure includes deploying a customized repository users and administrator guide and establishing roles and responsibilities to manage the evolution of the LTM. The LTM, over time, becomes outdated if it is not refreshed with changes in the physical, logical, and business environment.

C.1 LTM Baseline Object Definitions

ATTRIBUTE

Description:

Defines an attribute within an entity relationship or logical data model.

Relationships:

ATTRIBUTE_DESCRIBES_ENTITY

ATTRIBUTE_DESCRIBES_RELATIONSHIP

ATTRIBUTE_MAPS_TO_ATTRIBUTE

ATTRIBUTE_MAPS_TO_ELEMENT

SUBJECT_AREA_CONTAINS_ATTRIBUTE

BUSINESS_AREA

Description:

Defines a cross-section of the organization that comprises one or more information systems.

Relationships:

ER_DIAGRAM_REPRESENTS_BUSINESS_AREA

LOCATION_IS_LOC_FOR_BUSINESS_AREA

OBJECT_DIAG_REPRESENTS_BUS_AREA

SYSTEM_SUPPORTS_BUSINESS_AREA

CHANGE_REQUEST

Description:

Manually entered request to upgrade the system. Relation to system is implied through related object relationships. If used, relationships must be maintained as the request backlog changes.

Relationships:

CHANGE_REQUEST_AFFECTS_COPYBOOK

CHANGE_REQUEST_AFFECTS_ELEMENT

CHANGE_REQUEST_AFFECTS_FILE

CHANGE_REQUEST_AFFECTS_JOB

CHANGE_REQUEST_AFFECTS_PROGRAM

CHANGE_REQUEST_AFFECTS_PROCESS

CHANGE_REQUEST_AFFECTS_RECORD

CONSTANT

Description:

Defines a literal that can be embedded in a program, on a form or other system object. Users can rename this as a LITERAL, depending on in-house terminology.

Relationships:

CONSTANT_MAPS_TO_ELEMENT

FORM_CONTAINS_CONSTANT

PROGRAM_USES_CONSTANT

COPYBOOK

Description:

Defines a reusable component accessible through features in the compiler such as the COBOL COPY library and related reference. Preferred over hard-coded, nonreusable definitions, particularly for data records.

Relationships:

COPYBOOK_DEFINES_RECORD

COPYBOOK_INCLUDES_COPYBOOK

COPYBOOK_IS_USED_BY_PROGRAM

COPYBOOK_IS_CONTAINED_IN_LIBRARY

CHANGE_REQUEST_AFFECTS_COPYBOOK

PROC_INCLUDES_COPYBOOK

RECORD_INCLUDES_COPYBOOK

DATABASE_DEFINITION

Description:

Defines physical and logical database structures, including IMS, DB/2, and other physical objects required to define physical DBMS. If this is an IMS database, this object represents a DBD. A relationship to a segment (PSB) object serves as a pointer to a logical view of this physical definition.

Relationships:

DATABASE_DEFINITION_DEFINES_SEGMENT

DATABASE_DEFINITION_DEFINES_FILE

DATABASE_DEF_MAPS_TO_DATABASE_DEF

DATABASE_DEF_IS_CONTAINED_IN_LIBRARY

DFD

Description:

Represents existence of a data flow diagram (DFD) that supports logical documentation of a system or subsystem. Typically, the DFD represents high-level data store flow and usage across and between systems and subsystems.

Relationships:

DFD_DEFINES_SUBSYSTEM

DFD_DEFINES_SYSTEM

DFD_MAPS_TO_DFD

DFD_REFERENCES_FILE

ELEMENT

Description:

Defines physical element within current application. Initial analysis will lead to redundantly defined definitions being repeated under differing names. These are represented by an element-points-to-element relationship. Rationalization would reduce number of element instances. Records or other group definitions are considered special cases of an element. Users may choose to refine this relationship, based on in-house repository standards. Automated population, given that this level of detail is applied, is required for this LTM object.

Relationships:

ELEMENT_CONTAINS_ELEMENT

ELEMENT_MAPS_TO_ELEMENT

CHANGE_REQUEST_AFFECTS_ELEMENT

CONSTANT_MAPS_TO_ELEMENT

ATTRIBUTE_MAPS_TO_ELEMENT

FIELD_REPRESENTS_ELEMENT

FILE_CONTAINS_ELEMENT

RECORD_HAS_KEY_ELEMENT

RECORD_USES_REC_TYPE_ELEMENT

RECORD_REPRESENTS_ELEMENT

SEGMENT_CONTAINS_DATA_ELEMENT

PROGRAM_DEFINES_ELEMENT

PROGRAM_NEEDS_PARAMETER_ELEMENT

TABLE_CONTAINS_ELEMENT

TABLE_DEFINES_ELEMENT

ENTITY

Description:

Represents an entity as defined in an entity relationship diagram or logical data model. This definition may have been extracted from a current application or created as a top-down component of a target model.

Relationships:

ENTITY_MAPS_TO_RECORD

ENTITY_MAPS_TO_ENTITY

ENTITY_MAPS_TO_OBJECT

ATTRIBUTE_DESCRIBES_ENTITY

ER_DIAGRAM_CONTAINS_ENTITY

FUNCTION_USES_ENTITY

PROCESS_USES_ENTITY

RELATIONSHIP_FROM_ENTITY

RELATIONSHIP_TO_ENTITY

SUBJECT_AREA_CONTAINS_ENTITY

ER_DIAGRAM

Description:

Defines a collection of entities and relationships as defined in an entity relationship model.

Relationships:

ER_DIAGRAM_CONTAINS_ENTITY

ER_DIAGRAM_MAPS_TO_ER_DIAGRAM

ER_DIAGRAM_REPRESENTS_SYSTEM

ER_DIAGRAM_REPRESENTS_BUSINESS_AREA

EVENT

Description:

A happening in the business that changes the state of an object through invocation of a business rule operation. Events are linked through an event diagram, which could be re-created through event-precedes-event relationship.

Relationships:

EVENT_DIAG_ DEFINES_EVENT
EVENT_TRIGGERS_BUS_RULE
EVENT_ PRECEDES_EVENT
EVENT_IMPACTS_OBJECT_STATE
FORM_DETERMINES_EVENT
JOB_INITIATES_EVENT
JOBSTEP_INITIATES_EVENT

EVENT_DIAGRAM

Description:

Physical diagram that connects a series of events defining an event-driven system.

Relationships:

EVENT_DIAG_ DEFINES_EVENT

FIELD

Description:

Represents a user view of an element on a screen or report (FORM). Typically, it is physically defined in an on-line map macro. Normally, only a subset of the attributes applies.

Relationships:

FIELD_REPRESENTS_ELEMENT
FORM_CONTAINS_FIELD

FILE

Description:

Represents the data definition name for a physical data set within a system. A file can interface directly with programs or can be the underlying file structure for a database.

Relationships:

FILE_CONTAINS_ELEMENT
FILE_MAPS_TO_FILE
FILE_IS_CONTAINED_IN_LIBRARY
CHANGE_REQUEST_AFFECTS_FILE

DATABASE_DEFINITION_DEFINES_FILE

DFD_REFERENCES_FILE

RECORD_DEFINES_FILE

PROGRAM_USES_FILE

SYSTEM_USES_FILE

FORM

Description:

Can represent an on-line screen or a report. This includes GUI definitions as well. If a physical screen map is defined outside an actual program, this should be the source of this object. A user can choose to define separate REPORT and SCREEN objects in place of the FORM object in a customized LTM model.

Relationships:

FORM_CONTAINS_CONSTANT

FORM_CONTAINS_FIELD

FORM_DETERMINES_EVENT

FORM_IS_INPUT_TO_SOURCE_PROGRAM

FORM_IS_OUTPUT_FROM_SOURCE_PROGRAM\

FORM_DEF_CONTAINED_IN_LIBRARY

FUNCTION

Description:

Can be interpreted as a planning-level entity used in Information Engineering (IE) methodology. Alternate development methods may define a function slightly differently.

Relationships:

FUNCTION_MAPS_TO_FUNCTION

FUNCTION_MAPS_TO_SOURCE_PROGRAM

FUNCTION_PRECEDES_FUNCTION

FUNCTION_USES_ENTITY

FDD_CONTAINS_FUNCTION

FHD_CONTAINS_FUNCTION

FUNCTION_DEPENDENCY_DIAGRAM (FDD)

Description:

Represents the sequential relationships among many functions within an IE development environment.

Relationships:

FDD_CONTAINS_FUNCTION
FDD_IS_PART_OF_SYSTEM
FDD_DECOMPOSES_INTO_PDD
FDD_IS_PART_OF_SUBSYSTEM

FUNCTION_HIERARCHY_DIAGRAM (FHD)

Description:

Represents the hierarchical relationships among many functions within an IE development environment.

Relationships:

FHD_CONTAINS_FUNCTION
FHD_IS_PART_OF_SYSTEM
FHD_DECOMPOSES_INTO_PHD
FHD_IS_PART_OF_SUBSYSTEM
FHD_MAPS_TO_FHD

INCLUDE

Description:

Special case situation of a Copy, used as a means of reusing code within library management systems.

Relationships:

INCLUDE_DEFINES_RECORD
INCLUDE_IS_CONTAINED_IN_LIBRARY
INCLUDE_IS_INCLUDED_IN_SOURCE_PROGRAM

JOB

Description:

Defines a group of execution steps within a batch system and may define IBM MVS job streams or other types of environmental, execution-control-language run streams.

Relationships:

> JOB_USES_PROC
> JOB_CONTAINS_JOBSTEP
> JOB_IS_CONTAINED_IN_LIBRARY
> JOB_IS_PART_OF_SUBSYSTEM
> JOB_IS_PART_OF_SYSTEM
> JOB_PRECEDES_JOB
> JOB_INITIATES_EVENT
> CHANGE_REQUEST_AFFECTS_JOB
> PROC_STARTS_JOB

JOBSTEP

Description:

Delineates steps within a job stream and is a key indicator of the sequence of batch system processes.

Relationships:

> JOBSTEP_EXECUTES_LOAD_MODULE
> JOBSTEP_PRECEDES_JOBSTEP
> JOBSTEP_INITIATES_EVENT
> JOB_CONTAINS_JOBSTEP
> PROC_CONTAINS_JOBSTEP

LIBRARY

Description:

Defines the cataloged name of a physical system component. It is the key link between various physical objects and location. If a physical, catalogued object is being used within the LTM and library applies, then link library with that object, using applicable relationship.

Relationships:

> LOCATION_IS_LOCATION_FOR_LIBRARY
> LIBRARY_USES_LIBRARY
> COPYBOOK_IS_CONTAINED_IN_LIBRARY
> DATABASE_DEF_IS_CONTAINED_IN_LIBRARY
> FILE_IS_CONTAINED_IN_LIBRARY

FORM_DEF_CONTAINED_IN_LIBRARY
INCLUDE_IS_CONTAINED_IN_LIBRARY
JOB_IS_CONTAINED_IN_LIBRARY
LOAD_MODULE_IS_CONTAINED_IN_LIBRARY
MACRO_IS_CONTAINED_IN_LIBRARY
CONTROL_TBL_FOUND_IN_LIBRARY
PROC_IS_CONTAINED_IN_LIBRARY
SEGMENT_DEF_CONTAINED_IN_LIBRARY
PROGRAM_IS_CONTAINED_IN_LIBRARY

LOAD_MODULE

Description:

The executable program, typically comprising one to many source modules.

Relationships:

LOAD_MODULE_CONTAINS_SOURCE_MODULE
LOAD_MODULE_IS_CONTAINED_IN_LIBRARY
JOBSTEP_EXECUTES_LOAD_MODULE
CONTROL_TBL_EXECS_LOAD_MOD
PROC_EXECUTES_LOAD_MODULE

LOCATION

Description:

Implies physical location. Location object is particularly applicable for organizations with multiple computer sites or distributed environments. Objects are linked to location via library objects.

Relationships:

LOCATION_IS_LOCATION_FOR_LIBRARY
LOCATION_IS_LOCATION_FOR_SYSTEM
LOCATION_IS_LOC_FOR_BUSINESS_AREA

MACRO

Description:

Defines reusable code accessible through features in assembler compiler. May be standard or user-defined, based on environment.

Relationships:

> MACRO_IS_USED_BY_PROGRAM
>
> MACRO_IS_CONTAINED_IN_LIBRARY

OBJECT

Description:

> An abstraction of certain business information, within a specific problem domain, that encompasses both data and processes associated with that information.

Relationships:

> OBJECT_IS_ASSOCIATED-WITH_OBJECT
>
> ENTITY_MAPS_TO_OBJECT
>
> EVENT_IMPACTS_OBJECT_STATE
>
> OBJECT_DIAGRAM_CONTAINS_OBJECT
>
> BUS_RULE_IMPACTS_OBJECT

OBJECT DIAGRAM

Description:

> Defines each object and associations among these objects. This object modeling approach is based on the Martin/Odell object modeling paradigm.

Relationships:

> OBJECT_DIAGRAM_CONTAINS_OBJECT
>
> OBJECT_DIAGRAM OBJECT
>
> OBJECT_DIAG_REPRESENTS_BUS_AREA
>
> OBJECT_DIAGRAM BUSINESS_AREA

ONLINE_CONTROL_TABLE

Description:

> Controls the execution of system load modules based on on-line transaction invocation. Examples are CICS PCT or IMS ACB definitions.

Relationships:

> CONTROL_TBL_EXECS_LOAD_MOD
>
> CONTROL_TBL_FOUND_IN_LIBRARY
>
> CONTROL_TBL_PART_OF_SYSTEM

PROC

Description:

An IBM JCL term that allows for the reuse of control language statements with a substitution facility. PROCs are recognized because they are a physical component of the system that impacts analysis. Non-IBM environments likely use a similar construct, and this should be reflected where applicable.

Relationships:

PROC_CONTAINS_PROC

PROC_EXECUTES_LOAD_MODULE

PROC_INCLUDES_COPYBOOK

PROC_IS_CONTAINED_IN_LIBRARY

PROC_CONTAINS_JOBSTEP

PROC_STARTS_JOB

JOB_USES_PROC

PROCEDURE

Description:

Represents a block of code delineated by a paragraph name or label (depending on source type). Business rules are generally mapped to current source code procedures, depending on the project and paradigm being used.

Relationships:

PROCEDURE_DEFINED_IN_PROGRAM

PROCEDURE_RELATED_TO_PROCEDURE

PRAD_DEFINES_PROCEDURE

PROCESS_MAPS_TO_PROCEDURE

PROCEDURE_ACTION_DIAGRAM (PRAD)

Description:

IE-based diagram showing procedures defined at the design level. Because IE procedures are very close to implementation-level representations, they are not defined as objects within the LTM. If an IE procedure is to be traced back to an existing system for derivation purposes, the process action diagram (PAD) mapping to PRAD can be used to identify processes and their respective links to legacy source code.

Relationships:

PRAD_DEFINES_PROCEDURE

PRAD_REPRESENTS_SYSTEM

PRAD_REPRESENTS_SUBSYSTEM

PAD_DECOMPOSES_INTO_PRAD

PROCESS_ACTION_DIAGRAM (PAD)

Description:

An IE-based decomposition of analysis-level business rule representations. This diagram explodes a process, as defined in the IE methodology. Links to legacy source code can be traced through the PROCESS/BUS_RULE object mapping to source code procedure logic.

Relationships:

PAD_DEFINES_PROCESS

PAD_DECOMPOSES_INTO_PRAD

PAD_REPRESENTS_SYSTEM

PAD_REPRESENTS_SUBSYSTEM

PROCESS/BUS_RULE

Description:

Can represent an IE-based analysis object called a process, an event-driven business rule implementation, or other instantiations of business rules as defined by other development paradigms. This is a key component of the LTM for redevelopment transition mapping. Redundancy is defined by the mapping relationship between PROCESS/BUS_RULE objects with the same current_target_indicator setting.

Relationships:

BUS_RULE_MAPS_TO_BUS_RULE

BUS_RULE_MAPS_TO_SOURCE_PROGRAM

PROCESS_USES_ENTITY

BUS_RULE_IMPACTS_OBJECT

BUS_RULE_DECOMPOSES_INTO_BUS_RULE

BUS_RULE_MAPS_TO_PROCEDURE
    CHANGE_REQUEST_AFFECTS_PROCESS
    EVENT_TRIGGERS_BUS_RULE
    PAD_DEFINES_PROCESS
    PDD_CONTAINS_PROCESS
    PHD_CONTAINS_PROCESS

PROCESS_DEPENDENCY_DIAGRAM (PDD)

Description:

An IE-based dependency representation of analysis-level business rule representations. This diagram is a collection of processes as defined in the IE methodology.

Relationships:

    PDD_CONTAINS_PROCESS
    PDD_REPRESENTS_SYSTEM
    PDD_REPRESENTS_SUBSYSTEM
    FDD_DECOMPOSES_INTO_PDD

PROCESS_HIERARCHY_DIAGRAM (PHD)

Description:

An IE-based hierarchical representation of analysis-level business rules. This diagram is a collection of processes as defined in the IE methodology.

Relationships:

    PHD_CONTAINS_PROCESS
    PHD_REPRESENTS_SUBSYSTEM
    PHD_REPRESENTS_SYSTEM
    PHD_MAPS_TO_PHD
    FHD_DECOMPOSES_INTO_PHD

RECORD

Description:

Defines a group of data elements that are input to or output from a program. A record can define one or more physical files and be defined identically to other records (duplicate records). A record can be a record because it has direct correlation to an input or output record, even if it is not used directly in I/O.

Relationships:

RECORD_CONTAINS_RECORD

RECORD_HAS_KEY_ELEMENT

RECORD_USES_REC_TYPE_ELEMENT

RECORD_INCLUDES_COPYBOOK

RECORD_IS_DEFINED_IN_PROGRAM

RECORD_REDEFINES_RECORD

RECORD_REPRESENTS_ELEMENT

RECORD_DEFINES_FILE

RECORD_DEFINES_SEGMENT

CHANGE_REQUEST_AFFECTS_RECORD

COPYBOOK_DEFINES_RECORD

ENTITY_MAPS_TO_RECORD

INCLUDE_DEFINES_RECORD

PROGRAM_HAS_PARAMETER_RECORD

PROGRAM_USES_RECORD

RELATIONSHIP

Description:

Defines the connection between entities within an entity relationship diagram or logical data model.

Relationships:

RELATIONSHIP_FROM_ENTITY

RELATIONSHIP_MAPS_TO_RELATIONSHIP

RELATIONSHIP_TO_ENTITY

ATTRIBUTE_DESCRIBES_RELATIONSHIP

SUBJECT_AREA_CONTAINS_RELATIONSHIP

SEGMENT

Description:

Database-specific term that applies to hierarchical (e.g., IMS), network (e.g., IDMS) or other database structures and defines a logical view of a group of elements. It would be defined by an IMS PSB, for example. Other database definitions should use this object to represent a logical view of a physical data structure, as required. Renaming this object to be more specific is an option open to the user analyst.

Relationships:

SEGMENT_CONTAINS_DATA_ELEMENT

SEGMENT_DEF_CONTAINED_IN_LIBRARY

DATABASE_DEFINITION_DEFINES_SEGMENT

RECORD_DEFINES_SEGMENT

SOURCE_PROGRAM

Description:

A delineated block of production source code, represented in a variety of language types, that can be compiled into an object module. One or more object modules are generally linked into an executable load module.

Relationships:

PROGRAM_CALLS_PROGRAM_ENTRY_POINT

PROGRAM_DEFINES_ELEMENT

PROGRAM_HAS_PARAMETER_RECORD

PROGRAM_IS_CONTAINED_IN_LIBRARY

PROGRAM_NEEDS_PARAMETER_ELEMENT

PROGRAM_USES_CONSTANT

PROGRAM_USES_FILE

PROGRAM_USES_RECORD

BUS_RULE_MAPS_TO_SOURCE_PROGRAM

CHANGE_REQUEST_AFFECTS_PROGRAM

COPYBOOK_IS_USED_BY_PROGRAM

FORM_IS_INPUT_TO_SOURCE_PROGRAM

FORM_IS_OUTPUT_FROM_SOURCE_PROGRAM

FUNCTION_MAPS_TO_SOURCE_PROGRAM

INCLUDE_IS_INCLUDED_IN_SOURCE_PROGRAM

LOAD_MODULE_CONTAINS_SOURCE_MODULE

MACRO_IS_USED_BY_PROGRAM

PROCEDURE_DEFINED_IN_PROGRAM
RECORD_IS_DEFINED_IN_PROGRAM
SYSTEM_CONTAINS_SOURCE_PROGRAM

SUBJECT_AREA

Description:

A very high level definition of data within the IE methodology. Addition of a SUBJECT_AREA_DIAGRAM object may be warranted depending on the situation.

Relationships:

SUBJECT_AREA_CONTAINS_ATTRIBUTE
SUBJECT_AREA_CONTAINS_ENTITY
SUBJECT_AREA_CONTAINS_RELATIONSHIP
SUBJECT_AREA_MAPS_TO_SUBJECT_AREA

SUBSYSTEM

Description:

Describes a delineated group of physical components that an organization defines as belonging to a larger group called a system. For example, pay processing may be a subsystem within a human resources system. This is user defined and not a requirement to the use of LTM.

Relationships:

SUBSYSTEM_INTERFACES_WITH_SUBSYSTEM
DFD_DEFINES_SUBSYSTEM
FDD_IS_PART_OF_SUBSYSTEM
FHD_IS_PART_OF_SUBSYSTEM
JOB_IS_PART_OF_SUBSYSTEM
PRAD_REPRESENTS_SUBSYSTEM
PAD_REPRESENTS_SUBSYSTEM
PDD_REPRESENTS_SUBSYSTEM
PHD_REPRESENTS_SUBSYSTEM
SYSTEM_CONTAINS_SUBSYSTEM
SYSTEM_INTERFACES_WITH_SUBSYSTEM
SSC_REPRESENTS_SUBSYSTEM

SYSTEM

Description:

Describes a delineated group of physical components that an organization defines as belonging to or being maintained by a specifically defined group within the enterprise. For example, human resources is an example of a system. System is the key delineator within a business area or enterprise.

Relationships:

SYSTEM_CONTAINS_SOURCE_PROGRAM

SYSTEM_CONTAINS_SUBSYSTEM

SYSTEM_INTERFACES_WITH_SUBSYSTEM

SYSTEM_INTERFACES_WITH_SYSTEM

SYSTEM_SUPPORTS_BUSINESS_AREA

SYSTEM_USES_FILE

DFD_DEFINES_SYSTEM

ER_DIAGRAM_REPRESENTS_SYSTEM

FDD_IS_PART_OF_SYSTEM

FHD_IS_PART_OF_SYSTEM

JOB_IS_PART_OF_SYSTEM

LOCATION_IS_LOCATION_FOR_SYSTEM

CONTROL_TBL_PART_OF_SYSTEM

PRAD_REPRESENTS_SYSTEM

PAD_REPRESENTS_SYSTEM

PDD_REPRESENTS_SYSTEM

PHD_REPRESENTS_SYSTEM

SSC_REPRESENTS_SYSTEM

LOCATION_IS_LOCATION_FOR_SYSTEM

SYSTEM_STRUCTURE_CHART (SSC)

Description:

Defines an overall structural decomposition of a system within an IE-based environment.

Relationships:

    SSC_REPRESENTS_SUBSYSTEM
    SSC_REPRESENTS_SYSTEM
    SSC_MAPS_TO_SSC

TABLE

Description:

Defines a relational DBMS-based table definition. Program record tables are defined in RECORD objects with repeating groups.

Relationships:

    TABLE_CONTAINS_ELEMENT
    TABLE_DEFINES_ELEMENT

UPGRADE UNIT

Description::

A logical combination of systems or subsystems that can be made Year 2000 compliant and moved into production as a logical unit of work within the context of a single migration project.

Relationships:

    UPGRADE_UNIT_INCLUDES_SYSTEM
    UPGRADE_UNIT_INCLUDES_SUBSYSTEM

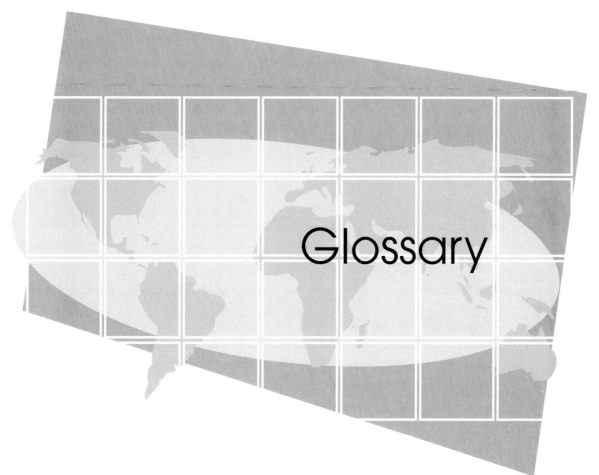

Glossary

API

Application Programming Interface (API) is a routine that expands or contracts data formats during on-line application execution to reconcile expanded or unexpanded data formats between an application and shared data store.

blueprint

A detailed approach, containing generic and tool-related, step-by-step guidelines, for developing, upgrading, improving, or replacing application systems. Also called a "methodology."

bridge

A routine that expands or contracts batch data files to reconcile data format differences between expanded and unexpanded data stores in a Year 2000 project.

business area

A functionally distinct corporate division or strategic business unit that is supported by one or more application systems.

century date change

The impending Year 2000 millennium change and its resultant impact and potential *disruptions* of business services, information databases, and application systems. Same as Year 2000.

century-date compliant

Status of a given unit of software if it correctly handles comparisons, calculations, and sorts that use date data spanning both sides of the century boundary. The goal of a Year 2000 initiative is to achieve century-date compliance for all of the software in a company's portfolio.

century midpoint

An application parameter representing the 2-digit year upon which the century date will toggle in a Year 2000 procedural workaround project. Any 2-digit year higher than the century midpoint would be assumed to have a "19" in the century field, and those lower than or equal to the century midpoint would be assumed to have a "20" in the century field.

certification

The process of testing a given application or set of programs to determine if they correctly handle century dates. This process must be performed before assuming any application is century-date compliant. Certification is performed before migration activities for applications that are thought to be century-date compliant and is the final step of the validation process for noncompliant applications that have been migrated.

data name rationalization

The process by which data element definitions are modified so that each element retains the same name and characteristics throughout an application system. This process has a tendency to dramatically reduce the actual number of record groups and physical data names within a system by creating reusable Copy or Include code blocks for a given record, segment, or table definition.

event horizon

The amount of time before a Year 2000 migration effort for a particular application must begin.

expansion

1. The removal of a COPY statement from a program during restructuring process and the placement of the statements from the COPY member into the program without reference to their origin.

2. The increase in physical or logical size of a record or element definition or the corresponding physical data that is referenced by that element or record.

external system file

A file or data store received from or passed to an interface system.

interface system

Any system or upgrade unit that receives data from or sends data to a system or upgrade unit currently undergoing an assessment or conversion effort.

I/O record group

A record group (*see* record group) that contains at least one record definition used in an input/output transaction.

junction

Interface point where a system with expanded fields passes data, receives data, or otherwise interacts with another system whose corresponding fields have remained unchanged.

legacy transition meta-model (LTM)

An entity relationship model representing current and target system components and relationships among those components. It is usually customized for a given project and requires an open repository to support practical use. It is used to cross-reference, trace, track, and audit physical, logical, and externally defined system components before, during, and after a redevelopment project.

local data element

A data element that accomplishes an intermediate task or calculation within a program and only within that program.

logical record

The full aggregation of attributes with no redundancy describing an I/O record in the context of the programming language being used. There can be many physical records used to describe a single logical record.

LTM

See legacy transition meta-model

methodology

A detailed approach, containing generic and tool-related, step-by-step guidelines, to developing, upgrading, improving, or replacing application systems. Also called a "blueprint."

parsing

The conversion of physical system components into data structures suited to code transformations within a software engineering tool. All tools used to document, analyze, import, improve, reverse, or in any other way process existing source or executable object types of any nature require this facility. An example of a tool containing parsing technology is a source code compiler.

physical system components

The actual pieces that constitute an executable production system. Examples are JCL, load modules, source code, screen maps, and related items.

quality assurance

The critical review process required to ensure that a century-date compliance task was adequately and correctly performed, existing functionality was not unintentionally altered, and century-date compliance was achieved. This process includes monitoring coding quality, performing validation tests, and measuring compliance to standards.

record group

A group of elements (such as a COBOL 01 level) or I/O records that have been grouped together according to common lengths, underlying record structure, or verb transfer usage (e.g., Move, Read Into)

repository

An information storage facility or central database that contains all meta-data relevant to the management, design, implementation, and transition of one or more information systems or for the enterprise.

scenario

A project-oriented, assessment, and implementation work plan template that incorporates required blueprint/methodology steps into prepackaged solutions to address century-date migrations. Scenarios provide a means for organizations with little or no experience in large-scale migrations to rapidly deploy methodology techniques for their century-date compliance projects.

software reengineering

The use of tools and techniques to facilitate the analysis, improvement, redesign, and reuse of existing software systems to support changing business and technical information requirements.

subject matter expert

One who is knowledgeable in the functional or technical aspects of an application system or other area of study, such as redevelopment; also called an SME.

synonyms

Data elements that map to the same physical data but have a different definition and a different data name. Synonyms are usually valid redefinitions of data elements and are used for various purposes, such as for reporting and computations.

systems redevelopment

The process of significantly modifying or rebuilding application system(s) that essentially replaces portions or all of one or more existing systems through the use of software reengineering technology.

task

1. A low-level activity that begins and ends.

2. A collection of related steps within a Year 2000 methodology that contains objectives, entrance criteria, rolls/skills, inputs, tools support, deliverables, quality checks, metrics, exit criteria, and generic and tool-based guidelines.

testing

The process of executing one or more programs in a system to verify that functional capability of that system meets the user requirements specified during a prior development or maintenance modification.

tool

A software product that supports one or more century-date compliance project tasks or steps. Tools are generally off-the-shelf, commercially available software products that assist with the analysis, upgrade, improvement, or rearchitecting of legacy applications.

upgrade unit

A system, or group of related systems, treated as a single unit of work for purposes of a given redevelopment project scenario. One common application of upgrade unit segmentation is for enterprise-wide, century-date change projects.

validation

The process for testing the results of a century-date compliance project to ensure their correctness. It is accomplished by processing a series of tests that show (1) the modified applications or programs correctly handle century dates, and (2) existing functionality has not been adversely affected by the project.

Year 2000

The impending Year 2000 millennium change and its resultant impact and potential *disruptions* of business services, information databases, and application systems. Same as Century Date Change.

Year 2000 Project Office

The core IT project team that coordinates century-date compliance projects across an enterprise. Their responsibilities include communication, skills transfer, tool management, central infrastructure issues, and third-party relationships.

Index